The Devil's Wheels

To Sean,
Keep riding

Sasha Diskes

Explorations in Mobility

Series Editors:
Gijs Mom, Eindhoven University of Technology
Mimi Sheller, Drexel University
Georgine Clarsen, University of Wollongong

The study of mobility opens up new transnational and interdisciplinary approaches to fields including transport, tourism, migration, communication, media, technology, and environmental studies. The works in this series rethink our common assumptions and ideas about the mobility of people, things, ideas, and cultures from a broadly understood humanities perspective. The series welcomes projects of a historical or contemporary nature, and encourages postcolonial, non-Western, and critical perspectives.

Volume 1
Atlantic Automobilism
The Emergence and Persistence of the Car, 1895–1940
Gijs Mom

Volume 2
The Devil's Wheels
Men and Motorcycling in the Weimar Republic
Sasha Disko

Volume in Preparation
Driving Modernity
Technology, Experts, Politics, and Fascist Motorways, 1922–1943
Massimo Moraglio

The Devil's Wheels

Men and Motorcycling in the Weimar Republic

Sasha Disko

berghahn
NEW YORK • OXFORD
www.berghahnbooks.com

Published in 2016 by
Berghahn Books
www.berghahnbooks.com

Library of Congress Cataloging-in-Publication Data

A C.I.P. cataloging record is available from the Library of Congress

British Library Cataloguing in Publication Data

A catalogue record for this book is available from the British Library

ISBN 978-1-78533-169-5 hardback
ISBN 978-1-78533-170-1 ebook

For C.S.

Contents

List of Illustrations

Images

Tables

Preface

Many years ago now, first seized by a drive to explore the relationship between consumption practices and the construction of modern German masculinities, I went about outlining a study centered on the automobile. After all, at least to a significant degree, the automobile's pedigree is German. A principal realm for male consumption, researching the automobile promised to provide insights into the manifold social conflicts and contradictions of classical modernity and, particularly in relation to the construction of gender in Weimar Germany, it appeared understudied. After initial visits to the archives, however, I discovered the numerical dominance of motorized two-wheelers and was moved to take the project in a different direction. My focus on motorcycling thus stems not from a personal connection to or fetish for these undeniably aesthetically powerful objects. Indeed, I am the only sister of three never to have possessed a motorcycle license. Instead, my motivation has been intellectual, arising from a desire to capture the specificity of motorization in Germany and thus to be better able to analyze its impacts on the broadest range of users, including working-class motorists. Motorcycles offered a cipher to decode modern mobility.

Visitors to Berlin's German Historical Museum may have come across Lotte Laserstein's 1929 oil portrait of a motorcyclist that hangs prominently in the gallery devoted to everyday life in the Weimar Republic. Painted in a New Objectivity style, Laserstein's motorcyclist, who stands solidly in front of a motorcycle and assorted tools, is leather clad and resolute, yet his class status is unclear. With this image, Laserstein rendered an iconic figure of the era—the motorcyclist—in its striking ambivalence. Like her painting, this book represents my attempt at reading these motorcyclists' stories to portray everyday life in uncertain times.

Acknowledgments

The pursuit of this endeavor was generously enabled by a number of institutions. A fifteen-month research fellowship at the Berlin Program at the Freie Universität Berlin as well as a short-term follow-up visit, funded by the German Academic Exchange Service, DAAD, allowed me to gather a great deal of the material that forms the basis for this study. Two years at the Center for Metropolitan Studies at the Technischen Universität Berlin, and a ten-month Angsar-Rummler fellowship at the Wissenschaftskolleg zu Berlin helped me build on and retool my initial findings, and, importantly, gave me time to craft a polished product. New York University, Berlin allowed me space and time to conclude this project. I would also like to thank those people, institutions, and corporations that agreed to reproductions of the illustrations in this book. While institutional assistance was essential, intellectual support was equally, if not more important. Gijs Mom challenged me to engage more deeply with mobility studies, and convinced me that it provides a useful framework for my study. The TELEUNIT group, a virtual community, kept me on track during the long haul of rewrites and edits. The editors at Berghahn Books, especially Caroline Kuhtz in Production, have been supportive in helping me get to the finish line.

For engaging with this project during various stages along the meandering journey, I thank in particular Hillary Angelo, Elisabetta Bini, Dorothee Brantz, Maggie Clinton, Ray Daniels, Sarah Ehlers, Atina Grossmann, Samara Heifetz, Stefan Höhne, Sabine Horlitz, The Hysterical Materialists, Bruce Kogut, Nathan Marcus, Shane Minkin, Khary Polk, Sherene Seikaly, Quinn Slobodian, Frank Steinbeck, and Anne Vogelpohl. I was blessed by the guidance of Mary Nolan and Manu Goswami, who stand out both as mentors and as friends. Manu Goswami continually spurred me to question deeply the connections between shifts in social and spatial relations, the process of motorization, and the contours and contradictions of modernity. More than anyone else, Mary Nolan committed her acute attention to helping me shape this project over the many years between its incipience and its completion.

From the San Francisco Bay area to New York City, Munich, Bremen, Hannover, Hamburg, Berlin, and places between, family and friends, far too many to mention by name, gave me encouragement. My sisters, Monika Bhushan and Gitanjali Denley, my brother-in-law, Orion, the Teutsch and Schmidt families, and my parents, Cybele Lo Vuolo Bhushan and Abhay Bhushan, cheered me on, even though my interests rarely seemed to overlap with their own. To my wonderful friend Andy Pollack, who has been here when I needed him most. I dedicate this book to my truly beloved husband and wonderful partner, Christopher Schmidt, who always helped kick start my engine whenever it stalled. It has been my greatest privilege and pleasure to ride through life with you. I miss you. Finally, I wish to commend the persistence of my young friend Oskar Beez. Although it will take a few more years of learning English until he can read this book, he never failed to ask, *"Ist Dein Buch schon fertig?"* Well, Oskar, here it is.

List of Abbreviations

ADAC	Allgemeiner Deutscher Automobil-Club [Nationwide German Automobile Club]
AIZ	*Arbeiter-Illustrierte Zeitung* [Workers' Illustrated Newspaper]
ATG	Automobiltechnische Gesellschaft [Automobile Technological Society]
AvD	Automobilclub von Deutschland [Automobile Club of Germany]
AVUS	Automobil-Verkehrs- und Übungsstrasse [Automobile-Trafficand Test Track]
BMW	Bayerische Motoren Werke [Bavarian Motor Works]
DAF	Deutsche Arbeitsfront [German Work Front]
DDAC	Der Deutsche Automobil-Club [The German Automobile Club]
DIW	Deutsche Industrie-Werke [German Industry Works]
DKW	Zschopauer Motorenwerke J.S. Rasmussen Aktiengesellschaft DKW Zschopau [Zschopau Motor Works, J.S. Rasmussen Corporation DKW Zschopau]
DMV	Deutscher Motorradfahrer-Verband [German Motorcyclists' Union]
DNVP	Deutschnationale Volkspartei [German National People's Party]
DTC	Deutscher Touring–Club [German Touring Club]
FKZ	*Fahrrad und Kraftfahrzeug Zeitschrift* [Bicycle and Motor Vehicle Magazine]
HJ	Hitler Jugend [Hitler Youth]
KPD	Kommunistische Partei Deutschlands [Communist Party of Germany]
NSDAP	Nationalsozialistische Deutsche Arbeiterpartei [National Socialist German Workers' Party]
NSKK	Nationalsozialistische Kraftfahrerkorps [National Socialist Motorist Corps]

NSU	Neckarsulmer Motoren Werke [Neckarsulm Motor Works]
Reichsbanner	Reichsbanner Schwarz-Rot-Gold [Black-Red-Gold Banner of the Reich]
RDA	Reichsverband der Automobilindustrie [Reich League of the Automobile Industry]
RDT	Reichsbund Deutscher Technik [Reich Union of German Technology]
RM	Reichsmark (currency of the Weimar Republic)
SA	Sturmabteilung [Storm Troopers]
SPD	Sozialdemokratische Partei Deutschlands [Social Democratic Party of Germany]
SS	Schutzstaffel [Protection Squadron]
TT	Tourist Trophy
VDDI	Verein Deutscher Diplom-Ingenieure [Association of German Academic Engineers]
VDMI	Verein Deutscher Motorfahrzeug-Industrieller [Association of German Motor Vehicle Industrialists]
VDI	Verein Deutscher Ingenieure [Association of German Engineers]
VLI	Verband der Leichtkraftrad-Industrie e.V. [League of Small-Powered Motorcycle Industry]

Introduction

Does the Man Make the Motorcycle or the Motorcycle the Man?

> Someone, or something, sowed the flaming desire in your young male heart to become a disciple of motor sport.... Your desire was initially borne of envy at the daily experience of seeing a friend race noisily by on his jalopy, while you must travel cumbersomely and slowly by foot.... The desire eats and gnaws and nourishes itself from thence on within your breast ... Fills all of your senses and thoughts ... Follows you in your dreams.
>
> —Alexander Büttner, *Motorrad-Sport, -Verkehr und -Technik*

Loosely crafted in the form of a Bildungsroman, Alexander Büttner's short story from 1924 portrays a male protagonist in his journey from pedestrian to motorcyclist, culminating in his evolution into a "real man."[1] Sparked by an irresistible desire, the "motorcyclist's development" is punctuated by acts of consumption, first by ordering catalogs, then in purchasing a motorcycle. Once a motorcycle owner, a number of accessories suddenly appear indispensible to the rookie motorcyclist. "You mount the bike and race through the city ... and all the while you notice that a hundred things are missing that you absolutely need: a gruff horn, an odometer, a speedometer, and especially electric lights, and good tires ... spare parts and a well-sprung pillion seat."[2] Participation in consumer culture was a requirement for the overwhelmingly male owners of motor vehicles during the Weimar Republic. Yet most contemporary observations, as well as subsequent analyses, have consistently linked consumption to femininity, while studies of masculinity during the Weimar Republic have focused predominantly on militarized masculinity as the hegemonic form.[3] Indeed, in Büttner's short story and in the discourse of motorcycling as a whole, proper masculinity was rhetorically disassociated from conspicuous consumption. The act of masculine consumption was concealed behind the twin pillars of modern manliness: production and possession. As the motorcyclist progresses through the stages from "novice" (intoxicated with speed until he crashes) to "connoisseur" (a gourmet of beauty in both landscapes and motorcycles), he is not depicted as merely consuming passively. Instead, the motorcyclist is portrayed as mastering time, space, and the machine. The emphasis is on acquiring skills and knowledge, rather than new gadgets or accessories.

While the "motorcyclist's development" may appear idiosyncratic at first glance, the themes Büttner addresses are emblematic of modernity and masculinity in Germany during the first decades of the twentieth century.[4] Although the dream world of mass automobility was in its infancy, increasingly affordable, domestically manufactured motorcycles swelled the ranks of German motorists. The number of two-wheelers, including two-stroke motorcycles with low engine capacity, steadily rose, surpassing the number of automobiles on German roads in 1926.[5] By the end of the 1920s, with motor vehicle registrations totaling well over a million, motorcycles outnumbered automobiles by three to two.[6] While individual automobile ownership continued to be a privilege of the upper classes, by the late 1920s the working classes were taking to motorcycling in droves.[7] Skilled and unskilled laborers, alongside new white-collar workers so astutely analyzed by Siegfried Kracauer in *The Salaried Masses: Duty and Distraction in Weimar Germany*, were able to participate in motorization through buying mass-produced two-wheelers, sometimes making use of layaway plans or the extensive used-motorcycle market. This book explores how the everyday choices that men and women made expressed their desires to partake in the social and spatial mobility offered by motorization, and how their actions also produced and reflected anxieties about inhabiting an increasingly elastic and plastic world.

Possessing a dazzlingly seductive power over citizens of the new republic, motorcycles midwifed mass motorization in Germany. As one contemporary journalist put it, "it was then that the motor vehicle was 'performed', it became fashion, a pipe dream, a great craving and desire for bourgeois ownership among thousands from all social strata."[8] After World War I, the formal abolition of aristocratic privilege, the founding of a democratic republic grounded in a progressive constitution, and the granting of universal suffrage promised political and economic modernity for all German citizens. The degree to which a society was motorized was understood as an indicator of the ability of a society to fulfill the promises of consumer modernity, greater individual freedom, and increased mobility, both spatial and social.[9] Above all in terms of how it altered both lived environments and social rhythms, motorization was a source of both enthrallment and anxiety.[10] The dreams and fears generated by these freedoms are central to different interpretations of Weimar history, from those who celebrate it as a unique site of social and cultural experimentation to those who demonize it as a precursor to the horrors of National Socialism.[11]

Like their contemporaries around the globe, Germans during the Weimar Republic were fascinated by motorization and obsessed with technology, regardless of whether they embraced, condemned, or were ambivalent about these changes.[12] On a par and in step with radio, cinema, fashion, and sports, the "emergent culture" of mass motorization was an important terrain on which complex struggles over changes in gender and class relationships were played out.[13] In a 1929 photo-reportage titled "Motorcycle-Radio Weekend," for example, the author, a white-collar worker, described a motorcycle weekend getaway with a female friend to a lake on the outskirts of Berlin. His female companion, Hilde, a "lady's helper," at one point exclaimed excitedly, "We'll have the radio waves, the waves of the lake, and my brand new permanent wave!" Once the radio was set up, the couple tuned into the following variety program: Sports news of the day, followed by a popular love ballad, a jazz song (a so-called "black bottom" which caused Hilde to dance "a little jig"), a Spanish one-step, a segment in which an elderly lady discussed meat prices and infant care, and a report on a "rationalized beauty regimen." The end of the story described how "the two sit in the sunshine in front of their tent and listen, listen. On the headphones, Hawaiian songs are broadcast from the Savoy Hotel in London and frogs croak industriously in the reeds close by."[14] Steeped in a culture of consumption and leisure, these weekenders epitomized the "new man" and "new woman"—futuristic ideal-types of masculinity and femininity of a globally scaled, consumer-driven industrial economy. Furthermore, their casual relationship signaled the rise of new forms of heterosociability and sexual exploration. Because motorization facilitated spatial, social, and sexual mobility and flexible everyday rhythms for Germans, it represented both a social threat and a social boon.

Modernity, Mobility, Masculinity

The Devil's Wheels explores how, in both tangible and intangible ways, motorization changed German society during the fifteen years of the Weimar Republic, visibly transforming cityscapes and landscapes, and intensifying and altering the patterns of circulation of people, goods, and capital.[15] Although driving had not yet become routine for the masses, motorization was already influencing the experience of the everyday. As Kristin Ross has argued for the case of post–World War II France: "the centrality of the car ... precedes the car's becoming

Image 0.1. New Forms of Leisure. *BMW-Blätter*, cover July 1930. BMW Group Archive.

commonplace … As such the discourse, on the whole, is futuristic: anticipatory and preparatory in nature, fascinated or horrified, but generally permeated with anxieties."[16] In fantasy and reality, the process of motorization shaped social relations, and motor vehicles served as carriers of multiple social meanings. In this book, the category of modernity is employed to express interlinked processes of accelerated social and physical mobility. It follows in the tradition of historians who view it as superfluous if not misleading to speak of modernity without speaking of the profound contradictions that modernity produces.[17]

With the physical and social world in upheaval during the Weimar Republic, many Germans were overwhelmed by the sense that they were living through times of perpetual political instability and chronic economic crisis in a society untethered from long-standing social truths, stable categories, and predictable life trajectories. A convergence of historical events and social processes made gender relations appear particularly precarious during the Weimar Republic. The first years of the republic were marked by the defeat of the military and the loss of Germany's overseas colonies. A series of political and social revolutions and counterrevolutions testified to the inherent instability of the republic. Following almost a decade of steadily rising inflation, the acute phase of hyperinflation in the early 1920s caused a massive redistribution of wealth. Creating new groups of the wealthy and the poor, hyperinflation partially eroded the social stratification that had defined imperial German society. During the period of so-called "stability," the expansion of rationalized industrial production gave rise to new types of both white- and blue-collar work, and continued the decline of traditional craft industries. Profound structural changes unfolded in the context of social and political upheaval, and were reflected in rearticulated categories of both femininity and masculinity. Attempts to construct a stable form of modern manliness appropriate to the altered conditions represented one strategy to counter the perceived loss of traditional anchors of masculinity. *The Devil's Wheels* shows that citizens of the nascent democracy did not react to the series of crises uniformly. Instead, contesting models for society and choices of lifestyle proliferated, if only briefly. When the World Economic Crisis hit Germany especially hard, it impacted all sectors of society, and politically polarized calls for alternate routes became more insistent.[18]

Philosophers, scholars, and theorists have marshaled motorized mobility to analyze changes in social and spatial constellations ever since the early days of motorization.[19] In more recent years, cultural and social historians, sociologists, and geographers, united under the banner of mobility studies, have been building a growing body of innovative interdisciplinary research around the concept of "automobility" and "automobilism."[20] By examining how motorized traffic in everyday life transformed social and physical space in the United States and contributed to reinvigorating a national identity grounded in rugged republican selfhood, and by dissecting struggles over the governance of the new technology and its attendant infrastructures, scholars have demonstrated the high social and political stakes of automobility in the US.[21] Fine-grained analyses of the intersections of class, gender, and motoring invoke the concept of "habitus" to show how the car both demarcated and blurred social distinctions.[22] Mobility studies scholars have also probed identity formation within distinct user cultures, for example among "tinkerers" and early women motorists.[23] Other studies that explore novelties such as speed, risk taking, and their complementarities, safety and encapsulation, add to our understanding not only of the "timings and spacings" of motorized societies, but also of the sensation of driving as an "embodied sensibility" and of transformations in the sensual and haptic experience of motorized travel.[24] These scholars and many others have placed motorization and mobility firmly on the agenda of academic inquiry, and have created a rich body of evidence and analysis. By exploring the complex ways that motorization impacted the organization of everyday life, *The Devil's Wheels* engages with debates around the "social construction of technology," drawing on insights developed in previous studies of motorized mobility.[25]

With few exceptions, however, existing studies focus exclusively on the car and its uses, producers, and consumers.[26] The tenacious grip of the automobile on the historiography of motorization in Germany, and more globally, both signals and perpetuates the ideological dominance of the model of motorization based on Ford's Model T.[27] Thus, rather than reflect a normative bias towards a portrayal of economic and industrial development based on the exceptional situation of the United States (or of other settler colony settings including Canada, Australia, and South Africa), I narrate the emergence of mass motorization in Germany foremost from the vantage point and through the voices and actions of its primary objects and subjects—motorcyclists.[28] Due to constraints on the economy during the Weimar Republic, the German automotive industry never successfully manufactured or marketed an equivalent of Ford's Model T, a fact that can be attributed partly to inadequate capital investment.[29] Moreover, wartime inflation and the subsequent hyperinflation throttled the buying power of the middle classes. The uneven socioeconomic structure and the wealth gap influenced the pattern of demands, and contributed to the motorcycle industry gaining a competitive advantage.[30]

Faced with seemingly insurmountable economic and political challenges to producing a Volkswagen, the German industry and press
championed the two-stroke motorcycle as "the people's vehicle" due
to its affordability, its German production, and its lack of tax and licensing restrictions.[31] In contrast, in the United States and in France the
automobile was by far the dominant form of individual motorized
transport. Even in Great Britain, considered the "motherland of motorcycling" during the 1920s, the transition to four-wheeled motor vehicle
occurred earlier, allowing the German motorcycle industry to take over
England's position as the global leader in motorcycle manufacturing
by the end of the Weimar Republic.[32] In Italy, by the end of the 1930s,
there was only one-tenth the number of motorcyclists there was in
Germany, despite Mussolini's personal passion for motorcycling and the
motor-obsessed aesthetics of the Futurists.[33] Within the skewed competitive environment of the German automotive industry, motorcycle
manufacturers took the lead in manufacturing affordable motor vehicles, partially through successfully adopting and implementing Fordist
production techniques, such as the assembly line. Frank Steinbeck's
recent monograph delves into the details of how economic, political,
and juridical factors coalesced to favor the expansion of motorcycling
in Germany.[34]

Yet the significance of the motorcycle cannot be completely understood through economic constraints or political interventions. Instead,
as a "cultural commodity," the motorcycle is saturated with meaning
beyond "the thing itself."[35] Martin Heidegger employed the motorcycle
as a heuristic device on numerous occasions to explain his phenomenological philosophy to students at the University of Freiburg. In order,
for example, to elucidate the concepts of "hearkening," or the difference
between "entities" and "beings," Heidegger invoked the motorcycle as a
peculiar object.[36]

> How does it stand with Being? Can we see Being? We see beings—the
> chalk here. But do we see Being as we see color and light and dark? Or
> do we hear, smell, taste, or touch Being? We hear the motorcycle roaring
> along the street. We hear the grouse flying off through the mountain
> forest in its gliding flight. Yet really we are only hearing the noise of the
> motor's rattling, the noise that the grouse causes. Furthermore, it is hard
> and unusual for us to describe the pure noise, because it is precisely not
> what we generally hear. We always hear more [than the mere noise].[37]

Heidegger presented the motorcycle, an everyday object, as possessing
a form of existential authenticity comparable to a wild bird, verging on
acquiring a quality beyond its lifeless materiality.

Motorcyclist and mobility scholar Jeremy Packer argues that motor-cycling offers a "phenomenological validation," including its quality of appearing to provide an unmediated experience, "being in touch with the world around you, particularly the beauty of nature." Time appears compressed, in terms of "having a heightened sense of being in the moment – being 'more alive.'" The authenticity of the experience is augmented through "knowing and understanding one's machinery in a more intense and extensive fashion than the average motorist." And performance is key—"looking and feeling tough; being noticed and cre-ating a scene; and certainly, not least of all, experiencing the thrill of speed."[38] In his classic essay on motorcycling as popular culture, John Alt writes that motorcycling fulfills "ambiguous social needs," combin-ing "sensuous experiences (ecstasy, exhilaration, virility) and conceptual images (freedom, individualism) which are denied in everyday life, but which can be rediscovered and relived through a particular assemblage of metal, rubber, and plastic." Thus, as a "symbolic representation of the modern search for meaning and experience," the motorcycle is often imbued with mythical and metaphysical qualities.[39]

Given its symbolic baggage, focusing on motorcycling thus offers new grounds for exploring how gender and class intersected. New forms of mobility were discursively and materially linked to new forms of consuming, with consumer culture increasingly organizing "struc-tures of meaning and feeling."[40] While scholars of technology and of mobility have shown the automobile to be gendered in complex ways, when analyzed at all, the motorcycle has been coded as decidedly and aggressively masculine.[41] Furthermore, although a rich body of histor-ical studies on consumption and gender during the Weimar Republic exists, it focuses almost exclusively on constructions and representa-tions of femininity.[42] Although mass consumption had not fully arrived in Weimar Germany, consuming exerted a growing influence on the formation of modern subjects, disrupting relationships between class and gender.[43] Motorized mobility promised transformation, as Cotton Seiler and other scholars have argued, not only of women, but impor-tantly also of men.[44] Thus, in *The Devil's Wheels* I hope to provide a contribution to understanding how consumption shaped not only constructions of modern femininity, but of modern masculinity as well.

Consuming, however, is never the only, or even the most signifi-cant act involved in producing and reproducing gender. Motorcycling masculinity combined consumption and production, aesthetics and technology. Multiple and relational, yet historically produced within concrete social contexts, masculinities (and femininities) are both "made" and "making."[45] During the Weimar Republic, economic and political upheavals destabilized traditional sources of institutional and cultural power, threatening the smooth reproduction of "hegemonic masculinity" and thus challenging the gender order.[46] Struggles over definitions of normative masculinity reveal conflicts over the organization and regulation of social relations, for example in heated debates on technology, sports, and delinquency. Motorcycling, in the sense of Judith Butler's "doing and undoing gender," thus offers a site to explore enactments and embodiments of masculinities and femininities, of modern men and modern women.[47] When viewed through the lens of motorcycling, often-contradictory repertoires and representations of gender, and masculinity in particular, were made available through the emerging mass consumer society. On the one hand, motorcycling created spaces for masculine self-fashioning beyond an occupational or confessional basis; on the other hand, motorcycling was a practice that generally served to disguise acts of masculine consumption under a veil of masculine-coded skilled labor or the conquest of space, time, and women. And, as an icon of female masculinity, the figure of the active female motorcyclist challenged conceptions of proper femininity.[48]

In the hierarchy of transportation vehicles, when compared to automobiles, motorcycles were inferior status symbols. The chorus regularly denouncing Weimar Germany's alternate path to motorization was large and loud. Industrial and political leaders, as well as everyday Germans, expressed negative attitudes towards motorcycles and motorcyclists, reflecting more general anxieties regarding the rise of the United States as an industrial powerhouse and the weakened position of Germany's economy and society after the defeat in World War I. Whether phrased in terms of rationalization, conspicuous consumption, crass materialism, or masculinized women, unease over social changes was often framed as a critique of "Americanism." To compensate for the motorcycle's inadequacy as a marker of social class status and national wealth, an image of the motorcycle as a marker of "iron-hard" masculinity became increasingly dominant, in part promoted by the motoring industry and press, and in part self-ascribed by motorcyclists. Similar to the way in which Weimar contemporaries saw "silk stockings and permed hair" as the modern woman's "weapons in the struggle for survival," the masculine motorcycling community evaluated qualities such as "risk-taking" and "weather-proofed" as necessary attributes for surviving the vicissitudes of modern life.[49]

Nonetheless, the masculine world of motorcycling was a collective less adequately characterized by homogeneity than by its internal distinctions.[50] Although motorcyclists in Germany shared particular experiences and practices, a range of masculine "ideal types" existed for

Weimar-era motorcyclists to draw upon.[51] Indeed, in contrast to David Gartman's proposal that the "cultural logic of car consumption" has progressed through the three stages of distinction, obscuration, and differentiation, I would argue that these three "logics" were at play simultaneously and in competition with each other within the motorcycling culture of the Weimar Republic. This reflected a more general expression of the lack of consensus around meaning-making though consumption.[52] As the number of motorcyclists grew over the course of the 1920s, trade journals, clubs, and motorcyclists attempted to delimit the community by creating self-disciplining mechanisms and through circumscribing acceptable behavior. However, descriptions of motorcycle ideal types, such as the "Pure Unadulterated Sportsman," the "Grease Monkey," the "*Halbstarke*," and the "Leather Jacket," reveal deep schisms not only over which practices and behaviors were accepted as constituting appropriate masculinity within the motorcycling community internally, but also in the Weimar Republic in general.

The Devil's Wheels makes three discrete interventions in the historiography of the Weimar Republic—into the history of motorization, consumption, and gender. I do not limit my focus to militarized masculinity, nor do I look exclusively at femininity and consumption. Instead, the relationship of masculinity to consumption in a particularly masculine-coded milieu, motorcycling, is at the center of this investigation. By exploring representations and performances of gender and class in the "emergent culture" of motorization, and motorcycling in particular, I both extend and amend standard interpretations of class and gender in the Weimar Republic. With the destabilization both of class boundaries and the undermining of the naturalized equation of man as producer, consumption and leisure emerged as important practices in the construction and enactment of modern masculinity. The modern man participated in the emergent consumer society, and his masculinity was defined not only by what he produced, but also by what and how he consumed.

If "automobility" can be understood as a "forge of subjects," then this study hopes to contribute to comparative discussions of modern mobility and the fashioning of modern masculinity under historically specific material and social conditions.[53] In the United States, the case Cotten Seiler studied, driving an automobile facilitated a reconsolidation of republican individualism in the face of Taylorism and Fordism. Citizens of the newly minted Weimar Republic faced a different set of issues. Wracked with insecurities over the defeat in war and loss of status as an imperial power, they were filled with anxiety over the constant volatility of the economy and the tattered fabric of the nation.[54] On the one hand, resentment over being excluded from full participation both in the ideal form of mass consumption symbolized by Henry Ford's Model T and on the world power stage dominated political debates during the Weimar Republic. On the other hand, deep unease over an uncertain present and future existed alongside tentative pride over manifestations of Germany's own modernity and great expectations for a technologically driven advancement of society. Exploring openings and obstacles, barricades and byways, *The Devil's Wheels* inquires into the reworking of relationships between class, gender, production, and consumption through the emergent practice of motorcycling during a period of acutely perceived social, political, and economic instability.

Sourcing the Fuel of History

Writing a history of motorization that accounts for the economic, social, and cultural context required consulting a broad archive of materials. First, the motor vehicle industry and the motoring clubs were the institutional pillars that produced and promoted the process of motorization. Sources from, and about, prominent manufacturers during the Weimar Republic offered material on the organization of production and the workforce, engineering and design, marketing and sales strategies, and the role industrial organizations and cartels played in state decisions on regulating the new technology. Motoring clubs, such as the Allgemeiner Deutscher Automobil-Club (ADAC) and the Deutscher Motorradfahrer-Verband (DMV), constituted an institutional factor crucial to popularizing motorization. Clubs, alongside industrial actors, exerted pressure on politicians to promote the progress of motorization and to forward the interests of motorists over other forms of transportation. On the consumption side, clubs published journals for their members, and offered insurance policies, maps, and international drivers' placards. In addition, sometimes together with industry, they sponsored races and rides. Above all, they provided an organized space of (homo) social consumption for their members.

Grounding this study sociologically also meant compiling ownership statistics. Registration records provided raw data on the sex and occupation of motorists, which were essential for evaluating the class and gender composition of those who had access to motor vehicles. A legal framework was constructed at the state and local level, albeit haltingly and unevenly, to regulate the process of motorization. Legal records provided evidence of struggles over uses of public space and private property, and the task of managing the social risk of motorization.

Differences in legislation and enforcement varied according to the type of motor vehicle, testifying to the class and gender biases of the emerging legal structure. Political, institutional, and industrial archives provided important insights into how motor vehicles came to dominate individual transportation in industrial societies.

Records left by government and other official institutions cannot, however, adequately capture "non-rational, symbolic, social or psychological choices."[55] In order to grasp how imaginations and emergent practices reworked understandings of class and gender through the intertwined practices of consumption, production, technology, and aesthetics, it was necessary to consult an archive of less-official renderings of the process of motorization in Germany. As symbols of modernity, the car and the motorcycle (often featured with a sidecar) became increasingly present in film and graphic representations, and in print media that represented different sectors of society and political directions. Indeed, the bulk of sources analyzed in this book were produced through the initiative of private individuals participating in the growing media sector, many of whom remain anonymous. The numerous journals for motoring enthusiasts that flourished during the Weimar Republic show how motorization was being sold and consumed on an everyday level.[56] These journals, with their letters to the editor, travelogues, and advice columns shed light on everyday mentalities and routines, intimating at gestures and bodily practices, and illuminating the shadowy contours of social relationships, from class to gender and generation. Lively debates held on a wide range of topics, from the effects of motorcycling on women's health to the problems of youth, from acceptable levels of violence to who qualified as a "true" sportsman, testify to a culture of public discussion and social negotiation.

The social and material culture of the motorcycling milieu was also recorded in innumerable fictional sources published in motoring magazines during the Weimar Republic.[57] Short stories, jokes, poems, and song lyrics, all popular forms of literary expression in this period, enriched the social terrain of motorization. In addition, the "motorcycling" novels *Garage 13*, *PS-Narr*, and *Rennfieber* were serialized in the most prominent independent motorcycling magazine during the late 1920s.[58] Although demonstrating differences in style and interpretations of modern men and women, these fictional works often share a similar repertoire of preoccupations and presumptions about social identities, gender relations, and motorized modernity. They also provide rich material for exploring the figure of the engineer, the relationship between industry, sports, and the nation, and especially courtship and sexuality.

Signposting the Territory: Chapter Outline

To show how relationships between the state, economy, and society shifted during the Weimar Republic, the first chapter rides the bumpy but not uphill road on the German motorcycle industry's journey "From Pioneers to Global Dominance." During the fifteen-year span of the first German republic's often-tenuous existence, the economy was a fractured space, fraught with competing visions. The fortunes of the German motorcycle industry, for which I provide a chronological history until 1933, reflected the political, social, and economic turmoil of the era, whereby the motorcycle industry attained a relative advantage vis-à-vis the automobile industry. By tying consumption to production, the growth of the motorcycle industry can be understood through important changes in design and manufacturing that made motorcycles increasingly more affordable and reliable. Furthermore, the state was deeply implicated in the promotion of mass-motorized two-wheelers. By providing incentives, such as tax and licensing advantages, the state fostered an environment that helped to expand the domestic market for motorcycles.

The second chapter, "Engineering and Advertising a Motorized Future," probes the crucial role of engineers and advertisers in the production and consumption of motorcycles. The figure of the engineer, materially and intimately involved with both the production of the industrial economy and the nation, provides an example of the conflicts over modern masculinity.[59] Motorization, alongside industrialization and urbanization, enabled this new professional group to present themselves as the principal actors of modernity and the protagonists of the modern nation. Engineers positioned themselves as experts able to determine the proper relationship between culture and technology, and as arbiters between the German "spirit" and the material world. The second half of the chapter explores advertising—a growing profession central to creating a public image of both motorcycles and motorcyclists. It looks at advertising agencies and the establishment of customer service departments as well as at the spaces, techniques, strategies, and motifs of advertising the motorcycle and the sidecar. The shiny visions of a motorized society that advertisers often produced, however, rarely reflected the everyday difficulties of motorcycling or the often-harsh reality of economic and social instability in the Weimar Republic.

Through analyzing motorcycling as a distinctive yet variegated habitus, the third chapter, "Motorcycles and the 'Everyman,'" shows the motorcycling community during the Weimar Republic as a predominantly masculine collective replete with internal distinctions. Statistics compiled on motorcycle and automobile ownership (ridership inevitably remains a gray area) uncover how the sociological landscape of the motorized changed over time. Motor sport clubs and the trade press were essential for constructing a motorcycling habitus. Sartorial fashioning, motorcycle touring, and tinkering were also central practices that shaped the motorcycling milieu. An analysis of competing ideal types of motorcycling masculinity, drawn from descriptions in motorcycling journals, demonstrates how acts of male consumption were incorporated into a repertoire of distinctly masculine practices and behaviors. Close readings of sources such as poems and short stories underscore my central argument that the modern man of the Weimar Republic can be firmly located within consumer society.

The field of sports exploded during the Weimar Republic. The fourth chapter, "Is Motorcycling Even Sport?," traces a particularly contentious debate within the motorcycling community. The discussion over the meaning and value of sports gave voice to both anxieties about and hopes for engineering individual bodies and reformulating the nation in the context of severe economic, political, and social ruptures. Sports provided a space for men to both assert their masculinity and create distinctions within masculinity. Competing visions of what defined a sport or a sportsperson provide insight into how motorcyclists attempted to negotiate their identities as modern men during a period in which the primacy of production was giving way to the growing importance of consumption. Germany's uneasy and partial transformation into a consumer-driven industrial capitalist society was reflected in manifold iterations of discomfort with materialism. The massive and seemingly uncontrollable social changes produced disruptions that Germans often countered by framing the contradictions and challenges of modernity within the realm of the spiritual. For example, motorcyclists attempted to veil their participation in consumer society through employing the concept of struggle to define sports, a struggle that was naturalized and envisioned as primordial. By invoking "iron-hard masculinity" as a marker of motorcycling, motorcyclists also sought a means to escape the feminization associated with consumption and to obviate the threat of being characterized as superficial.

Central sources of social conflict throughout the process of motorization, such as drunk driving, joyrides, violence, accidents, and noise, are the topic of the fifth chapter, "Deviant Behaviors." Public attitudes towards motorcyclists, and motorcyclists' reactions to the problems prompted by motorization, are explored by looking at how different social groups thought these conflicts could be managed and the risks be fairly distributed socially. Often-heated debates reveal contestations, both between the non-motorized and motorized, and within the motorized community, over the right to define appropriate comportment in public spaces. For example, in 1928 another lively debate was held in *Das Motorrad* over whether it was appropriate or not to run over dogs. While no consensus was reached, the debate shows how motorization forced issues around acceptable levels of violence, and the relationship between ownership and violence. This chapter also deals with attempts on the part of the state, the police, and motoring clubs to mediate conflicts between the motorized and the non-motorized, as well as the motorcycle communities' own attempts to regulate motorcyclists' behavior. While problems with motorization were sources of strife in an ever-more industrialized, urbanized, and mobile mass society, the specific conflicts between motorists and non-motorists also served as a pretext for expressing anxieties over the instable social, economic, and political conditions during the Weimar Republic. Unevenness and abrupt shifts in the organization of the economy produced struggles around public and private; dynamics of inclusion and exclusion became increasingly relevant in a society that confronted democracy and consumerism with profound ambivalence.

"Motoring Amazons?," the sixth chapter, focuses on active female motorcyclists and female motorcycling authors by paying attention to their relatively scant voices in the pervasively masculine world of motorcycling. By looking at both fictional and factual examples of female motorcyclists, this chapter explores the strategies women employed in order to participate in the modern activity of motorization, as well as the challenges they faced in their attempts. An exemplary figure was Hanni Köhler, who not only raced alongside men and won competitions such as the North–South Race in 1924, but also undertook a nine-month 20,000 km motorcycle expedition from Sri Lanka to Germany in 1931, a remarkable feat for any person at that period of time. While her achievements were often celebrated within the trade journals, her insistence on active female motorcycling made her vulnerable to claims of not being properly feminine, of upsetting gender norms, and of being what motorcycle magazines called a "Motorcycle Amazon." Furthermore, the predominantly male-generated discourse around women and motorcycling was couched in terms of debates on women's health and on women's technological aptitude—or their ostensible lack thereof—and women encountered institutional obstacles when they took the steering wheel or handlebars. Nevertheless, although sexism was institutional and class and social rank were less important than gender when it came to driving motor vehicles, women motorcyclists found ways to assert their needs and desires, and ultimately transformed definitions of proper femininity.

Tracing the intricate webs of male–female sexual intimacy on and off the road, from mere voyeurism to tentative selection, taking a test drive and the rituals of purchase, and trading in the old for the new, the final chapter, "Sex and the Sidecar," analyzes the ticklishness of gender, sexuality, motorization, and consumption during the Weimar Republic. The motor vehicle's potential offer of (sexual) liberation was often portrayed as its greatest asset. In the mostly fictional sources analyzed in this chapter, the motorcycle usually occupies both a material and a symbolic role, as an instrument that facilitates sexual experiences on the one hand and as an enhancer of male sexuality on the other. Motorcycles, with their promises of freedom and mobility, represented a modern form of male-dominated sexually potent capital. The opportunities opened by motorized mobility were perceived, sometimes with great anxiety, as catapulting both men and women headlong into precipitous sexual intimacy and as accelerating sexual relations. For one side, it was an acute threat to marriage and the moral fabric of society; for the other, it was simply a new technology that produced new forms of age-old behaviors. This ambivalence mirrored the instability of economic and sexual relations during the Weimar Republic.

If the oft-invoked metaphor of a "laboratory of modernity" is a fitting vehicle to describe the Weimar Republic, then motorization was an important field of social experimentation. For many Germans during the Weimar Republic, motorcycling became a vehicle for negotiating the modern world. The motorcycle was a source of both fear and fascination: "When you curse the thundering cloud of dust kicked up through this land by the devil's wheels, you feel that this eerie singing roar has something provocative, daring, yes seductive about it."[60] Motorcycles propelled German men and women headlong into modernity. "The thundering motor is the heart of this new world, it shares its speed with the humans, and they test themselves against it."[61] Or, as one skeptical police captain wrote in 1931 to the Prussian Minister of the Interior: "Dear Honorable Minister! If one day a 'necrology' of these wonderful times are written, then it shouldn't be forgotten that it was characterized by the 'mellifluous' motorcycle."[62]

Notes

1. Alexander Büttner authored motoring manuals and wrote a great number of articles for the motoring press: Alexander Büttner, "Motorradfahrers Werdegang," *Motorrad-Sport, -Verkehr und -Technik*, no. 10, 1924, 11–13. This story was reprinted in *Das Motorrad*, 1925: 109–11.

2. Büttner, "Motorradfahrers Werdegang," 11–13. A similar story, "Werdegang," written in the form of a poem, also highlights the role of male consumption in becoming a motorcyclist:

"In a jiffy, you buy a leather vest,
Racing helmet, crash helmet—should sit tight—
Also long boots, gloves, goggles.
And with a proud elation,
In first-class gear you stand,
You only have the best."

—Karo, "Werdegang," *Motorrad-Sport, -Verkehr und -Technik*, no. 25, 1928, 25.

3. Klaus Theweleit's classic, *Male Fantasies*, has long set the tone for inquiries into masculinity during the Weimar Republic. Klaus Theweleit, *Male Fantasies* (Minneapolis: University of Minnesota Press, 1987). George Mosse's work has likewise been very influential: George L. Mosse, *The Image of Man: The Creation of Modern Masculinity* (Oxford: Oxford University Press, 1996); George L. Mosse, *Fallen Soldiers: Reshaping the Memory of the World Wars* (Oxford: Oxford University Press, 1990). See also Todd Ettelson, "The Nazi 'New Man': Embodying Masculinity and Regulating Sexuality in the SA and SS, 1930–1939" (PhD diss., University of Michigan, 2002). Notable exceptions to the exclusive focus on the Männerbund and militarism are Jens Schmidt, *Sich hart machen, wenn es gilt: Männlichkeitskonzeptionen in Illustrierten der Weimarer Republik* (Münster: LIT-Verlag, 2000); Erik Norman Jensen, *Body by Weimar: Athletes, Gender and German Modernity* (Oxford: Oxford University Press, 2010); and Tanja Paulitz, *Mann und Maschine: eine genealogische Wissenssoziologie des Ingenieurs und der modernen Technikwissenschaften 1850–1930* (Bielefeld: transcript Verlag, 2012). One edited volume explores the construction of "hegemonic (white) masculinity," around 1900: Ulrike Brunotte and Rainer Herrn, eds., *Männlichkeiten und Moderne: Geschlecht in den Wissenskulturen um 1900* (Bielefeld: transcript Verlag, 2008), which focuses primarily, but not exclusively, on the constitutive relationship between militarization and masculinity in Germany. For a sample of literature on the Männerbund, militarism, and masculinity in modern Germany, see Thomas Kühne, "Männergeschichte als Geschlechtergeschichte," in *Männergeschichte – Geschlechtergeschichte: Männlichkeit im Wandel der Moderne*, ed. Thomas Kühne (Frankfurt am Main: Campus Press, 1996), 7–30; Ute Frevert, "Soldaten, Staatsbürger: Überlegungen zur historischen Konstruktion von Männlichkeit," in Kühne, *Männergeschichte*, 69–87; Nicholas Sombart, "Männerbund und Politische Kultur in Deutschland," in Kühne, *Männergeschichte*, 136–55; Ute Frevert, *Mann und Weib und Weib und Mann: Geschlechterdifferenz in der Moderne* (Munich: C.H. Beck, 1995); Bernd Widdig, *Männerbund und Massen: Zur Krise Männlicher Identität in der Literatur der Moderne* (Opladen: Westdeutscher Verlag, 1992); Berndt Weisbrod, "Military Violence and Male Fundamentalism: Ernst Jünger's Contribution to the Conservative Revolution," *History Workshop Journal* 49 (Spring 2000): 68–94; Stefanie Schüler-Springorum, "Flying and Killing: Military Masculinity in German Literature, 1914–1939," in Karen Hagemann and Stefanie Schüler-Springorum, eds. *HOME/FRONT: The Military, War and Gender in 20th Century Germany* (Oxford: Berg, 2002), 205–32; Thomas Kühne, *Kameradschaft: Die*

Soldaten des nationalsozialistischen Krieges und das 20. Jahrhunderts (Göttingen: Vandenhoeck & Ruprecht, 2006); Thomas Kühne, *Belonging and Genocide: Hitler's Community, 1918–1945* (New Haven, CT: Yale University Press, 2010).

4. Ilse Lundberg, a prolific female author, published a similar story, "When a Lady Rides a Motorcycle," about the development of a female motorcyclist. This story is discussed in Chapter 6, "Motoring Amazons?" Ilse Lundberg, "Wenn eine Dame Motorrad fährt," *Das Motorrad*, 1927: 527.

5. Helmut Braun and Christian Panzer, "The Expansion of the Motor-Cycle Industry in Germany and Great Britain (1918–1919)," *Journal of European Economic History* 32, no. 1 (2003): 52; Heidrun Edelmann, *Vom Luxusgut zum Gebrauchsgegendstand: Die Geschichte der Verbreitung von Personenkraftwagen in Deutschland* (Frankfurt am Main: Verband der Automobil Industrie, 1989), 108, 126; Reiner Flik, *Von Ford lernen? Automobilbau und Motorisierung in Deutschland bis 1933* (Cologne: Böhlau Verlag, 2001), 81.

6. *Tatsachen und Zahlen der Reichsverband der Automobilindustrie*, 1930.

7. Wolf-Dieter Lützen, "Radfahren, Motorsport, Autobesitz. Motorisierung zwischen Statuserwerb," in *Die Arbeiter: Lebensformen, Alltag und Kultur* (Munich: C.H. Beck, 1986), 369–77. See also, Edelmann, *Vom Luxusgut zum Gebrauchsgegendstand*, 108.

8. Bielefeld, "Krisis im Motorradgeschäft," *Motor-Kritik*, no. 3, 1931, 56.

9. Consumption is a central element of twentieth-century citizenship. Cotton Seiler makes this point, for example, in regard to automobile ownership and African American claims to full citizenship. Cotten Seiler, *Republic of Drivers: A Cultural History of Automobility in America* (Chicago: University of Chicago Press, 2008), 114–28. More generally, see Susan Strasser, Charles McGovern, and Matthias Judt, eds., *Getting and Spending: European and American Consumer Societies in the 20th Century* (Cambridge: Cambridge University Press, 1998); Victoria de Grazia and Ellen Furlough, eds., *The Sex of Things: Gender and Consumption in Historical Perspective* (Berkeley: University of California Press, 1996), especially Part 3: "Empowering Women as Citizen-Consumers." Also see Kathleen Canning's overview in *Gender History in Practice: Historical Perspectives on Bodies, Class, and Citizenship* (Ithaca, NY: Cornell University Press, 2006), 1–62, especially 29–32.

10. Brian Ladd addresses the phenomena of "the love–hate relationship" with automobiles in *Autophobia: Love and Hate in the Automotive Age* (Chicago: University of Chicago Press, 2008).

11. In a provocative essay, Adelheid von Saldern considers the Weimar Republic as period not only of economic crisis, but "one entailing a conflict of attitudes to culture in a phase of developing mass culture," exploring motorcycle racing as one terrain of conflict. See Adelheid von Saldern, "Cultural Conflicts, Popular Mass Culture, and the Question of Nazi Success: The Eilenriede Motorcycle Races, 1924–39," *German Studies Review* 15, no. 2 (1992): 317–38, here 317. Her analysis draws on Detlev Peukert's particularly astute analysis of the Weimar Republic, which above all stresses its profound contradictions; see Detlev J.K. Peukert, *The Weimar Republic: The Crisis of Classical Modernity* (New York: Hill and Wang, 1989); Eric Weitz also foregrounds the "tension-bound world of modernity" in Eric D. Weitz, *Weimar Germany: Promise and Tragedy* (Princeton, NJ: Princeton University Press, 2007), 4.

12. See Bernhard Rieger's excellent comparative analysis of the relationship between technology and modernity in Germany and Britain from the end of the nineteenth century through the end of World War II. Bernhard Rieger, *Technology and the Culture of Modernity in Britain and Germany, 1890–1945* (Cambridge: Cambridge University Press, 2005).
13. The term "emergent culture," taken from Raymond Williams, denotes a space where novel representations and performances of gender and class are possible. Raymond Williams, *Marxism and Literature* (Oxford: Oxford University Press, 1977), 121–27. See also, Rudy Koshar, "On the History of the Automobile in Everyday Life," *Contemporary European History* 10, no. 1 (2001): 149–50.
14. Isle Lundberg, "Motorrad-Radio-Wochenende," *Das Motorrad*, 1928: 466–68.
15. Decades before Jean Baudrillard asserted that everything you needed to know about the United States you could learn "from an anthropology of its driving behavior," Henri Lefebvre asserted that motorization was a key site of the "bureaucratic society of controlled consumption," and automobiles a "leading object" in his investigation of "everyday life in the modern world." Jean Baudrillard, *America* (London: Verso [1968] 1988), 54; Henri Lefebvre, *Everyday Life in the Modern World* (New Brunswick, NJ: Transaction Publishers, [1968] 1994), 103. For American case studies of the spatial and social transformations brought about by motorization, see Clay McShane, *Down the Asphalt Path: The Automobile and the American City* (New York: Columbia University Press, 1994); and Peter D. Norton, *Fighting Traffic: The Dawn of the Motor Age in the American City* (Cambridge, MA: MIT Press, 2008). In his study of motorization in France, Germany, and Switzerland, Christoph Maria Merki considers the impacts of shifts from non-motorized to motorized traffic and travel. Christoph Maria Merki, *Der holprige Siegeszug des Automobils, 1895–1930, Zur Motorisierung des Straßenverkehers in Frankreich, Deutschland und der Schweiz* (Vienna: Böhlau, 2002). See also Peter Kirchberg, "Die Motorisierung des Straßenverkehrs in Deutschland von den Anfängen bis zum Zweiten Weltkrieg," in *Die Entwicklung der Motorisiserung im Deutschen Reich und den Nachfolgestaaten*, ed. Harry Niemann and Armin Hermann (Stuttgart: Franz Steiner Verlag 1995), 9–22. Moreover, *Atlantic Automobilism*, Gijs Mom's recent expansive study and the first volume in this series, provides an analytically driven synthetic account of the first four and a half decades of car cultures within seven distinct national contexts, including Germany. Highlighting both differences and commonalities, Mom firmly positions the car as a cultural and technological commodity. Importantly, he reads the car and its antecedents, accouterments, and outgrowths (both material and immaterial) as something to be explained rather than as something that explains, thus, as *explanandum* rather than *explanans*. Gijs Mom, *Atlantic Automobilism: Emergence and Persistence of the Car 1985–1940* (New York: Berghahn Books, 2015).
16. Kristin Ross, *Fast Cars, Clean Bodies: Decolonization and the Reordering of French Culture* (Cambridge, MA: MIT Press, 1995), 27.
17. Susan Buck-Morss, *Dreamworld and Catastrophe: The Passing of Mass Utopia in East and West* (Cambridge, MA: MIT Press, 2002); Harry Harootunian, *Histories Disquiet: Modernity, Cultural Practice, and the Question of Everyday Life* (New York: Columbia University Press, 2001); David Harvey, *The Condition of Postmodernity: An Inquiry into the Origins of Social Change* (London: Blackwell Publishers, 1989); Mary Nolan, *Visions of Modernity: American Business and the*

Modernization of Germany (Oxford: Oxford University Press, 1994); Wolfgang Schivelbusch, *The Railway Journey: The Industrialization of Time and Space in the 19th Century* (Berkeley: University of California Press, 1986). I draw upon a number of methodologies, from historical anthropology and material culture studies to social histories of technology and the sociological concept of the habitus, in order to complicate simplistic gender and class readings of gender, motorization, and modernity in the Weimar Republic. My approach follows Arjun Appadurai's appeal to investigate "the social life of things." Appadurai calls for looking at the historical moments in the object's social life from "production, to mediation, to reception." Arjun Appadurai, ed., *The Social Life of Things: Commodities in Cultural Perspective* (Cambridge: Cambridge University Press, 1986). See also: Daniel Miller, *Material Culture and Mass Consumption* (Oxford: Blackwell Publishers, 1987); Daniel Miller, *Car Cultures* (Oxford: Berg, 2001); Pierre Bourdieu, *Distinction: A Social Critique of the Judgment of Taste* (London: Routledge, 1984); Michel de Certeau, *The Practice of Everyday Life* (Berkeley: University of California Press, 1984); Helmut Lethen, *Cool Conduct: The Culture of Distance in Weimar Germany* (Berkeley: University of California Press, 2002).

18. Eric Weitz provides an extremely good and readable overview of politics, culture, and society in the Weimar Republic. Weitz, *Weimar Republic*.

19. A few prominent examples are Thorstein Veblen, Werner Sombart, Antonio Gramsci, Roland Barthes, Henri Lefebvre, Paul F. Lazarsfeld, Herbert Marcuse, Pierre Bourdieu, and Jean Baudrillard.

20. For a concise definition of "automobility," see Jeremy Packer, *Mobility without Mayhem: Safety, Cars, and Citizenship* (Durham, NC: Duke University, 2008), 293n4. For a sociological approach towards "automobility," see "Special Issue on Automobilities," *Theory, Culture & Society* 21 (October 2004), ed. Mike Featherstone, Nigel Thrift, and John Urry. On the concept of "automobilism," see Mom, *Atlantic Automobilism*, 37–38. For a critical account of the development of mobility studies, and the differences between "automobility" and "automobilism," see Mom, *Atlantic Automobilism*, 7–27.

21. McShane, *Down the Asphalt Path*; Norton, *Fighting Traffic*; Seiler, *Republic of Drivers*; Packer, *Mobility without Mayhem*.

22. Merki, *Der holprige Siegeszug*; Sean O'Connell, *The Car and British Society: Class, Gender and Motoring 1896–1939* (Manchester: Manchester University Press, 1998). Lewis S. Seigelbaum has also looked at role of "light vehicles" in the development of Soviet society: Lewis S. Siegelbaum, *Cars for Comrades: The Life of the Soviet Automobile* (Ithaca, NY: Cornell University Press, 2008).

23. Kathleen Franz, *Tinkering: Consumers Reinvent the Early Automobile* (Philadelphia: University of Pennsylvania Press, 2005); Virginia Scharff, *Taking the Wheel: Women and the Coming of the Motor Age* (New York: Free Press, 1991); Georgine Clarsen, *Eat My Dust: Early Women Motorists* (Baltimore, MD: John Hopkins University Press, 2008).

24. Kurt Möser's recent monograph on "driving and flying" probes what made "mobility machines"—cars and airplanes, but also bicycles, motorcycles, motor boats, canoes, skis, surfboards, sleds, and so on—the object of intense fascination from 1890 to 1930. Kurt Möser, *Fahren und Fliegen in Frieden und Krieg: Kulturen individueller Mobilitätsmaschinen 1880–1930* (Heidelberg: Verlag Regionalkultur, 2009). On "timings and spacings" and "embodied sensibilities," see Peter Merriman,

Mobility, Space and Culture (London: Routledge, 2012). On speed, see Paulo Virilo, *Speed and Politics: An Essay on Dromology* (New York: Semiotext(e), 1977); Mimi Sheller, "Bodies, Cybercars and the Mundane Incorporation of Automated Mobilities," *Social & Cultural Geography* 8, no. 2 (2007): 175–97. On discourses of safety, see Packer, *Mobility without Mayhem*. On encapsulation and cocooning, see Gijs Mom, "Encapsulating Culture: European Car Travel, 1900–1940," *Journal of Tourism History* 3, no. 3 (2011).

25. On the "Social Construction of Technology," see Wiebe E. Bijker, Thomas Parke Hughes, and T.J. Pinch, eds., *The Social Construction of Technological Systems: New Directions in the Sociology and History of Technology* (Cambridge, MA: MIT Press, 1987).

26. Gijs Mom recovered a less-known trajectory—once abandoned, but now again celebrated as a necessary alternative—of the electric vehicle for the history of motorization. See Gijs Mom, *The Electric Vehicle: Technology and Expectations in the Automobile Age* (Baltimore, MD: John Hopkins University Press, 2012). Through its broad interpretation of "mobility machines," Kurt Möser's *Fliegen and Fahren* represents an exception and Jeremy Packer has one chapter on motorcycling and another on trucking in his study, *Mobility without Mayhem*. Mom's *Atlantic Automobilism* also pays some attention to other forms of motorized transport, including the motorcycle.

27. For academic literature on the automobile in Germany, see: Edelmann, *Vom Luxusgut zum Gebrauchsgegendstand*, 108, 126; Flik, *Von Ford lernen?*; Uwe Fraunholz, *Motorphobia: Anti-automobiler Protest in Kaiserreich und Weimarer Republik*, (Göttingen: Vandenhoeck & Ruprecht, 2002); Alexa Geisthovel, "Das Auto," in *Orte der Moderne: Erfahrungswelten des 19. und 20. Jahrhundert*, ed. Alexa Geisthovel and Habbo Knoch (Frankfurt am Main and New York: Campus, 2005), 37–46; Barbara Haubner, *Von Nervenkitzel zur Freizeitvergnügen, Automobilismus in Deutschland, 1860–1914* (Göttingen: Vandenhoeck & Ruprecht, 1998); Koshar, "On the History of the Automobile"; Rudy Koshar, "Cars and Nations: Anglo-German Perspectives on Automobility between the World Wars," *Theory, Culture & Society* 21 (2004): 121–44; Merki, *Der holprige Siegeszug*; Kurt Möser, "World War I and the Creation of Desire for Automobiles in Germany," in *Getting and Spending: European and American Consumer Societies in the 20th Century*, ed. Susan Strasser, Charles McGovern, and Matthias Judt (Cambridge: Cambridge University Press, 1998), 195–222; Kurt Möser, *Geschichte des Autos* (Frankfurt am Main: Campus, 2002); Wolfgang Sachs, *For the Love of the Automobile: Looking Back into the History of our Desires* (Berkeley: University of California Press, 1992); Angela Zatsch, *Staatsmacht und Motorisiserung am Morgen des Automobilzeitalters* (Konstanz: Hartung-Gorre, 1993).

28. While Frank Steinbeck's recent monograph, *Das Motorrad*, is an important exception to an exclusive focus on the automobile in the history of motorization in Germany and his research partly overlaps with the interests of the present book, his stated purpose is to provide an explanation for Germany's two-wheeled 'special path' (what he terms a *Sonderweg*) to motorization. His work, valuable in its own right, nevertheless pays very little attention to cultural or social conflicts, or to shifting understandings of class, gender, and sexuality. See Frank Steinbeck, *Das Motorrad: Ein deutscher Sonderweg in die automobile Gesellschaft* (Stuttgart: Franz Steiner Verlag, 2012), here 9–11. A few articles have also been published on production and the economic side of motorcycling in Germany:

Braun and Panzer, "The Expansion of the Motor-Cycle Industry"; Rainer Gömmel and Helmut Braun, "Aufstieg und Niedergang der deutschen Motorradindustrie," in *Struktur und Dimension. Festschrift für Heinrich Kaufhold zum 65. Geburtstag*, vol. 2, ed. Hans-Jürgen Gerhard (Stuttgart: Franz Steiner Verlag, 1997), 167–94. Motorcycling culture in England has been given more attention by mobility and transport scholars. See, for example, Christopher Thomas Potter, "An Exploration of Social and Cultural Aspects of Motorcycling during the Interwar Period" (PhD diss., Northumbria University, 2007); Steve Koerner has also published a number of articles on motorcycling in England: Steve Koerner, "Four Wheels Good, Two Wheel Bad: The Motor Cycle versus the Light Motor Car 1919–1939," in *The Motor Car and Popular Culture in the 20th Century*, ed. David Thoms, Len Holden, and Tim Claydon (Aldershot: Ashgate, 1998), 151–76; Steve Koerner, "Whatever Happened to the Girl on the Motorbike? British Women and Motorcycling, 1919 to 1939," *International Journal of Motorcycling Studies* (March 2007), accessed 28 June 2007, http://ijms.nova.edu/March2007/IJMS_Artcl.Koerner.html. Indeed, a small, Anglo-American-dominated cultural studies subfield of "motorcycling studies" has been initiated by a group of interdisciplinary scholars. See the "only peer-reviewed journal devoted to motorcycling": *International Journal of Motorcycle Studies*, http://ijms.nova.edu. Two of the editors of the IJMS published a monograph on the motorcycle from a broadly conceived "object design" perspective: Steven E. Alford and Suzanne Ferriss, *Motorcycle* (London: Reaktion Books, 2007).

29. In fact at least two automobile companies, Opel and Hanomag, did implement partial assembly line production at their plants, but their cars were still too costly, especially in terms of operating costs, to be affordable to the masses seeking to motorize. On the efforts of rationalization in the automobile industry during World War II, see Anita Kugler, "Von der Werkstatt zum Fließband, Etappen der frühen Automobilproduktion," *Geschichte und Gesellschaft* 13, no. 3 (1987): 324–28.

30. See Flik, *Von Ford lernen?*, especially 199–201, 221–29. Furthermore, the depressed real wages for workers in Germany impeded the implementation of a Fordist model of production based on mass consumption. See also Nolan, *Visions of Modernity*, 78–80, 162–65.

31. "Zur Frage des Volksmotorrades," *Das Motorrad*, 1927: 372–73.

32. The 1931 yearbook of the National League of the German Automobile Industry reported that, "already in 1928, the German motorcycle industry had moved up to the top position in world production of motorcycles with 162,000 units. In 1929, with the production of 200,000 units, the German motorcycle industry solidified its position as the global leader, responsible for more than a third of global production." *Jahrbuch der Reichsverband der Automobilindustrie*, 1931, 124–25; Braun and Panzer, "Expansion," 49–50.

33. Andrea Rapini, "La Vespa: histoire sociale d'une innovation industrielle," *Actes de la recherche en sciences sociales* 4 (2007): 76. A 1932 article in *Das Motorrad* claimed: "Mussolini is himself an enthusiastic motorcyclist. It is not seldom that he roars out of the side gate of the Palazzo Venezia, rushing through Rome to take the street to Ostia in a record tempo – the relaxation and recreation of a dictator." G.R. "Italienischer Motorsport und italienische Industrie: Konzentration und Zusammenarbeit: ein Ziel aufs innigste zu wünschen – für Deutschland," *Das Motorrad*, 1932: 1250.

34. Steinbeck, *Das Motorrad*.

35. John Alt proposed reading the motorcycle as a "cultural commodity." While I do not apply a "culture industry" based reading of motorcycling to the Weimar Republic as he does in terms of motorcycling in the 1980s, many of the tropes Alt proposed were present already during the Weimar Republic. See John Alt, "Popular Culture and Mass Consumption: The Motorcycle as Cultural Commodity," *Journal of Popular Culture* 15, no. 4 (Spring 1982): 129–41.

36. See, for example, Martin Heidegger, "Von Wesen und Wirklichkeit der Kraft," in *Die Grundbegriffe der Metaphysik, Aristoteles: Metaphysik IX 1–3* (Frankfurt am Main: Vittorio Klostermann, 1981), 517.

37. Martin Heidegger, *Introduction to Metaphysics*, trans. Gregory Fried and Richard Polt (New Haven, CT: Yale University Press 2000), 36. See also, Hans Ulrich Gumbrecht, *In 1926: Living at the Edge of Time* (Cambridge, MA: Harvard University Press, 1997), 454.

38. Packer, *Mobility without Mayhem*, 133.

39. Alt, "Popular Culture and Mass Consumption," 134, 138. See also the 1970s pop-philosophy classic, Robert M. Pirsig, *Zen and the Art of Motorcycle Maintenance: An Inquiry into Values* (New York: Morrow, 1974).

40. See Victoria de Grazia's introduction to the *Sex of Things*. De Grazia and Furlough, *The Sex of Things*, 7.

41. As Judy Wacjman put it: "Even more markedly than the car, the motorcycle is a symbolic object that represents physical toughness, virility, excitement, speed, danger and skill. Their conspicuous bodywork and mechanics resonate with their original military use, and speak of aggression and virility. Along with leather jackets, riders wear grease-stained jeans to express their technical competence. The experience of riding a bike encapsulates the outdoor, roving life of the wanderer with no ties. It also symbolizes a form of man's mastery of the machine; a powerful monster between his legs which he must tame." Judy Wajcman, *Feminism Confronts Technology* (University Park: Pennsylvania State University Press, 1991), 134. Notable exceptions that look at the British case are Koerner, "Whatever Happened to the Girl on the Motorbike?"; and Potter, "Social and Cultural Aspects of Motorcycling."

42. "In Western societies, acts of exchange and consumption have long been obsessively gendered, usually as female." De Grazia and Furlough, *The Sex of Things*, 1. On gender, especially femininity during the Weimar Republic, see: Katharina von Ankum, ed., *Women in the Metropolis: Gender and Modernity in Weimar Culture* (Berkeley: University of California Press, 1997); Atina Grossmann, *Reforming Sex: The German Movement for Birth Control and Abortion Reform, 1920–1950* (Oxford: Oxford University Press 1995); Patrice Petro, *Joyless Streets: Women and Melodramatic Representation in Weimar Germany* (Princeton, NJ: Princeton University Press, 1989); Jennifer M. Lynn, "Contested Femininities: Representations of Modern Women in the German Illustrated Press, 1920–1945" (PhD diss., University of North Carolina, Chapel Hill, 2012); Nina Sylvester, "'Das Girl': Crossing Spaces and Spheres: The Function of the Girl in the Weimar Republic" (PhD diss., University of California, Los Angeles, 2006). See also the global implications of the "new woman": Alys Eve Weinbaum et al., *The Modern Girl around the World: Consumption, Modernity and Globalization* (Durham, NC: Duke University Press, 2008), especially the essay by Ute G. Poiger, "Fantasies of Universality? *Neue Frauen*, Race and Nation in Weimar and Nazi Germany," 315–44.

43. See also Christopher Breward, *The Hidden Consumer: Masculinities, Fashion and City Life 1860–1914* (Manchester: Manchester University Press, 1999), 1–2.
44. Seiler, *Republic of Drivers*, 54. On the gendering of technology in general, see Roger Horowitz and Arwen Mohun, eds. *His and Hers: Gender, Consumption and Technology* (Charlottesville: University of Virginia Press, 1998); Roger Horowitz, ed., *Boys and Their Toys? Masculinity, Technology and Class in America* (New York: Routledge, 2001). On the automobile, see, for example, Sachs, *For the Love of the Automobile*, 32–46; Merki, *Der holprige Siegeszug*, 257–64, 286–94; O'Connell, *The Car and British Society*, 43–76. On the motorcycle, see: Dick Hebdige, "Object as Image: The Italian Motor Scooter Cycle," in *Hiding in the Light: On Images and Things* (London: Comedia, 1988), 77–115.
45. "Gender is a political category, not only through the hierarchical differ-ence between men and women, but also through the conflict-ridden rivalries between different imaginations of masculinity (and also femininities) – within one time, in one society, one man." Kühne, "Männergeschichte als Geschlechtergeschichte," 19.
46. Although in decline during the Weimar Republic, older institutions, such as the church and the family, continued to assert considerable influence over gender norms, while militarization and labor became more important rhe-torically as their position to materially reinforce normative masculinities in everyday life was weakened. See Raymond C. Sun, "'Hammer Blows': Work, the Workplace, and the Culture of Masculinity among Catholic Workers in the Weimar Republic," *Central European History* 37, no. 2 (2004): 245–71. On hege-monic masculinity, see R.W. Connell, *Masculinities* (Cambridge: Polity, 1995); and R.W. Connell, "Hegemonic Masculinity: Rethinking the Concept," *Gender & Society* 19, no. 6 (2005): 19.
47. On "doing and undoing gender," see Judith Butler, *Undoing Gender* (London: Routledge, 2004); also Ulrike Brunotte and Rainer Herrn, "Statt einer Einleitung. Männlichkeiten und Moderne–Pathosformeln, Wissenskulturen, Diskurse," in *Männlichkeiten und Moderne*, ed. Brunotte and Herrn, 9–24, here 11.
48. For a discussion of female masculinities during the Weimar Republic, see Katie Sutton, *The Masculine Woman in Weimar Germany* (New York: Berghahn Books, 2011).
49. On the modern woman, see: Gabriele Tergit, *Atem einer anderen Welt: Berliner Reportagen*, ed. Jens Brüning (Frankfurt am Main: Suhrkamp, 1994), 46. On attri-butes of the modern man, see: "Öffentliche Meinung 216: Motorradfahren stei-gert das Allgemeinbefinden," *Das Motorrad*, 1929: 116. Kurt Möser argues that automobilism, both before and after WWI, provided a "conditioning for modern life." Kurt Möser, "The Dark Side of 'Automobilism', 1900–30: Violence, War, and the Motor Car," *Journal of Transport History* 24, no. 2 (2003): 243–46. See also, Joachim Radkau, *Das Zeitalter der Nervösität: Deutschland zwischen Bismarck und Hitler* (Darmstadt: Wissenschaftliche Buchgesellschaft, 2002).
50. Distinctions between different types of motorists, for example between motorcy-clists and automobile owners, were created and perpetuated based on class and gender. For example, Heidrun Edelmann asserts that the automobile industry tried to maintain an elite aura, whereas with motorcycles, and especially smaller types, the "mass character" became a selling point. "Thus, the motorcycle, 'the motor vehicle of the working population,' for whom it was possible to 'do with-out individuality' (*auf Individualität verzichtet werden konnte*), rationalization of

constructions and the production process progressed especially far." Edelmann, *Vom Luxusgut zum Gebrauchsgegendstand*, 109.

51. My use of habitus draws upon both Pierre Bourdieu's formulation of the habitus as a "structuring structure," but also goes back to draw upon contemporary Weimar sociologist Theodor Geiger's concept of lifestyles and habitus. See Pierre Bourdieu, *Distinction*, 170; Theodore Geiger, *Die soziale Schichtung des deutschen Volkes. Soziographischer Versuch auf statistischer Grundlage* (Stuttgart: Ferdinand Enke Verlag, 1932), III–IV, 13, 77–82.

52. David Gartman, "Three Ages of the Automobile: The Cultural Logics of the Car," in *Theory, Culture & Society* 21, no. 4–5 (2004): 169–95. Although also structured in terms of "stages," the argument Gijs Mom offers in *Atlantic Automobilisms* supports a more complicated reading of car consumption during this period. See Mom, *Atlantic Automobilism*, 647.

53. Seiler, *Republic*, 60.

54. On driving as compensation for a loss of individualism in the United States, see Seiler, *Republic*.

55. Kurt Möser, "Dark Side of 'Automobilism,'" 238.

56. For the twentieth-century history of the motoring press in Germany, see Ulrich Kubisch, Andreas Curtius, and Joachim Dufner, *Das Automobil als Lesestoff: zur Geschichte der deutschen Motorpresse, 1898–1998.* Vol. 29 (Berlin: Staatsbibliothek zu Berlin, 1998).

57. Gijs Mom also makes extensive use of fictional sources, a body of literature Mom terms "autopoetics," to trace the development of a "grammar" of automobilism; see Mom, *Atlantic Automobilism*, 133–204.

58. Fred Petermann's *PS-Narr* was serialized in *Das Motorrad* in 1927, Julius Donny's *Garage 13* in 1929, and Fritz Pullig's *Rennfieber* in *Motorrad-Sport, -Verkehr und -Technik* in 1929–30. A further novel, Walter Julius Bloem's *Motorherz*, was published in 1927 and reviewed in motorcycle magazines. See Chapter 3 on the motoring trade press. For more information on the reading culture during the Weimar Republic, see: Gideon Reuveni, *Reading Germany: Literature and Consumer Culture in Germany before 1933* (New York: Berghahn Books, 2006).

59. Bruce Seely has explored the habitus of the US highway engineer. Bruce E. Seely, *Building the American Highway System: Engineers as Policy Makers* (Philadelphia, PA: Temple University Press, 1987).

60. "Auto oder Motorrad," *Auto-Magazin*, no. 8, 1928, 578–82, here 578.

61. "Review of Walter Julius Bloem, Motorherz, Verlag Scherl, Berlin, 1927," *Der deutsche Motorfahrer*, no. 1, 1928, 24.

62. As quoted in Paul Friedmann, "Pest von Vehikeln – Lärmritter der Straße!," *Das Motorrad*, 1931: 1767–68.

CHAPTER 1

From Pioneers to Global Dominance
The First Forty Years of the German Motorcycle Industry

In 1928, the "rationalization" craze had a firm grip on German society. *Theory and Praxis of Rationalization*, its cover designed by avant-garde artist John Heartfield, was Soviet professor Ossip Ermanski's second book published in German translation. An expert on fatigue and a strong critic of Frederick W. Taylor, Ermanski debated the benefits and drawbacks of the reorganization of labor based on Taylor's principles of scientific management. Unable to find a diagram of the layout of the Ford factory in Cologne, Ermanski instead used the layout of the Stock motorcycle factory in Berlin to illustrate the principles of flow production and the assembly line, thus acknowledging how efficiently production was organized at the motorcycle factory: "The result of the whole organization is that every four minutes a complete motorcycle leaves the assembly line. The net costs of this German manufacture have been pushed so low that it is even competitive on the export market."[1] Ermanski's discussion of advanced production methods reveals a number of aspects salient to this chapter. First, the book itself is a telling artifact, demonstrating the global fascination with productivist ideologies and modernist aesthetics, which was markedly pronounced in the Weimar Republic.[2] Second, it rehearses the standard association of the assembly line with automobile production and Ford in particular. Third, and if only by accident, Ermanski's use of the Stock motorcycle factory to illustrate the "praxis of rationalization" points to how, by 1928, the motorcycle industry was one of the most advanced branches of German industry.

The road the German motorcycle industry took to becoming a model of "rationalized" production was, however, neither smooth nor direct. Due to internal and external pressures, the fortune of the German motorcycle industry fluctuated wildly, contributing to a "deviant path" of German motorization.[3] Rather than motorizing via the automobile, as for example was the case in the United States, by the end of the Weimar Republic, Germany had both the highest per-capita ownership and was the world's largest manufacturer of motorcycles.[4] The industry developed haltingly alongside the bicycle and car industries from the late nineteenth century through World War I. The first crisis years of the republic and hyperinflation had mixed effects on the industry, leading to the simultaneous growth and rationalization of the industry during the so-called "golden years" of 1924–1929. Finally, the World Economic Crisis deeply impacted German motorcycle production.[5] This chapter examines the salient aspects of the first four decades of motorcycle manufacturing in Germany, from finance to design to government subsidies, and from the types of motorcycles that were manufactured to the production process of individual companies. Through tracing the development of the motorcycle industry in Germany in the first decades of the twentieth century, I demonstrate the centrality of the motorcycle in the process of motorization in Germany, exploring why this phenomenon was a matter of such great concern for contemporaries.

A set of historically specific economic and legal circumstances facilitated the rise of the German motorcycle industry following World War I, making it *the* vehicle to individual motorization during the Weimar Republic. Its development and its subsequent rise to predominance must be situated in the context of the larger automotive industry and the economy as a whole, including how it was located within shifting global markets. Alongside juridical and financial incentives provided by the state, advancements in technology, changes in production, and competitive pricing and sales strategies resulted in motorcycles being the only viable and affordable means of personal motorized transportation for both productive and recreation purposes for most Germans. Revisiting the potholes and patches on the German motorcycle industry's road to global dominance demonstrates how mobility choices were shaped by politics and the economy, both of which were fractured and ambivalent spaces, fraught with competing visions.

The Beginnings of an Industry: Motorcycle Production prior to World War I

Origin stories of the motor vehicle were and most often are still recounted as heroic tales of pioneers who dared to challenge the constraints of nature. Indeed, as many mobility scholars have argued, the conquest of nature is one of the most persistent foundational myths of motorization. In reality, during the nineteenth century, motor vehicles were clumsy, awkward affairs that were neither practical nor reliable. Furthermore, they did not appear out of nowhere, but rather were developed within the context of older technologies. The bicycle, for example, was central to the development of both the motorcycle and the automobile as forms of individual transportation, as of course were horse-drawn vehicles. Advancements in engine-driven mobility during the nineteenth century were moreover dominated by the implementation of steam-powered technologies, most visibly in the form of the railway locomotive and the steamship, and the first self-propelled road vehicles were steam- and electric-driven.[6] In the 1880s, German engineers and inventors, however, were at the international forefront of applying the mechanics of internal combustion to transportation. According to mobility historian Kurt Möser, "In this decade, new mobility technologies were either invented or older forms were socially and technologically reconstructed, user groups were identified and expanded, new socialization and organization forms were tried out or adopted, stable cultural patterns for usage were established, and finally patterns of perception and representation were stabilized."[7]

Often cited as the "first" motorcycle, Gottlieb Daimler and Wilhelm Maybach developed a one-cylinder internal combustion engine in 1883 that they installed on a two-wheeled vehicle, improving the vehicle over the course of three years. Even though Daimler and Maybach called their vehicle a "riding car" rather than a motorcycle, the two-wheeled vehicle powered by an internal combustion engine was claimed as a German invention.[8] The "triumphal procession" of combustion engine–powered vehicles was, however, "bumpy," rather than smooth.[9] Even after advances in developing the internal combustion engine, both steam and electric power for individual vehicles continued to be viable technological options.[10] Even Henry Ford first dabbled in steam engines, before he was inspired by German innovations in internal combustion.[11]

In his 1929 dissertation on the German motorcycle industry, Willi Christenn, a 28-year-old doctoral candidate in political economics (*Volkswirtschaft*) at the Ludwig-Maximilians University in Munich and a summer intern at BMW, championed the idea that the motorcycle was a German invention, and that powering it with an internal combustion engine was essentially a technologically determined fait accompli. Noting that the steam engine was not a feasible alternative for powering the smaller frame of a motorcycle, Christenn asserted, "So a vehicle had to be constructed that would eliminate the misshapenness and difficult handling of the steam-powered vehicle (*Dampfwagen*), as well as the exhaustion of the driver, as is the case with bicycles. So one came upon a bicycle with a built-in motor as its source of power: this thought was … first conceived in Germany and the precursors of all of today's motorcycles and mopeds originate from this idea."[12] While Christenn's boastful stance on Germany's role in advancing motorcycle design implies a steady, steep ascent, this was not the case. On an international scale, however, the last decades of the nineteenth century and the first decade and a half of the twentieth century did witness many new mechanical and technical innovations that increased the reliability and power of the new combustion engines. Nonetheless, these advances were applied mainly to developing airplanes and the four-wheeled automobile rather than to the two-wheeled motorcycle.[13]

To commemorate the thirtieth anniversary of the invention, F. Paul Fritsche, a high-ranking member of the leading motorcycle associations in post–World War I Germany and an academically trained merchant, wrote on the origins of the German motorcycle industry, providing a more sober assessment of its development: "The classification 'motorcycle' first appears in the year 1894, in which Hildebrand and Wolfmüller mounted their much-improved four-stroke engine and patented this vehicle under the name 'motorcycle.' Around the turn of the century, a few leading bicycle manufacturers took up the idea of motorcycle construction and after some stubborn attempts the actual development of the German motorcycle industry began."[14] Neckarsulmer Fahrzeug AG [Neckarsulm Motor Vehicle Company, NSU], located in in Swabian Württemberg, and the Wanderer Werke [Wanderer Works] in Chemnitz, Saxony, were both important producers of bicycles before adding motorcycles to their product line, and were instrumental in the early years of the German motorcycle industry.[15] Between 1901 and 1903, according to Christenn, whose language often reproduces the conception of the inventor/engineer as the hero of the process of motorization, these two manufacturers were engaged in a "tenacious struggle to gain dominance." Christenn hyped the manufacturers, claiming that through "standardized production and producing more motorcycles through efficient fabrication from the lessons learned from previous experiments," NSU and Wanderer had attempted, even before World War I, to "design a rationalized make of motorcycle."[16]

While there were no more than two thousand motorcycles on German streets in 1903, that number had quadrupled by 1905, making it possible to speak of a "motorcycle boom."[17] A considerable number of technological improvements on the motorcycle had been made in the decades since its invention, such as electric magneto-ignition with spark plugs replacing the hot bulb. The introduction of gear transmission with clutch and chain, belt, or flexible shaft harnessed engine power more effectively. The invention of drum brakes, pneumatic tires, and front forks with suspension improved safety, reliability, and comfort.[18] It was during this time that a new technological style developed that was, in turn, tied to a new culture of mobility.[19] During the prewar era, the symbolic and cultural valence of motor vehicles—cars, motorcycles, and airplanes—coalesced around a combination of "archaic heroic ideals of knighthood and courage with specifically modern qualities, especially a personal relationship with technology."[20] As Cotten Seiler noted, "Early twentieth-century popular culture, art, and political philosophy also celebrated the car as a force-multiplier of the self, facilitator of a gratifying, thrilling transgression, and a fosterer of self-control."[21]

During the decades preceding World War I, actively partaking in the culture of motorized mobility was limited to a small yet global elite. Even more than cars, motorcycles were a novelty item for the rich and/or inventive. They remained costly—the price of a Hildebrand & Wolfmüller motorcycle was the equivalent of the annual salary of a skilled worker.[22] Motorcycles were also mechanically unreliable and thus in need of constant repair and upkeep. In addition, the condition of most streets in Germany was abysmal; rural roads were unpaved, rendering them dusty when dry and impassably muddy when wet. After the short boom period in the first decade of the twentieth century, in which motorcycles outnumbered cars approximately five to three, the sale of motorcycles in Germany stagnated in comparison to that of automobiles (see Appendix: Table 1). The comparative numbers of automobiles, trucks, and motorcycles reflected the relative strength of the German Empire's pre–World War I economy.

Furthermore, in the ten years preceding the outbreak of World War I, foreign manufacturers made more advances in the production of the two-wheeler than the Germans. The French (Dion-Bouton), Belgian (Fabrique Nationale), North American (Harley Davidson and Indian) and British (Excelsior, Matchless, Royal Enfield, and Triumph) industries gained a considerable competitive edge by producing sturdier and more reliable motorcycles than did Germany's indigenous industry. The stronger motorcycles—primarily US and British—however, represented a considerable expense and thus were less likely to be purchased than automobiles. During this period, automobiles also became more reliable and were preferred by those who could afford the purchase and upkeep of a motor vehicle for their relative comfort and as highly visible and powerful status symbols, both material and psychological.[23] Indeed, NSU, one of Germany's major prewar manufacturers, had such a difficult time drumming up domestic demand for their motorcycles that two-thirds of the prewar production was exported.[24] Even prior to World War I, the motorcycle was considered to be the "stepchild" among the available transport methods.[25]

Motorcycles and the Military in World War I

Although the Imperial Army integrated the motorcycle as early as 1904 into its *Kaisermanöver* (an important military maneuver held on a rotating basis in the different states of the relatively recently united German Empire, and named such because of the presence of the Kaiser), the Imperial Army, for all intents and purposes, did not pursue a strategy of motorization prior to the outbreak of World War I.[26] Despite the establishment of a "Volunteer Automobile and Motorcyclist Corps" before the war, from all accounts, the motorcycle only found hesitating acceptance in the Imperial Army: "Even our military authorities had little trust in this method of transportation [motorcycles], and extensive propaganda work by interested parties . . . was necessary to get military posts to actively promote the motorcycle."[27] The Imperial Army, in contrast to the truncated Reichswehr of the Weimar Republic as will be discussed later, appeared to have had very little interest in developing the motorcycle for military use. Trucks, however, were promoted as military vehicles and were deployed as troop, munitions, and provisions carriers.[28]

During World War I, the French, British, and US armies relied on motorcycles far more heavily than did the German army. For example, while the British Army had more than sixty thousand motorcycles in use in 1918, only approximately five thousand were ever deployed on the German side. Instead, bicycles were a far more common form of "mechanized" individual transport for the German Army than any type of motor vehicle.[29] The primary military use of the motorcycle was for delivering messages to and from the front by soldiers designated as "motorcycle couriers." In photographs of World War I motorcycle couriers, these soldiers emanated bureaucratic blandness in their uniforms and their vehicles, lacking militaristic and masculine sex appeal, and appearing more like postal workers than modern warriors. Standing in exotic visual contrast to motorcycle couriers, however, were "motorcycle gunners," who operated motorcycles with special sidecar machine-gun mounts that NSU built from 1915 to 1918, and who were celebrated during the Nazi era as "Hussars of the Infantry."[30] The newness of the machine technology enhanced the "motorcycle gunners" appearance as strong, modern men, and images of these troops on cigarette cards, postcards, and in magazines served to promote motorization, during and especially after World War I.

With motorized mobility still in emergence, World War I provided a prominent if morbid showcase for its potential uses. Historians have often pointed to the symbolic importance of the fighter pilot in fueling male desire for motorized masculinity in post–World War I Germany.[31]

While the fighter pilot was indeed an important and influential cultural icon, the representation of masculinity that the fighter pilot embodied shifted over the course of the Weimar Republic.[32] Overemphasizing the figure of the fighter pilot also obscures the significance of alternate icons of motorized masculinity, such as motorcycle and automobile racers who were also glorified during the Weimar Republic as heroic figures. Constructions of motorcycling masculinity were more heterogeneous than a focus on militarized motorcycling masculinity would suggest, and both masculinity and the symbolic import of motorcycling were flexible and changed over time.

After the outbreak of World War I, factories involved in the manufacturing of motor vehicles were required to halt civilian production, and the state was permitted to requisition private vehicles for military purposes. Indeed, the number of civilian motor vehicles on German roads dropped significantly over the course of the war. The 1920 encyclopedic work *Technology in World War* evaluated the use of technology primarily in the German Army. The author of the chapter on the role of motor vehicles in the German army, claimed: "While most of the implements of war are specially conceived and designed for the purpose of the army, the motor vehicle is without doubt definitely a peacetime creation. It is possible to say that during the war it did not undergo any significant modification."[33] Instead of meeting consumer demands, automotive manufacturers were obliged to increase overall production to meet the demands of the army. To fill the order of approximately seventy-five thousand motor vehicles contracted by the army, the industry introduced serial production, and, following initial difficulties reorganizing the production process, the motor vehicle industry was able to accommodate the demands of the German army. In terms of the automotive industry, conditions were transformed through the shift to wartime production, the most important vehicle being the truck.[34].

In 1929, with the hindsight of ten years, Christenn provided a drastic description of the effects of the war on the German motorcycle industry: "In all areas of the economy the war was a terrible consumer (*furchtbarer Verbraucher*), certainly, at least partially, of a rather unproductive nature. With the scarcity of raw materials, the motor vehicle industry had to place all its reserves on the sacrificial altar of the war god." Forced to switch production lines to manufacture munitions for the war, Christenn claims that "those few companies able to rescue themselves through the war could not realize their ideas for further developing [the motorcycle] due to the lack of necessary raw materials that were either completely unavailable or else were subject to requisition by the army."[35] Rather than being able to use resources for further technical innovations, the motorcycle industry was forced to devote its energies to implementing serial production of prewar models and standardized norms. On a material level, the war, rather than aiding the cause of motorization in Germany, had a negative impact on motorcycle production, and on the automotive industry generally.[36]

The First Crisis Years of the Republic

November 1918 brought the definitive end to Wilhelmine Germany with the capitulation of the Imperial German Army, the dethroning of the emperor, the dissolution of regional monarchies, the abolition of all formal feudal privileges, and the birth of the German Republic. It also ushered in a new era and a gradual reversal of fortunes for the flagging motorcycle industry. Due to the centrally directed and severely restricted wartime economy, the German motorcycle industry, to a large extent, lay in shambles. The only German motorcycle manufacturers able to survive were NSU and Wanderer, both of which had lucrative wartime contracts supplying motorcycles to the army.[37] In the months following demobilization, a number of decommissioned and surplus military motorcycles became available (including foreign models, such as Fabrique Nationale, Harley Davidson and Indian). Yet, due to the chaotic political, economic, and institutional situation in Germany following the war—with revolution and rebellion, strikes and putsch attempts on the daily order—the German industry faced severe impediments to growth. It was not until the end of 1920 that fuel, rubber, and oil ceased to be rationed, and it was not until 1921 that a new law was issued that officially allowed the civilian use of motor vehicles.[38]

At the end of the war, seeking an outlet to put their factories to work, German industrialists identified an emerging market for a relatively cheap form of individual motorized transportation.[39] Thus, during the course of the transition to a peacetime economy, numerous armament manufacturers took up the production of motorcycles. For example, the Bayrische Motoren-Werke [Bavarian Motor Works, BMW] in Munich, having manufactured airplane motors before and during the war, had switched production over to motorcycle engines by 1921, manufacturing their first complete motorcycle in 1923. The state-owned Heereswerkstätten Spandau [Army Workshops Spandau] in Berlin had manufactured weapons and munitions before and during the war, and began manufacturing D-Rad motorcycles between 1919 and 1921. Zündapp in Nuremberg, founded during World War I as the Zünder- und Apparatebau GmbH [Fuse and Apparatus Manufacture] began production of motorcycles marketed at the "everyman" by 1922.[40] The motorcycle industry, according to Willi Christenn, "sought to build on the hopes from the prewar era." The war had dramatically altered the economic situation, as Christenn argues, "because although the purchasing power of the public was weaker, the demand for private methods of transportation was greater than before, especially because in the immediate postwar era the reliability of the railways and also the tramways left much to be desired."[41] Out of this set of circumstances—which included the still decreased purchasing power of the German population, the scarcity of the raw materials (including rubber and petroleum) necessary for the everyday use of motor vehicles, and insufficient capital for investment-intensive industries, such as the automobile industry—a number of German manufacturers began to concentrate on developing a lightweight, low-power (often meaning a two-stroke engine with a higher cubic capacity and lower displacement) motorcycle.[42]

Constraints on both the supply and demand side thus favored the two-stroke engine design, which gained in popularity within the German motorcycle industry and also among consumers.[43] Nevertheless, although the two-stroke engine was cheaper to produce and theoretically less expensive and easier to maintain, it had the reputation of being noisier and messier, as well as less fuel-efficient than the four-stroke engine. When a not-insignificant portion of Germany's overall motorcycle industry took up or shifted over to the production of two-stroke engines, a major debate arose among industrialists and riders alike around which engine design was preferable.[44] One champion of the two-stroke engine, Curt Hanfland, syndic of the Verband der Leichtkraftrad-Industrie e.V. [League of Small-Powered Motorcycle Industry, VLI] and author of numerous technical publications, celebrated the "blossoming of a new industry." Referring to auxiliary motors for bicycles and small-powered motorcycles, Hanfland claimed, "Thousands upon thousands of motorcycles were demanded, manufactured, and sold monthly."[45] While production and ownership of four-stroke motorcycles remained higher than those with two-stroke engines until the late 1920s, the growing production and demand for the engines with less cylinder volume was driven to a large degree by the conditions of economic constraint that characterized the Weimar Republic.

The rapid postwar development of the motorcycle industry was also in part a result of the inflationary economy that ended only in 1924 with a radical currency reform.[46] While inflation had been creeping upward since the declaration of war in August 1914, by the beginning of the 1920s the inflationary trend could no longer be ignored and took on gross proportions by the summer of 1923.[47] Although the short acute period of hyperinflation in the last months of 1923 had a dampening effect on the motorcycle industry, the years of moderately increasing inflation between 1920 and the middle of 1923 witnessed a rash of growth.[48] Between 1919 and 1924, the number of German motorcycle manufacturers mushroomed from 35 to over 350. Most of these firms were very small operations in which one to five workers would assemble frames and motors purchased from other manufacturers, often from English companies such as Matchless or JAP.[49] "Alongside bicycle manufacturers, dealers and machinery shops, metalworking shops, iron dealers, foundries, and instrument-makers" also took on the title of "motorcycle manufacturer."[50]

The explosion in the number of motorcycle manufacturers in 1921–1923 can be attributed to the "flight into fixed capital," or "fixed capital mania" as one contemporary critic called it—meaning the rapid conversion of currency into capital investment.[51] "The period of inflation demanded quick investment of cash sums. There was no other option—operating capital had to be transformed into fixed capital. Wasting time meant asset erosion and quick merchandising decisions meant asset accretion, or at least asset preservation."[52] Indeed, motorcycle manufacturers profited from the easy availability of state bank credit for capital investment and the ability to wipe out debt based on speculation on further currency devaluation.[53] In 1931, Paul Friedmann, an engineer with an academic title and the editor-in-chief of *Das Motorrad*, the leading motorcycling journal during the Weimar Republic, wrote on the effects of inflation on the motorcycle industry: "Before (and during) the war only two firms ... existed that built motorcycles in noteworthy numbers. An extensive motorcycle industry only emerged through 'promoterism fury' [*Gründerwut*] during the period of inflation. Those whose money did not stretch far enough for 'an automobile factory' at least founded a motorcycle factory. Every metalworker felt himself to be an industrialist."[54] Another side effect of inflation that contributed to the growth of the German motorcycle industry was that foreign imports were beyond the means of almost every German, and the devalued currency also meant a more favorable export climate.[55]

The inflationary economy, as traumatic as it was, stimulated decisions in terms of the design, production, and consumption of motorcycles. The German motorcycling industry organization Verein Deutscher Motorfahrzeug-Industrieller [Association of German Motor Vehicle Industrialists, VDMI] claimed: "As a result of the rapidly advancing inflation, calls for a lightweight motorcycle grew louder, which, in relation to its purchase price and running cost, would still be relatively affordable.

A large portion of the industry heeded this call and began building lightweight, reliable motorcycles."[56] On the demand side, runaway inflation led to a pervasive sense of economic instability, which in turn influenced the options weighed and choices made by individual men from all walks of life across Germany. In turn, on the supply side, the often inchoate and undirected interplay between the economy and politics influenced the design of motorcycles and the choices available to consumers.

At the beginning of the period of extreme currency devaluation, F.A.E. Martin, an engineer and contributing editor of *Das Motorrad*, waxed optimistic on the rapid development of the small-powered motorcycle industry: "A completely new, powerfully flourishing branch of industry established in Germany after the war continues to develop: the small-motor and low-powered motorcycle industry." Blaming the economic situation, which made "a vehicle cheap in purchase price, and in operation quick as well as comfortable, almost indispensable," Martin argued that smaller motorcycles were essential in the impoverished population's "fight for survival."[57] While Martin did not go so far as to allege that the industry was profiteering from financial maneuvering made possible by the inflationary economy, he acknowledged that postwar economic instability significantly contributed in particular to the development of the small-motorcycle industry. Indeed, in contrast to the "victor states" of the U.S.A., Great Britain, and France, where heavier motorcycles continued to be the preferred model both in terms of production and consumption, in Germany, the production of motorcycles, with its growing focus on small, lightweight versions, reflected the impact of the postwar economic development on the development of the automotive industry and the available choices for motorized mobility. Thus, the economic crises expressed in increased competition, speculation, and inflation resulted in a heightened pace of innovation in the motorcycle industry and furthered the diffusion of new technologies.

Notwithstanding the jolt they gained from the postwar economic situation, the leaders of the motorcycle industry often complained about the restrictions of the Versailles Treaty, which they viewed as unduly harsh. Despite a comparative price advantage due to inflation, automotive industrialists harped about the treaty's hampering effects on their ability to secure an export market for their products.[58] More generally, the sentiment that the reparation payments were humiliating and the settlement unjust permeated Weimar society and found expression in the official government policy to seek renegotiation of the terms of reparation obligations, leading some historians of the era

to speak of a "Weimar Revisionism Syndrome."[59] Even following mon-
etary stabilization in 1924, the motorcycle trade press continued to
criticize the effects of the Versailles Treaty on the industrial recovery
of Germany in general.[60] Nonetheless, it did not escape their notice
that the German motorcycle industry retained a competitive advantage over the automobile industry due to the economic constraints
of the period. Reflecting on the inflationary period, a commentator in
an editorial remarked: "In common effort, industry and science have
worked together to catch up with the lead that foreign countries had
taken." More than any other branch of the automotive industry, the
motorcycle industry and motorcycle sport were, according to the editorial, seemingly preordained to improve the transportation situation
in Germany: "For a long time to come, the scarcity of money and
the difficult burden of our treaty will hinder the automobile, becoming widespread among the entire population unlike in the victor
states. The motorcycle, however, with its smaller units is the future
means of motorized transport for the entire population, because its
price is affordable for the less well-to-do."[61] The German motorcycle
industry's attitude towards the terms of the peace was fraught with
ambivalence.

Furthermore, the automotive industry, with its competing branches,
was neither a cohesive entity nor did it speak with a unified voice
throughout the fifteen-year duration of the Weimar Republic.[62] A contentious issue was whether protectionist policies would benefit or damage
the motorcycle industry. This question surfaced in the postwar period in
the context of motorcycling exhibitions and races that the industry put
on in order to court the public.[63] The first major motorcycle and automobile exhibition after World War I, held in Berlin in September 1921,
coincided with the first major race held on the Automobil-Verkehrs- und
Übungsstrasse [Automobile Traffic and Test Track, AVUS], Germany's
first road built exclusively for motorized traffic and for promoting motor
sports.[64] Feeling at a disadvantage vis-à-vis the more developed US,
British, and French automobile industries and in response to the exclusion of the German automotive industry at international automobile
exhibitions held in Paris, London, and Brussels, the umbrella organization for the interests of the German industry, the Reichsverband der
Automobilindustrie [National League of the Automobile Industry, RDA],
limited the exhibition to a purely "national" composition.[65] Leading
members of the RDA displayed nationalistic political leanings, including the director of the RDA, Dr. Curt Sperling, as well as RDA speaker,
Dr. Gomoll; however, nationalism and economic protectionism were
hardly unique to Germany.[66]

Nationalistic posturing in the Weimar Republic was in part due to a concern over tariff policies and relative competitiveness in the global market. That tariff politics were generally filled with nationalistic rhetoric during this era, regardless of the nation involved, was a point German industrialists often made when justifying their call for greater protective measures: "The newest customs amendment of the United States is justified on the basis that the American high protective tariff [*Hochschutzzoll*] is one of the major foundations upon which the incredible growth of the industrial and agricultural sectors in America rests. It facilitates—according to their own statements—the proverbial wealth of the American people and allows the businessmen to pay the highest wages in the world."[67] The question of US unilateral trade agreements becomes particularly salient following the currency reform and the renegotiation of the reparations agreement through the mediation of the US banker Charles Dawes in 1924.[68]

The percentage of imported vehicles versus the percentage of domestically produced vehicles on German roads was a matter of intense interest to both the public and industry throughout the Weimar Republic.[69] RDA director Sperling registered the globally pervasive, national, anti–free market, semi-autarkic context in his reflections on the "Automotive Industry as a National Industry": "Italy, France, England, Belgium, and America follow the development of their domestic automobile industries with a particular fondness and are proud of their achievements in promoting above all that it is a matter of patriotism not to drive a foreign car. In Italy, England, and France there are only relatively few foreign cars, not to speak of the situation in America."[70] The number of motorcycles imported to Germany in comparison to those domestically produced, nevertheless, remained very low, especially when compared with the import and export figures for automobiles.[71] The positive trade balance for motorcycles in comparison to automobiles was mostly due to the fact that most of the automobiles manufactured by Germany were out of the affordable price range for all but the very wealthy or turned out to have an unreliable design, whereas the motorcycle industry was largely able to fulfill market demands with well-developed and economical products.

Indeed, manufacturers of the small-powered motorcycle championed it for being a German product that would bring motorization to all Germans. The Zschopauer Motoren Werke [Zschopau Motor Works, known as DKW] lobbied the Bavarian minister of the interior, emphasizing the Germanness of their product: "The concept of a small-powered motorcycle industry is a German one, because in postwar Germany a powerfully blossoming and strong small-powered motorcycle industry is now established, which emanates from the idea, with the smallest motor power, of providing the widest range of road users with a means of transport for the people [*Volksverkehrsmittel*] in the true sense of the word." The plea to the minister to intervene in raising the license-free status of motorcycles from three-quarters horsepower to one horsepower was based on the argument that it would benefit "only those classes of employed ... whose economic situation does not allow them to buy either a heavier motorcycle or a small car."[72]

Although motorcycles with four-stroke engines with a higher engine displacement dominated the market until the late 1920s, lightweight motorcycles, in particular those with two-stroke engines, eventually developed into an important feature of the industry.[73] In the inflationary period, auxiliary motors that could be mounted on bicycle frames witnessed their first boom, representing the easiest and cheapest way to enter the world of personal motorized transportation.[74] The government's decision, when pressured by the motorcycle industry and motorists' interest groups, to exempt the smallest of the small-powered motorcycles from the luxury tax and from licensing requirements provided further momentum in particular to the process of motorization through the two-wheeled motor vehicle.[75] Under the 15 March 1923 revisions of the law regulating small-powered motorcycles, the owner was no longer required to register the vehicle or to have a number plate; however, in 1925 this regulation was amended to again include this class of motorcycles in terms of registration (see Appendix: Table 2).[76]

1924–1929: The Golden Years? Rationalization: Between Expansion and Contraction

The "wonder of the Reichsmark" in 1924 worked by "re-establishing the Reichsmark on gold at its prewar parity against the dollar," thus bringing hyperinflation to an end.[77] Nonetheless, the 1925 New Year's editorial of *Das Motorrad* claimed 1924 was "a year of the greatest worries for the motorcycle industry." Instead of real growth, the currency conversion had brought forth a bubble in the industry that the editor called a "sham boom." By the end of 1925, however, the motorcycle industry had begun to revive. The 1925 German Automobile Exhibition, postponed from September 1924 to December 1925, represented a turning point, and "demonstrated to skeptics" that the industry was both "healthy and viable."[78] For example, one visitor to the 1925 exhibition remarked on the motorcycles on display: "It is as if here the hardships of these times have not disastrously swept away the good belief in a better future. Confidence in their own performance and a hope for the victorious overcoming of the present economic crisis seem to almost confront the visitor in a way as if [the motorcycles were] alive."[79] The exhibition featured new constructions by D-Rad and DKW, which included "a ton of modern novelties," brought forth by innovations in "mass and serial fabrication." DKW's 1925 model earned particular praise, "the powerful, compact, stabile, and solid form gives justified reason to hope that the new type of DKW will definitively influence the motorization of German economic life."[80]

The year 1924 was indeed a tumultuous one for the motorcycle industry. Currency reform and the implementation of the Dawes Plan, which readjusted Germany's reparations payment, paved the way for the German economy to enter a phase of stabilization, even if it was not immediately perceptible, especially within the motorcycle industry. In fact, the recalibration of the German motorcycle industry took place in the context of a wave of "dying off" of many of the firms that had been founded during the inflationary period—a period when a number of industrialists and engineers already viewed the mushrooming number of firms as detrimental for the overall composition of the industry. For example, in 1923, Emil Fischer, an engineer at D-Rad, called for an "internal process of recovery [*innere Gesundungsprozeß*]" from the influx of poorer quality products resulting from deficient engineering on the part of the "inflation profiteers [*Inflationsgewinnler*]."[81] The implementation of the currency reform set the process of contraction in motion. Real prices for all automotive products began a steady decline as the currency market stabilized and the Reichsmark appreciated. Export markets dried up completely as the exchange rate was adjusted to Germany's relative disadvantage. A process of attrition and consolidation took place within both the motorcycle and the automobile industry, and by 1927 only 139 motorcycle manufacturers existed in Germany, as compared with 367 two years prior.[82]

Hanfland, advocate of the small-powered motorcycle industry, made the following suggestions on the steps the motorcycle industry needed to take in order to prosper in a post–currency reform environment: "We should aim to build on a new foundation, to let new life blossom on old ruins and through active work on design, rational methods of fabrication, and rationalization to the furthest extent, correct what aggravations the last years brought our industry in this respect, and I am not just speaking of the motorcycle industry."[83] "Rationalization," a buzzword during the Weimar Republic, "meant increasing productivity by integration and consolidation, technological modernization and labor process reorganization, the assembly line, and the time-and-motion studies of Frederick W. Taylor."[84] Although already applied at least piecemeal in isolated motorcycle factories since World War I, rationalization gained momentum in the phase of post–currency stabilization, meaning that, as capital began flowing again, in part in the form of US loans, productive capacity increased and production costs decreased. Having benefited from familiarity with larger unit batches due to experience in either the bicycle industry or the armament industry, retrofitting factories for assembly line production entailed a lower investment barrier for many more motorcycle manufacturers than was the case for automobile manufacturers.[85] Furthermore, automotive engineers were at the forefront of the push for standardization, taking up this cause even before World War I.[86]

The case of D-Rad provides an interesting, although somewhat atypical, example of the relationship between the motorcycle industry, the state, and rationalization. During the war, the Imperial Army–owned munitions factory in Spandau was a hotspot of the German rationalization movement. Under the aegis of German rationalization wonder workers Georg Schlesinger, Otto Kienzle, and Heinrich Schaechterle, an independent engineering office was set up to accelerate the process of mass production and standardization.[87] In the wake of demobilization and the conversion to a peacetime economy, the state-owned and state-operated munitions factory in Haselhorst was first refitted as a motorcycle factory.[88] From 1919 to 1925, the D-Rad factory was operated by the state-held Deutsche Industrie-Werke [German Industry Works, DIW]. Its managers built upon wartime rationalization efforts and implemented assembly lines in their production process as early as 1922. The state-owned factory was the first German automotive manufacturer to rationalize production methods based explicitly along Fordist lines of flow production.[89] One visitor described the factory in glowing terms: "The individual factory rooms of the DIW speak eloquently of the unconditional and consistent implementation of the latest innovations in technology that take into account the manufacturing methods of the Fordist style, and in every workroom one feels how the individual piece fits into the whole, and knows that one has a fundamentally purposeful and harmoniously built corporation." Despite the celebratory rhetoric of having implemented Fordist production methods, the description of the D-Rad factory incorporated elements that point more to adaptation than wholesale adoption.[90] German rationalization was conceived in different terms than the "American method of production." The D-Rad factory was presented as an organic whole, and the purpose of automation was not to eliminate German quality labor. Instead the factory represented a futuristic merging of machine and man, with the machine nonetheless "setting the tempo" of the man.

Indeed, the state-owned factory adopted some elements of the Fordist method of production, its organization relying both on modified Taylorist methods in terms of the division of labor and on the partial implementation of a continuous assembly line. "The piecework is executed with the utmost attention to detail; in all departments one sees special machines built for a specific purpose—for example, automatic gearwheel, cylinder, and crankshaft grinders and many-spindled drilling installations—which, without the need to continually readjust the machines, enable all drilling on one piece to be completed in one operation with the most exact precision." In other areas of the factory, automation was more completely implemented; for example, in the painting shop, "two huge, completely autonomously operating dipping-lacquering-ovens especially constructed for the DIW" reduced the number of workers substantially by replacing manual labor with a mechanized dipping technique. "Special machines and the transport paths with the hanging swings that bring the individual parts to the workstation set the tempo for the worker." The author went on to extol the results of implementing what he called "Fordist" production methods: "The results that large series production can achieve is proven by the motorcycle production of the DIW, which in an 8-hour shift at current rates can produce two thousand motorcycles monthly. These are indeed first-class precision machines that enjoy the best reputation internationally and, furthermore and most importantly, are completely absorbed by the consumer market."[91] Reporting dubiously high production numbers, the author clearly intended to hype the new production method rather than to present the reality.[92] And what the author also failed to belabor upon was whether or not the D-Rad workers received equivalent wages to the workers at Ford's factory. Nonetheless, the government subsidized motorcycle factory represented an early example of the partial adoption of "American methods of production" and Fordist principles of production and consumption, while maintaining the organic rhetoric of German quality work. The example of D-Rad and the DIW thus indicates the extent to which the state was invested in promoting the contentious process of rationalization and automation in the motorcycle industry.[93] The early implementation of the assembly line and the modernity of the factory reflected modern ideas of management and the firm belief in rationalization within official state policy.

Willi Christenn's analysis of the German motorcycle industry in his 1929 doctoral thesis in the field of political economics also stressed the need for "rational" production methods to increase the profit margins of motorcycle factories. During the university recess periods, Christenn gained practical experience in both technical and commercial aspects of motorcycle production through working at a motorcycle factory in Munich.[94] Based on his practical experience, he claimed that the "complete secret to thriving production," was precisely arranging "the operative sequence in respect to the individual operations" so that "no friction or difficulties arise in execution." By stressing that "the operative sequence must always be—yes, on an hourly basis—scrutinized by professional controllers, so that interruptions can already be identified in the preliminary stages, and deficiencies in the operation can be eliminated without ado," his approach to rationalization in the organization of the shop floor owed more to Taylorism, with its constant surveillance of the operative sequence, than to Fordism with its stress on implementing technologies such as the assembly line to improve productivity.[95] "If difficulties should occur, even though the preparatory work has been undertaken with adequate precision, it is possible to identify with relative certainty the point at which any deficiencies arise and also whether a defect has been caused by a material deficiency. If a defect can be identified as worker related, meaning it emerges that it is the fault of a worker, then, in so far as the legalities permit this, the costs for the eventual damages must be collected from the worker at fault."[96] In contrast, however, to Taylorism's emphasis on bonuses, Christenn recommended punishment for negligent workers, fashioning an oppressive vision of a management- and machine-driven workers' dystopia.

Indeed, while rationalization was a method widely discussed in political debates and promoted within engineering and managerial circles during the Weimar Republic, it was decidedly not to follow the Fordist model of higher wages for workers. One editorial in *Das Motorrad* quite explicitly refuted the applicability of the Fordist model to the German postwar situation. Pointing to the "unlimited" raw materials and resources available for North American industry to exploit, the author argued: "We live as a small nation-state with a national industry and a national market in between states of the same type. We cannot produce *mass commodities*, but at most *serial commodities*. The desire to raise the wages of German workers to the level of US workers is therefore unjustified." Another problem the author saw with switching from serial to mass production was in Germany's difficult postwar economic situation: "As a poor country we are forced to manufacture exportable commodities that support the foreign-exchange value of the domestic currency. The increase in cost due to serial production versus mass production also has to be taken into consideration in the future. The financial burdens from the lost war resemble a high interest rate that the German state has to pay over with its entire manpower to foreign states." This "high interest rate 'impacts' every individual and reduces the standard of living of the entire German people. Only slowly and gradually is improvement possible, if the increase in production creates higher revenue, and high revenues allow for a decrease in taxation. This would benefit all, and increasing production must therefore be the goal in the coming years."[97] Observers of the German automotive and motorcycle industry saw multiple factors at play in terms of the inapplicability of the Fordist model for German industry, some of them being financial, such as above. Skepticism towards Fordist modes of production was also reflected in dominant trends in economic engineering during the Weimar Republic, and mirrored Germany's uneasy relationship with the United States, the economic powerhouse of the 1920s.

By 1926, the German industry judged motorcycles manufactured in Germany as sufficiently reliable technically for consumers at a price that could be competitive on the global market. The RDA cited design improvements and innovations in production technologies as reasons for the decline in prices in Germany. This allowed the German motorcycle industry to develop their designs "independently from foreign tendencies," which for the RDA displayed "a much more harmonious self-contained whole than most foreign motorcycle constructions and is so thoroughly developed in its organs that it unqualifiedly belongs to the class of quality machines."[98] The RDA thus also promoted a vision of the industry being an organic whole to which the pieces were subsumed. Indeed, ideas about German "quality work" and rhetoric of an organic culture of production resonated in the discourse on motorization as well as rationalization well before the onset of the World Economic Crisis in 1929.[99] The opposition between an organic, harmonious, and spiritual Germany was most often juxtaposed against an inorganic and superficial materialism in the United States, and these debates as well found their way into debates about the production of motor vehicles.[100]

Despite or perhaps because of the successful early implementation of mass production methods, industry experts feared a saturation of the market for motorcycles in Germany. The motorcycle industry was beginning to stagnate in both England and France, not to speak of North America where motorcycles had ceased to play a significant role in motorization, at least since the introduction of Henry Ford's Model T.[101] The primary reason offered by experts, both then and today, for the impending obsolescence of the motorcycle as a means of personal motorized transportation was that when wages rise, consumers switch over to automobiles. Economic historians Braun and Panzer have identified this as "a peculiar feature" of the demand side of the motorcycle market: "If wealth or real income surpasses a critical but not quantifiable level, the demand for motorcycles switches to a more convenient but expensive substitution product, the automobile, as a competing vehicle for individual transportation."[102] During the 1920s, German automotive manufacturers were called on both by industry organizations and the trade press to develop a *Volkswagen*, a "people's car," along the lines of Ford's Model T.[103] The belief in the inevitability of the eventual dominance of the automobile and the eventual demise of the motorcycle shaped industry-dominated discourse about the process of motorization. During the Weimar Republic, the RDA devoted little attention to the most saleable and financially liquid of its branches.[104]

Nevertheless, a number of institutional organizations were established during the Weimar Republic, including state-directed initiatives, to facilitate the diffusion of the new technology.[105] In July 1924, the Beirat für das Kraftfahrwesen im Reichsverkehrsministerium [Advisory Committee for Automotive Affairs in the Transportation Ministry] was formed in the Reich Transportation ministry in order to promote the interests of the automotive industry within government policy. At their first meeting, held in December 1924, a number of topics relevant to motorcycles were discussed including speed limits, exhaust gases, exhaust noises, warning signals, and licensing for small powered motorcycles.[106] A further point considered by the industry as vital to both the quality of constructive elements as well as for the overall efficiency of the motor vehicle industry was the creation of standardized norms. While initiated before the war and generally established during the war and the period of inflation, the process was only formalized with the establishment of the Fachnormenausschuss Kraftfahrzeuge [Automotive Standards Committee, FAKRA] in the Deutsche Normen Ausschuß [German Standardization Committee, DNA] in March 1925.[107] Standardization organizations, while technically non-governmental, nonetheless wielded considerable power as they made decisions and recommendations that found expression in national and international laws, and shaped the everyday lives of consumers.

Industrialists also joined together to lobby for the interests of the motorcycle industry. In 1923, the VDMI united with the umbrella organization RDA, the VLI, the Verband Deutscher Motorrad-Händler e.V. [League of German Motorcycle Dealerships], and the Reichsverband Deutscher Fahrrad-, Nähmaschinen- und Motorfahrzeug-Händler e.V.

[National League of German Bicycle, Sewing Machine, and Motor Vehicle Dealers] to promote two-wheeled motorized vehicles.[108] Following a suggestion by a number of automobile and motorcycle clubs, a working group for automotive affairs was also founded in 1925. This group addressed "questions related to motorized transportation, motor vehicle taxation, as well as questions on legal protections," and served also in an advisory function to the government's Beirat für das Kraftfahrwesen im Reichsverkehrsministerium [Committee for Automotive Affairs]. Acting together with the RDA, the group's explicit aim was to promote the cause of motorization by having a "beneficial propagandistic effect in the interest of motorized transportation in the press." The group also sought "to take steps against the many unjustified attacks against automobile owners and drivers, as well as to explain and educate the general public."[109] Reflecting the continued emphasis in the German school of economics on the importance of an interwoven state and economy, industrial and state actors undertook concerted efforts to promote the process of motorization. These institutional arrangements were not only central to facilitating the introduction of motorized traffic in Germany, but such early efforts at cooperation and integration also foreshadow the Nazi-era near-complete entwinement of the automotive industry and the state.[110]

The industry's lobbying efforts were not without effect and, over the course of the Weimar Republic, the interests of the state and the interests of the motorcycle industry increasingly overlapped. The state repeatedly made concessions to the motorcycle industry by providing incentives to purchase small-powered motorcycles, which helped generate a steady upswing in the number of increasingly affordable and reliable two-stroke machines on German streets during the 1920s and 1930s. In doing so, the state, regardless of which coalition was ruling, did not shy from taking an interventionist approach. Through lowering hurdles to mass motorization for the less well to do and by promoting the motorcycle, the state claimed to be pursuing a politics of the "little man."[111] It was especially the 1928 amendment to the law regarding motor vehicle transportation, which stipulated the cubic capacity of the engine as the taxation assessment basis and exempted all motors below 200 ccm, that led to an increase in demand for the two-stroke engines favored by German motorcycle manufacturers. Through the enactment of incentives and regulations, a strong correlation can be observed between the activities and interests of the state and the development of the industry.[112]

Beyond promoting the interests of the industry through making motorcycles more accessible and affordable, the state introduced the motorcycle into a number of government-controlled institutions. A report on "prestigious visitors" to the NSU factory in 1932 reported that government officials from Stuttgart, including those from the postal ministry, the railroad ministry, the finance ministry, and the employment office, as well as Reichswehr officers, toured the factory with an eye toward procurement.[113] As a result of the continual growth of motorized traffic in Germany, a number of police departments introduced motorized methods of policing traffic in the mid-1920s.[114] Motorcycles were also incorporated into the fleet of another large state employer, the postal service, alongside trucks and other vehicles.[115] Furthermore, public works and forestry departments across Germany purchased motorcycles for official purposes.[116] Above all, the Reichswehr became an increasingly important customer for a number of major motorcycling companies towards the end of the Weimar Republic. Beginning in the early 1930s, BMW included reports of its "success with the Reichswehr" in its company journal.[117] With the onset of the World Economic Crisis, the Reichwehr ministry took on an overtly exclusionary nationalistic approach, banning the requisitioning of all foreign-manufactured vehicles and parts.[118] In their support for organizations such as the Reichskuratorium für Wirtschaftlichkeit [National Productivity Board, RKW] and the Deutsches Institut für technische Arbeitsschulung [German Institute for Technical Labor Training, DINTA], the state often followed a technocratic and corporatist course both in terms of implementing motorization and within their larger aim of rationally organizing society.

The so-called "golden years" of the Weimar Republic did indeed bring an upward trend to the fortunes of the German motorcycle industry. Its resurgence was based in part on improved constructive elements that made motorized two-wheelers both more dependable and less expensive to operate and maintain. Numerous intermediary organizations located between the state, the industry, and the consumer also created an institutional framework to regulate and regularize the experience of motorization. Rationalization increased the productivity, if not the profitability in the short run, of the factories that were able to survive the process of post-inflationary industrial contraction. The relatively low capital investment threshold to implementing rationalized production methods gave the motorcycle sector of the German automotive industry a substantial competitive edge over the automobile sector. The state also actively intervened to promote the motorcycle as the vehicle to mass motorization. By 1929, the German motorcycle industry, as a global leader in motorcycle production, saw itself "no longer in need of a 'crutch.'"[119]

In contrast to the previous years of severe economic instability, real wages increased for workers and remained relatively stable for members of the middle classes over this period. Thus, while for most the desire for an automobile remained outside of the realm of the possible, the motorcycle came to be understood as the only form of individual motorized transportation suitable for the budgets of the many potential consumers who desired to participate in motorization.[120] As the automotive industry came to be seen as a symbolic indicator of the material wealth of nations, some concluded that the flourishing motorcycle industry indicated Germany's imminent recovery. The rhetoric around individual motorized transportation, caught between the trauma of hyperinflation, the ensuing fetishization of austerity, and desires to take part in modern consumer fantasies of freedom, speed, and power, increased the importance of the motorcycle industry during the period of relative economic stability (see Appendix: Table 3).

Byway I: DKW: The Small Wonder

The story of the Zschopauer Motoren Werke, J.S. Rasmussen, and the DKW Corporation—the motorcycle manufacturer that grew to be the world's largest in the late 1920s—is illustrative of the various stages and changing methods of production in the early phase of German motorization. Founded in 1906 by Danish entrepreneur Jørgen Skafte Rasmussen, the firm began by manufacturing household and workshop machines as well as automobile accessories in a former cloth factory in Zschopau, close to Chemnitz in Saxony. As was the case for most other manufacturers, during World War I production was shifted to meet military demands. Alongside manufacturing of grenade detonators, an attempt was made in 1917 to promote a viable steam-powered automobile because of the war's blockade-induced gasoline shortages. Although the attempt failed, the acronym DKW—*Dampfkraftwagen* (steam-power-wagon, indicating the proximity of the train and other steam technologies to the development of the motor industry)—stuck.[121]

At the end of World War I, Rasmussen developed a two-stroke engine for toys that he presented at the Leipzig Convention in 1919. This two-stroke motor was the next milestone in the firm and the acronym's history—the motor was dubbed *"Der Knaben Wunsch"* (The Boys' Wish). In 1920, using the basis of the two-stroke motor, DKW began producing auxiliary motors for bicycles. While at first scoffed at, these small motors energized a public eager to participate in motorization by virtue of their sturdiness and their relative power. DKW transitioned its production line to the smaller two-stroke engine and consequently the acronym was reinterpreted for a third time as *"Das Kleine Wunder"* (The Small Wonder), from which copywriters created the catchy slogan *"DKW, das kleine Wunder, läuft bergauf wie andere runter"* (DKW, the small wonder,

Image 1.1. *"Das Kleine Wunder"*—The Small Wonder. DKW Advertisement, ca. 1919, Audi Corporate Archives.

rides uphill like others ride downhill).[122] By depicting the young devil on a bicycle with an auxiliary motor, the image hints that the youngster will one day graduate to become a full-grown devil on a full-powered motorcycle.

In 1922, production of actual motorcycles (2,000 DKW motorcycles, and 20,000 DKW auxiliary motors) commenced, and within two years 50,000 motorcycles had been built in Zschopau.[123] In addition, in 1924, the firm began offering installment plans, and classes and workshops in post-purchase assembly and repairs. This was a path-breaking innovation and of great importance for the supply side for promoting the motorcycle to the wider public: "DKW offered not only technological improvements for cheaper, but still high quality motorcycles, but also the financial innovation of payment through installments."[124] Some of the standard technological innovations that the company offered as inclusive within the purchase price were headlights, air-filled tires, and an adjustable suspension. These innovations made the motorcycle considerably safer and more comfortable. With the displacement capacity advantage of the two-stroke engine as well as easy maintenance, DKW offered an attractive vehicle for cash-strapped consumers.

In 1921, Rasmussen made a study trip to the United States in order to gather firsthand knowledge of the newest automotive production techniques, including assembly-line production.[125] In 1926, the firm undertook a "far-reaching rationalization," beginning assembly-line production of two-cylinder, two-stroke motorcycles. Beside the actual assembly line, various transport and feed mechanisms were implemented, the longest of which was 1,500 meters long. In 1927 and 1928, Rasmussen purchased a number of other companies, including refrigerator and automobile machinery factories, in order to diversify the production line. During this period, he also pursued a strategy to expand the firm's interest in motor vehicle production by becoming majority shareholder of Schüttoff AG Chemnitz (a motorcycle manufacturer), by buying the iron foundry Erla, and by taking over the entire stock portfolio of Audi-Works AG Zwickau. In 1929, another manufacturing innovation was introduced by switching the production of frames to a pressed-steel profile, a move that further simplified large series production.

By the end of the 1920s, DKW had grown to be the world's largest motorcycle factory—in the years 1928–29 over 100,000 motorcycles, mainly two-stroke tax- and license-free models (200cc and under), rolled off the production line. In 1928, the firm employed over 2,300 workers, but by 1929 it was over double that number, and daily production levels reached between 300 and 350 motorcycles a day (or one motorcycle every seventy-eight seconds). DKW exported its products as far away as Japan and South Africa.[126] Over the course of the 1920s, Zschopau became a factory town: "You almost want to call it 'Rasmussen City' or 'DKW-Town.' Between the administrative offices and the factory yard, five stories below, offices, offices, offices. A giant apparatus, organization wherever you look."[127] Alongside its own foundry for light metals and cast iron, a factory for hubs, screws, nuts, fittings, saddle-seats, there was a large stamping press and a workshop for magnet and light installations. Numerous neighboring towns also benefited economically from the booming motorcycle factory in Zschopau. In addition, construction on a workers' housing settlement, begun in 1919, was completed in 1928, and provided housing for approximately fifty families.[128]

Economists and journalists alike viewed the innovations in production methods implemented by Rasmussen with interest. According to a pamphlet produced by the Deutsche Wirtschafts-Archiv [German Economic Archive] about the company in the middle of the 1920s: "Every worker executes one and the same operation in piece-work under the strictest supervision."[129] In the general discourse of rationalized production, the benefits of assembly-line production remained controversial. A 1929 article provided a glance inside the "world's largest motorcycle factory" and its working conditions. Echoing Ford's assessment of the assembly line, the author insisted that the implementation of mechanized production was not detrimental to the workers, yet he added a German twist: "The joy in work is not diminished, but rather becomes livelier through the necessary mutual working-together [*Ineinanderarbeiten*]; and because the individual motions are completely mechanized, less physical energy needs to be expended and more time is left for free thinking than is the case in individual assembly." In summing up the success of the factory: "Zschopau is the first town in Germany where German quality labor and American production methods were implemented without making the former suffer."[130] Zschopau thus served as a model of a distinctly German form of rationalized production.

In 1929, DKW introduced a new two-cylinder, two-stroke motorcycle model that it called the *Volksrad*, "The People's Motorcycle," underscoring the particular importance of the smaller cubic capacity engines to the existence of the German motor industry and to the process of motorization in Germany. An advertisement for "The People's Motorcycle" claimed that it was "hardly more expensive than a bicycle with an auxiliary motor!" "A motorcycle in its own right," the advertisement acknowledged its "somewhat simple design" while stating that it "evenly matches other DKW-motorcycles." Above all, it was the "appropriate vehicle" for the people, built to accommodate small budgets, "precisely for the thousands of employed, who travel their daily route

to work by bicycle or on foot." The advertisement praised its low running costs—"less than the cost of riding the train in the third class"—and
touted its ability to afford more mobility and independence: "Besides
its advantage of reaching the workplace quickly and independently
of public transportation, during leisure time it offers the joys of pleasant excursions and motor sports." Moreover, a tax- and license-free
Volksrad could be acquired on "the best layaway plan available."

DKW presented itself confident enough in 1929 to report that it had
overcome the threat posed by its main competitors: "The English and
American competition, which has a great deal of say in the German
market, hardly makes itself noticeable with *us*, as our pricing policy has
made us just as affordable while at the same time providing the same
quality, and the only circle of consumers whom we have not been
able to capture are those with so-called 'foreign-mania.'"[131] Through
manufacturing reliable vehicles using rationalized production and providing installment purchase plans, DKW was able to offer motorcycles
at approximately half the price of their competitors, and thus make the
dream of individual motorized transport realizable for a broad spectrum
of German society.

From early attempts at constructing a steam-powered car to joint-
development projects with Slaby-Beringer, a Berlin auto manufacturer,
which in 1919 offered a small electric car commanding much public
attention, Rasmussen was also actively involved in the production of
four-wheeled motor vehicles. In 1924 he took over Slaby-Beringer,
and in 1928 he presented a two-cylinder, two-stroke, fuel-run, rear-
wheel-drive small car with a wood frame (model P15), an endeavor
that met with limited commercial and critical success. Through the
Audi takeover in 1928, Rasmussen hoped to be able to expand into the
middle and luxury class automobile market. None of DKW's attempts
at manufacturing four-wheelers proved as profitable as manufacturing two-wheelers. In addition, the intense capital investments required
for these unsuccessful projects meant the Zschopauer Motor Works
had spread itself very thin financially. Heavily indebted, by the end of
the 1920s the State Bank of Saxony held the majority of shares of the
corporation.[132]

The World Economic Crisis hit Zschopau hard. Despite slashing prices
for all of their models in 1931, DKW, as was true for the entire motor vehicle industry and indeed all industry in Germany, experienced a drastic
drop in sales, as potential consumers were lost to the masses of the
unemployed. At the 1930 annual DKW shareholders meeting, despite
balanced books for the year of 1929, the board reported that, "as a consequence of the generally opaque economic situation, it is impossible

to give a prognosis for the current year. Hope was expressed that the government would foster the automotive industry through appropriate tax and tariff policies."[133] Due to the lack of demand, DKW was forced to reduce employment at the factory from over 6,000 in 1930 to 850 in 1932. A protocol from the DKW board of directors meeting from 1931 reported that "the motorcycle enterprise had developed unfavorably," and considering expected sales of only twenty thousand motorcycles for the entire year of 1931, "Zschopau will not survive."[134] With such a drastic drop-off of sales and with Saxony facing the highest number of unemployed in Germany, in 1932 the State Bank of Saxony stepped in and DKW ceased to exist as an independent company.[135] With 6 million Reichsmark credit, the four largest motor works in Saxony were merged by the state to form Auto Union. The merger of the four companies, Zschopauer Motor Works (DKW), Audi, Wanderer and Horch, into Auto Union are still represented in the four rings of the Audi logo. Audi is the only brand that continues to exist today, although it is now a subsidiary of Volkswagen.[136]

1929–1933: World Economic Crisis

The World Economic Crisis had an enormous impact on all branches of German industry. The previous years of relative economic stability and industrial rationalization allowed the motorcycle industry to thrive both vis-à-vis the indigenous automobile industry as well as the international motorcycle industry. The automotive industry and interest groups most often sought to expand state incentives to other classes of motor vehicles, citing the potential economic stimulus and hence the social benefits for society. At other times, however, automobile manufacturers attacked what they deemed unfair advantages that manufacturers of smaller motorcycles enjoyed. Motoring trade journals regularly weighed the pros and cons of Germany's specific process of motorization, and articles such as "The Small Car and Beyond It," "The Small-Powered Motorcycle Must Die," "The Threatened Small-Powered Motorcycle," and "The Catastrophe in the Politics of Motorization," displayed the dissonance and disorder within the automotive industry in a period of increasing economic uncertainty.[137] The implementation of rationalized methods of production in the motorcycle industry remained a contentious issue during the World Economic Crisis. One observer of the crisis claimed that the "depression (or, more generously, the World Economic Crisis) was not solely responsible for the situation," but rather that the "monstrous hypertrophy of the means of production," effected by expanding capacity was the true underlying cause of the crisis of the motorcycle industry.[138] The surge in output in the second half of the 1920s pointed to the market for motorcycles having long surpassed the saturation point.[139]

Although the discourse around motorization had long contained nationalist overtones, the collapse of domestic and global markets, from credit to export to labor, increased the volume and persuasive power of already loud protectionist voices within the German automotive industry. Although the German motorcycle industry overall continued to fare comparatively well in the first year of the crisis, calls for more far-reaching protectionist measures became more urgent, while nationalist cries for "Germans buy German" grew more vociferous.[140] As with all areas of German life, with the deepening of the crisis, the discourse of motorization became increasingly politicized. In 1931, one motorcycling journalist, who viewed the crisis as "not alone a material crisis, not a temporary crisis of an economic body or its individual branches, but rather an ideational crisis, a crisis of the entire complex of economic, political, social, and ethical systems," saw a form of "state capitalism" emerging, in which large-scale industry "had come under increasingly strict control of the state and the authority of the national-bounded 'society.'"[141]

Yet determining which party represented pro-motorization interests was not entirely self-evident. In an article that, on one hand, sang the praises of the democratic electoral system of the Weimar Republic for giving the people a representative voice, on the other hand, it chastised the "progressive republic of Germany" for not having a party that adequately represented motorists' interests: "The greater community of motorcyclists has no representative in the Reichstag. The progressive Republic of Germany has not gone far enough because here politics and party politics are the only things of consequence; in the end, however, economic politics are all that can be allowed."[142] Increasingly, motoring journals published articles calling for motorists to use their collective strength as consumers to influence the political process, and *Das Motorrad* went so far as to suggest that the German economy would benefit from being organized along the lines of the Fascist political economy in Mussolini's Italy.[143]

Yet political claims for motorists' rights were most often made within the context of an understanding of a democratic, parliamentary system. Walter Ostwald, a long-time motorist, trade and scientific journalist, and industrial chemist responsible for promoting the benzol-gasoline mixture, published "An Appeal to Motorists for the Reichstag Election," in which he claimed, "under the German constitution every German is free to drive on German roads. And all Germans are supposed to be treated equally. There is nothing in the constitution that states that motorists are an exception." Ostwald asserted that German motorists had "much to complain about": "The German motor vehicle code is a complicated science that is impossible for a simple motorist to understand. Nowhere else in the world do people allow this. Everyone knows from practical experience how complicated registration, taxation, international driver's licenses, etc. are, because even in the smallest German village there is at least one motorcycle." Ostwald believed a political solution was possible: "And therein lies the only hope of ending the misery of German motoring. The German people must, want to, and will drive. And during the Reichstag election meetings now, there will always be a motoring man or motoring woman who stands up and asks the candidate: 'What is your position and the position of your party towards German motoring?'"[144] Motor vehicle owners' fears of anti-motoring politics were not completely unjustified: the Deutsch Nationale Volkspartei [German National People's Party, DNVP] had resubmitted a petition to reinstate taxation and licensing requirements for all motorcycles, including those under 200 ccm, in 1929.[145] Proponents of motorization viewed the DNVP's petition as "hostile to industry and transportation" and as "a death blow" to the small-powered motorcycle.[146]

While demand for motorcycles only declined slowly until late 1930, when demand dropped, it dropped radically. By the end of 1930, the drastic effects of the World Economic Crisis were evident in the motorcycle industry. Yearly sales at DKW, for example, underwent a precipitous decline, and the larger non-tax exempt division was hit the hardest (see Appendix: Table 4). As more and more men lost their jobs, fewer were able to afford the operating costs of a motorcycle, especially of heavier types. Thus, in the face of the severe downturn in the overall economic situation in Germany, motorcycle manufacturers reacted by changing their product offerings. BMW, for example, designed the downsized R2 four-stroke, 198 ccm tax-exempt model, which went on the market in 1931. Other manufacturers again turned to constructing bicycles with auxiliary motors.[147] In 1931, NSU launched the "Motorsulm," a motorized bicycle capable of speeds up to 35 km/h, declaring it the "People's Bike for Everyone!"[148] In addition, another manufacturer of auxiliary motors, Fichtel and Sachs, was able to sell approximately one million of their motors over the course of the crisis.[149] The decision on the part of the motorcycle industry to revert to producing motorized bicycles reflects both the severity of the economic crisis in Germany and the continued importance of the influence of the consumer on design and production decisions. Despite the severity of the crisis, the mobility provided by motorized transport had increasingly become a part of everyday life. Appearing requisite to living a modern life, the number of new registrations of limited cubic capacity motorized two-wheelers grew throughout the crisis era, whereas all other types of vehicles, including motorcycles with non-tax-exempt higher power motors, witnessed a decline (see Appendix: Table 5).

Byway II: NSU in 1933

In the middle of the World Economic Crisis, in 1932, NSU was chosen as a "showcase firm of the German economy" in a book series designed to prove that "German industry and German trade had again taken its place in the first row of the world economy."[150] After addressing the development of the firm from its prewar beginnings and the development of NSU's motorcycles, especially during World War I, business writer Julius Schmitt then described the manufacturing process, the physical space of the factory, and the service division in detail, concluding the book with a discussion of the "spiritual bond between factory leadership and its employees." Discipline and a latent threat of punishment characterized the "spiritual bond" between the factory and its young apprentices, who were judged "not only for their mental maturity and their practical talent" but also on the basis of their "physical health": "The mission embarked upon does not end with the training of a skilled worker with a high productivity level." Instead, apprentices were simultaneously guided "to be independent-minded employees," and educated "to be useful members of the factory community." Furthermore, a "love of order" needed to be fostered:

> Every apprentice has a production schedule at his workstation. He exactly monitors his use of time, recording every operation and every absence from his workstation. Understanding is thus awakened, and self-discipline is set on the proper path. The large firm is founded on order, and therefore the primary mission of the educators must be to develop a love of order that is not always innate.[151]

Merely instilling its workers with a sense of factory time discipline was not sufficient, and despite the room for "independent thinking," order was key to NSU's project of creating productive workers.

Schmitt offered a hierarchical, patrimonial, and corporatist vision of society. An organic vision of the production process was presented in the variance diagram, "Soll und Ist" (Should Be and Is, see Image 1.2), showing the "stages of development." The "thinking organ"—the construction office, the fabrication office, and the materials used in fabrication—were

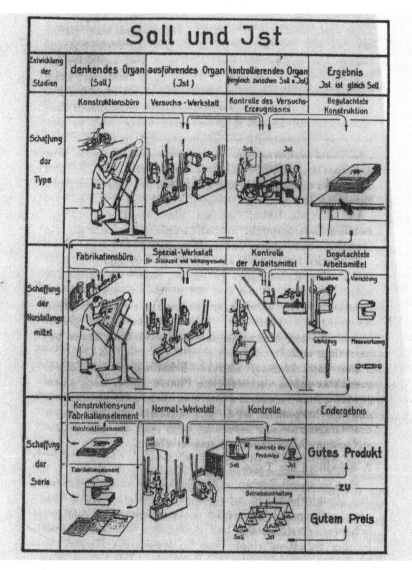

Image 1.2. Industrial Relations in the late Weimar Republic: NSU "Variance Analysis," Audi Corporate Archives.

portrayed as the "should be"; the "executive organ"—the test lab, the special workshop, and the normal workshop—were portrayed as the "is"; and the "controlling organ"—control of the test results, control of the work methods, and general control—were portrayed as the "comparison between should be and is." Reflecting how new management techniques had been adopted and adapted in the German context, the illustration also demonstrates that hierarchical ordering of worker relations was intrinsic to the NSU company philosophy: "The more intense specialization and mechanization in production processes become, the more monotonous individual work is for the hand, the stronger the spiritual bond must be, which joins the employees from the director to the apprentice in a working community [*Arbeitsgemeinschaft*]."[152] As the economic crisis worsened, providing continuing education not only for workers but also the unemployed, "who should stay in contact with their profession and at the first opportunity should join as fully valued workers," was a strategy NSU employed in order to foster company loyalty.[153] Housing was another form of company patrimonialism, as were leisure programs such as sports activities and facilities. Together with the residents of the town of Neckarsulm, the factory was imagined as "producing the healthy and moral soil [*gesunden und moralischen Boden*] for the further development of the industry."[154]

An ode to the New Year, published in the January 1933 issue of the NSU journal, waxed lyrical on the possibility of a new consumer-driven harmonious society organized along corporatist lines. The tone reflected the desperate economic situation, as the previous year's poem had, yet it also provided a positive conception of a motorized future of consuming Germans.[155] It spoke of 1932 as being a year of crisis, but hoped that the New Year would bring a transformation, and "though it isn't yet raining ducats, everywhere action is being taken, and deeds are expected of us as well." The fusion of D-Rad and NSU is portrayed in terms of NSU "taking in a friend": "And now both factories stand twice as powerful, equipped for better times." The poem showered praise on bicycles with auxiliary motors and "motorcycles with pillion seats which the ladies like so much":

> Now the race is over,
> Now better times begin,
> Just do it, buy a motorbike!
> Time, money, and the world you'll win.
>
> And though I don't know the future, I do see,
> I'd be better off if I was riding astride –
> That's why: Nineteen hundred and thirty-three,
> On an NSU, off into a better time![156]

The future envisioned as a fraternal yet hierarchically ordered society of satisfied consumers loomed large in the imagination of NSU in January 1933.

Conclusion

By the beginning of the 1930s, the German motorcycle industry had developed into a global leader in production. Despite humble prewar beginnings and interceding obstacles, motorcycle manufacturers during the Weimar Republic were successful in capturing the largest share of the market, vis-à-vis foreign competitors as well as other forms of personal motor vehicles. While the prevalence of the motorcycle in Germany was largely attributable to Germany's relative post–World War I economic instability, the successful implementation of rationalized production techniques allowed the motorcycle industry to offer consumers a variety of quality products at affordable prices. Furthermore, due to incentives provided by the state, motorcycles held an even greater advantage for financially strapped Germans eager to join the ranks of the motorized. Although industrialists in the Weimar Republic promoted a decidedly pro-technology outlook, tensions remained over the role and form of a modern German nation in a world economy of global players competing on uneven ground. The relatively good fortune of the motorcycle industry was at once a source of worry that it was a sign of Germany's continued economic deformation, and a source of pride for the hopes of a resurgent Germany in the global market.

Notes

1. J. Ermanski, *Theorie und Praxis der Rationalisierung* (Berlin: Verlag für Literatur und Politik, 1928), 386–87 and Figure 74.
2. On Soviet fascination with Taylorism and Fordism, see Buck-Morss, *Dreamworld and Catastrophe*, 104–11.
3. Steinbeck, *Das Motorrad*. Steinbeck details many of the issues raised in this chapter.
4. Flik, *Von Ford lernen?*, 81.
5. Helmut Braun and Christian Panzer have compared the growth of the motorcycle industries in Germany and England in terms of the three "Schumpeterian stages." The first stage is the stage of "invention" (the late nineteenth century), the second stage is "innovation"(1894–98, with the introduction of the motorcycle as an exchangeable commodity), and the third stage is "diffusion" in which "imitators" (firms building motorcycles) and "adaptors"(motorcycle riders) diffuse the technology. Braun and Panzer, "The Expansion of the Motor-Cycle Industry," 24–26.
6. Mom, *Atlantic Automobilism*, 63–65. Möser, *Fahren und Fliegen*, 36–42.
7. Möser, *Fahren und Fliegen*, 38.
8. See Steinbeck, *Das Motorrad*, 29; and Merki, *Der holprige Siegeszug*, 39. Also Curt Hanfland's chapter in his volume on the development of bicycles and motorcycles: Curt Hanfland, "Die Entwicklung der Fahr- und Motorräder," in

Das Motorrad und seine Konstruktion unter Berücksichtigung des Fahrrad-und Seitenwagenbaues sowie der Sonderkonstruktion (Berlin: M. Krayn Verlag, 1925), 1–19.

9. See Merki, *Der holprige Siegeszug.*

10. Mom, *The Electric Vehicle.*

11. Henry Ford (with Samuel Crowther), *My Life and Work* (Garden City, NY: Doubleday, 1923), 25–32.

12. Willi Christenn, "Die deutsche Motorrad-Industrie und ihre Steuerliche Belastung" (diss., Ludwig-Maximillians-Universität, 1929), 2, 11.

13. Steinbeck, *Das Motorrad*, 30–32.

14. F.P. Fritsche, "Die Entwicklung des deutschen Kraftrades," *Motorrad-Sport, -Verkehr und -Technik*, no. 3, 1924, 21.

15. Both NSU and Wanderer Works can be considered flexible production factories. Alongside bicycles and motorcycles, they also manufactured a number of other mechanical and motorized devices, from sewing machines to typewriters to automobiles. See Steinbeck, *Das Motorrad*, 23. See also David Hounshell, *From the American System to Mass Production, 1800–1932: The Development of Manufacturing Technology in the United States* (Baltimore, MD: Johns Hopkins University Press, 1984).

16. Christenn, "Die deutsche Motorrad-Industrie," 13.

17. Merki, *Der holprige Siegeszug*, 65–66.

18. Steinbeck, *Das Motorrad*, 39–40.

19. Mom, *Atlantic Automobilism*, 111–13; Möser, *Fahren und Fliegen*, 69–75.

20. Möser, "The Dark Side of 'Automobilism,'" 43.

21. Seiler, *Republic of Drivers*, 45.

22. Steinbeck, *Das Motorrad*, 39–40.

23. The French automobile industry was dominant from 1898 to 1905, at which point the US automobile production began its steep ascent to global dominance. James M. Laux, *The European Automobile Industry* (New York: Twayne Publishers, 1992), 8, 34; Christenn, "Die deutsche Motorrad-Industrie," 13–14. In addition, in the prewar era, the German automobile industry had begun to produce viable smaller vehicles that were favored by the professional classes. See "Zusammenschluß und Selbständigkeit im Motorradwesen," *Das Motorrad*, 1923: 1–3. Also Merki, *Der holprige Siegeszug*, 67. For the Dutch case, see Mom, *Atlantic Automobilism*, 83.

24. Prior to World War I, NSU had branches in London, Moscow, and New York City, but they closed at the outbreak of the war, never to reopen. Dr. Julius Schmitt, *Musterbetriebe deutscher Wirtschaft*, vol. 27, *Die Motorradfabrikation, NSU Vereinigte Fahrzeugwerke AG, Neckarsulm/Württbg* (Leipzig: J.J. Arnd, Verlag der Übersee-Post, 1932), 8.

25. Steinbeck, *Das Motorrad*, 53–65. Here Steinbeck addresses above all the legal framework that many industrialists and enthusiasts saw as an impediment, and the changes that were sought but not implemented until after World War I.

26. Möser, "The Dark Side of 'Automobilism,'" 250–53. Steinbeck, *Das Motorrad*, 66–67. There is some discrepancy in the reporting of the first official use of the motorcycle in the army maneuvers: Christenn dates the first official use of the motorcycle in 1907. Christenn, "Die deutsche Motorrad-Industrie," 15.

27. "Zusammenschluß," 1–3; Christenn, "Die deutsche Motorrad-Industrie," 15. Braun and Panzer note that "in Imperial Germany [there was] no appreciation

of [the motorcycle] by those who had the means to buy it." Braun and Panzer, "The Expansion of the Motor-Cycle Industry," 26.

28. Steinbeck, *Das Motorrad*, 66–68.

29. See ibid., 67–69.

30. For Nazi era representation of World War I motorized troops, see the 1936 cigarette card album: *Das deutsche Heer im Manöver* (Dresden: Cigaretten Bilddienst, 1936). See also Steinbeck, *Das Motorrad*, 69; and Peter Schneider, *Die NSU-Story: Die Chronik einer Weltmarke* (Stuttgart: Motorbuch Verlag, 1999), 23.

31. Möser, "World War I," in Strasser et al., *Getting and Spending*, 210. See also Möser, *Fahren und Fliegen*.

32. Stefanie Schüler-Springorum counters the interpretation posited by Peter Fritzsche in *A Nation of Fliers: German Aviation and the Popular Imagination* (Cambridge, MA: Harvard University Press, 1992). According to Schüler-Springorum: "If we read the works on pilot literature in chronological order, it becomes clear that the construction of the pilot-hero tended to be an open-ended process – as opposed to Peter Fritzsche's interpretation – and that the image of the pilot so firmly established nowadays as a masculine ideal was much more heterogeneous in the beginning and had to be re-created for each generation." Schüler-Springorum, "Flying and Killing," in Hagemann and Schüler-Springorum, *HOME/FRONT*, 223.

33. The author of the chapter was Hauptmann Fries. Max Schwarte (ed.), *Technik im Weltkriege*, (Berlin: E.S. Miller, 1920), 243. Interesting is that in the entire 610-page-plus illustrations work, the only reference I found to motorcycles in the service of the military was: "Ambulance trucks took over the transport of wounded from the battlefront to the hospital, [and] motorcycles and 'dispatch' two-seaters were employed in the service of relaying commands." Schwarte (ed.), *Technik im Weltkriege*, 223.

34. Merki, *Der holprige Siegeszug*, 84–87; Mom, *Atlantic Automobilism*, 241-242; Möser, "World War I," 203; Steinbeck, *Das Motorrad*, 68–72; Schwarte (ed.), *Technik im Weltkriege*, 235.

35. Christenn, "Die deutsche Motorrad-Industrie," 16

36. See, for example, Fritsche, "Die Entwicklung des deutschen Kraftrades," 21. See also Steinbeck's analysis, *Das Motorrad*, 72–80.

37. Steinbeck, *Das Motorrad*, 72–74. Both NSU and Wanderer were able to profit to a considerable extent due to their military contracts (Wanderer also provided automobiles for the officer corps), although this did not increase their competitiveness following the war.

38. Steinbeck, *Das Motorrad*, 81.

39. Fritsche, "Die Entwicklung des deutschen Kraftrades," 21; Hanfland, *Das Motorrad und seine Konstruktion*, xvii. See also Steinbeck, *Das Motorrad*, 81–90.

40. By the end of 1924, Zündapp had already manufactured ten thousand motorcycles. *Der Motorradsport; motorsportliche Mitteilungen bayrischer Motorrad Klubs*, Vereinigung Nürnberg-Fürther Motorradfahrer eV, December 1924. Furthermore, Nuremburg developed into a center of motorcycle production, with six major motorcycling firms—Ardie, Hercules, Mars, Triumph, Victoria, and Zündapp—located in the provincial capital of Franconia, alongside a burgeoning motorcycle accessory industry, which together employed over five thousand workers in 1925. Michael Diefenbacher and Rudolf Endres, eds., *Stadtlexicon Nürnberg* (Nürnberg: W. Tümmels, 2000), 1219–20. In 1931, one

German motoring magazine called Nuremburg "Germany's Coventry" in reference to the strong hold of the British motorcycling industry. "2,400 Kilometer: Reportage von Unterwegs," *Motor-Kritik*, no. 21, 1931, 484. Another article claims Nuremburg to be the "German motorcycle metropolis": "Die Nürnberger Motorrad-Industrie," *Motorrad-Sport, -Verkehr und Technik*, no. 5, 1925, 17–18.

41. Christenn, "Die deutsche Motorrad-Industrie," 16. The reparations agreement also stipulated that Germany immediately surrender 5,000 locomotives that were in working condition as well as 150,000 railway cars. See Edelmann, *Luxusgut zum Gebrauchsgegendstand*, 27–29.

42. Engine or piston displacement is based on the cylinder volume (cubic capacity) measured in cubic centimeters. Two-stroke engines today can be found in many chainsaws and lawnmowers, and are recognizable for their telltale high-pitched operating noise.

43. Steinbeck, *Das Motorrad*, 88–89.

44. See F. Paul Fritsche, "Zweitakt oder Viertakt," *Klein-Motor-Sport*, no. 5/6, 1923, 30–31; F.A.E. Martin, "Die Zschopauer Motoren-Werke, eine interessante Einblick in die Kleinmotoren-Großfabrikation," *Das Motorrad*, 1923: 198–99. See also, Steinbeck, *Das Motorrad*, 141–70.

45. Hanfland, *Das Motorrad und seine Konstruktion*, xvii–xviii.

46. The new currency, the "Rentenmark," which the government claimed legitimacy through tying it to the supposed "net worth" of Germany's agricultural, commercial, and industrial sectors, was devised in the fall of 1923 and began circulation in November 1923. We can observe the effects of hyperinflation in the pricing of the trade journal: the April issue of *Das Motorrad* was priced at 600 Mk; on 30 September 1923, the price for a single issue (No. 18) was 5 000 000 Mk; and issue No. 23 from 14 December 1923 cost 25 Goldpfennig. For more on the effects of hyperinflation on the motorcycle industry, see: "Zum neuen Jahre," *Das Motorrad*, 1925: 1–2.

47. Hans-Ulrich Wehler, *Deutsche Gesellschaftsgechichte 1914–1949* (Munich: C.H. Beck, 2003): 246–47. For an extensive analysis of the phenomenon of hyperinflation in Germany, see Gerald Feldman, *The Great Disorder: Politics, Economics, and Society in the German Inflation, 1914–1924* (New York and Oxford: Oxford University Press, 1993).

48. See "Aus der General-Versammlung des VDMI," *Das Motorrad*, 1923: 82.

49. Steinbeck, *Das Motorrad*, 90.

50. Gömmel and Braun, "Aufstieg und Niedergang," 171.

51. Bielefeld, "Krisis im Motorradgeschäft," *Motor-Kritik*, no. 3, 1931, 56.

52. Hanfland, *Das Motorrad und seine Konstruktion*, xviii.

53. "The social groups that gained included, first, the entrepreneurs. They obtained cheap credits and were able to undertake sizable investment projects and to build up big commercial empires." Peukert, *The Weimar Republic*, 65.

54. Paul Friedmann, "Kleinkrafträder," as quoted in Flik, *Von Ford lernen?*, 82.

55. For example, in 1923 the motorcycle industry imported 265 and exported 8,265 motorcycles. By 1925 Germany was importing four times the number of motorcycles it was exporting (4,117 imported vs. 1,371 exported; Czechoslovakia was the biggest importer of German motorcycles). Table X "Der Außenhandel mit Kraftfahrzeugen," in Wilhelm Scholz, *Festschrift der Reichverband der Automobilindustrie zum fünfundzwanzigjährigen Bestehen 1901–1926* (Berlin: Reichsverband der deutschen Automobilindustrie, 1926), 148–49.

56. "Die Entwicklung der deutschen Motorrad-Industrie," *Das Motorrad*, 1923: 32–33.
57. Martin, "Die Zschopauer Motoren-Werke," 198–99.
58. "Zum neuen Jahre," *Das Motorrad*, 1925: 1–2.
59. Michael Salweski, "Das Weimarer Revisionssyndrom," *Aus Politik und Zeitgeschichte* 2, no. 80 (1980): 14–25.
60. "Zum neuen Jahre," 1–2.
61. "Zum Geleit," *Das Motorrad*, 1924, 350. Another relevant aspect of the reparation payments that affected the German motor vehicle industry was the government commissions awarded to the motor vehicle industry to fulfill the requirements of the reparations agreement. This practice only came to a halt in mid-1923, when the period of acute hyperinflation commenced and the government was no longer making payments to the motor vehicle industry on the reparations deliveries. On "reparations payments," see RDA, *Jahrbuch*, 1925, 11.
62. One commentator believed that "international integration" should be the greatest priority for Germany: "For a Germany that is still working on the reconstruction of its industry that was destroyed by both the war and the inflation and is burdened with the Dawes obligations, international integration is more of a necessity than it is for almost any other country." "Darf man ausländische Kraftfahrzeuge kaufen?," *Klein Motor-Sport*, no. 21, 1928, 450.
63. A number of motorcycle races, as well as sport and industry-related exhibitions and conferences held between 1922 and 1923 were announced in *Rad-Welt*.
64. Merki, *Der holprige Siegeszug*, 277. The Deutscher Motorradfahrer-Verband (DMV) organized a race on the newly opened AVUS on 24 June 1923, described in *Der Motorradsport; motorsportliche Mitteilungen bayrischer Motorrad Klubs*, VNFM, June 1923, 6.
65. "Die deutschen Automobil-Ausstellungen," *Festschrift der RDA*, 99–102.
66. "Ein Betriebsunfall beim RDA," *Klein-Motor-Sport*, no. 14, 1928, 300–302. See also the strong critique of the RDA's nationalistic tendencies in *Klein-Motor-Sport*: "Ein neues Mittel, den Luftdurchtritt durch Automobilkühler zu behindern; Das Kennzeichen für deutsche Kraftfahrzeuge," *Klein-Motor-Sport*, no. 21, 1928, 441–43; "Darf man ausländische Kraftfahrzeuge kaufen?," *Klein-Motor-Sport*, no. 31, 1928, 445–49.
67. RDA, *Jahrbuch*, 1929, oa–ob.
68. See Flik, *Von Ford lernen?*, 50–52.
69. This type of rhetoric resurfaced in the 1927 motorcycling novel *Motorherz* by Walter Julius Bloem: "No man from the Deutschen Motorrad-Club will ride a foreign make as long as the foreigners refuse to ride a German motorcycle … We don't find it proper to ride foreign machines. Step by step, free trade as trade between the free … And even if foreign machines were better, I would only buy the best that my country has to offer—as long as this country is oppressed and exploited by the whole world." Walter Julius Bloem, *Motorherz* (Berlin: Julius Scherl-Verlag, 1927), 173. Following the readmittance of the German automotive industry in the Union Internationale Contructeurs d'Automobiles in 1927, German manufactures were once again exhibited abroad. See Merki, *Der holprige Siegeszug*, 301. See also Steinbeck, *Das Motorrad*, 199–200, on the RDA's campaign, "Deutsche kauft Deutsche Wagen," to promote domestic consumption of motor vehicles.

70. Dr. Curt Sperling, "Die Automobilindustrie als nationale Industrie," in RDA, *Jahrbuch*, 1926, 8.
71. See "Aufteilung des Kraffahrzeugbestandes in deutschen Anteil und ausländischen Anteil" in RDA, *Tatsachen und Zahlen*, 1930, 19.
72. DKW (Zschopauer Motoren Werke) J.S. Rasmussen an das Bayrische Innenminister von 25 February 1925, MInn 66416 (1923–1924), Ministerium des Inneren, Bayerisches Hauptstaatsarchiv.
73. Steinbeck, *Das Motorrad*, 202–3.
74. Two leading manufacturers of auxiliary motors for bicycles at this time, DKW (in Zschopau in Saxony) and Snob (from the Rhineland), staged massive advertising campaigns to promote the advantages of their product over the competitor. This campaign was centered around the 1922 ADAC Reichsfahrt, about which DKW and Snob both took out many pages of advertising in numerous sporting and trade journals, each accusing the other of having cheated by taking the train for part of the many-days-long endurance trial. See advertisement "DKW-Reichsfahrt-Sieger; Snob fährt Eisenbahn!," *Das Motorrad*, no. 20, 1922. Auxiliary motors became less fashionable in the second half of the 1920s, but experienced another boom starting in 1928 and continuing throughout the 1930s. See Steinbeck, *Das Motorrad*, 239–55.
75. "Ist ein Führerschein für Kleinkrafträder notwendig?," *Klein-Motor-Sport*, no. 10, 1923, 71–72.
76. Statistics on motorization during these first years of the Weimar Republic should be examined with quite a bit of caution, as it is unclear which classifications of power-driven cycles were included. It is highly unlikely that the statistics, even in 1926, contain the actual number of motorized cycles on German roads. On the change in the regulation, see RDA, *Jahrbuch*, 1925, 24–25.
77. Adam Tooze, *The Wages of Destruction: The Making and Breaking of the Nazi Economy* (New York: Penguin, 2006), 6.
78. "Zum neuen Jahre," 1–2.
79. H.-A. König, "Deutsche Automobilausstellung 1925! Zur Motorradschau in Berlin," *Motorrad-Markt*, no. 147, 1925, n.p.
80. Alexander Büttner, "Das Motorrad auf der Deutschen Autoschau: Ein Überblick über Konstruktionsneuheiten und –Neuerungen," *Motorrad-Markt*, no. 148, 1925, n.p.
81. Emil Fischer, "Entwicklungen im deutschen Motorradbau," in RDA, *Jahrbuch*, 1926, 535. See also Braun and Panzer, "The Expansion of the Motor-Cycle Industry," 32, in which they discuss the effects of businesses founded during the inflationary period on the motorcycle industry in general. The small manufacturers invested little capital in either R&D or advertisements. Instead they simply purchased parts, assembled them, and then sold them with a new brand name. "This kind of production allows quick entry into the motorcycle market with negligible capital costs, and a quick exit from it as well, if profit margins decline." Firms in related branches of industry, for example, "sewing machines, bicycles or even a simple blacksmith, could make a 'hit-and-run' on the motorcycle market with products of poorer quality usually for local markets at low prices. These extremely ready-made manufacturers compete with reputable and innovative firms with their more expensive but high quality brand-producers." Also, see the above discussion on the effects of an inflationary economy on the motorcycle industry.

82. Braun and Panzer, "The Expansion of the Motor-Cycle Industry," 24.
83. Hanfland, *Das Motorrad und seine Konstruktion*, xix. Alongside suggesting the sinking of prices through the adoption of modern methods of manufacturing, including the adoption of the assembly line, Hanfland's suggestions also included making motorcycle dealers more knowledgeable.
84. Nolan, *Visions of Modernity*, 6. See also, Charles S. Maier, "Between Taylorism and Technocracy: European Ideologies and the Vision of Industrial Productivity in the 1920s," *Journal of Contemporary History* 5, no. 2 (1970): 27–61.
85. Jürgen Bönig, *Die Einführung von Fließbandarbeit in Deutschland bis 1933: Zur Geschichte einer Sozialinnovation*, vol. 1 (Münster: LIT-Verlag, 1993), 402–3, 412–21.
86. Edmund Levy, "25 Jahre ATG," *Der Motorwagen*, no. 9, 1929, 184.
87. Bönig, *Die Einführung von Fließbandarbeit*, 89–93. See also Steinbeck, *Das Motorrad*, 192.
88. "Rationalisierungsprogramm der Deutsche-Industrie-Werke," *ADAC-Motorwelt*, no. 1, 1928, 25; see also Steinbeck, *Das Motorrad*, 189–98.
89. Richard Lang, plant manager at Daimler's Untertürkheim facility, had implemented Taylorist measures already in 1919. Flik, *Von Ford lernen?*, 225.
90. The fact that the factory adapted rather than "adopted" Fordist methods was noted by an author who visited the plant in 1927. See "Rationalisierungsprogramm," 25.
91. "Technik und Wirtschaft bei den Deutschen Kraftfahrzeug-Werken Akt.-Ges., Spandau," *Motorrad-Sport, -Verkehr und -Technik*, no. 4, 1926, 17–18.
92. Steinbeck, *Das Motorrad*, 193–94.
93. In 1926, the firm was reconstituted as the shareholders' corporation Deutsche Kraftfahrzeug-Werke Aktien-Gesellschaft [German Motor Vehicle Works, Ltd.]; see W. Caspar "Fließende Reihenfertigung von Krafträdern," in *FKZ*, no. 29, 1926, 5–6. Despite the shift to private ownership, the D-Rad factory continued to be subsidized by the state, a measure that members of the Nuremburg industrial and trade chamber took issue with, fearing that the "continued state subvention of this factory" presented a real danger to Nuremburg's motorcycle industry. See *Geschäftsbericht der Handelskammer Nürnberg*, 1926, 19.
94. Christenn, "Die deutsche Motorrad-Industrie," curriculum vitae. Willi Christenn was born in 1901 in Kulmbach in northeast Bavaria, the son of a factory owner. He died in 1944.
95. For a discussion in English on the reception of Taylorist ideas and methods in Weimar Germany, see Nolan, *Visions of Modernity*, 42–50. See also Anson Rabinbach, *The Human Motor: Energy, Fatigue, and the Origins of Modernity* (Berkeley: University of California Press, 1992), 253–58, 271–78.
96. Christenn, "Die deutsche Motorrad-Industrie," 45.
97. "Zum neuen Jahre," 1–2.
98. "Die Entwicklung der deutschen Motorradindustrie," in RDA, *Festschrift 1926*, 49.
99. For example: "Deutsche Arbeit, Qualitätsarbeit!," *FKZ*, no. 37, 1927, 5–6; "Ford und Wir," in *FKZ*, no. 37, 1927, 8–9; "Made in Germany," *FKZ*, no. 39, 1927, 41.
100. E. Bieringer, "Serien- oder Einzelfabrikation," *ADAC-Motorwelt*, no. 1, 1926, 1–2. For a discussion in English on "The Cultural Consequences of Americanization," see Nolan, *Visions of Modernity*, 108–27.
101. For a discussion of the British motorcycle industry between the wars, see Koerner, "Four Wheels Good, Two Wheel Bad." For a comparative analysis of

Germany and England based on the "Schumpeterian" model of diffusion, see Braun and Panzer, "The Expansion of the Motor-Cycle Industry." For a discussion of the French and Swiss motorcycle industries, see Merki, *Der holprige Siegeszug*, 120–25. See also Steinbeck, *Das Motorrad*, 91–99, 185–204.

102. Braun and Panzer, "The Expansion of the Motor-Cycle Industry," 32.

103. "'The Interest in the Transportation Industry, Can the German Automobile Industry Cover the Demands?' This demand can be completely satisfied by the German industry, and especially through the so-called utility cars, therefore in cheap cars, also called the "Volkswagen.'" See "Das Interesse der Verkehrswesens. Kann die deutsche Automobilindustrie den Bedarf decken?" in RDA, *Jahrbuch*, 1930, 6. Flik also discusses the question of the *Volksautomobil*, in Flik, *Von Ford lernen?*, 57–60. For a discussion in English on the popularity of Ford and the Fordist model in Weimar Germany, see Nolan, *Visions of Modernity*.

104. For example, in the commemorative book celebrating the 25-year existence of the RDA, forty-one pages are devoted to the history of the German automobile industry and a mere eight to the development of the German motorcycle industry. This lack of recognition of the motorcycle industry can also be attributed to: (1) the relatively fewer numbers of workers employed in the motorcycle industry (the 1927 RDA yearbook cited the total number of workers employed by the motorcycle industry in 1925 at 6,315 and the total number of workers at automobile factories at 71,328); (2) the relatively lower profit margins of the motorcycle industry (comparative pro-unit profits were approximately 1:100); and (3) the relatively lower worth, as the RDA cited the 1925 total worth of the motorcycle industry at 49.9 million Reichsmarks, and the total worth of the automobile industry at 663.3 million Reichsmarks. See RDA, *Tatsachen und Zahlen*, 1927, 6, 15. Statistics used by the RDA on the motorcycle industry are not inclusive, as only forty-three of the two hundred plus motorcycle firms that existed in Germany during 1925 were included. See Christenn, "Die deutsche Motorrad-Industrie," 36.

105. Haubner, *Von Nervenkitzel zur Freizeitvergnügen*, 12. Haubner presents a forceful argument that structures (state, economic, and institutional) that greatly facilitated the motorization of Germany were already being actively implemented in the Wilhelmine era.

106. RDA, *Jahrbuch*, 1926, 31.

107. Flik, *Von Ford lernen?*, 230–32. On the ineffectiveness of standardization attempts within the automobile industry, see Nolan, *Visions of Modernity*, 151–53. Kugler, "Von der Werkstatt zum Fließband," 324–28.

108. Some of these organizations, like the RDA, predated the war. In addition, there were numerous other industrialists' organizations that promoted the interests of the motor vehicle industry in general, as well as its related industries, including: Deutsche Automobil-Händler-Verband, e.V. [German Automobile Dealers' League]; Deutschen Kraftfahrer-Verband [German Professional Drivers' League]; Reichsverband der Deutschen Fahrzeug und Karosserie-Industrie, e.V. [National League of German Motor Vehicle and Chassis-Building Industry]; Vereinigung Deutscher Automobil-Zeitschriften-Verleger [Organization of German Automobile Magazine Publishers]; Reichsverband der Garagenbesitzer [National League of Garage Owners]; Verband der Deutschen Kraftfahrzeig-Ueberwachungs-Vereine [League of German Motor Vehicle Monitoring

Associations]; Reichsverband des Kraftfahrzeugshandels und Gewerbes [National League of Motor Vehicle Trade and Industry]; Verbandes der Besitzer von Kleinkraftdroschken e.V. [League of Owners of Small-Powered Taxi Cabs]; and Kraftfahrer-Vereinigung Deutscher Aerzte [Motorists' Association for German Doctors]. This list is certainly not complete. See Gustav Braunbeck, *Braunbecks Addressbuch der Motorfahrzeug- und verwandten Industrie für Deutschland* (Berlin: Verlag Gustav Braunbeck G.m.b.H., 1925/1929).

109. The following organizations had agreed to work together in the working group, including: the RDA; Automobilclub von Deutschland [Automobile Club of Germany, AvD]; Automobiltechnische Gesellschaft [Automobile Technical Society, ATG]; Allgemeiner Deutscher Automobil-Club [Nationwide German Automobile Club, ADAC]; *Deutsche Auto-Liga* [German-Auto-League]; Deutscher Motorradfahrer-Verband [German Motorcyclists Association, DMV]; Deutscher Touring-Club [German Touring Club]; Deutscher Verkehrsbund (Reichsabteilung für Kraftfahrer) [German Transportation Association (National Division of Drivers)]; Kraftverkehr Deutschland G.m.b.H. [Motorized Traffic Germany, Ltd]; Reichsverband für Kraftfahrzeughandel und Bedarf [National League for Motor Vehicle Trade and Necessities]; Verband der Berliner Großgaragen-Besitzer [League of the Berlin Large Garage Owners]; and the Verband deutscher Motorradhändler [League of German Motorcycle Dealers]. See "Arbeitsgemeinschaft für das Kraftfahrwesen," RDA, *Jahrbuch*, 1926, 45–46.

110. Merki also provides a discussion of the organizational integration of the motor vehicle industry with the state. See Merki, *Der holprige Siegeszug*, 256–64.

111. Steinbeck, *Das Motorrad*, 141.

112. Ibid., 132–70, 313.

113. *NSU-Mitteilungen*, no. 102, 1932, 2789.

114. Munich was supposedly the first city to equip their traffic police with motorcycles with sidecars, *Motorrad-Sport, -Verkehr und -Technik*, no. 18, 1925, 22. Also "Die Pflicht zur Disziplin: Ein Erziehungsbeitrag. Die polizeiliche Überwachung des Verkehrs mit Krafträdern," *Motorrad-Sport, -Verkehr und -Technik*, no. 45, 1930, 5.

115. "Das Motorrad als Nutzfahrzeug," *Motorrad-Markt*, no. 147, 1925, n.p. See also Kirchberg, "Die Motorisierung des Straßenverkehrs," 16–17.

116. *Strasse und Verkehr*, 1929.

117. "BMW-Wagen im Dienst der Ostpressischen Reichswehr," *BMW-Blätter*, no. 6, 1931, 7–9; "Ein neuer BMW-Erfolg bei der Reichswehr," *BMW-Blätter*, no. 13, 1932, 9.

118. Paul Friedmann, "Was ist eigentlich deutsch?," *Das Motorrad*, 1931: 1607.

119. Paul Friedmann, "Deutschland c/a Ausland," *Das Motorrad*, 1929: 1633.

120. Jürgen Kocka, "Zur Problematik der deutschen Angestellten 1914–1933," in *Industrielles System und Politische Entwicklung in der Weimarer Republic*, ed. Hans Mommsen (Düsseldorf: Droste, 1974), 792.

121. Flik, *Von Ford lernen?*, 83.

122. Interestingly, in 1919, the first motorcycles built in Bologna had DKW motors. Antonio Campigotto and Enrico Ruffini, "Le veterane degli anni '20; Agli albori dell'industria motociclistica Bolognese," *Scuola Officina: Museo del Patrimonio Industriale di Bologna* 1 (2004): 10–11.

123. Six hundred "returned soldiers" were employed at the factory by 1922. MZ Zschopau, "1922–2002: 80 Jahre Motorrad und Motorradbau in Zschopau," brochure (Zschopau, 2002), n.p.

124. Braun and Panzer, "The Expansion of the Motor-Cycle Industry," 43.

125. Immo Sievers, *Jørgen Skafte Rasmussen: Leben und Werk des DKW-Gründers* (Bielefeld: Delius Klasing Verlag, 2006), 85.

126. D. Wolf, "Die Entwicklung der DKW-Werke, der größten Motorradfabrik der Welt," *Motor-Tourist*, no. 16, 1929, 10–11; Brochure, MZ Zschopau.

127. "Zschopau," *Motor-Kritik*, no. 16, 1930, 354.

128. Sievers, *Jørgen Skafte Rasmussen*, 60.

129. DKW – Zschopauer Motorenwerke J.S. Rasmussen AG (Sonderdruck aus Deutsches Wirtschafts-Archiv) Akte 34: 30170, Bestand Zschopauer Motorenwerke J.S. Rasmussen AG (DKW), Zschopau 1913–1932, Sächsisches Staatsarchiv Chemnitz.

130. Wolf, "Die Entwicklung der DKW-Werke," 10–11. Ford, *My Life*, 105–6.

131. "Fragebogen der Enquete-Ausschuß," Akte 104, Firmengeschichte, 31070, Bestand Zschopauer Motorenwerke J.S. Rasmussen AG (DKW), Zschopau 1913–1932, Sächsisches Staatsarchiv Chemnitz.

132. Flik, *Von Ford lernen?*, 217–18.

133. "Zschopauer Motorenwerke J.S. Rasmussen Aktiengesellschaft DKW Zschopau," *Der deutsche Motorfahrer*, no. 9, 1930, 20.

134. "Auszugsweise Abschrift des Protokolls der Sitzung des Aufsichtsrates der Zschopauer Motorenwerke J.S. Rasmussen Aktiengesellschaft, Zschopau, am 11. März 1931 in Zschopau i. Sa.: 2, Akte 1, 31070, Bestand Zschopauer Motorenwerke J.S. Rasmussen AG (DKW), Zschopau 1913–1932, Sächsisches Staatsarchiv Chemnitz.

135. DKW was not the only manufacturer to lose its autonomy through the contraction caused by the world economic crisis. D-Rad entered into a strategic partnership with NSU in 1932. Steinbeck, *Das Motorrad*, 195.

136. Audi AG (ed.), *Das Rad der Zeit, Die Geschichte der Audi AG* (Bielefeld: Verlag Delius Klasing, 2000).

137. "Der Kleinkraftwagen – und am ihn vorbei," *Der deutsche Motorfahrer*, no. 4, 1930, 1–4; Otto Lüders, "Die Kleinkraftrad soll sterben!," *Der deutsche Motorfahrer*, no. 12, 1929, 11–12; "Der bedrohte Kleinkraftrad," *Motorrad-Sport, -Verkehr und -Technik*, no. 46, 1929, 4–5; "Die Katastrophenpolitik im Motorfahrwesen," *Der deutsche Motorfahrer*, no. 7, 1930, 3–6.

138. Bielefeld, "Krisis im Motorradgeschäft," *Motor-Kritik*, no. 3, 1931, 55.

139. "Stagnation und Finanzielle Schwierigkeiten," *Der deutsche Motorfahrer*, no. 31, 1930, 3–5.

140. "Öffentliche Meinung 253, 'Deutsche kauft Deutsche Räder,'" *Das Motorrad*, 1929: 405. "Die Erdrosselung der deutschen Wirtschaft," *Der deutsche Motorfahrer*, no. 9, 1930, 3–5; "Deutsche kauft deutsche Autos! Und was hinter der Reklame steht," in *AIZ*, no. 18, 1929, 4–5.

141. Bielefeld, "Um die deutsche Motorrad-Industrie?," *Motor-Kritik*, no. 20, 1931, 446.

142. "Die Katastrophenpolitik im Motorfahrwesen," 3.

143. Paul Friedmann, "Dacho-Kraft," *Das Motorrad*, 1931: 1223.

144. Walter Ostwald, "Erdrosselung der deutschen Kraftfahrt; Ein Apel an die Kraftfahrer für die Reichstagswahlen," *Motorrad-Sport, -Verkehr und -Technik*, no. 33, 1930, 4–5.

145. Another instance of anti-motorcycling politics was when, in 1925, eight members of the Bayerische Volkspartei [Bavarian People's Party] submitted a petition to the Bavarian parliament asking: "What new measures has the government considered taking in order to effectively make transportation on public streets safe from the collective risk presented by speeding motor vehicles?" Bayerischer Landtag, Kurze Anfrage 212, 14 July 1925. Kraftfahrzeug allgemein, Ministry of Interior 66418 (1 July 1925, 1 November 1925), Bayerisches Hauptstaatsarchiv.
146. Otto Lüders, "Das Kleinkraftrad soll sterben!," 11–12.
147. Steinbeck, *Das Motorrad*, 239–41.
148. "Das Volksrad für Jeder!," *NSU-Mitteilungen*, no. 101, 1932, 2773.
149. Manfred Nabinger, *Deutsche Fahrradmotoren, 1898 bis 1988* (Brilon: Pozdun Motorbücher, 1988), 7.
150. Preface from the series editor, in Schmitt, *Musterbetriebe*, 3.
151. Schmitt, *Musterbetriebe*, 67.
152. Ibid., 66. This position was, for example, also held by DINTA, the German Institute for Technical Labor Training, who "combined an acceptance of economic modernity with an admiration of right-wing militarism and a conservative ideology of leadership." See Nolan, *Visions of Modernity*, 192.
153. Schmitt, *Musterbetriebe*, 68.
154. Ibid., 69–70.
155. The 1932 poem, "The True Employer," followed the logic of consumer-driven growth by pointing its finger at the lack of consumer demand as the cause of the economic problems: "No steel factory trust, no coal monopoly / no Ford, no IG, no Deterding / has as much power / brought together / in his hands / as the largest employer in the world / YOU!; Why do so many chimneys not smoke / and why do so many boats not sail? / Why welfare? / Why unemployed? / Why is everything at a standstill? / Because some don't want to buy! / YOU!.; "Der wahre Arbeitgeber," *NSU-Mitteilungen*, no. 101, 1932, 2757.
156. Oskar Pfeiffer, "Zum neuen Jahr!," *NSU Mitteilungen*, no. 103, 1933, 2826.

CHAPTER 2

Engineering and Advertising a Motorized Future

Ernst Neumann-Neander was a distinctively modern man.[1] His life united the spheres of motorization, engineering, and advertising. Connecting art and technology was central to his life-long passion for design—of poster art, motorcycles, and lightweight cars. At the turn of the twentieth century, he was a member of the Munich avant-garde cabaret *Die 11 Scharfrichter*. He then lived in Paris for several years before moving to Berlin in 1908 to open an atelier called "Workshop for the Art of Engineering and Advertising." Joining the influential indus-trial arts group *Werkbund* in 1912, his philosophy on designing motor vehicles stressed the importance of the eye:[2] "The human eye does not want only to optically register the movement of the vehicle, but also to experience it, to grasp its demonstration. So the form should speak of the movement. Body and motor power should coincide inside a unified complex of feeling."[3] As an artist, Neumann-Neander was prominent enough to be the leader of his own "school," and was the teacher of Weiland Herzfelde and his brother John Heartfield, among others.[4] One critic attributed the success of his advertisements and poster art to "a skillful import of well-tested American advertising tricks."[5]

During the early inflation years of the Weimar Republic, Neumann-Neander, who became known as N², constructed motorcycles with both lightweight Duralumin frames as well as steel-pressed frames that achieved cult status as an example of perfection in form.[6] Neumann-Neander rode one of his own constructions in the February 1924 Deutschlandfahrt, a 3,000-km ride through "ice and snow" that, accord-ing to his account, demanded the utmost of the man and the machine.[7] Continuing to perfect his designs, he built motorcycles that won countless races in the mid-1920s. His motorcycle frame designs were so successful in international competitions that the most advanced German automotive manufacturer, Opel, bought a license to produce a standardized frame in 1928.[8] Neumann-Neander, who adopted the name "Neander" to express an entire philosophy of life around the creative potential of the "new man," embodied a mutually constitutive

Image 2.1. The Engineer, Adman, and Motorcyclist Ernst Neumann-Neander, 1904.

relationship between technology, masculinity, and the practices of engineering and advertising in the era of classical modernity.

The transformation of industry led to a growth of engineering activities in the design of both products and production systems, as well as to innovations in sales and service strategies and departments, creating new occupational groups. Alongside the workers and the factory owners, engineers and admen were central to producing and promoting both motorization and the motorcycle. Admen and engineers played a vital role in imagining, organizing, and realizing a modern society of consumers. This chapter looks at the figure of the engineer, who historian Charles S. Maier judged as "central to the new industrial gospel ... not so much as a master of machines" than "as a potential manipulator of all industrial relationships."[9] The automotive engineer in particular represented a symbolically powerful variation of masculinity, intimately involved, both discursively and concretely, with the production of the industrial economy and with shaping the nation. During the Weimar Republic, however, engineering was still a profession very much in the making, and relationships between various factions—engineers holding academic degrees vs. self-taught engineers vs. technicians—were highly contentious. Engineers were also at the center of debates over the relationship between culture and technology, the spiritual and the material. Politically heterogeneous, the sole unifying principle behind the engineering profession's identity was a vision of a technological future. The second half of the chapter explores the world of advertising the motorcycle, from advertising agencies and customer service to the spaces, techniques, strategies, and motifs of advertising the motorcycle and the sidecar. The shiny visions of a motorized society that advertisers often produced, however, reflected neither the everyday difficulties of motorcycling nor the often-harsh reality of economic and social instability in the Weimar Republic. In the manufacturing and selling of desires, unfulfilled promises of motorized modernity were manifest.

Engineering a Motorized Society

Due to a similarly high personal and professional investment in technological progress, engineers, like motorcycling manufacturers, were indeed among the most active promoters of the process of motorization and were central to giving the project direction.[10] Engineers proclaimed their era the "Age of Technology" or the "Age of the Motor," and pictured themselves as leaders of the modern world. They proclaimed technology to be a "great power, a power over other powers that are all more or less dependent on technology."[11] Regularly rehearsed idolization involved transforming engineers into prophets through proclaiming technology as a panacea for all social ills: "Motorization means revival; it means invigoration, uplift, and intensification of the economy. Motorization is the way to increase performance, which therefore leads to improved earning of the individual and increased prosperity of the nation."[12] Many engineers also accorded technology an incomparable influence over "modern life"—over "politics, press, science, economy, and the bodily and spiritual constitution of mankind."[13] They presented themselves as capable "new men," destined to take on the challenges of modernity.[14] In reference to motorcycle engineer and head technical director at DKW, Richard Blau, one journalist pithily remarked, "Even the Gods at Zschopau appear to be men, with whom you can

communicate fairly decently in German."[15] "Ethical and idealistic," engineers claimed they were "humanity's benefactors."[16] Possessing not
only technical knowledge, but also "intellect and reason, moral sentiment and thinking, appearing as a refined and unified harmony," engineers understood themselves to be ideal "*Kulturmenschen*."[17] Within the
engineering community in Germany and internationally, the identity of
engineers as "men of deeds" closely associated their masculinity with
both technology and productive labor.[18]

Yet despite sharing a similar habitus, the professional status of engineers in Germany remained unclear and fraught with internal distinctions, heightening a sense of insecurity over their role in society.[19]
Engineers struggled over how to define the profession of engineering,
and whether to institute standard qualifications and legal protections.
They also argued over the benefits and drawbacks of rationalizing industry and the economy, and over the relationship between technology
and culture. Despite their self-image as shapers of modern society, they
often expressed the view that society in general did not accord them
proper recognition.[20] Their putative sense of misrecognition stemmed
in part from greater shifts in the occupational structure and the lack of
unity among the various technological professions in Germany, and it is
to this point that I now turn.

Although technical achievements were seen as a central pillar of
Germany's rapid rise to industrial strength in the late nineteenth century, engineering was late to develop as a profession and thus lacked the
internal cohesion more pronounced among other professional groups
such as lawyers and teachers.[21] Moreover, the profession of engineering
was riddled with internal distinctions. Unlike lawyers and teachers, it
was possible for any person to claim the occupational title of "engineer."
A letter to the technical advisor of *Der Schlossermeister* [Master Metal
Worker], a journal to which motorcycle mechanics and want-to-be
motorcycle engineers often wrote letters, indicated the—for German
standards perhaps surprising—laxity in terms of the professional title of
engineer. A reader posed the question of whether "anyone can legitimately add the title 'engineer' to their name and use it on printed material etc. if he is qualified but has not attended an engineering school?"
The editors replied: "The title 'engineer' is not legally protected, in contrast, for example, to the title of 'master' in connection with a craft ...
The efforts of German engineers to create a legal basis for the use of
the title 'engineer' only for those who have completed their studies at a
technical school have not yet been successful."[22]

In fact, the question of the legal protection of the title "engineer"
during the Weimar Republic was a highly contested issue that major

professional groups did not agree upon and that remained unresolved until the 1970s.[23] The largest professional organization for engineers, the Verein Deutscher Ingenieure [Association of German Engineers, VDI] was against a restriction of the term to those who had completed engineering school because it "feared the loss of non-academic members," whereas the younger association, the Verein Deutscher Diplom-Ingenieure [Association of German Academic Engineers, VDDI], as the inclusion of *Diplom* (academic) in its name may suggest, was the most active proponent for instituting a legal protection of the title. Another reason for the disunity in engineering was the fast growth rate of the profession in the first decades of the twentieth century. Indeed, the numbers of academically trained engineers increased substantially over the course of the Weimar Republic, nearly doubling in the period between 1925 and 1933.[24] At the same time, the introduction of modern management methods, the steadily increasing level of mass production methods, and the rationalization hype all worked together to create the appearance of demand for well-trained mechanical engineers. As engineering schools turned out graduates at an unprecedented rate, the labor market was eventually unable to absorb the available pool of trained technical workers. Rationalization thus had the dual consequence of thrusting engineers into the forefront of modernizing the economy and society while diminishing employment opportunities for those in the technical professions, both in terms of numbers and job quality.[25]

Consolidating engineering as a profession was also hampered by its uncertain position between manual and mental labor. Engineers during the Weimar Republic continued to quibble over whether or not engineering was related more closely to the arts or to the natural sciences.[26] Carl Weihe, engineer, passionate motorcyclist, admirer of Schopenhauer, and editor of the popular science journal *Technik und Kultur*, claimed that "technical creation includes not only mental but also manual and machine labor, and both, the ideational and the practical sides, are so intertwined that there is no such thing as manual labor without mental labor."[27] Weihe sought to distance engineering from its intellectual professional image by emphasizing the technical nature of engineering while at the same time presenting the engineer as a god-like creator.[28] The strong association between engineers and the figure of the genius inventor, alongside the fact that many engineers, including such successful motorcycle engineers as Ernst Neumann-Neander, claimed that engineering knowledge could best be acquired through autodidactic methods, diminished the drive to require academic training across the board for engineers.[29] In what can be understood as part of an effort to reign in the disorder wrought by industrialization and accelerated social mobility, numerous attempts were initiated with the aim of professionalizing and regulating the field of engineering, and professional groups for engineers proliferated.

Already prior to World War I, the increasing importance of motorization as an engineering field led to the founding of the Automobiltechnische Gesellschaft [Automobile Technological Society, ATG]. A professional organization specifically for motor vehicle engineers, it was established in 1904 "out of the urgent necessity of the times, namely to unite all those forces active in the then still young field of automotive technology in collective scientific labor."[30] On the occasion of its twenty-fifth anniversary in 1929, ATG stated that its role was to promote the "exchange of ideas" between its seven hundred members, a heterogeneous group that included "office and fabrication engineers, chief engineers, technical directors, and a few sales directors."[31] The ATG claimed to be the main organization promoting the cause of rationalization within the automotive industry, even beating the American Association of Automotive Engineers in designing industry standard-norm sheets.[32] Mirroring the auto-centric attitude of the RDA, the ATG was similarly dismissive of the motorcycle in relation to the automobile, the truck, and the airplane.[33]

Members of the ATG were employed both as constructors of motor vehicles and their accessories, and, as jobs for constructors became more competitive due to the glut of engineering graduates, they joined the "rationalized field of repair."[34] Another area of employment for graduates of engineering schools developed within the field of regulating motorization as technical experts qualified in assessing the new technology. A part of the growing state apparatus, engineers found positions, for example, with the "Official Examination Bureau for Motor Vehicle Traffic." These new expert institutions were key actors in establishing norms and regulating the process of motorization. Responsible for evaluating the new technologies and making recommendations, the engineers employed by these new institutions exerted substantial influence on shaping the process of motorization. Signed by two engineers, for example, the following recommendation to the government of Upper Bavaria regarding the 1924 exemption of small-powered motorcycles from licensing and number plates, provides a generally negative assessment of two-stroke motorcycles. The engineers employed their expertise not only in terms of determining technical specifications, but also weighed in on appropriate motoring behavior: "Many of the small-powered motorcycles are being driven in a noticeably inconsiderate manner. In addition, the noise made by the exhaust systems of these small-powered motorcycles is unreasonably loud and has a disrupting and disturbing effect on the rest of traffic."[35] While the anti-motorcycling stance taken by the engineers acting as expert consultants to the state may appear antithetical to the overall project of motorization, it provides evidence of how engineers evaluated different technologies and is indicative of their investment in the more general discussion on the appropriate path to motorization.[36]

Thus, like the general public, engineers' attitudes to specific technologies of motorization were not uniform. Some engineers expressed a sense that the motorcycle was an inferior instrument for motorizing society, and that it was only an "unfortunate reflection of the postwar poverty of German society."[37] Others, including Carl Weihe, claimed that the motorcycle was the foremost technical instrument of "liberation," possessing decisive advantages over both the bicycle and the car. "How much freer are we on a motorcycle! … The motorcyclist is the freest person, hardly surpassed by the pilot, who can be affected by bad weather in the nastiest way." Weihe conceived the benefits of motorcycling not only as material, but as spiritual and psychological as well: "With the freedom of the body, the soul is also freed. Everyday worries disappear, the odds and ends of life are lost, the oppressive heartache that has weighed on us for so long leaves us, and we become free and want to ride out into the world cheering."[38] In a utopian vision, another engineer wrote, "a new era will dawn with the motorcycle of the future." Hailing the motorcycle as a panacea for the world's problems, the author claimed: "In future days, motorcycles will have an unimagined influence on the development of humanity. People will get to know each other and respect each other without anything getting in between. Horizons will be widened. A drivers' license will authorize the free movement of peoples across borders. People will become multilingual, and thoughtfully they will make comparisons and learn from each other. Humanity will grow closer and understand each other better."[39] Despite differences in individual engineers' attitudes towards specific instruments of motorization, however, the common belief in the primacy of technology for shaping the future of Germany and the world was central to the Weltanschauung of engineers.[40] "Increasing the degree of efficiency," the unofficial slogan of German engineers, was also an oft-cited advantage of motorized transportation over non-motorized forms.[41]

Byway I: The Literary Figure of the Engineer

Representing an archetypal new man, engineers were also popular literary figures during the Weimar Republic.[42] Similar to the ways in which the role of the engineer in society was discussed in *Technik Voran!*, the literary figure of the motorcycle engineer was filled with vitality, creativity, and a technocratic vision of a better future society.[43] Engineers could, however, also be portrayed in a Faustian, almost demonic light. In Fred Petermann's 1927 "sports-novel" *Der PS-Narr* (Horsepower Fool), Thomas Weiland, the main protagonist, personifies both of these aspects of the literary figure of the engineer. Inarguably a "new man," the character of Thomas Weiland embodies the Weimar era "homo faber." In *PS-Narr*, Petermann addressed the relationship between sports, industry, and the nation through the figure of the engineer, providing a revealing, if somewhat atypical, variety of motorcycling masculinity.

The driving plot element is Thomas Weiland's successful construction of a *perpetuum mobile*, in the form of a motor able to harness the energy of the sun. After Weiland wins his first race with the "Thomas Motor" on the newly constructed AVUS racetrack in Berlin, soundly smashing the international competition, "the flag was raised and the orchestra played the German anthem. Carried away, thousands sang along."[44] Connecting engineering feats to the strength of the German nation, Weiland, the engineer and motorcyclist, embodies a resurgent Germany. In a flashback, Petermann revealed why Weiland was driven to invent the motor. As a youth, he had desired to be a winner: "Motor vehicles and the longing to one day take part in a race, and at the end to come out the laurel-wreathed winner, ruled him completely."[45] Technological ambition is coupled with personal ambition. Explicitly connecting sports to the furthering of engineering and industry, Weiland's personal victory possesses the potential to enhance the standing of the nation.

Petermann's Weiland is not an engineer by training—rather he is an inventor, indeed an often-mocked genius, hence the nickname "Horsepower Fool." The character of Weiland represents the popular literary figure of the inventor/engineer with a "will to control nature unconditionally," who Petermann portrays in both a positive and a negative light.[46] Producing "the effect of a revolution," Weiland's "Thomas Motor" turns the world upside down:

> What had once ruled in solitary heights was smashed. A spirit blew through the world and ripped everything down. Despite its potential benefits for humanity, the invention has a cataclysmic impact on the global economy. The stocks of energy and transportation, which had been so sought after yesterday, flooded the market. Everyone wanted dump stocks that had been made worthless by the Thomas Motor. Within 24 hours, the consequences were horrible. Stock market indexes dropped rapidly, banks went bankrupt, fabulously wealthy people became paupers. The world

had never experienced such a thing. Like a ghost hovering over the chaos stood the name Thomas Weiland.

The "revolution" sparked by Weiland's invention is, on the one hand, a panacea for the problem of energy scarcity, and, on the other, an economic scourge with "horrible consequences." While a plot that revolves around the idea of a *perpetuum mobile* can clearly be situated in the genre of science fiction, the idea of harnessing the physics of fusion and fission was soundly within the realm of the imaginable during the Weimar Republic. In fact, energy scarcity was already a perceptible issue, and atom fission and fusion were wildly speculated on as being probable energy sources of the future.[47] Although published serially in *Das Motorrad* in 1927, before the onset of the World Economic Crisis, the traumas of recurrent intense political and economic dislocations were familiar to all Germans. Despite the period of relative stabilization between 1924 and 1929, a feeling of permanent economic, political, and social uncertainty permeated German society.

In the figure of Thomas Weiland, Petermann provided a particularly ambivalent representation of German masculinity. While Petermann most often described Weiland as a new man, his face "manly, handsome, and powerful,"[48] even in his moments of triumph, Weiland is portrayed as having shaky nerves and being susceptible to crying fits: "Away from the bandstands, away from the people, and alone in nature, Thomas Weiland dismounted his motorcycle and ripped the helmet from his head. Then he sat down next to his bike and cried . . . From that hour, Thomas Weiland was a different person. His carefree, joyful way of being was gone. The serious, nerve-whipping hours left their trace on him."[49] From that point on, Weiland's character begins to undergo a transformation Petermann linked not only to his invention, but, more importantly, to Weiland's relationships to women. Despite the fact that Weiland is an ingenious inventor, his "destiny" depended on women: "Yes, you women are my destiny! Only through you can I be human again. . . . You are my sun, women, and I must also conquer you. And you must all lay at my feet, and the most beautiful will be mine, today—tomorrow—forever."[50] The first woman to be seduced by Weiland, Ruth, enters his life right after he won his first race. The second woman is Vilma, the wife of Thomas Weiland's best friend, Ralf. After Ralf dies defending Weiland and his invention from sinister gangsters in America, Vilma is portrayed as reawakening Weiland's desire to live. As with Ruth, Weiland soon wearies of Vilma's affections. The third woman, Lya Monte, an industrialist's daughter and movie star, is the final proof of Weiland's godliness in her submission to him. His triumph over Lya Monte again alters his character: "The nighttime hours spent with Lya Monte filled Thomas Weiland with fortitude. His word was now an order, his wish dictatorial."[51]

At this point in the narrative, Weiland's character takes a decisive turn: from often emotional, insecure, indecisive, and dependent on women, to cold, obsessed, and controlling, transforming him from a "Horsepower Fool" into a "Horsepower God": "Day and night the Thomas Works operate before the gates of Berlin. New factory buildings have to be built . . . the demand for Thomas Motors of all types was so unbelievably large that daily production was increased at a frightening tempo." Accompanying the expansion of the factory, Weiland's character also undergoes a metamorphosis:

> Cold and calculating stood the motorcyclist of yesteryear at the peak of his power, the zenith of his fame. He felt that the whole world was addicted to him and his work. This knowledge made the man clever and conniving in all questions about life . . . With a cold smile, Thomas Weiland became the ruler. He had made the world happy, so it should lay down at his feet in gratitude . . . Ever since the moment he conquered Lya Monte, he despised women, those who he had once wished to lay at his feet.[52]

Losing his drive for women, they become merely a means to produce an heir to his invention and his power. Weiland, however, had to reckon with the desire for revenge on the part of the disappointed women. Each realizing that Weiland was only using them, they unite together and plan to take their revenge. Their first attempt, shooting him at a motorcycle race, is unsuccessful. Their second attempt, blowing up a ship that he was sailing on, is more successful. Although Weiland survives the bombing, his brain is irreparably damaged so that in the end the genius inventor has lost both his mind and his spirit ["*sein Geist verloren*" "*Ja – der Geist fehlt*"]—the "Horsepower God" was reduced again to a "Horsepower Fool."[53] Petermann provides a strikingly ambivalent depiction of the relationship between genders: on the one hand, the women are portrayed as having ruined the "Horsepower God" and as having robbed the world of a great invention; on the other hand, Weiland's need to conquer women is depicted as essentially sociopathic, harmful for the relationship between the sexes, and thus contrary to the natural order of society.

In Weiland's alternate incarnations as "Horsepower Fool" and "Horsepower God," Petermann critiques the Faustian, demonic man as creator. In contrast to previous literary analyses of the profession of engineering and the construction of masculinity during the Weimar Republic, *PS-Narr* put a new spin on the relationship between masculinity and technology.[54] Rather than celebrating the "relationship between technological power and the traditional entitlement of the man to conquer the woman," the figure of Weiland was intended as a warning against exactly that relationship between engineering masculinity and the conquering of nature and women.[55] Petermann's depiction of the darker side of "homo faber" is, however, rather atypical for Weimar literary representations of engineers, with the literary figure of the engineer/motorcyclist often being portrayed as an ideal man and citizen, mirroring the self-image of engineers as the ideal rational and objective *Kulturmensch*.[56] Nevertheless, the figure of the engineer/motorcyclist Weiland provides a vivid expression of the anxiety around the effects of technology on society, including on gender and sexuality.

The Politics of Engineering a Motorized Future

With a belief that the principle of efficiency could equally be applied to social contexts, similar to colleagues in the United States and around the world, automotive engineers during the Weimar Republic officially supported a vision of a rationalized and streamlined economy, society, and state.[57] A group of engineers organized in the Reichsbund deutscher Technik [Imperial Union of German Technology, RdT] proposed establishing a state "Ministry of Technology and Transportation." Based on the idea that only a technocratically organized state could ensure both economic prosperity and social harmony, in a proposal submitted to the Reichstag in October 1925, the authors claimed such a ministry would be the "expression of a rational merging of tasks" that had until then been inefficiently administrated by disparate ministries. Instead, the new ministry would be responsible for issues ranging from regulating transportation and traffic on rails, roads, waterways, and in the air, to exploring and allocating energy resources, building and maintaining housing stock, and surveying land. Beyond specific calls for increased efficiency through rationalization, its initiators believed that establishing a Ministry of Technology and Transportation would further the German people as a whole. In order to emphasis their point, they cited Reichverkehrsminister [Minister of Transportation] Oeser's technocratic view of the modern world: "Railroads, radios, and aviation deny political borders. Technology covers the whole world and, with the increase of transportation, it will be the duty of technology to spread its achievements throughout the world."[58] Concluding with far-reaching hopes for implementing a technocratic approach to society, the engineers organized in the RdT believed a ministry could restore Germany's position in the world as a technical leader: "Imbued with a social and economic spirit, the Ministry of Technology and Transportation will become a vital aid in leading the German people to renewed heights of its former inner-greatness, and to make it an equal and free member of the society of people [*Gesellschaft der Völker*]."[59] In the declaration of its purpose, the RdT defined itself as a "*civil union* of technicians of *all* types and degrees and *all state-loyal* parties. It aims to build a united front of all technicians for the purpose of intervening in the state functioning [*Staatsgetriebe*] in the interest of the entire people."[60] Technology was thus conceived of as standing above politics, and was presented as an alternative to politics. German engineers promoted a technocratic approach that they believed could serve to replace politics and that would culminate in the rational ordering of the polity.

Although many engineers argued their work was apolitical and should not be aligned with any particular ideology, others recognized the capacity for technology to be employed in the service of politics.[61] In a debate in *Technik Voran!* (Technology to the Fore!), the influential journal of the RdT, one side maintained that technology itself should be the "worldview of a new era," while the other side argued that it was the use of technology that determined whether it would be for the harm or the good of humanity: "Technology, science, and, to name a third, politics, as the art of designing social systems, are only worth as much as the will of those who use it is worth. Knowledge in itself is not good, but the will to knowledge is; technology in itself is not good, but only the pure free will to technology is, to have control over the power of nature. Good is perhaps the will to power, but power itself, like knowledge and technology, have often enough been used detrimentally."[62] On the whole, engineers tended to see their role as outside politics, and some even viewed "politicians as their greatest enemy."[63] In their recommendations to their members regarding voting, the RdT maintained "the interests of technology in the economy are, in their nature, above party politics and are not bound to any party program," and asserted that "if technology progresses then the people will progress too."[64]

In the wildly fluctuating political and social climate during the Weimar Republic, however, engineers felt called upon to take part in debates about the role of technology in the shaping of modern society. Even within the professional engineering journals, it was possible to find an attitude of cultural pessimism reminiscent of Oswald Spengler. "Culture is life. Technology is death. The cliffs, the trees, the river speak their living language, but the factory smoke stacks, the machines are mute, and, when they speak, they announce death. Whatever kind of material technology touches, whether stone, water, wood, it is dehumanized." Looking to the future, the author asked: "How long will it be until machines arrange pro-creation? That would be a barbarous end to humanity. There is no room for compromise. Technology transforms everyone that engages with it ... into a slave."[65] Positions among engineers, as well as among phi-losophers and sociologists, varied from those who were unconditionally enthusiastic about a technological future to those who were wary of the potential impacts of technology. Discussions over the role of technology in society often revolved around whether a dichotomy existed between culture, connected to the "spiritual" and carrying a positive valence, and technology, connected to the "material" and portrayed as destructive to the "spiritual." Engineers, as Jeffrey Herf noted, sought to legitimate technology "without succumbing to Enlightenment rationality."[66] For example, Heinrich Hardensett, an engineer who wrote prolifically on the relationship between technology and society, proposed overcoming this opposition by suggesting that technology contained a metaphysical dimension that would provide meaning in the future: "Out of our con-crete objectivity a new sense of life will arise, without pathos, creative, objective, and thus also metaphysical and rationally magic."[67] The engi-neers' debates should be understood in the context of the larger debate over technology and culture in German society. While these debates had their origins before World War I, the mechanization of warfare during World War I, the acceleration of social and physical mobility, and the everyday proliferation of mass-produced, mechanically operated objects and reproduced images during the Weimar Republic lent them a new sig-nificance and urgency.[68] The intensity and longevity of the debate over technology and culture is testimony to the force of changes wrought by industrialization and the deep uncertainties over its social impacts.

Engineers echoed broader discourses when they framed the opposi-tion between technology and culture by positing a fundamental distinc-tion between European, sometimes specifically German, society, and Anglo-Saxon, often American, society. Hardensett, for example, argued that while technology in the United States was stripped of its greater social purpose, in Germany technology represented the reconciliation between the material and the spiritual.[69] Not all engineers, however, agreed with Hardensett's juxtaposition of specifically American and spe-cifically European expressions and uses of technology. One contributor to the debate in *Technik Voran!* argued: "It is without question bizarre to contrapose two educational strengths, associating Americanism with the content of life—business sense, technology, and sport—and Europeanism with the form of life—Christianity, humanity, and national character."[70] The debate about the proper role of technology in shaping human society in the wake of World War I was, of course, not unique to

Germany, and was a discussion with international dimensions. Bruce Seely has investigated how American highway engineers invoked the notion of progress and scientific authority when asserting the right to reshape the American landscape. He cites Thomas McDonald, the chief of the Bureau of Public Roads, as claiming in 1926 that "if the [engineer] is making progress, if he is succeeding, if he finally proves beyond all doubt the ability of the engineer to master and thus to lead in a new and major translation in our national life, it will be through research."[71] German engineers shared with their professional colleagues across the Atlantic at the Bureau of Public Roads, in large part, a "belief that unbiased, technically trained specialists were the ideal shapers of society."[72] Although often looked at askance, as a way of life, "Americanism"—associated with applying technical answers to social questions—was not universally condemned. German reception of American ideas could also include praise of an American-style application of technological solutions to social questions.[73] Many in the Weimar Republic, in particular most engineers, embraced the idea that technology should play a central role in designing modern society.[74]

Despite their affinity for technical resolution to economic and political questions, engineers maintained an ambivalent position towards implementing "American methods of production" in motorcycle factories. On the one hand, their equivocations were leveled against potentially negative economic effects. While their critiques sometimes also encompassed Taylorist methods, most often they were directed against assembly-line Fordism: "One look in the factories demonstrates that everywhere work is being done to improve quality and to reduce production costs. One does not have to insist offhand that motorcycle manufacturers must switch over to American production methods. First of all this method requires an exact study of every individual operation, and then the transition takes much too much time, which, despite the future benefits, we cannot sacrifice."[75] Towards the end of the Weimar Republic, engineers, who had often been the initiators and strongest supporters of rationalization, began to re-evaluate their position on the effects of rationalization on the economy. In a 1929 article on "What Rationalization Looks Like in Practice," the author compares pre-rationalization and post-rationalization businesses to two types of motorcycle engines.

> Let us make a rather material comparison ... A touring motor is like a manually operated business. Obstacles and fluctuations in economic activity are overcome through warehousing. The slow pace of manufacturing does not allow for the amassing of large stocks. The racing motor,

on the other hand, presents a comparable picture to highly developed, face-paced manufacturing. Although the touring motor appears weaker at first glance, the racing motor cannot achieve the same moment of force that its relatively weaker brother possesses.[76]

With a matter of fact reference to the relative performance of motor-cycle engines, the author illustrated the drawbacks that many German businesses experienced after implementing mechanized manufacturing methods such as inflexibility due to over-capacity and non-amortization of production machinery. By the early 1930s, the negative effects of rationalization both on the economy and on the engineering profession, visible above all in capital-intensive projects to modernize production processes rendered superfluous by the World Economic Crisis, damp-ened the initial enthusiasm of some German engineers. Skepticism towards a wholesale adoption of the Fordist model of production was a dominant trend in economic engineering during the Weimar Republic, and the tendency to look to alternate models ran strong.[77]

Thus, while engineers promoted technology as an instrument for shaping the future, the question of what kind of future engineers imag-ined remained open. The RdT's proclaimed goals for 1929 highlight how engineers thought that finding solutions to social problems required applying technical approaches: "We seek to integrate technology into the life of the individual and into the civic life of the people [*das staatsbürger-liche Leben seines Volkes*]. Technological progress should be understood as an absolutely necessary instrument for unifying the world, for creat-ing a culture that has a universal characteristic." Shifts in political and economic structures were seen as bringing about a crisis that need to be responded to by engineers: "We also want to illuminate the great exter-nal and internal difficulties of our economic life, the crisis of our spiritual life, the shifting of political structures under the pressure of technical forces ... because we believe it is necessary to interweave technology into general human knowledge."[78] Believing in technocratic solutions to achieving a harmonious society was a principle that German engineers shared with engineers around the world. Nevertheless, engineers in the Weimar Republic proved politically opportunistic: "The vision that it was technical experts who should be in power in order to shape society in the interest of the common good, based on purely technical criteria, took the place of democratic decision-making processes and consti-tutional reconciliation of interests ... The belief in the rule of experts and on one best technical solution was not consistent with pluralistic opinion making."[79] Many engineers were notably quick to give up on the democratic experiment when the World Economic Crisis hit.

Advertising: The Making and Selling of Desire

Alongside engineering, advertising was a central motor of the emerging system of mass consumption. Advertising developed as a branch of industry prior to World War I and was central to mediating Germans' encounter with global capitalist modernity.[80] In the mass media era of the Weimar Republic, advertisements that "Germans interacted with on a daily basis" mirrored "the promise of the new era: a youthful, socially mobile, and technologically modern society." Like motorization, "advertising was one language of experimentation" in the "crucible of modernity."[81] A 1929 editorial in *Das Motorrad*, written on the occasion of the opening of the "International Congress of Advertising" in Berlin, claimed advertising to be "one of the most important factors in the global economy."[82] Advertising became increasingly sophisticated as German admen in part adopted and transformed American techniques: "The German industry and trade were only converted to this modern worldview when a clever person removed the word 'publicity' ['*Reklame*'] from the German language usage and replaced it with 'sales promotion' ['*Werbung*']. Since then, a new scientific and artistic branch of industry has developed. There are 'advertising agencies,' 'advertising experts,' 'artistic advertising,' 'market analysis,' etc., and all of this serves the obvious purpose: 'If you don't let the public know you have good commodities for sale, they can't know about them.'"[83] An aesthetic understanding of advertising as an art was mixed with an understanding that the advertising was necessary to sell products, and should be approached in a scientific manner. As another magazine stated: "Whoever renounces propaganda is like a man without an apartment, no one can find him."[84]

New Landscapes and New Media

Advertising was central to the symbolic and real landscape of the new republic.[85] As the process of motorization picked up speed during the 1920s, the physical territory of the Weimar Republic was not only increasingly marked by the necessary material infrastructure, such as asphalt streets, traffic signals, gas stations, dealerships, and repair shops, but it was also inundated by images and slogans of motorization. The AVUS, Berlin's newly constructed paved expressway where many motorcycle and automobile races were held, became a space saturated with advertisements for various automotive products. Motor vehicles of all types, including motorcycles with sidecars, also provided space for mobile advertising. Buses and streetcars in Berlin and other major cities displayed advertising, providing an extra source of income for the transportation authorities. Weimar advertising experts saw mobile advertising as "an important element of advertising in the street; it is seemingly created for the purpose of imprinting itself on the memory of the passerby, with the brain quickly storing the image, color, and name, for it to be recollected later ... *The influence of the subconscious is one of the primary tasks of street advertising.*"[86] Small business owners who could afford a motorcycle with a trailer often used the space available on the trailer to advertise their wares or services. Larger firms also developed new marketing strategies. For example, by retrofitting a truck that toured around Germany showcasing their newest motorcycle models, DKW demonstrated its innovativeness in finding novel ways to attract new customers. Outdoor advertising melded physical space into symbolic and real landscapes of consumption.

Highly popular mass-sporting spectacles, motor sport races were exploited in a variety of ways to engender interest in the motorcycle as both a viable means of individual transportation and an exciting and modern sporting good. A significant number of prominent races took place during the Weimar Republic that attracted crowds that sometimes numbered in the tens of thousands.[87] No less than three major international racetracks opened in Germany during the Weimar Republic: alongside the AVUS in Berlin, the Nürbergring in the Eifel west of Koblenz and the Hockenheim Ring between Heidelberg and Karlsruhe were constructed during this period.[88] Races held on streets and in parks turned public space into advertising space. For example, beginning in 1924, an annual race was held in the Eilenriede, Hanover's urban forest. Co-sponsored by the Hanover-based tire manufacturers, Continental and Excelsior, by 1926 the Eilenriede race was increasingly professionalized and commercialized. Viewer grandstands were named after firms, and advertisements for a variety of automotive products were plastered throughout Hanover's "green-lung." Record-breaking performances and stunning falls increased the sensational appeal of the race. Whereas in 1929 the race had around fifty thousand spectators, in the following year almost double that number came to witness the spectacle.[89] Not only were motor sports central to promoting motorcycling every weekend at racetracks, but motor sport victories were also a central motif of motorcycling advertisements. Manufacturers portrayed their champion machines both to provide evidence of the quality of their products and, importantly, to associate their products with struggles over machine and nature. The racetrack provided an important backdrop to staging motorcycling as heroic and modern.

As motorization came to stand for modernity and as the aesthetic principles of expressionism gave way to New Objectivity, motorization and advertising were casted for roles on the theater stage and the silver screen. Leon Feuchtwanger's 1927 play *Die Petroleuminsel* (The Petroleum Island) features both an automobile race and tire advertising. A theater critic writing in an advertising trade journal claimed that Feuchtwanger sought "not an aesthetic surprise, but the closest approximation to reality, the air and the ground, the roots of people today, the life-form of the twentieth century in whose sociological structure advertising inextricably belongs. That is why he promotes, in the context of an automobile race, Gloria Tires."[90] Motor vehicles, especially automobiles, were also featured prominently on the silver screen.[91] *Die Drei von der Tankstelle* (The Three from the Filling Station), in which a gas station plays a prominent role, was a massive hit in Germany and Europe in 1931. Siegfried Kracauer, a preeminent film critic during the Weimar Republic, called it "a playful daydream woven of the materials of everyday life." Kracauer found the film particularly "refreshing" in the way that it transferred the "operetta paradise from its traditional locales to the open road."[92] Three of the best-known silent films from the era, *Asphalt*, *Berlin – Simphonie einer Großstadt* (Berlin – Symphony of a Great City) and *Menschen am Sonntag* (People on Sunday), all feature motor vehicle traffic as a central motif. While Joe May's *Asphalt* was filmed in the Babelsberg film studios, and *Berlin – Simphonie einer Großstadt* and *Menschen am Sonntag* were filmed on site at various locations in Berlin, all three films used traffic to stage the ideal city, the flows of traffic being testimony to its modernity.[93]

Newsreels shown in theaters provided another modern medium for displaying motorization. Motorcycle races were so ubiquitous that Kraucauer was prompted to make the following, albeit critical, remark: "The newsreels spliced together by various well-known companies— shots of ship christenings, destructive fires, sports events, parades, and idyllic scenes of children and animals—may well contain items of current news, but certainly not events worth watching a hundred times. One need hardly mention that the various motorcycle races look so similar it's enough to drive you to despair."[94] Not only did weekly newsreels cover motorcycle races, a number of motorcycle manufacturers also produced films specifically to advertise their products, which were shown at the beginning of the newsreels.[95] DKW, NSU, and Zündapp were particularly adept at taking advantage of the popularity of the new medium, producing both documentary and animation films for this purpose.[96]

Beginning in 1922, cinemagoers could have seen any number of films made to promote DKWs products. The films often show highlights from racing events at which DKW takes top prizes or other sporting events that demonstrate the reliability of their product. The films, however, also sell motorcycling as a modern form of sociability. One clip, for example, documents an excursion of the Grünewald Police Department's motorcycle club to a local forest, where the policemen and their female companions play games and dance to a portable phonograph. Another clip highlights the freedoms that individual forms of mobility offer. Opening with a title card, "When you are dependent on the railway," a man is shown running through snow after a train as it pulls out of a station. In the next scene, he is at the front of the Warneuchen station outside Berlin where a motorcyclist is parked. The next title card asks, "When will the next train arrive?" The motorcyclist, a female, gestures to her motorcycle, and the next title card announces, "Next train won't come for a long time. Hop on my pillion seat and I'll take you." The man climbs on and the two drive off. The next shots, filmed from a moving vehicle, show the motorcycle racing a train and passing it. The female motorcyclist then drops off her passenger, "Mr. Busy," in an urban area. The next title card has "Mr. Busy" saying, "If I had a motorcycle I could get five times as much accomplished during a day." The clip ends with "Mr. Busy" inside the motorcycle dealership, inspecting the different DKW models. The advertisement, perhaps unintentionally, subtly undermined gender norms by normalizing the somewhat unlikely scenario of a woman offering a ride to a man.

Advertising films could subvert or confirm social norms. In contrast to the DKW one, an animated NSU advertisement transmits an obvious and trite message that a motorcycle can be a decisive factor in attracting women. A young man in a paperboy's cap on a motorcycle picks up a blond woman as his passenger. This action catches the attention of a policeman who makes googly eyes and toots his whistle, leading the motorcyclist to stop his motorcycle. The sequence ends with an admiring crowd gathering around the spectacle of the young man, the young blond, and the NSU motorcycle. In the final shot, the young man is shown winking at the camera/audience. In order to attract a range of potential customers, the plots of motorcycle advertisement films pointed to the different benefits a motorcycle could provide to its owner. "Master and Dog," another animated NSU short from 1929, produced by Epoche film, however, took a different approach. Rather than targeting new buyers, it was directed towards persuading motorcycle owners of the superiority of their product, underscoring the ease of operating the NSU motorcycle and its reliability. The film's opening sequence shows a heavy-set man with a moustache and knickerbockers in what appears to be a typical Berlin rear courtyard with a garage on the ground floor. His dog waits in the courtyard as the man frantically attempts to repair his old motorcycle in the garage. Parts begin flying through the air, hitting the dog. As ever more pieces hit the man's dog, the dog runs off through the city to a motorcycle store. The dog returns to his owner, riding the new NSU motorcycle. At the end of this sequence, the man appears convinced of the superior qualities of the NSU bike that is obviously easy to operate. While both NSU advertisements rely heavily on clichés, they also demonstrate the motorcycle industry's savvy in understanding the appeal of the new medium.[97] Reflecting the variety of motorcyclists and potential motorcyclists, the films invoke different masculine types, from the young man interested in a love charm to the older, experienced motorcyclist interested in reliability. The films circulated images that linked motorcycling to success in the modern world, both in terms of business and sexual pursuits.

Other films embedded advertising elements within a documentary format. For example, in 1929, Ufa, the most prominent German film studio, released *Das Motorrad und Wir* (The Motorcycle and Us). Produced by Zündapp, the film premiered in Berlin at the gigantic new cinema Ufa-Palast am Zoo. Mixing the mediums of animation and live action, the film begins with an animated segment that shows the construction of the new Zündapp factory in Nuremburg. Switching over to live-action shots, it then shows the division of labor in the new, partly automated factory. In a tracking shot that moves from workstation to workstation, the rhythm of the assembly line is synched with the rhythm of the filmic media. As mobility and technology scholar Kurt Möser argues, production itself became aestheticized. Films like *Das Motorrad und Wir* contributed to producing an aesthetic of mass production through reproducing images of uniformity and "geometric patterns of half-finished products."[98] Framing the modern factory as an object of fascination, films were a powerful means for idealizing assembly-line production and adding to the allure of modern means of mobility.

Zündapp's advertising slogan, "the motorcycle for the everyman," links the two halves of the film. After showing how the motorcycle for "the everyman" was produced, the film then focused on how "the everyman" uses his motorcycle. In a review that itself was almost an advertisement for Zündapp, the author praised how the film depicted the many uses of the motorcycles, both professional and leisure: "Alongside images of the ride to work and pretty shots of the weekend, the film also showed a number of short takes from this year's six-day race through the Alps. These splendid images have perhaps led some who wished to own a motorcycle to the decision to buy one."[99] The motifs and images in the film—the factory sequences, the sequences of motorcyclists riding through towns and rural landscapes, and the shots of motorcycle races—aestheticize both new production techniques and the experience of motorcycling. Within this celebration of the modern, Zündapp places its product in the foreground, with the intention of producing the specific association of its products with the advancements of modern industry and the pleasures of motorcycling.

In times of recurring economic turbulence combined with a highly competitive environment, motorcycle manufacturers adopted sophisticated advertising strategies in order to drum up sales. DKW placed a greater emphasis on education and information rather than entertainment in their 11-minute short, *The Steel Horse*, touted as the "great motorcycle film of 1932."[100] Made in the midst of the economic depression, it seeks to show viewers the importance of both motorcycling and the motorcycle industry for the well-being of Germany and Germans. Filmed at the DKW factory in Zschopau, this quasi-documentary advertisement film, produced by the state-owned Sachsen Film, intended not only to awaken consumers' desires for owning a motorcycle, but also to appeal to consumers' consciences regarding their vital role in the German economy. Scenes from the shop floor highlight DKW's innovative engineering and its "rationalized" and "thoroughly modern" assembly line montage—yet DKW's mixed form of serial and mass production is presented as dependent on the quality of craftsmanship. This "quality craftsmanship" is then linked to the success of DKW's products on the racetrack. While emphasizing the quality of German labor and precision instruments, it insists on the strategic importance of the motorcycle industry, and in particular DKW, "the world's largest motorcycle factory," for providing "work and bread" for countless Germans. With the State Bank of Saxony holding majority shares in both Sachsen Film and DKW, the makers of the film intended to boost the sales of one company in particular: DKW. Through the extensive use of product placement, *The Steel Horse* thus aimed at stirring the conscience of the consumer to buy DKW motorcycles in order to promote German industry and employ the unemployed masses.[101]

Sophisticated advertising campaigns, such as those of Zündapp and DKW, point to the increasing skill necessary to reach potential consumers and survive in the competitive market. Although the advertising industry had reached a high degree of development during the Wilhelmine era, during the Weimar Republic the profession continued to develop and expand. Rudolf-Mosse-Service, one of the larger advertising agencies in Berlin, produced print campaigns for Zündapp motorcycles together with the in-house advertising and sales department. The Rudolf-Mosse-Service claimed to "work together in an ideal manner with a staff of suitable scientists, psychologists, salesmen, authors, draftsmen and news media experts."[102] Other large manufacturers, such as DKW, established internal advertising departments in which they employed "advertising engineers," who would be capable of presenting the technical aspects of the product.[103] Indeed, advertising formed a not insubstantial portion of manufacturers budgets; for example, in the first nine months of 1929, DKW reported spending nearly a million Reichsmark on "propaganda," including advertisements, brochures, posters, prize money, films, and photos.[104] Furthermore, in 1927, the RDA established an internal press agency, Auto-Presse-Dienst, alongside a "propaganda fund." The RDA fund and press service were created to deliver propagandistic articles to the daily papers and the trade press and to explicitly promote the German motor industry.[105] In-house magazines popped up as another popular way of generating interest. While the format of this promotional material was nearly identical to independent and club-sponsored journals—with poems, short stories, news from sales representatives and clubs, reports on competitions of various sorts, as well as special issues that targeted specific groups such as students, the military and police, and women—the items published in these magazines were designed solely to shed the best possible light on a specific brand and to thereby create a positive product image.[106]

Sales and advertising departments, however, were involved with more than just writing flattering accounts and designing advertisements, they also took a keen interest in how products were displayed and sold in stores across Germany. BMW also encouraged its official sales representatives to create attractive sales displays so that the "customer can become acquainted with all the innovations without obligation, and be instructed about the advantages of BMW motorcycles and cars."[107] Window dressing was a central component for capturing the attention of potential customers. The journal for the bicycle and motorcycle shop owners' association also regularly published articles on "attractive, modern" designs for shop windows, stressing clarity and modernity in design. An aesthetic presentation of the product was the key to creating an attractive window display. By building a podium and placing the motorcycle in front of a backdrop of black cloth, "the motorcycle will appear like a painting." At night, the motorcycle was to be illuminated with electric lights, so that it would have a "striking effect."[108] Shop windows, as Rachel Bowlby has noted, are particularly effective because of their visual immediacy. The shop window "is a setting for stylish modern art; and it simply shows the object itself. It is framed, aesthetic, for looking at; and it is just the things as they are, making a direct appeal to the potential purchaser. It is for contemplation and it is for action. You can admire it at a distance, and you can go in and get it right now."[109]

Byway II: Zündapp—Advertising the Motorcycle for the "Everyman"

In 1929, with hopes of increasing sales, especially vis-à-vis its main competitor, DKW, Zündapp developed a detailed strategy to foster its relationship with its salespeople across Germany. A pamphlet entitled "Instructions to Sales Representatives" accompanied this campaign, and provides ample evidence of the sophistication of advertising and sales tactics during the Weimar Republic. Produced by the advertising and sales department, the brochure outlines the five most important areas in terms of advertising and sales: "The Product; Our Advertisements; Your Advertisements; The Test-Ride; Customer Service." The admen claimed that implementing strategies for each of these would provide sales representatives with the "weapons needed to survive the competitive battle."

In "The Product," descriptions of new features of the 1929 model make clear that Zündapp took their slogan of "The Motorcycle for the Everyman" seriously, in terms of both design and advertising. When discussing the adjustable handlebars and foot pegs, the advertisement department instructed the sales representatives to highlight the new features when showing the motorcycles to potential customers. "The Zündapp customer will no longer have to crouch with a crooked back over the handlebars like a racer, nor will he have to sit up straight like a high school student in front of his strictest teacher."[110] The design of the machine was modified to accommodate various performances of masculinity—from the racing sportsman to that of the upright citizen. The openness of this advertising and sales strategy attests to the openness of the category of motorcyclist, even if it was, with few exceptions, consistently gendered masculine.

Next, the brochure pointed to the importance of Zündapp's in-house advertising department's strategy, "because there is no name brand product in the whole world that can have success without advertising." The advertising department stressed that "name recognition" was not sufficient to move potential customers to purchase. Instead, the product must appear "interesting" and "sympathetic." While acknowledging that "familiarity" could breed "sympathy," they asserted that a modern advertisement should "lead its audience to make a purchase, meaning that the advertisement should have a similar mechanism in terms of purchase as the sales representative." In order to provoke "interest" in and "sympathy" for the Zündapp brand, the advertising and sales department claimed that the advertisements they designed "demonstrate to the audience what the Zündapp motorcycle is, what it offers, and what relief it brings. We say to him insistently: 'Look, the Zündapp motorcycle will give you this and that; when you buy a Zündapp motorcycle you get this and that advantage, this relief, this enjoyment.'"[111] The strategy of the sales department was again to highlight wish fulfillment, the vessel of which was the motorcycle; the specific content of the desire to be fulfilled, however, was left to the individual customer.

Individual sales representatives also played a key role in Zündapp's advertising strategy. In the section "Your Advertisement," the marketing department highlighted the importance of window dressing and made suggestions for creating an attractive display: "From time to time, hang reports of Zündapp victories or photographs of your sports friends on our machines in your shop window and describe them in a few words. This will awaken the passerby's interest and direct their attention to your business. With a little bit of love, even the smallest store can be tastefully decorated." The local businessman's cooperation was needed to successfully implement the company's strategy. In tandem with advertisements designed by the sales department that appeared in newspapers and magazines with nationwide distribution, individual sales representatives were urged to take out advertisements in local newspapers to support the national campaigns. Local representatives were also asked to actively support local Zündapp motorcycling clubs.[112]

"The Test-Ride" was considered to be one of the most decisive moments in bringing a potential customer, who was consistently gendered male, to the point of making a purchase. The sales and advertising department first advised the sales representatives to keep the test-ride motorcycle in "tip-top condition"—a "clean appearance and a well-running machine is most important." They then went on to describe the ideal execution of a test-ride:

> Choose a day with good weather, so that the ride is actually enjoyable. Pick him up at his residence, invite him to take a seat on the pillion seat, so that he is seated comfortably and has the feeling of absolute safety ... Make sure the machine starts the first time you use the kick-starter. Use streets that are in good repair so that the customer doesn't get shaken up, and pick a particularly pretty area to awaken in your passenger the joys of motorcycling.

The phrasing of this advice reveals the elaborate staging necessary in order to hide the problematic aspects of motorcycling and to make the experience seem effortless, comfortable, and carefree. After the test-ride, the sales representative should "invite him right away to come to your shop," and pressure him into making the purchase: "Heat the iron so long until it's hot and then present him with the filled-out contract that just needs his signature."[113] The goal of the test-ride was to fan the flames of desire until the thought of not possessing a motorcycle was unbearable.

Post-purchase customer service was the final issue addressed in the pamphlet. "Make sure you have satisfied customers! Every satisfied customer is an advertising organ for you: he speaks well of you and in this way leads new customers to you regularly." Following other manufacturers, such as DKW, Zündapp established a Germany-wide "thick web" of Zündapp sales and repair locations that were to service the post-purchase needs and desires of customers in an age when customers were increasingly less likely to have the necessary skills to repair their own motorcycles, let alone handcraft spare parts. The advertising and sales department instructed their sales representatives to carry all kinds of spare parts and accessories in order to "fulfill all of his wishes and needs through timely and prompt service."[114]

Alongside providing detailed instructions for sales representatives, Zündapp's advertising and sales department, which included outsourced divisions, produced printed matter, films, photographs, posters, and clichés, prepared materials for exhibitions and other events, and produced promotional items for clubs and other enthusiasts.[115] Their total budget for all advertising in 1929 was 600,000 RM, and used approximately 4.5 percent of Zündapp's total revenue in 1930.[116] Furthermore, the department made detailed lists of which kinds of press were suitable to advertise in, including press targeted at "blue- and white-collar workers."[117] The advertising and sales department also began tracking their buyers by occupation and region, so that they would have more precise knowledge to decide which groups to target in their campaigns.[118] All of these tactics added up to a modern advertising strategy, one that would produce wishes and dreams to be fulfilled through consumption.

Bonds that Last: The Creation of Consumer Desire

Major motorcycle manufacturers encouraged local dealerships to cultivate brand awareness and to be inventive in their approaches to attracting new customers. NSU urged its sales representatives to remember their motto when selling their Depression-era "Motosulm" brand bicycle with auxiliary motor: "Save time in this world. He who saves time saves money."[119] Both NSU and BMW recommended that dealerships promote their brands through "propaganda rides."[120] NSU reported that a dealer in the Ruhr area let his "14-year-old son, who knows as much about engines as an old-hand mechanic and is as good at sales as an experienced department store salesperson," ride around in the city district on a "Motosulm." His "propaganda rides" were described as attracting the attention of "hundreds of spectators" and resulted in "many new customers for his proud father."[121] Zündapp, as we saw earlier, encouraged its dealerships to allow potential customers to take a long test-ride so that the potential buyer could become convinced of the advantages of their product.[122]

Another aspect of the developing service industry was customer service, as we saw in the case of Zündapp. By assisting customers with their post-purchase needs, not only were customers tied more closely to the brand but the automotive industry and its sales representatives across Germany were also brought into a closer relationship. DKW developed a chart that they asserted would enable sales representatives to identify nearly any mechanical defect, and that together the sales representative and the manufacturer would be able to resolve the problem. By the early 1930s, both DKW and NSU were operating repair service schools on-site at their factories to train sales representatives in repairs. The idea of "customer service," like so many advertising and sales strategies, was, according to the advertising experts during the Weimar Republic, supposedly American in origin. Indeed, Henry Ford drummed up the concept of "service" in his world-best-selling autobiography.[123] "Customer service" (*die Dienst am Kunde*) interpreted the moment of the sale as only the beginning of a relationship between the consumer and the manufacturer.[124]

Motor vehicle owners were generally considered to possess both consumer strength and consumer desire, and were therefore especially targeted by advertisers. The Institut für Konjunkturforschung [Institute for the Research of Economic Cycles] published a special pamphlet on the automotive industry that offered market observations in the context of "American methods" and "German teamwork," and that saw "the creation of a central statistic for the registration of motor vehicles" as essential to understanding consumer behavior.[125] During the last years of the Weimar Republic, a special magazine, *Straße und Verkehr* (Street and Transportation), assembled and published all of the official lists of newly registered motor vehicles and the names of their owners in Prussia (excluding Berlin). The fact that *Strasse und Verkehr* took out an advertisement in the journal *Die Reklame* (The Advertisement), a professional journal for advertisers, hints at how interconnected advertising and motor vehicle ownership had become.[126]

Alongside market analysis and customer service, branding is another important technique that was employed during the Weimar Republic, as the case of Zündapp neatly illustrates. Branding is more than mere product name recognition. Indeed, Weimar advertising experts believed the key to selling goods was in the construction of a "spiritual bond" between consumer and commodity. Franz Findeisen, a notable promoter of branding as a marketing technique and a professor of business administration at the business school in Nuremberg, wrote: "To speak of the soul and the commodity together appears surprising at first glance. Thinking, however, of the most important marketing tool, publicity, which is capable of psychological engagement, then a relationship between the soul and the commodity is discernible. The human soul will always be particularly sensitive when it notices that it has come in contact with another soul." Elaborating on this quality, Findeisen pointed to the bond between the motorcycle rider and his machine:

> Some may object that a dead good, as the commodity is depicted, can have no influence on the soul. But let us observe a motorcyclist, how lovingly he treats his machine, how he knows all her attributes and all her moods. Filled with joy he tells us how, in a tough struggle, despite all forces against him, he was able to get an idea of the essence of his machine and that he does not feel as well or secure riding on any other. The machine has a spiritual significance for him. She is his friend.

In Findeisen's analysis of the relationship between the "soul and the commodity," the bond between the motorcyclist and the machine needs to be rendered "natural," even "spiritual," and in a sense effortless, thus hiding the labor of producing both the motorcycle and the bond.[127] The branding of motorcycles, however, was an operation that required a conscious and concerted effort, and motorcycling manufacturers and the advertising agencies hired by the companies employed a variety of elaborate strategies in order to create desire and forge customer loyalty.[128] What Findeisen importantly points to is the potential profitability of the creation of such a bond, calling it the "noblest duty of a brand. The brand-name commodity speculates on the spiritual connection between the commodity and the soul."

Already targeted in the pre–World War I era as threatening the purity of German culture, advertising professionals continued to be confronted with vocal critiques that they promoted materialism and the Americanization of German society.[129] Siegfried Seher, a trade journalist and director of motor sport films who visited the United States, provided a particularly disparaging view of the over-commercialization of American society. In "Happiness?," his "short balance sheet on a trip to America," he strongly criticized the dominance of "sales leadership, advertising bosses, and sales promoters": "Fast advertising bosses and sales experts inculcated the idea that you have to have a car, naturally—if you don't then you are backward. Vanity is added to the mix, the bedazzlement, the rampant self-deception in America. Ridiculously low payment plans are a seduction to close the deal. In St. Louis I saw that it was possible to buy a Ford with a down payment of just ten dollars. Who would be able to resist?" Seher found that a real critique in America was missing, one that recognized the emptiness of materialism, and that, while American manufacturing methods and even advertising methods could inspire much enthusiasm, Germany should not follow the same path as the United States.[130] During the Weimar Republic, critics regarded both American advertising methods and the path to motorization in the United States with ambivalence. While American technological advancement and abundance were often admired, American advertisers and motor vehicle industrialists were attacked for promoting a materialist outlook that many, including Seher, regarded as evidence of a lack of spiritual depth and social commitment.[131]

These critiques, although prevalent during the entire span of the Weimar Republic and even before, gained particular potency with the deepening of the global economic crisis in 1930.[132] As in the case with German engineers and industrialists, advertisers struggled with the question of the "Americanization" of German society. Complicating matters, American advertising agencies had set up shop in Germany above all to market cars that remained out of reach for all but a very small minority of Germans. German and American advertisers came with a different approach and aesthetic to advertising, and both had difficulties accepting the others advertising culture.[133] Moreover, critics saw postwar Germany as being systemically disadvantaged vis-à-vis the enormous capital resources available to American firms, and castigated German advertisers for "worshipping and parroting" America. Arguing for a qualitative difference between German publicity (*Werben*) and American advertising, one critic of the Americanization of the German advertising industry pointed his finger at the motor vehicle industry in particular: "We demand an adjustment to the German mentality (and a retreat away from 'advertising'). Level of education and mentality are two different things, however, they overlap at their end zones. This zone is important as the romping place of advertising. The average German person, indeed the great majority, is more educated than the average American . . . Americans chew gum, Germans ruminate problems."[134] He pointed directly to the relationship between eroticism and the selling of desire: "Masked, veiled, hidden, and prudishly deceptive eroticism is one of the main foundations of advertising. (You only have to think of the role the weekend ride with a female passenger has in motorcycle advertising.)"[135] The author bemoaned the pernicious influence of supposedly American values in the use of erotic images and the lack of objectivity in marketing strategies. He concluded by making a pitch for "naked objectivity" in contrast to the emotive appeal of kitsch. German advertisers thus perceived the world in terms of differences in national character, and sought to address their advertisements to a specifically German audience that inhabited an aesthetic sense not based on emotions, but rather on objectivity. While, by the end of the Weimar Republic, many argued against the indiscriminate adoption of American advertising techniques and for a German advertising vernacular, the nationalist turn by no means signaled the wholesale repudiation of commodity capitalism.

Capturing Markets, Capturing Modernity: Visions of Motorcycling Modernity

By and large, motorcycles, like many other industrial consumer durables, were aspirational commodities during the Weimar Republic. Thus,

Image 2.2. Dreaming of a Commodity. NSU Advertisement, 1928, Audi Corporate Archives.

before brand loyalty could be exploited, manufacturers first had to make the motorcycle attractive to consumers by employing a variety of strategies to entice new buyers, from producing films to holding propaganda rides and sponsoring races. Above all, print advertisements that filled the pages of motoring magazines and beyond targeted groups judged likely to be attracted to motorcycling. Advertisers designed and combined images and texts in a way they hoped would speak to potential buyers. Operating in a competitive market, a large number of firms vied for the patronage of a limited number of consumers able and willing to purchase into the promise of motorized modernity.

In order to expand the market for motorcycles, motorcycling advertisements were thus often geared towards the "Twelve Million Bicyclists in the German Empire," who, by virtue of their experience with two-wheeled mobility, were viewed as potential owners of a motorized version. Motorcycle manufacturers took out full-page advertisements in various bicycling magazines, highlighting the attractiveness of a motorcycle for a public already familiar with riding two-wheeled vehicles. In one such advertisement, Zündapp portrayed the motorcycle as inevitably being more "modern" than the bicycle, due to its capacity to attain higher speeds and thus keep up with the tempo of the times. Moreover, the motorcyclist was portrayed as having an advantage over the bicyclist, as he was free from having to exert his own energy in order to propel himself forward: "Everyone has the need for greater speed, to be quicker on level ground and no longer to have to push uphill, and that is why, sooner or later, you will need a motorcycle in order to keep up with the times." The advertisement praised its design, claiming it "does not require any special advance knowledge and whose construction is especially designed for the practical needs of daily use. It has to be a simple and beautiful machine that always runs, because you earn your money slowly and with difficulty, and therefore you need to be spared needing to make repairs."[136] The appeal to bicyclists was predicated on a limited budget and presumed need to save time and money. The motorcycle, an extension of the man, was presented as providing maximum mobility and thus delivering full access to the benefits of modern life. Stock, another manufacturer of small-powered motorcycles, pointed to the "side-benefits" of owning a motorcycle—a motorcyclist would be able to beat out bicyclists in the competition over women.[137] Advertising strategies aimed towards recruiting potential customers among the ranks of bicyclists remained prominent throughout the Weimar Republic.

Motorcycle advertising campaigns also targeted students as a category of youth who were generally from wealthier backgrounds and who would be willing to invest in a status symbol. For example, an article in BMW's own journal made an argument that "the young academic and sportsman should form an inseparable concept … Sport should also educate the spirit and form in joyful movement manly self-discipline." Advertisements for motorcycles were, not surprisingly, frequently geared towards catching the attention of young men. For example, "fellow female students will be more likely to join in on weekend plans, because the motorcycle has long enjoyed a reputation as a dating intermediary." Advertisers clearly believed that spending on advertising campaigns directed towards students was money well spent: young men in the financial position to follow a course of studies at a university or technical school clearly belonged to the category of potential buyers of motorcycles.[138]

By the closing years of the 1920s, as the price of motorcycles dropped, they were also targeted specifically at workers, both white and blue collar, who would supposedly benefit from having an easier way to work than walking, riding a bicycle, or relying on public transportation.[139] In fact, wages for skilled working-class men in general remained stable or even increased over the 1920s, making the purchase

Image 2.3. Motorcycles for Workers. NSU Advertisement in the illustrated workers' weekly newspaper *AIZ*, 1929, Audi Corporate Archives.

Image 2.4. Motorcycles for Workers. DKW Advertisement in the illustrated workers' weekly newspaper AIZ, 1930, Audi Corporate Archives.

of a motorcycle, especially on a lay-away plan, within the realm of the possible.[140] In the closing years of the Weimar Republic, major motorcycle manufacturers, including DKW, NSU, and Zündapp, placed advertisements in publications that were directed specifically at the working classes, such as the *Arbeiter-Illustrierte-Zeitung* [*AIZ*] and *Concordia*. The advertisements all tended to stress the physical relief a motorcycle would bring the user, whether used as transportation to work or as a recreational vehicle. They also appealed to longings to fully belong to modern society; for example, one advertisement for Stock's inexpensive mopeds asked, "Do you want to continue to be backward?"[141] Catering to the readership of the *AIZ*, a weekly illustrated close to the Communist Party, advertising departments even paid tribute to Internationalist politics. For example, DKW placed an advertisement in which the image, with its Kremlinesque towers, and the message: "Will you come along? The DKW rider knows no borders—foreign countries are their destination" invoked the USSR.[142] Advertising departments spread the dream that even workers could take part in the motorized future.

Advertisers also increasingly recognized the importance of women as consumers, including as consumers of durable goods. In a 1929 article on the "Equality of Man and Woman in Advertising," the female author remarked that women were more interested in items such as "fountain pens, typewriters, radios" than the advertisements for these products, "which are aimed exclusively at men," suggested. She strongly recommended that advertisers attend to this problem by redesigning their advertisements to appeal to women as well.[143] Following the lead of British manufacturers, such as Ariel, German motorcycle manufacturers recognized women as potential consumers, and Stock, NSU, and BMW all specifically targeted women. Advertisers' appeals towards women stressed distinctly "feminine" criteria for selecting a motorcycle. For example, in designing their motorcycle, Schüttoff claimed to have been motivated to conform "in every respect" to the "demands of the ladies' world." Emphasizing comfort and safety, Schüttoff maintained they had constructed their suspension so that even a "sensitive lady will not easily tire," and had designed a seat that "almost feels like an armchair."[144] BMW's advertising department also persistently courted prospective female customers.

> A BMW is constructed to meet the high demands of a lady and to satisfy her highly critical eye: a fabulous classy 'iron horse.' Harmoniously contoured, the engine has the advantages of an automobile engine. Its absolute safety is known to all those who drive a BMW. The machine can, when cared for properly, be ridden wearing delicate clothing. It rides smoothly and quietly at the highest and lowest tempos. BMW is right for the lady who is looking, beyond just a method of transportation, for sport and beauty.[145]

By emphasizing the aesthetic aspects of the product, its safety, and its compatibility with "delicate clothing," BMW's advertisers repeated characteristics generally considered important to the female consumer in particular. Motorcycling advertisements targeting women also often assumed they would prefer to purchase a car. Yet similar to the way that motorcycles were sold to men, one BMW advertisement also stressed the sporting characteristic of the vehicle as well as its relative affordability: "There are so many thoroughly trained, healthy women and girls who could use a motor vehicle for their occupation or in the interest of motor sports, but who cannot afford a car."[146] And in sponsoring a handful of female motorcycle racers, German manufacturers provided visible role models for everyday women who desired racing a motorcycle of their own. Rights granted to women at the end of World War I, as mobility scholar Georgine Clarsen points out, allowed women to "avidly embrace commodity consumption as a means of expanding their lives," and advertising departments clearly understood the importance of capitalizing on expanding markets.[147]

Sidecars were relatively costly accessories that, when attached to a motorcycle, could dramatically extend a motorcycle's potential uses in terms of carrying passengers and goods. By allowing motorcyclists to transport more than one other person, for example, advertisements presented sidecars as enhancing the sociability of the (male) motorcyclist: "Only the fewest are such oddballs that they absolutely want to spend their recreation hours alone. Whether for an excursion, a weekend party, or a camping trip, the sidecar always makes it possible to bring along a male friend or a good female friend."[148] Beyond leisure, sidecars could also be employed for business purposes. Advertisements claimed that country doctors, the police, small business delivery firms, and peddlers could all benefit from a sidecar. Sidecar manufacturers thus often marketed their products according to their design and their use, from travel models that were equipped with extra space for luggage and a side door for easy access, to models that were fully enclosed and claimed to be as weatherproof as an enclosed automobile, to models that were expressly designed to carry goods, not people. Due to their range of uses, selling sidecars required a variety of rhetorical strategies. Advertisements for sidecars varied from those that emphasized the form—"racy," "perfected," "elegant"—to those that made a connection to technological aspects, claiming their sidecars to be "advanced," "the acme of technical performance," and "modern." Other manufacturers praised their models as articles for mass consumption: "a joy for everyman!" and "cheap," whereas others stressed comfort that afforded the "most pleasant riding for both motorcyclist and sidecar passenger."[149] Still others advertised their products by citing their successes in racing events or on cross-continental expeditions.[150] Sidecars were thus sold with an eye towards sports enthusiasts, families, and as a way for traveling salesmen to increase business.[151]

Sexualized images were common advertisement motifs. The product was placed in such a manner as to suggest that the attractiveness of the male consumer would increase if he bought one. For example, an advertisement for a BMW motorcycle with sidecar employs sexuality as a way of both attracting the male viewer's attention and indicating that the consumer of the object would be privileged to enjoy increased female attention.[152] The image seductively mirrors the gaze of the consumer and of the female spectator. The female, her back turned to the viewer, is focused on the male motorcyclist and the empty sidecar seat. The focus on the female's shapely backside provides the advertisement with a decidedly sexualized note. The modern dress of the female emphasizes the motorcycle as the modern man's necessary accessory in order to be desirable to the modern woman. As the adage goes, sex sells. The product is enacted in such a manner as to suggest that the attractiveness of the male consumer would increase if he were to buy one. Advertisements directed at male consumers sold the hope that enhanced sexual opportunities would result from purchasing the proper products.

Riding either solo or with a female passenger on his pillion seat, motorcycle advertisements during the Weimar Republic enacted modern masculinity and visualized the modern man. Indeed, the modern man of motorcycling advertisements, invariably clean-shaven with strong, angular features, bears similarities to depictions of the "modern girl."[153] The motorcyclist speeds into the frame, his velocity indicated through streaks, his modernity beyond question. Enhanced masculinity was an unspoken yet prominent element in advertisements that fetishized speed and victories over time and space. One ubiquitous strategy in advertisements that highlighted motor sport victories was the presentation of a motorcycle as a "naked" commodity, without a ride, as an object capable of creating a racing hero out of any man. Modern man was linked to the modern machine. Modern man could also be portrayed as merging with the machine. For example, to announce Ernst Henne's 1931 world-record-breaking ride, BMW produced a stylized advertisement, featuring a blurred, fractal image portraying Henne on a BMW wearing a futuristic white suit and cone-shaped helmet, hurtling through space and catapulting through time. (See Image 2.6). The design plays on the imagination of a cyborg-machine man, the energy of the man finding its extension in the machine.[154]

What motorcycling advertisers often denied in their visualizations of a motorized future were the hazards and annoyances of traveling on a vehicle that was both relatively fast and exposed to the elements. In references to reliability and comfort it was, however, possible to perceive the motorcycle as unreliable or uncomfortable. Safety was also only rarely directly addressed in advertisements. When advertisements did make note of the difficulties that could be encountered when motorcycling, there was often a disjuncture between the text that pointed to the problems and the illustrations that showed only happy and satisfied countenances.[155] The noise, grease, and possible threats to life and limb were thus virtually silenced in the advertisers' enticing visions of freedom, beauty, sexual prowess, comfort, and speed, claiming to "bring the fulfillment of all wishes."[156] The fragile relationship between the advertised dream and the lived experiences of motorcycling mirrors the

Image 2.5. "The Most Elegant and Reliable German Sidecar Machine." BMW Advertisement, 1927, BMW Group Archive.

Image 2.6. Ernst Henne as a Cyborg. BMW Advertisement, 1929, BMW Group Archive.

elusiveness of the promise of motorized modernity for the masses of Germans during the Weimar Republic.

Conclusion

As members of the new white-collar professions that emerged at the end of the nineteenth century, both engineers and advertisers struggled with a tenuous sense of identity, caught between artistic invention and technical execution, and inhabited a precarious social status. Yet both engineers and advertisers helped create a society of mass production and mass consumption, contributing to the aestheticization and fetishization of modern technology. At the forefront of modern industrial capitalism, engineers and advertisers were key figures in conflicts over the reordering of society and the nation. Attacked as potential threats to Germany as a *Kulturnation*, both groups grappled with the influence of "Americanism" in their professions, while they simultaneously worked to build a modern and motorized German society. As makers of a modern, mobile world, engineers and advertisers were integral to forming both the surface and the substance of motorcycling during the Weimar Republic. Through designs, slogans, and images, engineers and advertisers helped shape motorcyclists as modern men and modern women.

Notes

1. Neumann-Neander's life (1871–1954) spanned from the founding of the German Empire, through World War I, the Weimar Republic and the Nazi Regime, and up to the establishment and consolidation of the two post–World War II German republics.
2. Sherwin Simmons, "Ernst Neumanns 'Neuwerte der bildenden Kunst': Kunsttheorie und –praxis um 1900," in *Ernst Neumann-Neander, 1871–1954*, ed. Reinhold Kraft, Thomas Müller, and Georg Solms (Düren: Hahne & Schloemer Verlag, 2004), 51–52.
3. Ernst Neumann, "Die Architekur der Fahrzeuge," from the *Werkbund Jahrbuch 1914* "Der Verkehr," reprinted in Kraft, Müller, and Solms, *Ernst Neumann-Neander*, 181.
4. Simmons, "Ernst Neumanns 'Neuwerte,'" 54, 59.
5. Fritz Hellweg, "Ernst Neumann und seine Schule," *Kunstgewerbeblatt* 22, no. 5 (1910): 34–36, as cited in Simmons, "Ernst Neumanns 'Neuwerte,'" 34.
6. Paul Simsa, "Ein Leben wie sonst keines," in Kraft, Müller, and Solms, *Ernst Neumann-Neander*, 73–74.
7. Ernst Neumann-Neander, "Mit dem Motorrad durch Eis und Schnee," in *Auf dem Motorrad durch Eis und Schnee: die Geschichte der Deutschlandfahrt, 1924*, ed. Cölner Club für Motorsport (Düsseldorf: Mittag-Verlag, 1924).
8. Thomas Trapp, "Ernst Neumann-Neander und die Fahrzeugtechnik," in Kraft, Müller and Solms, *Ernst Neumann-Neander*, 80–82. On the work process at Opel, see Kugler, "Von der Werkstatt zum Fließband," 324–28.
9. Maier, "Between Taylorism and Technocracy," 28.
10. Gijs Mom analyzes the role of engineers in the creation of an "automobile system." See Mom, *Atlantic Automobilism*, 565–606.
11. P. Fessler, "Die Großmacht Technik," *Technik Voran!*, no. 14, 1929, 13; and *Technik Voran!*, no. 15, 1929, 11. See also DKW engineer Reinhold Thebis' description of "The Age of the Motor," in Thebis, "ZIS-Motorrad – 'ein neues Motorrad für alle," *ADAC-Motorwelt*, no. 49, 1929, 9.
12. Wilhelm Conrad Gomoll, "Der Weg der Motorisierung, Die Automobil Industrie und die Frage der Motorfahrzeug-Verwendung," *Technik Voran!*, no. 21, 1929, 2.
13. Fessler, "Die Großmacht Technik," 13. Fessler signed the article with the title of "engineer." Another engineer proclaimed technology as the "the fourth realm," a new realm to be added to Kant's three realms of natural science, ethics, and aesthetics. See Ritter, "Das vierte Reich," *Technik Voran!*, no. 15, 1929, 2.
14. Heinrich Hardensett, "Magische Technik," *Technik Voran!*, no. 40, 1929, 11; also H. Döll, "Sachlichkeit, unsere Stärke und Schwäche," *Technik Voran!*, no. 33, 1929, 9. For a description of Hardensett's "ideal-typical technical man," see Jeffrey Herf, *Reactionary Modernism: Technology, Culture and Politics in Weimar and the Third Reich* (Cambridge: Cambridge University Press, 1984), 183–84.
15. Rolf Bielefeld, "2400 Kilometer Unterwegs, Zschopau," *Motor-Kritik*, no. 16, 1930, 354.

16. Siegfried Hartman, "Hebung des Ansehens," *Technik Voran!*, no. 11, 1929, 8.
17. While the term *Kulturmensch* is often translated as "civilized man," the author, an engineer with a doctorate, used it precisely to distinguish his attributes from those of a "civilized man" (*zivilisierter Mensch*). In his view, a view that carries anti-Semitic undertones, a *Kulturmensch*, in contrast to a *zivilisierter Mensch*, would "use the advantages of wealth and civilization for internal and external further development. He takes a critical position. Wealth—if used properly—helps him to advance culture more rapidly." Althof, "Technik und Kultur," *Technik Voran!*, no. 6, 1929, 4.
18. See Paulitz, *Mann und Maschine*, especially Part 2, "Praktische Rationalität und Männlichkeit." For a comparison with US engineers, see Lisa M. Frehill, "The Gendered Construction of the Engineering Profession in the United States, 1893–1920," *Men and Masculinities* 6, no. 4 (2004): 383–403; and Ruth Oldenziel, *Making Technology Masculine: Men, Women and Modern Machines in America, 1870–1945* (Amsterdam: Amsterdam University Press, 1999). For a discussion of the US engineers at the Bureau of Public Roads, see Seely, *Building the American Highway System*.
19. US engineers faced similar disunity, see Oldenziel, *Making Technology Masculine*: 70–78.
20. Echternach, "Staat und Technik," *Technik Voran!*, no. 4, 1929, 4. See also, Hartman, "Hebung," 8; Fessler, "Die Großmacht Technik," 13; "Eine anti-technische Regierung?," *Technik Voran!*, no. 8, 1927, 155.
21. On the lack of professionalization in engineering in contrast to teaching and practicing law in the Imperial era, see Konrad Jarausch, *The Unfree Professions: German Lawyers, Teachers and Engineers, 1900–1950* (Oxford: Oxford University Press, 1990), 17–22.
22. "Frage 547," *Der Schlossermeister*, no. 39, 1927, 689.
23. See VDI, eds., *Technik, Ingenieure und Gesellschaft: Geschichte des Vereins Deutscher Ingenieure 1856–1981* (Düsseldorf: VDI-Verlag, 1981).
24. See "Table A.4. Growth of the Professions" and "Table A.7. Development of Engineers" in Jarausch, *The Unfree Professions*, 237, 242.
25. Nolan, *Visions of Modernity*, 184–85.
26. See the report on the 1928 annual conference of the VDI in *Der Motorwagen* 9 (1928).
27. Carl Weihe, "Das Kraftrad als Befreier," *Motorrad-Sport, -Verkehr und -Technik*, no. 5, 1924, 13. For more on Carl Weihe's influence on engineering rhetoric during the Weimar Republic, see Herf, *Reactionary Modernism*, 171–78.
28. Paulitz, *Mann und Maschine*, 208–10.
29. Reinhold Kraft, "Ernst Neumann-Neander, 1871–1954." Self-published (Düren: 2003). On the importance of the "genius inventor" in early US motoring culture, see Franz, *Tinkering*, 76–84.
30. "Automobil- und Flugtechnische Gesellschaft (Technisch-wissenschaftliche Vereinigung) e.V.," *Der Motorwagen*, no. 9, 1929, 180.
31. Robert Conrad, "Autoindustrie und Automobiltechnische Gesellschaft," *Der Motorwagen*, no. 9, 1929, 181.
32. Edmund Levy, "25 Jahre ATG," *Der Motorwagen*, no. 9, 1929, 184.
33. See Chapter 1 on the RDA. My assessment of the ATG's attitude towards the motorcycle is based on the lack of attention to the German motorcycle industry in their journal, *Der Motorwagen*. Furthermore, in one of the few articles

that mentions motorcycles, many of the negative stereotypes about motor-cycles and motorcycle riders are invoked: "A particularly disgusting chapter … is provided by motorcycles. The number of poorly maintained, old, and … rattling motorcycles is legion … Motorcyclists are mostly young people, who have a noticeable lack of feelings of responsibility, paired with a sporting self-aggrandizement, and so are inconsiderate and thus necessarily have an impact on their compatriots." Prof. W. Hort, "Der Strassenlärm," *Der Motorwagen*, no. 9, 1929, 185–86.

34. R. Küpper, "Die Frage des Nachwuches," *Der Motorwagen*, no. 9, 1929, 184.
35. Kraftfahrzeug allgemein "Amtlitche Prüfungsstelle für den Verkehr mit Kraftfahrzeuge an die Regieriung von Oberbayern – Kammern des Innern, Betreff: Verkehr mit Kraftfahrzeugen, hier Kleinkrafträder, 21.1.1924 (gezeich-net: Dipl. Ing. Kaffl und Kleinmann)"; MInn 66416 (1923–1924), Ministerium des Inneren, Bayerisches Hauptstaatsarchiv.
36. For more on noise, see Chapter 5.
37. "Der Kleinkraftwagen – und am ihn vorbei," *Der deutsche Motorfahrer*, no. 4, 1930, 1–4.
38. Weihe, "Das Kraftrad als Befreier," 13.
39. Hans Pohlert, "Das Kommende Kraftrad (Ein Zukunftsbild)," *Motorrad-Sport, -Verkehr und -Technik*, no. 10, 1924, 18–19.
40. Jarausch, *The Unfree Professions*, 48. This position predated World War I. See Wolfgang König, "Die Ingenieure und der VDI als Großverein in der wil-helminischen Gesellschaft 1900–1919," in VDI, *Technik, Ingenieure und Gesellschaft*, 269–70.
41. "Steigerung der Wirkungsgrad" – Erwin Viefhaus, "Ingenieure in der Weimarer Republic: Bildungs- Berufs- und Gesellschaftspolitik 1918–1933," in VDI, *Technik, Ingenieure und Gesellschaft*, 329.
42. Katja Schwiglewski, *Erzählte Technik; Die literarische Selbstdarstellung des Ingenieurs seit dem 19. Jahrhundert* (Cologne: Böhlau Verlag, 1995), 6.
43. See, for example, the short story by civil engineer Engelbert Zaschka, "Die Dame und Das Motorrad," *Motorrad-Sport, -Verkehr und -Technik*, no. 4, 1924, 18–19.
44. Fred Petermann, *Der PS-Narr: Sportroman* (Berlin: Georg König Verlag, 1930), 14.
45. Petermann, *Der PS-Narr*, 19.
46. Schwiglewski, *Erzählte Technik*, 121.
47. See, for example: "One speaks perhaps of solar energy, of using the tides, and when someone wants to appear very knowledgeable and modern, he speaks of atomic energy." Siegfried Hartmann, "Unsere Zukunft und die Technik," *Technik Voran!*, no. 2, 1925, 13.
48. Petermann, *Der PS-Narr*, 17.
49. Ibid., 46.
50. Ibid., 97–98.
51. Ibid., 131.
52. Ibid., 131–32.
53. Ibid., 179–80.
54. Schwiglewski, *Erzählte Technik*, 146–60.
55. Ibid., 146.
56. Julius Donny's character of Kurt Wolff, in *Garage 13*, provides an example of the benevolent engineer. See Chapter 7 for a discussion of Donny's novel.

57. Bruce E. Seely, "Engineers and Government–Business Cooperation: Highway Standards and the Bureau of Public Roads, 1900–1940." *Business History Review* 58, no. 1 (1984): 51–77.
58. "Das Reichsministerium für Technik und Verkehr," *Technik Voran!*, no. 13, 1925, 181–96, here 186.
59. Ibid., here 193.
60. Emphasis in orginal. Arnoldt, "Was bietet der Reichsbund deutscher Technik [RdT] seinen Mitglieder?," *Technik Voran!*, no. 25, 1926, 381–82.
61. Jarausch, *The Unfree Professions*, 70.
62. This quote is from Karl Busse, "Technik und Weltanschauung," *Technik Voran!*, no. 7, 1926, 14.
63. "Technik und Politik," *Technik Voran!*, no. 24, 1927, 451. See also "Eine anti-technische Regierung?," *Technik Voran!*, no. 8, 1927, 155.
64. "Technik bei den Wahlen am 17.11.1929," *Technik Voran!*, no. 40. 1929, 15.
65. This quote is from Dr. Georg Lange, in "Technik und Weltanschauung," *Technik Voran!*, no. 14, 1926, 14. Georg Lange was a Munich-based author, a critic of industrialization and a staunch proponent of "German Culture." In 1928, he published a book on German culture, *Erziehung als Zeugung. Zum Aufbau deutscher Kultur.* He was also a founding member of the *Kampfbund für deutsche Kultur* [Combat League for German Culture] in 1929, a Nazi-loyal group including artists, writers, and publishers, which had been called into life by Nazi ideologue Alfred Rosenberg. See Jürgen Gimmel, *Die politische Organisation kulturellen Ressentiments: der "Kampfbund für Deutsche Kultur" und das bildungsbürgerliche Unbehagen an der Moderne* (Münster: LIT Verlag, 2001), 202–3.
66. Herf, *Reactionary Modernism*, 155.
67. Hardensett, "Magische Technik," 11. For more on Hardensett, see Herf, *Reactionary Modernism*, 181–86.
68. On the pre–World War I discussion, see: König, "Die Ingenieure und der VDI," 275–78. See also, Thomas Rohkrämer, *Eine andere Moderne? Zivilisationskritik, Natur und Technik in Deutschland 1880–1933* (Paderborn: Schöningh, 1999).
69. Herf, *Reactionary Modernism*, 185.
70. "Technik und Weltanschauung," *Technik Voran!*, no. 7, 1926, 14.
71. Bruce E. Seely, "The Scientific Mystique in Engineering: Highway Research at the Bureau of Public Roads, 1918–1940," *Technology and Culture* 25, no. 4 (1984): 827–28.
72. Seely, *Building the American Highway*, 226.
73. For example, US economist and engineer Stuart Chase's 1929 book, *Men and Machines*, was translated in 1931 into German. In a review of the book, the sociologist Theodore Geiger praised Chase's approach to the social role of technology: "[Chase] blesses the machine and therefore technologization in the sense of an intensive structuring of the economy and an easing of life … Despite an at times accentuated carefree Americanism, he has written a thoughtful and highly serious book on the philosophy of technology." Theodore Geiger, Book Review, "Moloch Maschine," *Die Arbeit*, 1932, 540.
74. Rohkrämer, *Eine andere Moderne*, 254–60. Uwe Day, "Mythos ex machina: Medienkonstrukt "Silberpfeil" als massenkulturelle Ikone der NS-Modernisierung." PhD diss., Kulturwissenschaften Universität Bremen, 2004, 81.
75. Fischer, "Die Entwicklung der deutschen Motorrad-Industrie," 535–36.

76. Hellmuth Hock-v. Casanova, "Wie sieht die Rationalisierung in der Praxis aus?," *Technik Voran!*, no. 5, 1929, 11.
77. See discussion in Chapter 1.
78. "*Technik Voran!* 1929," *Technik Voran!*, no. 1, 1929, 1.
79. Rohkrämer, *Eine andere Moderne?*, 262. As Jeffrey Herf has argued, a belief in shaping a technologically modern society and a politically reactionary stance were not exclusive of each other. Herf, *Reactionary Modernism*, 1–4. On the influence of "Nazi alternatives" on the engineering profession, see Jarausch, *The Unfree Professions*, 75, 89–90, 99–100, 108. Indeed, the Nazis were the "dual beneficiaries" of the rationalization movement; see Nolan, *Visions of Modernity*, 232. As rationalization brought crisis instead of prosperity, towards the end of the Weimar Republic, engineers, including the Jewish engineer and editor of *Das Motorrad*, Paul Friedmann, began to openly laud a state-capitalist or fascist political project along the lines of Mussolini's Italy. Paul Friedmann, "Dacho-Kraft," in *Das Motorrad*, 1931: 1223. Also, R. Bielefeld, "Um die deutsche Motorrad-Industrie?," *Motor-Kritik*, no. 20, 1931, 446–51.
80. Christiane Lamberty's research on the beginnings of mass-media advertising in Germany in the period from 1890 to 1914 demonstrates how many of the advertising tactics, and the debates around them, had their origins in the pre–World War I period. Christiane Lamberty, *Reklame in Deutschland 1890–1914, Wahrnehmung, Professionalisierung und Kritik der Wirtschaftswerbung* (Berlin: Duncker und Humblot, 2000). On advertising in the Weimar Republic, see Janet Ward, *Weimar Surfaces: Urban Visual Culture in 1920s Germany* (Berkeley: University of California Press, 2001), especially 191–240. See also the edited volume: Pamela E. Swett, S. Jonathan Wiesen, and Jonathan R. Zatlin (eds.), *Selling Modernity: Advertising in Twentieth-Century Germany* (Durham, NC and London: Duke University Press, 2007).
81. Pamela E. Swett, S. Jonathan Wiesen, and Jonathan R. Zatlin, "Introduction," in *Selling Modernity*, ed. Swett, Weisen, and Zatlin, 9.
82. "Reklame!," *Das Motorrad*, 1929: 1683.
83. Ibid.
84. "Wer auf Propaganda verzichtet, gleicht einem Manne ohne Wohnung; niemand kann ihn finden," *Motor und Sport*, no. 1, 1928, 41.
85. Ward, *Weimar Surfaces*, 93–94; Uwe Day, "Mythos ex machina," 49–50; Traugott Schalcher, *Die Reklame der Straße* (Vienna and Leipzig: C. Barth Verlag, 1927).
86. Emphasis in original. Schalcher, *Die Reklame der Strasse*, 78.
87. Merki terms races "event marketing before the invention of the concept," and calls automobile expositions "high-tech bazaars." Merki, *Der holprige Siegeszug*, 247–302.
88. The AVUS was first conceived of before World War I, but was only completed in 1921. The first race held was an automobile race, which Fritz von Opel won. During 1922–1926 the AVUS hosted many motorcycle races, the first being held on 11–12 June 1922. See Hans Aschenbrenner, "Mit einer Träne im Knopfloch," *Berlinische Monatsschrift*, no. 7, 2001, n.p. The Nürbergring, conceived as a way of creating jobs in the underdeveloped Eifel region and employing between two thousand and three thousand workers for the two years of its construction, opened in 1927, and the Hockenheimring opened in 1932. The Nürbergring and the Hockenheim are still in use today. See also Steinbeck, *Das Motorrad*, 124–32.

89. von Saldern, "Cultural Conflicts," 317–38; Richard Birkefeld, "Spektakel im Stadtwald: Die Motorradrennen in der Eilenriede," in *Wochenend und Sonnenschein: Freizeit und modernen Leben in den Zwanziger Jahren: das Beispiel Hannover*, ed. Adalheid von Saldern and Sid Auffarth (Berlin: Elefanten Press, 1991), 15–23. Other internationally notable annually sponsored races were the Bäderrennen held on the Baltic Sea coast, and the Solituderennen in the hills around Stuttgart.

90. Dr. Heinz Walter Placzek, "Reklame in Drama," *Die Reklame*, no. 3, 1929, 83.

91. Motoring and the new technology of the cinema were also a theme in motorcycling journals. See, for example, "Ein großer Tag auf der Avus: 'Flimmerfritzens Freud und Leid,'" *Motorrad-Sport, -Verkehr und -Technik*, no. 37, 1926, 18; and "Ein interessanter Motorradtouren-Film," *Motorrad-Sport, -Verkehr und -Technik*, no. 10, 1925, 20–23.

92. Siegfried Kracauer, *From Caligari to Hitler: A Psychological History of German Film* (Princeton, NJ: Princeton University Press [1947] 1974), 207.

93. See Ward, *Weimar Surfaces*, 162–63; also Sabine Hake, "Urban Spectacle in Walther Ruttmann's Symphony of the Big City," in *Dancing on the Volcano: Essays on the Culture of the Weimar Republic*, ed. Thomas W. Kniesche and Stephen Brockmann (New York: Camden House, 1994), 127–28.

94. Siegfried Kracauer, "Film 1928," in *The Mass Ornament* (Cambridge, MA: Harvard University Press, 1995), 311.

95. For example, "DKW Volksrad – 485 MK – auf DEKA-Reifen," *Emelka-Woche*, 1929, 18.

96. The first advertising film in Germany was produced in 1896. Continental, a tire manufacturer, was already using film to advertise its products before World War I, however Lamberty asserts that the genre of film advertising only took off during World War I. Lamberty, *Reklame*, 214–23.

97. "Herr und Hund," 1929, Bundesarchiv, Filmarchiv M17124.

98. Möser, *Fahren und Fliegen*, 410–12.

99. "*Das Motorrad* im Film," *Der Motor-Tourist*, no. 25, 1929, 20.

100. It was made by the Atelier Gerd Philipp. The film studio made another film in 1932 named *Panne und Pneu* (Breakdown and Tires).

101. *Das stählerne Pferd* – Bundesarchiv, Filmarchiv, Film 10302. See also "Das stählerne Pferd," *Der Motorsportler*, no. 2, 1932, 5.

102. Rudolf-Mosse-Service Advertisement: "Anderer Artikel – anderer Reklamestil," *Die Reklame*, no. 15, 1929, vii.

103. Schalcher, *Die Reklame der Strasse*, 75–76. See also, E.L. Antz, "Technik, Presse und Reklame," *Technik Voran!*, no. 1, 1925, 6–7.

104. Propaganda-Unkosten 1.1.29–25.9.1929, 31070, Bestand Zschopauer Motorenwerke J.S. Rasmussen AG (DKW), Zschopau, 1913–1932, Sächsisches Staatsarchiv Chemnitz.

105. The goal of the press agency, which enlisted the assistance of the German automotive industry, was to "promote motorization and to encourage the general public's interest." "Propagandafragen," in RDA, *Jahrbuch*, 1928, 66. This decision was not popular with all trade journals. See, for example, "Rund um den RDA" and "Ein Presseskandal durch den RDA? Der Verband unterstützt die Pressekorruption und pönalisiert unabhängige, wahrheitsgemäße Kritik," *Klein-Motor-Sport*, no. 18, 1928, 374–82.

106. *NSU Mitteilungen*; *BMW-Blätter*; *Dixi Magazin*.

107. Photographs in the article show examples of how different BMW dealerships created interest in BMW's product line. "Vertreter Nachrichten," *BMW-Blätter*, no. 3, 1930, 31.
108. "Zugkräftige Schaufenster," in *FKZ*, no. 10, 1926, 1–2. See also Ward, *Weimar Surfaces*, 198–223.
109. Rachel Bowlby, *Carried Away: The Invention of Modern Shopping* (New York: Columbia University Press, 2001), 60–61. She provides a gender-attentive analysis of shopping in France and the United States that is particularly good at explaining the shifts in marketing, packaging, salesmanship (and its eventual decline), and store design. For window displays and masculinity, see Bowlby, *Carried Away*, 70–71.
110. FA Zündapp I.2.004 AK B0269: "Vertreter-Instruktion-Zündapp" (ca. 1929), Stiftung Deutsches Technikmuseum Berlin, Historisches Archiv.
111. Ibid.
112. Ibid.
113. In the only nod to the possibility that a potential customer could be female, the advertising and sales department had the following advice: "Don't drive too fast, especially with women; otherwise the novice gets scared and easily comes to the conclusion that the motorcycle is very dangerous. For this same reason, do not take the curves too sharply." Ibid.
114. Ibid.
115. FA Zündapp I.2.004 AK B0199: Die Werbeabteilung, Stiftung Deutsches Technikmuseum Berlin, Historisches Archiv.
116. FA Zündapp I.2.004 AK B0201: Etat für 1929; FA Zündapp I.2.004 AK B0268: Reklame Unkosten im Verhältnis zum Umsatz im Jahre 1930, Stiftung Deutsches Technikmuseum Berlin, Historisches Archiv.
117. FA Zündapp I.2.004 AK B0902: Arbeiter- und Angestellten Presse, Stiftung Deutsches Technikmuseum Berlin, Historisches Archiv.
118. FA Zündapp I.2.004 AK B0898-B0899: Aufstellung der Verbraucher-Geschäfte in der Zeit vom 1.1.1929–31.7.1929; FA Zündapp I.2.004 AK B897: Liste der Privatkunden in Groß-Berlin, Stiftung Deutsches Technikmuseum Berlin, Historisches Archiv.
119. "Zur besondere Beobachtung der NSU-Vertreter," *NSU-Mitteilungen*, April/June 1932, 2773.
120. "Vertreter Nachrichten," *BMW-Blätter*, no. 3, 1930, 31; "Anregungen zu Propagandafahrten für rührige NSU-Vertreter," *NSU-Mitteilungen*, April/June 1932, 2770–71.
121. "Anregungen zu Propagandafahrten für rührige NSU-Vertreter," 2770–71.
122. FA Zündapp I.2.004 AK B0269: "Vertreter-Instruktion-Zündapp" (ca. 1929), Stiftung Deutsches Technikmuseum Berlin, Historisches Archiv.; see also: Zündapp Advertisement in *Concordia*, no. 1, 1929.
123. See Ford, *My Life and Work*, for example, 273.
124. "Kundendienst," in *Das Motorrad* (Vienna), no. 138, 1931, 9; Schmitt, *Musterbetriebe*, 56–65; "Kundenwerbung durch die Reparaturwerkstatt," *Die Reparaturwerkstatt*, no. 3, 1928, 37; P.H. Franke, "Dienst am Kunden," in *FKZ*, no. 14, 1926, 3–5; "'Dienst am Kunden' – in mancherlei Auffassung!" *Klein-Motor-Sport*, no. 22, 1927, 485–86.
125. Dr. R. Niptsch, *Marktbeobachtung und Wirtschaftsführung in der Kraftfahrzeugindustrie (Amerikanische Methoden und deutsche Gemeinschaftsarbeit)*,

edited by Institut für Konjunkturforschung (Berlin: Reichsverband der Auto-mobilindustrie, 1930), 3.

126. See *Die Reklame*, 1927.

127. Franz Findeisen, *Die Epoche: Das Magazine des Werbefilms*, no. 1, 1929, 7–10. This magazine was a special insert in *Die Reklame* 1929. Findeisen, who was a professor at the Handelshochschule (commercial college) in Leipzig, developed these ideas earlier; see Franz Findeisen, *Die Markenartikel im Rahmen der Absatzökonomik der Betriebe* (Berlin: Industrieverlag Spaeth & Linde, 1924).

128. On the role of psychology and "psychotechnics" in advertising during the Weimar Republic, see Ward, *Weimar Surfaces*, 96–101; and Corey Ross, "Visions of Prosperity: The Americanization of Advertising in Interwar Germany," in *Selling Modernity*, ed. Swett, Weisen, and Zatlin, 59–60.

129. Lamberty, *Reklame*, 443–46; and Ross, "Visions of Prosperity," 52–77.

130. Siegfried Seher, "Happiness? Kleine Bilanz eine Amerikareise," *Motor-Kritik*, no. 10, 1930, 197–201.

131. Ross, "Visions of Prosperity," 53–61.

132. Seher, "Happiness?," 197–201. See also Martin Wagner, "Städtebauliche Probleme in amerikanischen Städten und ihre Rückwirkung auf den deutschen Städtebau," *Sonderheft zur Deutschen Bauzeitung*, 1929; "Hetz-Tempo der Zeit," in *AIZ*, no. 1, 1930, 18–19; also "Gesichter der Strasse," in *AIZ*, no. 4, 1928, 4–5; Fritz Rostosky, "Als Kraftfahrhilfsdienstbeamter in Amerika," *Das Motorrad*, 1929: 155–56.

133. Ross, "Visions of Prosperity," 61–65.

134. Janus, "Werben oder Advertising? Eine allgemeine und spezielle Betrachtung," *Motor-Kritik*, no. 5, 1930, 110–14.

135. Ibid.

136. Advertisement: "Zündapp: Zuverlässig; die steuer- und führerscheinfreie Zündapp Z200," after 1928.

137. Text of advertisement in *Die Reklame*, no. 19, 1929: "On a Stock motorcycle with a girl, you can go uphill easily. Whoever has to push pedals, won't be able to keep up (as a love rival)."

138. "Der Student und *Das Motorrad*," *BMW-Blätter*, no. 11, 1929, n.p.

139. *AIZ*, no. 46, 1929, 15.

140. See Chapter 3 for more information on the occupational distribution of the motorcycle in the last years of the Weimar Republic.

141. *AIZ*, no. 15, 1927, 12.

142. *AIZ*, no. 36, 1930, 17.

143. Dr. [Käthe] Kurtzig, "Die Gleichberechtigung von Mann und Frau in der Reklame," *Die Reklame*, no. 19, 1929, 742–43

144. "Schüttoff – *Das Motorrad* der Dame," *Der Motor-Tourist*, no. 9, 1929, 10.

145. The motorcycle was described in German as a *"fabelhaft rassiges 'Eisernes Pferd'"* in "Motorrad und Dame," *BMW-Blätter*, no. 9/10, 1929, n.p.

146. Ibid.

147. Clarsen, *Eat My Dust*, 6.

148. St. v. Szenasy, "Das Motorrad mit Beiwagen," *Motor-Tourist*, no. 18, 1929, 10.

149. For example, Anfa praised their vehicle for providing "a comfortable ride for both passenger and driver," Hugo Kalinowski und Co. advertised their sidecar as having a "racy tear-drop form," Dessauer advertised their product as "cheap," Höhne & Jäger emphasized the qualities of "cheap and solid," and Pilot claimed

their sidecar was a "joy for everyman!" Primus claimed their products were "the most modern models," while Jewel touted their products as "elegant, racy, durable, and advanced." These advertisements were repeatedly published in the extensive advertising sections of motorcycling journals such as *Das Motorrad, Motorrad-Sport, -Verkehr und -Technik,* and *Klein-Motor-Sport.*

150. See advertisements, for example, for Stolz sidecars: The "acme of performance," citing "11 victories on one day that document its unparalleled superiority," including a race in Leipzig and a "Round about Scotland" race.

151. See, for example, "Das Mädchen für Alles," *Das Motorrad,* 1929: 778–79.

152. BMW advertisement in *Motor* (1927); NSU published a very similar one in *ADAC-Motorwelt,* no. 20, 1928, 21.

153. Schmidt, *Sich hart machen, wenn es gilt,* 69–72, 84–86; Weinbaum et al., *The Modern Girl around the World.* Advertisements for Snob, Zündapp, NSU, and DKW regularly featured "new men." "NSU," *Der Motorfahrer,* no. 18, 1924, 352; "Eine Probefahrt macht Sie zum Zündapp Freund," *ADAC-Motorwalt,* no. 17, 1929, 11; "DKW – So sollen Sie feiern," *ADAC-Motorwelt,* no. 47, 1927, 27.

154. Möser, *Fahren und Fliegen,* 363–66. Matthew Biro, "The New Man as Cyborg: Figures of Technology in Weimar Visual Culture," *New German Critique* 62 (Spring/Summer, 1994): 71–110. Mom, *Atlantic Automobilism,* 497–507.

155. NSU ran a series of advertisements in *ADAC-Motorwelt* that point to averting problems such as breakdowns through purchasing their vehicles. "Save yourself the annoyance that many motorcyclists know in surfeit." "Überdruss," *ADAC-Motorwelt,* no. 2, 1928, 28; also "NSU," *ADAC-Motorwelt,* no. 9, 1928, 23.

156. This was Zündapp's promise for their motorcycle—see "Die große neue Zündapp," *Motor-Tourist,* no. 16, 1929, 21.

CHAPTER 3

Motorcycles and the "Everyman"

Exploring the Motorcycling Milieu

In 1924, the year Zündapp, an up-and-coming manufacturer of small and mid-sized motorcycles, launched an advertising campaign declaring their motorcycles "The Motorcycle for Everyman." As part of the campaign Zündapp hired graphic artists, including the prominent designer Ludwig Hohlwein, to depict "the everyman."[1] One of the posters Hohlwein produced, a four-color lithograph, grouped five heads around the Zündapp logo. The faces ranged from an old man with a beard and metal-rimmed glasses to a man in a top hat, two men wearing working class caps, and a stereotypical flapper-style new woman coquettishly glancing aside. Who Zündapp's "everyman" could be was apparently very malleable. Their slogan was at once premature and anticipatory.

Recurring cycles of severe economic instability during the early years of the Weimar Republic hindered the emergence of a mass base of consumers, upon which the full realization of mass motorization would have relied. Above all, for reasons that were discussed in the first chapter of this book, ownership of an automobile remained out of reach for most. Instead, motorcycles, an alternative form of individual motorized transportation, continued to grow in popularity throughout the Weimar Republic. Indeed, the ownership of motorcycles expanded almost eightyfold during the Weimar Republic and, due to sinking costs and falling prices for motorcycles and rising real wages for workers, motorcycles gradually came to fulfill, at least partially, the dreams of motorization for "everyman."[2] By 1930, the widespread dispersion of the motorcycle as a form of motorized transportation led one commentator to call it "truly the most social of all means of transportation in our era."[3]

But who was the motorcycling "everyman" during the Weimar Republic? Forged through a variety of experiences, practices, and processes, motorcycling masculinity was by no means uniform. As Hohlwein's image indicates, a range of identities were possible, from the working-class man in a paperboy cap, to a gentleman in a top hat, the "everyman" motorcyclist was a heterogeneous category, and even included a female with bobbed hair. Most previous historical studies of masculinity in the Weimar Republic have focused on the *Männerbund* (literally "band of men") and militarism as crucibles of Weimar masculinity.[4] George Mosse's work on the formation of interwar masculinity focuses on the strength of "myth of the war experience," and Thomas Kühne has explored the centrality of the concept of comradeship, a "motor of masculine collectivization" in Germany.[5] The rhetoric and experience of homosocial bonding and militarism was undeniably important for a range of motorized masculinities. Motorization, a practice rooted primarily in individual consumption, however, opened up spaces in which hegemonic masculinity could potentially be transformed, if not subverted.

Building upon previous historical interpretations of masculinities, this chapter explores the specific sociological makeup and the discursively elaborated possibilities and boundaries of the "motorcycling milieu" in Weimar Germany.[6] First, I examine the shifting social demographic of motorcycle ownership, and the increasing ownership of motorcycles by members of the working classes. I then provide an outline of the primary institutional frameworks—the clubs and journals—in which motorcyclists were active participants and which were central to the construction of the milieu. These records, which contain expressions produced by the motorcycling milieu, point to how and where motorcycling masculinity was produced. The chapter concludes with a discussion of the discursive variations of masculinity and motorcycling, based on a consideration of ideal types of motorcyclists. What emerges from this analysis is that during the Weimar Republic the motorcycling community represented a masculine collective perforated by internal distinctions. In the context of structural transformation, occupational status became a less viable marker of masculine identity, and the modern male motorcyclist sought alternative moorings.

Searching for the "Everyman": The Shifting Demography of Motorcyclists

Transport historians and mobility scholars have paid little attention thus far to shifts in the socioeconomic structure of motorcyclists in Weimar Germany, an important indicator of the diffusion of motorized mobility.[7] Comparing a data sample from 1923–1924 to statistics from 1929 demonstrates the extent of the demographic shift in motorcycle ownership. Data from 1924 on the occupations of 499 members of the largest southern German club exclusively for motorcyclists shows that the majority of members belonged to what can be classified as bourgeois occupations (see Appendix: Table 6).[8] The most common occupation provided by members was that of merchant or shopkeeper, with one hundred and seventy identifying themselves as *Kaufmann* (general retailers or merchants), seventeen as *Fahrzeughändler* or *Fahrradhändler* (motor vehicle or bicycle retailers), four as other specified types of merchant, including in animal and raw products, three as *Großkaufmann* (wholesale retailers), one *kaufmännischen Vertreter* (sales representative), one *Geschäftsreisender* (traveling salesman), one *Generalvertreter* (general agent), and one representative of Motag, a motor vehicle company. Self-proclaimed retailers or merchants alone accounted for slightly more than 34 percent of the club's membership. Including *Prokuristen* (head clerks) and *Betriebsleiter* or *Geschäftsführer* (managers) brings the number of those involved in the sales and commercial sector to almost 40 percent. Within this group, it is probable that some representatives belonged to the new lower middle classes of clerks and accountants. In comparison to the 1925 census, in which merchants and businesspersons constituted only 16.4 percent of the general population in Germany, the commercial sector was overrepresented among this sample of motorcyclists.[9]

Seventy-eight members, or 13.5 percent of the total sample, identified themselves as mechanics, making them the largest single group of skilled and semi-skilled workers in this sample from the club's membership roster. If the eight members who identified themselves as *Monteure* (assemblers) are included, this group then represented 14.9 percent of the total sample. It is likely they would have been drawn to motorcycling because of their mechanical proficiency, as these machines were in need of constant repair. As in the case of mechanics, *Schlosser* (metalworkers), due to their occupational and cultural affinity with the practice of tinkering, were early adopters of motorcycles. This group included two *Schlossermeister* (metalworker masters), two metalworkers without specific titles, two *Motorradschlosser* (motorcycle mechanics), one *Schlossergehilfe* (assistant metalworker) and one motorcycle constructor (*Motorradbau*). Artisanal master craftsmen made up 6.1 percent of the total sample of club membership, the largest group identifying themselves as *Werkmeister* (foremen or master workers). Twenty more artisanal "master craftsmen" included four "master butchers." In addition to mechanics and metalworkers, skilled craftsmen were represented in the sample who did not claim the "master" title: for example, a file cutter, a bottler, and a roofer.

A third widely represented occupation that has an even less uniform profile was that of *Fabrikant*, a professional term that connoted manufacturer, industrialist, or factory owner. In the sample from the club's membership list, forty-one identified with the title *Fabrikant* (one as a *Maschinenfabrikant*), thirteen with *Direktor* (director) and seven with *Fabrikbesitzer* (factory owner), together representing 10.6 percent. This occupational grouping is particularly tricky to evaluate on a socio-logical class basis. In the nineteenth century, the term *Fabrikant* was also used to indicate a worker who was a member of the "industrious classes." By the 1920s, it is likely that a person who identified with the designation *Fabrikant* was an owner of a small manufacturing work-shop, and, given the significant number of small motorcycle manu-factories that mushroomed during the early inflationary years of the republic, it is not surprising that this group was widely represented in the club's membership rosters.

White-collar groups that can be labeled as belonging to the classic liberal professions, such as doctors, dentists, lawyers, and architects, did not constitute a significant proportion of the club's membership, representing only 2.8 percent of the sample. Their relatively low num-bers could possibly be attributed to being able to afford an automo-bile; however, given the inflationary economy, it is also possible that they could have afforded neither. Engineers and technicians, on the other hand, constituted over 5 percent of the sample. While most often listed without any special title, the sample also included four engineers with an academic title. Bank clerks represented a further 1.9 percent of the sample, and other members of service industries, such as barbers, chauffeurs, and artists, accounted for nearly 3 percent. Another nota-ble professional group was those connected directly to state power, such as policemen and members of the motorized divisions of the military, who accounted for more than 3 percent of the total sample. Students and interns, who can be presumed to have been young, made up 2.1 percent. In addition, eight women appear on the membership list, accounting for nearly 1.4 percent.[10]

Surveys of the occupations of motorcyclists from the end of the 1920s provide a vastly different picture of motorcycle ownership. The shift can partly be accounted for in that the first is drawn from a club roster, whose members can be presumed to have held a significant stake in motorcycling, whereas the second set of statistics is drawn from sales numbers and new registrations of motorcycles from the general population. Nonetheless, by the late 1920s motorcycle manufacturers offered products affordable to an ever-greater number of Germans, and state-supported juridical incentives made small-powered motorcycles a financially attractive means of joining the ranks of the individually motorized.[11] Finally, the extent of the change is substantial enough to draw general conclusions about the increasing socio-economic diversity of the motorcycling population, despite the necessary caveats both about the variance in the samples as well as the ambiguity of descriptive occupational categories employed in the samples and the difficulty of interpretive analysis of productive categories in an economy that was in the process of radical restructuring.

Thus, when the head marketing office of Zündapp decided in 1929 that they needed to know who bought their products and ordered their sales offices to send in biannual statistics on the occupations of consumers, the numbers showed that, increasingly, their motorcycle was indeed the motorcycle for "everyman." Among their customers in Cologne and Munich in the first half of 1929, almost 44 percent were either blue- or white-collar workers, split equally.[12] Independent craftsmen and merchants made up only 19 percent of the sample, and government clerks, teachers, and policemen accounted for 21 percent. Less than 10 percent of the recorded buyers belonged to the liberal professions. Thus, in the span of five years, the percentage of motorcyclists who belonged to independent labor halved, whereas the percentage of dependent labor more than doubled.

A statistical survey from 1930 underscores this demographic shift. Dr. Herbert Schmidt-Lamberg, an academically trained journalist who wrote on a wide spectrum of topics, presented his findings in an article on the "Distribution of the Motorcycle among the Various Occupational Groups." An analysis of new registrations for the "world city of Berlin" reveals 1,107 factory workers and 2,100 commercial agents and office employees had recently registered their vehicles. In addition, the "eastern peripheral areas of Neukölln, Tempelhof, Cöpenick [sic], Lichtenberg, Treptow, and Rummelsberg experienced an increase of 45 percent of new ownership of motorcycles." To Schmidt-Lamberg, these numbers demonstrated that "the motorcycle enjoys popularity as a means of transportation precisely among the broad social classes of craftsmen, tradesmen, and workers."[13]

The trend towards a broader occupational spread among motorcycle owners is also reflected in a 1929 sample of 471 of all new motorcycle registrations in Prussia, excluding Berlin (see Appendix: Table 7).[14] In this geographically heterogeneous sample, 46 percent fall into the category of skilled, semi-skilled, or unskilled labor, which is a slightly higher percentage in comparison with the census numbers on persons employed in the industrial and craft sectors of the economy, and represents an increase of approximately 30 percent over the 1924 statistical sample (see Appendix: Table 8).[15] This group included a far greater variety of workers, with miners making up the second largest group behind metalworkers, an occupational group that had taken to motorcycling early. Other widely represented categories of manual labor in the sample were masons, electricians, construction workers, and housepainters who would likely have used their motorcycle for work-related purposes. In addition, there were fourteen "workers" lacking any occupational specification within the sample. By 1931, the number of new registrations among workers and employees in the Rhineland had risen to almost 82 percent, including 23 percent who were officially unemployed.[16]

The commercial sector represented again a large segment of new registrations, constituting 16 percent, yet showing a significant decrease compared to the 1924 sample of motorcyclists' occupations. Within this occupational subset, merchants and retailers made up over three-quarters of the new registrations, with assistants and employees representing a little over 13 percent. Traveling salesmen and commercial agents accounted for the remaining 10.5 percent. Members of the commercial sector thus continued to represent a significant proportion of motorcycle owners. According to Schmidt-Lamberg's data, motorcycles were registered to 2,113 independent commercial businessmen in Hamburg, 1,884 in Cologne, and 1,749 in Munich. Hotfooted stock market operators were supposedly particularly fond of the motorcycle, and Schmidt-Lamberg painted a picture of the stock market district in Berlin as swarming with motorcycles: "Everyday in Berlin between 300 and 400 motorcycles ferry traders to the stock exchange."[17]

Craftsmen, including master artisans, represented another substantial subset, being 14 percent of the total sample. The numerically largest category of craftsmen was woodworkers, including carpenters and cabinetmakers (25 percent), followed by bakers (18 percent), smiths, and shoemakers (both 10 percent). The next largest subset, a little less than 10 percent, can be grouped in the amorphous category of "service industry," a category that includes waiters, carters, a doorman, and an orderly. Professional drivers were the largest group within this category, and if coachmen and carters are included within this group then they account for nearly half of the representatives of the service industry. Barbers represented almost a quarter of all service employees and photographers and artists made up one-fifth. Many independent economic actors may have found the motorcycle appealing because of its potential to provide mobility and a competitive edge in the market. Specially outfitted sidecars could also enhance business opportunities for many small-scale businessmen. Only 4 percent of motorcycles from the entire 1929 sample were registered to agricultural workers, a major, although generally declining, occupational category.

Outside of the commercial sector, members of what can be considered "white-collar" professions represented only a fraction of motorcyclists' occupations, making up 7 percent of the total sample, including engineers and "new white-collar" workers. State employees, members who belonged to the *Beamtentum* including policemen, constituted 4 percent of the sample, which included five teachers, three policemen, and three members of the provincial gendarmerie. By the end of the 1920s, however, "new white-collar" professionals, as both the Zündapp sales statistics and Schmidt-Lamberg's findings indicate, took to motorcycling in ever-greater numbers. The female stenographer who registered her motorcycle in Unterwesterwaldkreis near Koblenz in January 1929 stands as a cipher of social and occupational ruptures during the Weimar Republic.[18]

The enormity of economic and social shifts that took place in Germany during the period of rapid industrialization in the late nineteenth and early twentieth century, and the insecurity-driven politics after World War I, made labor a category at the fulcrum of the definition of social life.[19] The unevenness in the process of differentiation within the labor market was addressed by the trade journal of the metalworkers' association in terms of the question of "Worker versus Employee" (*Arbeiter oder Mitarbeiter*): "All people in the economy are divided into two large groups, in employers and employees [*in Arbeitgeber und Arbeitnehmer*]. Not rightfully, because the two terms are inadequate and do not cover the concept in any way."[20] The expansion of the tertiary sector and the growth of the number of industrial workers in the overall workforce precipitated conflicts over the valuation and definition of labor, as Siegfried Kracuaer's 1931 investigation, *The Salaried Masses*, vividly captures. The acceleration of mobility, both spatial and social, blurred occupational delineations, in some cases prompting an intensified identification with a collective as a strategy for shoring up boundaries between the self and the other.

The very real instability of the social structure of labor during the Weimar Republic was reflected in generalized anxiety about a social system based on relations of production divided along the lines of class. The severe disruptions in the political economy and the continued restructuring of the labor market and society through hyperinflation, rationalization, a general sense of political malaise, the misguided economic policies enacted to counter the effects of the World Economic Crisis and the ensuing political polarization, were tied to a long-term transformation of the concept of labor. Boundaries, for example, between "craft trades" and "industry" were not distinct.[21] Furthermore, the progressive mechanization of both agriculture and industry had the effect of making the population more mobile, while also leading to a devaluation of certain professions. On the other hand, this disorder simultaneously produced conscious and unconscious strategies and practices for anchoring masculinity in the tight coupling of productive labor and manhood.

The symbolic content of manual labor, according to Alf Lüdtke, involved attaching "meanings that are always multi-layered," formed through both everyday and eventful iteration and reiteration.[22] The

Image 3.1. Male Productivity and Motorcycling. "The Iron Foundry Worker," Max Schwammler, BMW Advertisement, ca. 1918, BMW Group Archive.

rhetoric of work during the Weimar Republic mirrored the language of motorcycling; workers were to be "knowledgeable masters of their machines," "in the work process, manual dexterity combined with sharp eyes, physical strength and 'toughness' with 'hard labor.'" [23] Like motorcycling, physical labor was consistently gendered masculine. Concurrently, the association of "dignity in labor" with "manual dexterity" could be transferred onto the practice of motorcycling, endowing the commodity with the symbolic capital to stand in for the lost social capital formerly embodied in labor.

If, as Cotten Seiler argues for the US case, Taylorism and the resulting shifts in the organization of labor led to a loss of autonomy for which the automobile partly provided compensation, then, in the German case during the Weimar Republic, as work became more routinized, mechanized, and automated through the introduction of new managerial practices and new industrial machines between 1924 and 1929, motorcycling, a practice that intertwined consumption, production, aesthetics, and technology, became increasingly important as a compensatory strategy. [24]

The Lifeworlds of Motorcycling

Analyses based on occupational statistics alone, however, do not provide "ultimate findings." Instead, as Theodore Geiger, "sociographer" of the Weimar Republic, argued, "symptoms of the external lives of people" are vital to assessing mentalities. [25] "Lifestyle, practices of consumption and other forms of structuring one's life, use of leisure time, taste in reading materials, forms of family life and sociability—in ensemble, a thousand details of everyday life make up the type of habitus, and this is an expression of mentality." [26] Clubs and journals constituted important spaces in which the habitus of the Weimar motorcyclist was produced and reproduced. [27] The lived everyday practices of setting the bounds of sociability and policing the community found their expression in club activities and in journal publications. Whereas in advertisements for "technologies of the self," including cosmetics and fashion, journals spread the idea of a purchasable modern masculinity, articles on tinkering helped to stabilize a hegemonic masculinity that was centered on productive labor and technological skill. By showcasing new leisure practices, articles on activities such as camping and motorcycle skijoring presented reconfigurations of relationships between time and space—in which the motorcycle allowed the rider to "bypass space and conquer time." [28] A closer reading of the "symptoms" of motorcycling provides insight into the formation of habitus and mentality of Weimar motorcycling masculinity.

Clubs: Homosocial Worlds of Motorcycling?

The largest motoring association in Weimar Germany was the Allgemeiner Deutscher Automobil-Club [Nationwide German Automobile Club, ADAC] that grew out of the 1903-founded Deutsche Motorradfahrer Vereinigung [German Motorcyclists' Union, DMV].[29] In 1911, the DMV changed its name to ADAC to reflect the changing demographic of its membership—by that year only one-fifth of the members of the club owned a motorcycle as opposed to an auto-mobile.[30] After the war, motorcycling members of the ADAC became increasingly disenchanted with both the financial leadership and with the supposed dismissal of their interests by the automobile-owning faction. This conflict resulted in the reestablishment of the DMV, a sep-arate interest organization for motorcyclists, in Halle in late February 1923.[31] At the time of its reconstitution, the DMV claimed to have over four thousand members organized in twenty-nine clubs across Germany.[32] Although animosity existed between the two clubs in the first years of their existence, by 1924 the DMV and the ADAC had agreed to work together in terms of organizing races under the newly founded Deutsche Motorrad-Sportgemeinschaft [German Motorcycle Sport Association, DMS].[33] The ADAC continued to organize a number of internationally prominent motorcycle races, including the annual Deutschlandfahrt. Although the ADAC claimed to represent more motorcyclists, the DMV was the largest single-interest association for motorcyclists throughout the Weimar Republic, boasting twenty thousand members in 1929.[34]

Alongside organizing races, the DMV published a journal from 1924 onwards, within which they not only reported on sporting events, but also discussed technical, legal, political, and financial issues, and pro-vided news of the various clubs that were organized under the umbrella organization. The DMV also used the journal to highlight their lobby-ing efforts, publishing letters that the association had written to police presidia and to ministries of the interior on behalf of the "less-well-off motorcyclists," often asking the states to reconsider taxation laws or to plead for less rigorous penalties for traffic violations.[35] Members also enjoyed other benefits, such as insurance and help with necessary paperwork for trips outside Germany. In addition, the DMV maintained it was their duty to "educate their members" by constantly reminding them to be responsible and considerate motorists. Furthermore, they organized annual gatherings, at which hundreds of motorcyclists from all around Germany would congregate in one town for a weekend in an event that combined social elements with organizational tasks.[36] The association thus coordinated a variety of efforts to increase the popularity and acceptance of motorcycling.

While buying a motorcycle did not mean automatic initiation into a "band of brothers," actively joining a club did imply membership as a comrade among other motorcyclists. The umbrella association saw itself as representing the interests of motorcycle sportspeople, and men in particular. In membership drives, the DMV claimed that it was "only interested in performance in sport" and "not in differentiating on the basis of social stratification."[37] Dr. Artur Vieregg, the long-time president of the DMV and a passionate motorcyclist as well as figure skater, asserted: "To be a DMV member is to be a sportsman." A club, according to Vieregg, was a "closed society" that should stand "together for one goal with strict discipline . . . One big family, irrespective of differences of opinions, all stand shoulder to shoulder loyal to the club, standing together in comradely encouragement . . . The great idea that joins us all together is the idea of comradeship, sticking together, readiness to help and the education of all motorcyclists in the interest of all motorcyclists."[38] Although the language of the president of Weimar Germany's largest motorcycling association would indicate that clubs fostered an exclusively homosocial environment, the reality of the motorcycling world was more diverse. Certainly for some veterans, joining together with other male motorcyclists offered an opportunity to relive the intense bonds of exclusively male camaraderie experienced on the front; however, motorcycling comradeship was a more inclusive concept than the purely masculine *Männerbund* experienced in the trenches in World War I. According to Thomas Kühne, during the Weimar Republic, comradeship was a hotly debated concept.[39] Although concepts of comradeship all revolved around visions of belonging, discipline, and sacrifice that sought to end class conflict, the nationalist iteration focused on submission to a racially imagined *Volksgemeinschaft*, while the socialist variant sought the transcendence of class through an international struggle to form a brotherhood of solidarity. Moreover, as Kühne argues, by 1930 the idea of female comradeship was accepted, "the concept of the female comrade was no longer a disturbance in the sexual hierarchy but rather its stabilizer."[40]

Thus, by invoking a vision of a family of comrades, Vieregg opened the concept of comradeship to encompass both sexes.[41] Indeed, women were not prevented from joining the DMV—that is as long as the subsidiary clubs organized under the umbrella association had no statute explicitly forbidding women from joining. Motorcycling clubs sometimes invited women to participate in their sporting activities; for example, a report from a 1925 "motor sports day" hosted by the Munich club, the Knatternde Gesell [Rat-a-tat-tatting Fellows], described two women competitors in a gymkhana contest that tested riders' skills in riding over a seesaw and weaving through obstacles.[42] Photographs and films of club outings almost always show a few women, at least as pillion seat riders.[43] And women were most often mentioned in invitations to club social evenings, providing evidence that motorcycle clubs were not exclusively homosocial. Within their statutes, however, many clubs did indeed prevent women from becoming "active members." The Motorrad Club München 1910 [Motorcycle Club of Munich 1910] stated that only "honest and respectable men who have completed their eighteenth year of life" could serve as active members.[44] While the largest motorcycle sport club in Munich, Sturmvogel [Storm Bird], allowed women to join for half of the membership fee, female members did not have the "rights or votes at meetings."[45] Thus, although women were most often not completely excluded from participating in motorcycle club life, they were almost always subjected to a subordinate position.[46]

Associational life was thus an important form of organized both homo- and heterosociability during the Weimar Republic, and often it was organized around political or confessional affinities. Beyond the DMV and the ADAC, there were numerous other supra-regional motoring associations, including the national-conservative Automobilclub von Deutschland [Automobile Club of Germany, AvD] and the centrist Deutscher Touring–Club [German Touring Club, DTC], all of which had been established prior to World War I.[47] The left-wing working-class sports associations also organized motorcyclists—both the communist-aligned sport club Die Fichte [The Pine] and the bicycle club Solidarität [Solidarity], that was closely associated with the Social Democratic Party (SPD), included motorcyclists within their ranks.[48] In 1930, an SPD sport journal reported that Solidarität had 24,000 motorcyclists, organized in 1,300 divisions. "With the growing number of motorcyclists, the 'Solidarity Cyclists Union' will soon surpass all bourgeois associations in this branch. It is already the strongest representative for the interests of the motorcyclist."[49] Concordia, the anti-Marxist working-class sporting organization, likewise welcomed motorcyclists in its cycling clubs.[50] With increasingly acerbic insistence, nationalists too tried to capture motorists for their cause. In 1929, under the patronage of Carl Eduard, the Duke of Sachsen-Coburg and Gotha, the retired general and

National Socialist parliamentarian von Epp, together with members of the right-wing Deutsch-Nationale Volkspartei [German National People's Party, DNVP] and the Reichswehr, founded an explicitly nationalist and revanchist automobile club. The club's insignia bore the imperial colors of black, red, and white in its insignia. Its founder claimed that, "given the ever-increasing significance of motorization for economic and cultural development and the increasing politicization that is encroaching upon the sphere of motor vehicle owner associations, the existence of a club that consciously stands on national grounds is a necessity."[51]

Indeed the volatile political landscape of the Weimar Republic during the late 1920s and early 1930s influenced the landscape of motoring sociability. The Reichsbanner Schwarz-Rot-Gold [Black-Red-Gold Banner of the Reich, Reichsbanner], a paramilitary umbrella organization established in 1924 to defend the Weimar Republic, formed a nationwide motorcycling organization, the Reichsverband republikanischer Motorradfahrer [Republican Motorcyclists' Federation of the Reich] in 1929.[52] In 1931, the National Socialists reorganized their motor vehicle association founded the year before, renaming it from Nationalsozialistisches Automobilkorps [National Socialist Automobile Corps, NSAK] to Nationalsozialistisches Kraftfahrerkorps [National Socialist Motorist Corps, NSKK], in order to reflect the growing number of motorcyclists in the association. In December 1931, the NSKK reported a membership of ten thousand, who they claimed were mostly also organized in the Motor-Sturmabteilung [Motor Storm Troopers, Motor-SA] and the Motor-Schutzstaffel [Motor Protective Squadron, Motor-SS].[53] Communists likewise organized motorized divisions that exercised both a sporting and a paramilitary function in the last near–civil war years of the Republic.[54] By the end of the Weimar Republic all mass-based political parties had motorized divisions.[55] Motorcycling was thus not aligned with any particular political group, and motorcyclists participated in political parades and demonstrations of all stripes and colors.

Consumer affinities, however, also gained in importance over the course of the Weimar Republic. Motorcyclists identified so strongly with their brand of motorcycle that a practice existed of greeting people riding on the same brand on rural roads by raising their left hand. This consumer-driven behavior was reported as being above all practiced by those who drove BMW, Harley, Indian, or Victoria motorcycles, all brand names that were more costly and were recognized as status symbols.[56] Owners of a particular brand sometimes joined together in clubs. The Berlin BMW club claimed the legitimacy of their bond to be based above all on the symbolic capital of the brand: "The BMW-rider, owner of the strongest and most famous machine in Europe and the most beautiful motorcycle in the world, can hardly join such a club that swarms about the country roads on ragtag and bobtail machines." Moreover, the club argued: "The BMW rider is rightfully proud of the unheard-of power that is in his machine and the enormous performance that it is capable of at all times; the furor that such a beautiful machine creates everywhere makes him reluctant to ride alongside machines of other brands." Such a stance, however, was not "arrogance or conceit, but rather this exclusivity is perfectly normal. The BMW-rider seeks equal opponents and equal riding comrades."[57] Brand bonding was not limited to owners of high-powered, heavyweight motorcycles; Zündapp clubs, for example, joined together riders of lightweight motorcycles.[58] Siegfried Kracauer commented on the prevalence of branding in leisure activities and sports in his analysis of the "new middle classes," using the example of the Berlin Industrial Race in which company-sponsored athletes competed against each other: "The fact that the fighting troops bore the names of their firms is not the worst advertisement; and at the same time it increases the feeling of solidarity."[59] The growing identification with the brand name of the motorcycle, and the formation of communities around brand names, points to the increasing importance of consumer practices in constructing modern masculine identities.

Nevertheless, most motorcyclists were not organized in a club. According to a 1926 propaganda article in the DMV's own journal, only one-tenth of all motorcyclists belonged to a club.[60] With the onset of the depression, despite the almost threefold increase in the number of motorcycles in Germany, the DMV began to lose members rapidly and to experience extreme financial difficulties.[61] The effect of motorcycling clubs on the construction of Weimar motorcycling masculinity should not, therefore, be overestimated. Although the clubs themselves had relatively limited influence on the everyday lives of the greater motorcycling community, they nonetheless reflected reconfigured patterns of fraternity, in which men formed bonds around their shared relationship to a consumer object that altered their experience of space and time.

Reading Motorcycling Mentalities

Gustav Braunbeck's 1929 "Address Book for the Motor Vehicle and Related Industries in Germany" listed ninety-one German language automotive trade journals, seven factory-issued journals, and ten journals related to automotive accessories.[62] Technical, legal, and industrial news dominated the content of the journals. Most discussions of technical and mechanical innovations and new motorcycle designs were illustrated, at the very least with technical diagrams. All reported extensively on the products displayed at motor vehicle exhibitions, in particular at the Olympia show held in London and the German Automobile Exhibition held in Berlin. Motoring journals consistently covered revisions to the law regarding motor vehicle traffic, as well as changes in taxation and stipulations regarding the registration of motor vehicles. Many provided travelogues, often illustrated with photographs of locations in Germany and as far abroad as Africa, India, and Japan. An important aspect of most journals, especially those that aimed for wider consumption, was the discussion of driving rules and etiquette. Indeed, instead of narrowly focusing on technical specifications, journals intended for consumption by the general public oriented their content towards issues of general social interest, including articles on competitive motorcycling, new gadgetry, and novel forms of leisure.

The less technical journals often ran short stories and serialized novels, in addition to fashion layouts. Quite a number of poems, songs, and cartoons were also included in the journals—surprising perhaps for a twenty-first-century reader, but in accordance with the popularity of both genres at the time. In addition, many journals also contained book and movie reviews of motor vehicle–related interest. Some provided reviews of books that were of more general interest, including reviews of novels, such as *College Girls*, as well as etiquette books for men, such as *Beauty Care for Men*.[63] In addition, the more "feuilleton" type journals often had a section of puzzles and jokes, as well as photographs and opinion letters sent in by their readers. All journals had extensive advertising sections. Most advertised goods related directly to motorcycling and the automotive industry more generally, however, occasionally hand creams, soaps, shaving devices, and even handguns were advertised. Portrayals of masculinity and femininity found in these journals are not uniform, and instead reflect the acceleration of social and spatial transformations. A selection of illustrated covers from 1930 issues of the DMV's journal (see Image 3.2) depicts various possible representations of motorized masculinity and femininity. Ranging from the futuristic, militaristic solo rider on his motorcycle to the solo female rider, the covers reflect the relative openness of enacting gender through the consumption of motorcycles in the Weimar Republic.[64]

Image 3.2. Covers of *Motorrad-Sport, -Verkehr und -Technik* from 1930.

Das Motorrad: Making Room for Debate

The leading German-speaking motorcycling magazine today, *Das Motorrad*, has arguably been the most important motorcycling journal since the Weimar Republic. In 1929, *Das Motorrad*'s long-standing editor, Paul Friedmann, a Jewish-German engineer residing in Berlin, claimed: "[It is] the largest specialty magazine in Germany, standing at the center of motorcycling life. It has drawn the attention of the widest circles. Through its neutrality, its honest and sincere treatment of all questions of the day, it has become *the* interest organ of German motorcyclists."[65] *Das Motorrad*'s editorial neutrality was evident in debates, for example over the role of violence or in terms of the "youth problem," in which the editors consistently published opinions from all sides, even when they noted their disagreement with an author's stance. Priding themselves on their neutrality, they provided extensive coverage on the full range of new products, both domestic and foreign, even in the increasingly nationalistic later years of the Weimar Republic.[66]

What made *Das Motorrad* so different from other mass motorcycling journals was that it neither represented the interests of any specific club or motorcycle brand, nor provided significant coverage of issues relating to automobiles or their drivers. Rather, it was an open forum catering above all to the interests of independent motorcyclists or those who hoped to join their ranks. On the other hand, through promoting accessibility, it allowed its readers to actively participate in producing motorcycling culture. Following a revamping, a new issue appeared every eight days beginning in 1927, and included a "public opinion" section, a "technical mailbox," a "legal corner," and a "tourist advice" page. Pursuing an inclusionary strategy, the magazine sponsored various competitions, for example, correctly identifying motorcycle parts or brands, the main prizes most often being a new motorcycle and organized excursions in the Berlin area. Encouraged by the editors, readers submitted photographs from their everyday lives, often of their wives and children, as well as travelogues, short stories, songs, poems, and illustrations. Women also contributed to *Das Motorrad* as letter writers and as authors of travelogues, how-to articles, and short stories. Thus, even if the bonds were not as close as with membership in a club, *Das Motorrad* contributed to creating a public that thought itself endowed with knowledge and understood itself as belonging to a community. The boundaries of that community, however, were always contested, as the public debates on the issues of violence, of sports, and of women, discussed in detail in later chapters, indicate.[67] Within its pages, evidence of an incipient consumer democracy can be found.

Byway I: Diet Regimes, Nivea Cream, and "Power-Tensing" Pills for the "Sportsman"

New men, with youthfully slim bodies, clean-shaven visages, and nerves of steel, surfaced as the new ideal of modern masculinity.[68] Advertisements for various personal improvement products, including slimming teas, Nivea skin cream, and pills to "increase the robustness of the body and increase performance," reveal shifts in practices of inhabiting the male body. Images and texts of advertisements published in illustrated magazines demonstrate how the "new man," like the "new woman" and the "modern girl," increasingly reached for mass-marketed commodities to fashion his identity.[69] As "symptoms" of the "lifeworld" of motorcycling, advertisements in motoring magazines present a modern masculine body reworked through the consumer world.

Dr. Ernst Richter's Frühstücks-Kräutertee, an herbal breakfast tea, manufactured by a pharmaceutical and perfume company in Munich, promised men they could "get slim without suffering." "Not only for twenty-year-olds"; their campaign in the *ADAC-Motorwelt* stressed youth and the successes it would bring in the user's "occupation, in sport, and in society." By claiming that "obesity is not destiny," the advertisers conceived of the body as the site on which social status was inscribed and on which to enact aspirations of change. At times marketed towards both men and women, advertisements for the diet tea promoted the cult of youthfulness and the ideal that the body of a modern woman or a modern man was thin, possessing "graceful slenderness" and "youthful suppleness."[70] Herbal tea was, however, only one product marketed at men's bodies. A rolling pin with suction-cups attached, the Punkt-Roller, a German invention also marketed in England, promised that the "joy of life would return." Illustrated with two men, one flabby and one taut, the advertisement exclaims: "They were both equally fat, but their dieting methods differed." The advertisement for the Punkt-Roller suggests that this "pneumatic method" is superior to "internal diet methods alone," and, referring to post-diet flabby skin, that any man who uses a Punkt-Roller will become "youthfully slender and strong."[71] Another advertisement for the device claims that users of the Punkt-Roller will live "10 years longer and become 10 years younger" without having to spend hours working out: "We all know that working out daily is necessary in order to stay fresh, slim, and healthy ... However, who has the time these days to do daily exercise for two hours?" Fitness is a modern preoccupation. Contrasting images provide evidence of the advantages of the product: on the left side of the image a male figure is contorted in a number of athletic and yogic positions, while on the right side a man and a woman, both topless and bearing the marks of the "new man" and the "new woman," leisurely self-massage their bodies with the Punkt-Roller. The Sascha-Selbstmassagegürtel, a "self-massaging belt" that promised to "immediately" give men a slimmer and more attractive figure, is a girdle-like contraption made from "a new special elastic material." Using the belt, a man would "not only look more slender, more graceful, and younger," but it would also help relieve a number of digestive and gastric troubles. "You feel new strength and energy, become nimble, and can execute every movement with no trouble at all." Claiming medical authority by marketing their product under the name of a doctor, the advertisement declares that men need not "weaken" themselves through "crash diets" or "strain" their hearts through "violent exercises and sweat baths." Instead, it pledges immediate results, a "quick and safe" method of losing belly weight.[72] Time was of the essence and youth was attractive—these were the messages that both motorcycle advertisements and diet advertisements disseminated in motoring magazines. Thus, not only did the new consumer society engender new forms of disciplining women's bodies, but men's bodies were, although to a lesser degree, targeted as well.

Concurrent to the emergence in the 1920s of a globalized "modern girl" style, a distinct "new man" style was developing.[73] The new modern ideal of beauty for both men and women was transmitted around the world through consumer products such as cosmetics.[74] Baiersdorff placed numerous advertisements for their Nivea creams and oils in motoring magazines that conjured up images of both new women and new men. In an advertisement that links Nivea to new forms of leisure, a man and woman, both bearing the markings of modernity, pour over maps while the text urges them not to forget to take Nivea along when traveling: "Air baths! Sun baths! Don't forget to first rub in Nivea cream or Nivea oil . . . Enjoy your vacation untroubled [by sunburn], and after only a few days you will be envied for your sporty and tanned looks."[75] Along with advertisements that portray new women behind the wheel of an automobile or sunbathing, advertisements for Nivea that praised the benefits of using the cream before shaving show men looking at themselves in mirrors, their clean-shaven angular jaws and well-groomed hands testifying to their modern sensibilities.[76] As with advertisements that featured modern women, different models of new masculinity were being made available, from the decidedly masculine to the dandy figure dressed in a bow tie with pomaded hair, plucked eyebrows, and wearing what appears to be lipstick on his broad smile.[77] The link to their uses for motorists was made in short promotional articles that gushingly recommended using Nivea to protect hands and as a means of preventing a cold, and in images of motorcycle racers applying Nivea skin cream during a winter "race on ice" event.[78] "Technologies of the self," so central to definitions of the "modern girl," likewise shaped the body of the "new man".[79]

Strength and potency belonged to the bodily attributes of new men, and numerous products were marketed to motorists to remedy "male impotency" and "sexual nervous disorders."[80] Okasa, a pill that "was awarded a gold medal at the Paris Grand Prix," promises men a "reliable" "sexual potency aid" that would help in the case of "premature conditions of weakness." While the advertisement screams out "Attention men!" it also pledges discretion concerning customer correspondence.[81] Products to increase the male libido were often veiled behind the language of "neurasthenia," a medical diagnosis of "sexual nervous weakness in men, combined with a dwindling of the best strength."[82] A modern man, again pictured here with the typical clean-shaven, angular jaw, short, parted and pomaded hair, and determined gaze,

Image 3.3. "Candiolin for Strong Nerves." Bayer Advertisement 1928, Bayer AG, Corporate History and Archives.

needed strong nerves: "Thinking and acting above all require healthy nerves."[83] The chemical and pharmaceutical corporation Bayer chose an illustration of a motorcycle race to pitch their product "Candiolin" in the *ADAC-Motorwelt*: "Are you really physically armed? Strengthen your muscles and nerves with Candiolin, the most appropriate power-tenser for the sportsman to increase bodily resistance and raise performance." Here motorcycling is linked to the conception of a potent "new man" with strong nerves.

Invoking words often found in motorcycling advertisements, such as "reliability" and "performance," these advertisements worked in concert to awaken dreams that modern manliness could be acquired through consumption.

Mobility, Masculinity, and Consumption

Weimar era media was loaded with images displaying the entwined relationship between mobility—understood as encompassing both social and physical mobility—and consumption. The growing trend towards orienting social relations around lifestyles fashioned through consumer goods was on display not only in advertisements and news stories in a range of publications and on film, but was present on virtually every page of the average motorcycle magazine. Performances of modern life, for example, were on parade in illustrated articles such as "Radio-Motorcycle Weekend" and in science fiction stories that linked the technologies of the present to a temporality of a utopian, and pervasively motorized, future.[84] Modern technologies and consumer goods were presented both as complementary to each other as well as essential for living a modern life.

Fashion layouts—seasonally centered advertisements of the newest styles for motorists—were published regularly. These spreads were sometimes illustrated with androgynous sketches, pictorial representations of the oft touted and potentially threatening "new woman" alongside images of the "new man."[85] Women's fashion has been read by historians of the Weimar Republic as playing "an important role in defining modern femininity, as a marker of economic status and social ambition, as an expression of female narcissism and beauty, and as the focus of consumerist fantasies and commodified versions of the self."[86] Anthropologists and scholars of material culture have claimed that clothing is not "simply reflecting given aspects of the self but, through its particular material propensities, is co-constitutive of facets such as identity, sexuality, and social role."[87] If sartorial questions are indeed constitutive of modern femininity, then it is necessary to examine how questions of dress effected and reflected the construction of modern masculinities.

While studies of pre–World War I and post–World War II masculinity have investigated the construction of a "new man" in terms of issues of dress and consumption, these questions have largely been neglected in historical studies of the Weimar era.[88] Julia Bertschik's study of the discourse of fashion and modernism in Germany that cursorily addresses male fashion during the Weimar Republic suggests that "during the short phase of stabilization between 1924 and 1929, the metropolitan masculine habitus converged with the feminine."[89] A number of magazines were devoted to male fashion, and illustrated weeklies such as the *Berliner Illustrirte Zeitung* covered male fashion, including the masculine type of the "inventive engineer, interested in machines, whose obligatory leather jacket even Brecht copied."[90]

Clothing, thus, also 'made the man,' and constructions of Weimar motorcycling masculinity found their visual assertions in clothing choices made by men. "On our weekend rides, Alex wears a beret; in the city he prefers to wear a cap. And someone is supposed to tell me that men aren't vain?"[91] The choice of clothing was an expression of an identity and a symbol of being part of a larger community. On the one hand, motorcyclists' attire could serve to bolster a romanticized masculinity. "Already the clothing, the stylish and practical leather suit with the many stitched pockets, with belt and helmet, give a certain je-ne-sais-quoi, the aura of a knight of the nimble guild."[92] Motoring fashion, however, was also associated with being modern. "Everywhere in these fast-paced times" the worshipful "dance around the motor [makes itself] externally visible in clothing. Whoever wants to participate in society today must be fashionably prepared for all situations." For "worldly people," whether they owned a motor vehicle or not, it was "absolutely necessary" that they owned "modern, elegant, representative" motoring attire.[93] Proper apparel signaled being a part of the motorcycling milieu: "One doesn't want to appear funny looking, but instead elegant, classy, and smart."[94] Leather caps and jackets, coveralls, protective outerwear, and goggles belonged to the standard outerwear recommended for motorcyclists.

Both men and women were often pictured wearing berets, newspaper-boy or baker-boy caps, knickerbockers, and silk scarves. Due to practical issues around clothing and motorcycling, with the rider being exposed to the elements—rain, snow, dusty or muddy roads, and the possibility of needing to make repairs—motorcycling clothing tended to account for more rugged conditions and inhered to a productivist ethos.[95]

Given the need of all motorcyclists, irrespective of gender, for protection against the elements, women's motoring wear was cut in a similar style as men's clothing. One example was the so-called *Kleppermantel*, the brand name of a rubber coat, an example Kurt Möser refers to in his discussion of clothing and mobility. "Originally an article of work and

Image 3.4. Motorcyclists' Fashion. Layout in *Das Motorrad*, 1929 © DAS MOTORRAD / Motor Presse Stuttgart GmbH + Co KG.

sport clothing, a functional piece of clothing for the outdoors," Möser argues that, in the 1920s, the *Kleppermantel* was no longer only a sartorial accessory for "the motorcycle subculture," but had become "everyday clothing for pedestrians, making an increasingly frequent appearance on city streets." The *Kleppermantel* "had a unisex quality, the motorcyclist and his pillion seat rider often bought the coat at the same time and wore the same model. Out of identical weatherproof clothing, pairs of motorcyclists became silhouettes in partner-look, lacking strong gender differentiation."[96] The androgyny associated with motorcycling clothing troubled the gendered dichotomy between production and consumption. One female observer commented, "With the 'masculinization' of the woman today, manifested particularly in sports, there is no great difference between male and female sport fashion."[97] A drawing with a short poem, "Modern Couple," that appeared in 1926 in the *Berliner Illustrirte Zeitung*, "featured two identically dressed young people on a motorcycle, in which the only indications of gender differentiation are a somewhat longer torso on the one and a slight curve of breasts on the other."[98] The accompanying rhyming verse underscores the disappearance of sexual difference: "Motorcycle, Pillion Seat / Pageboy hair of the same cut / Brown horn-rimmed glasses / Both bodies cambered / Both sweaters striped / Spring Idyll."[99] Weimar motorcycling clothing offered a "visual merging of male and female genders," and motorcyclists' choice of donning androgynous attire reveals the complicated and ambivalent relationship between gender, clothing, and technology during the Weimar Republic. Technologies of fashioning the modern self disrupted the neat equations of male as producer and female as consumer.[100]

Owning the newest gadgets was also introduced as a means of promoting male consumerism. Around Christmastime, for example, motoring journals published articles encouraging the gifting of automotive accessories, particularly often cameras.[101] Indeed, photography was often paired with motoring, and magazines as well as motoring companies regularly sponsored photo competitions.[102] Over five illustrated pages of detailed instructions of how the everyday motor tourist, motor sportsman, and motor sports spectator could achieve the best photographic results, one article maintained that "motor sports and the photo camera belong together."[103] Both the camera and the motor vehicle offered novel means of seeing and of apprehending the environment.[104] Living modern life thus required possessing the proper accessories, and the selling of these lifestyle accessories was directed towards men, targeting them as consumers. The language employed in such articles, however, implied that skills and constitutions associated with masculinity were necessary prerequisites for the use of both the camera and the motorcycle. In associating the use of these objects with skill and technical knowledge, an attempt was made to cleave the practice of consumption from masculinity.

Tinkering, Productivity, and Masculinity

New consumption practices, thus, did not on the whole upend normative gender definitions. Tinkering, a central topic in all of the journals and an activity that lent the motorcycling community internal coherence, helped to strengthen the formation of hegemonic masculinity "based on physical toughness and mechanical skills."[105] In the pre–World War I era, having some technological know-how and the ability to make at least some repairs was essentially a prerequisite to being a motorcyclist. Motor sports and possessing technical skills became linked and, as Kurt Möser argues, the "breakdown" was integrated into the culture of motorization. Qualities that were cited as necessary for "overcoming mechanical defects" were mirrored in attributes that characterized late nineteenth-century liberal bourgeois masculinity, especially within a colonial context, such as "self-discipline, proving oneself in adverse situations, self help removed from civilizational contexts, individual responsibility, [and] independence from infrastructures," and that likewise characterized the "habitus of the sportsperson." Proponents of motorized travel viewed acquiring technical skills as an educational tool that would bring about "a new type of person."[106] As Kathleen Franz has argued in the US case, "motorists used tinkering to redefine their cultural positions within American society," and "technological authority" was perceived "as a benefit of auto ownership."[107] By the late 1920s, however, improvements in motorcycle construction, which resulted in increased reliability, and the broader dispersion of both motorcycles and motorcycle repair shops meant that fewer and fewer motorcyclists had to (and thus were increasingly unable to) undertake major repairs on their motorcycles. Nevertheless, one aspect of belonging to the masculine-defined motorcycling community was tinkering, an activity often described as creating an almost mystical bond between the man and his machine.[108]

Emphasizing traits such as inventiveness, patience, skillfulness, and courage, Möser suggests that "maintenance, tinkering, and repairing could be integrated into the bourgeois value system and into the culturally acceptable canon of values. Thus manual labor did not appear as proletarian, but was presented as valuable and compatible with

»SAISONVORBEREITUNGEN« DES MOTORRADFAHRERS

Image 3.5. Masculine Tinkering. In *BMW-Blätter*, 1930, BMW Group Archive.

bourgeois values."[109] Thus, the ability to fix a flat tire was presented as a necessary skill in an age of abysmal roads, but it was also presented as a necessarily skill for the modern man and a pillar of normative masculinity. Other small repairs, such as changing sparkplugs or the oil, were portrayed as almost essential elements of the basic repertoire of knowledge and practices that defined a motorcyclist worthy of belonging to the motorcycling community. Motorcyclists were reminded to always bring a tool set along when embarking on a road trip. One of the cardinal rules espoused by the motoring journals was to always be prepared for a possible breakdown: "The only strong motorists are the ones that know the weaknesses of their machines; hours spent on repairs are like war years, they both count double."[110] Alongside diagnostic questions, the technical mailbox of *Das Motorrad* was filled with letters written by readers about the best way to tune their motorcycles—for example, how to increase the cylinder capacity of the engine, or how to construct a motorcycle from scratch, or how to refit bicycles with auxiliary motors.[111] Other letters included questions from disabled war veterans who wanted to know how they could adjust a motorcycle so that, as amputees, they could ride and steer.[112]

Tinkering was an activity that was clearly imagined and defined as masculine. Despite the existence of women tinkerers, such as Hanni Köhler, who were active motorcyclists and were also openly praised by their male colleagues for their technical knowledge, tinkering was nonetheless discursively firmly masculine, as the cover image of *Motorrad-Sport, -Verkehr und -Technik* demonstrates.[113]

Both the man and the woman are pictured with their gender-appropriate "tools"—his, a wrench, and hers, lipstick. In this image, the act of masculine consumption is rendered opaque by the aura of productivity of repairing the motorcycle, and the act of feminine "repair" is presented as frivolous consumption through the act of applying lipstick. Tools were purchasable objects of male fetishization, however, by virtue of their symbolic connection to the sphere of production, and the act of tinkering with tools served to conceal the act of male consumption. The form of hegemonic masculinity that evolved over the course of the Weimar Republic relied ever more on the identification of masculinity with technological authority and physical strength.[114]

Image 3.6. Tinkering, His and Hers. Cover *Motorrad-Sport, -Verkehr und -Technik*, June 1930.

Byway II: Drawing Distinctions on the Road

While tinkering was an activity that served to smooth over differences and solidify the contours of modern hegemonic masculinity, class divisions continued to disrupt the notion of a frictionless masculine motoring collective. Struggles portrayed in the motorcycling journals between different groups of road users illuminate the relationship between masculine consumption and the creation of social "distinctions."[115] Conflicts over the use of public space put motorcyclists at odds with other users of the road; motorcyclists positioned themselves vis-à-vis bicyclists, pedestrians, railroad and tram riders, and car drivers. Alongside demonstrating the fashionableness of Einstein's relativity theory in Weimar culture, the cartoon "Applied Relativity Theory," clearly demonstrated the hierarchy of road users in relation to class:

1. When he bought himself a bicycle, he looked down contemptuously upon the pedestrians.
2. When he bought himself a motorcycle, he felt sorry for the bicyclists.
3. When he bought himself a car, he pitied the motorcyclists.
4. But when he went broke . . . he bought himself a weekly ticket for the streetcar.[116]

Despite the fact that motorcyclists and car drivers shared a variety of specific concerns, from proposals of new laws regarding the use of

Image 3.7. Cartoon: "Theory of Relativity Applied," in *Das Motorrad*, 1929
© DAS MOTORRAD / Motor Presse Stuttgart GmbH + Co KG.

motor vehicles to the condition of the roads, conflicts between the two groups arose around the issues of safety, sport, class, and generation. Hans Kater's 1928 article, "'The Racing Motorcyclist' and the – Oh So Harmless – Automobile Driver," demonstrates the acerbity of the conflict between car divers and motorcyclists: "Don't our four-wheeled sports comrades feel themselves to be the masters of the rural roads, seeing not only 'women, cattle, and chickens' and chauffeurs as thorns in their side, but 'recently also us fleas of the country road.'"[117] Not only in frequent references to motorcyclists as "fleas," but also that they accused automobile drivers of grouping them together with other "lesser" groups—such as women and chauffeurs—underscored motorcyclists' self-perception as holding subservient position within the larger motoring community.[118]

The difference in cost of the different forms of individual motorized transportation no doubt reinforced the tendency to draw class-based distinctions between the users of the vehicles. In 1928, a two-seat car cost approximately 2,500 RM and a lightweight four-seat car 4,000 RM. In comparison, by the end of the 1920s, DKW offered a tax-free motorcycle that could carry two adults that could be purchased up front for less than 600 RM, or on layaway for 10 RM a week. Heavier types of motorcycles, despite being subjected to taxation, were still approximately one-third less expensive to operate per kilometer than the lightest-weight car.[119] Ownership of a personal car remained out of reach for almost all workers and new white-collar employees throughout the Weimar Republic, and indeed this was the case until the late 1950s.[120] While the automobile industry often attempted to maintain a feeling of exclusivity and to prevent their products as being understood as mass produced commodities, as we have seen, many German motorcycle manufacturers explicitly marketed their products as "the people's motorcycle" and "the motorcycle for everyman."[121]

As the class division between automobile drivers and motorcyclists grew, motorcyclists began to see automobile drivers less and less as "sporting comrades." While the sporting element that was attributed to the automobile in the pre–World War I years had almost completely disappeared by the late 1920s, many motorcyclists still felt that the act of riding a motorcycle was a sporting activity.[122] The growing animosity between the supposedly sporty motorcyclist and the non-athletic car driver was expressed in terms that explicitly linked wealth to deficient, "soft" masculinity. "Sporting stature, hard bodies, proper direction in every life situation and presence of mind? Who fits this more than a motorcyclist? ... I can certainly swing my leg higher than some car drivers with a double chin and two wallets. Even if I had more money,

I wouldn't want a car. Any horse-cart driver can be a car driver."[123] Questions around motoring as a sport fed the social conflict between motorcyclists and car drivers. In creating a distinction between the habitus of motorcycling and car driving, the author highlighted the lack of sports to emphasize the ostentatious and thus improper consumerism of the automobile community.

Another method of reinforcing the boundaries of the motorcycling community was distinguishing and creating a hierarchy between motorized and non-motorized cyclists. During the Weimar Republic, bicycles were posited as the "poorer older brother" to the motorcycle; bicycles had long since lost their status as "bourgeois" and were indeed the most commonly used form, besides walking, of individual transportation for the masses.[124] As automobile drivers began to look down upon motorcyclists, so too motorcyclists began to regard bicycles as inferior to motorcycles. Carl Weihe, in arguing that the motorcycle was a liberator, recognized that bicycles represented a "tremendous advance in individual transportation," while citing the "relatively limited radius of action" of the bicycle as a downside. Weihe argued that bicycles were "dependent on the quality of the work-performance of the peddler, whose job becomes more laborious with every hour, making it nearly impossible to summon up the energy for even the smallest uphill inclines." He continued by positioning the motorcycle between its "older brother," the bicycle, and its "wealthy uncle," the automobile, and claiming that the motorcycle "avoids the vices of the other and self-reliantly offers us all of its advantages."[125] Another motorcyclist commentator redirected the flea epithet by calling bicyclists "fleas of the rural road."[126] Although competition between men based on the engine strength of their motorcycles also existed, creating distinctions also between different forms of transportation helped in part to lend the motorcycling milieu a sense of internal coherence.[127] By framing the motorcycle as "a miraculous" machine that provided not only "material liberation, but mental and spiritual liberation," the motorcyclist possessed a panacea for the everyday troubles of the modern man: "With bodily freedom the soul is gradually freed. Everyday worries disappear, the odds and ends of life are lost to us, a heavy burden falls away; we are free, and relish our freedom in the world!"[128]

How Distant is the Everyday—Motorcycling and New Leisure Practices

"When the campfire crackles and sheds its restless glow, when in the west the last afterglow of the sunset is lost to darkness, then we find ourselves in a completely different world. How distant is the hustle and bustle of the everyday," lyrically waxed one motorcyclist when describing the enjoyment of camping and motorcycling.[129] Thus, despite productivist overtones, motorcycling belonged to a number of new leisure activities that gained popularity during the Weimar Republic years. Motorized modern leisure was a concept situated outside of the everyday world of work. In the mid-1920s, the idea of the "weekend excursion" took off in Germany. The relationship between the demands of the workweek and the rise of the weekend movement were explicitly addressed: "The aftereffects of the war with their great demands on all people, regardless whether brain worker or manual laborer, have convinced us of the need for the weekend."[130] The weekend was portrayed in the journals as providing workers with a necessary respite from the drudgery of work and the city. "Everyman fights desperately for his weekend, and those working in the stifling air of the big city justifiably insist on their right that their bodies can only tolerate the stresses and strains of the big-city noise and traffic chaos if given an appropriate weekly break."[131] In 1927, the Berlin Tourist Office held an exhibition on "The Weekend" in the Berlin Exhibition Halls and published a book of "practical suggestions" for weekenders.[132] While most city-dwelling Germans were still restricted to using bicycles or public transportation or both to travel to nearby recreation areas, motoring journals repeatedly published articles, travelogues, and short stories that extolled the pleasures of the motorized weekend getaway.[133]

One of the major selling points of motorcycling in the perspective of both the industry and the journals was thus the possibilities for leisure that the motorized weekend could provide. Leisure, in the form of the motorized weekend excursion, was depicted as necessary for the health, both mental and physical, of the modern man: "Sitting around at home or in the pub won't give you healthy nerves, but movement in fresh air will. That's why you should get out of the hazy hustle and bustle of the city into the fresh air of the weekend! The solid touring motorcycle for every wallet and every purpose is known throughout the world: Zündapp – The Motorcycle for Everyman!"[134] What it meant to be a modern "everyman," however, was not universal nor was it uniformly understood or experienced, despite the fact that everyman's everyday life was increasingly structured by the rhythms of commodity capitalism.

The division of life into urban weekday and rural weekend partly defined Weimar modernity, as Eric Weitz argues: "Life in the modern city has been alienated, segmented into the alienating workweek, and the lovely weekend full of life and pleasure."[135] The praxis of leisure during the 1920s evinced ruptures in the relationship between time and space in an unevenly industrialized and urbanized society, as Ernst Bloch philosophized in 1929. "Sentimentally the *town* gradually approaches, even its plush, its merely residual plush, becomes like false moss. The weekend in particular is increasingly liberating itself from mere diversion: the wish to become healthy through bathing boils as a cry and a protest." Bloch was acutely concerned with what he observed as the social state of "non-contemporaneity and intoxication" that for him was evidence of the temporal unevenness in German modernity, and a clue for understanding the rise of the National Socialist party. His analysis also included unveiling forms of escapism involved in the praxis of the weekend and the shifting relationship of urban to rural: "The employees of the city ... flee the empty mechanics that capitalism has already thoroughly bestowed upon them and in which, since the increasing bleakness of their labor and since the growing crisis, so few feel at ease in the city that for the first time they vault the trench of arrogance between city and country and allow the myth of the earth into their world: namely as an 'organic' machine breaker that replaces capitalism for them."[136] While motorcycling discourse did not self-consciously attempt to understand the contradictions of modernity, as Ernst Bloch and other Weimar intellectuals tried, it nevertheless often reproduced such spatial and temporal tensions: "The appeal of the motorcycle-touring ride is exactly to be aware of the freedom from time and the other constraints of civilized humanity [*Kulturmenschheit*] ... The appeal of motorcycle touring lies precisely in the freedom and independence from all timetables and other such chicaneries of modern civilization [*moderner Kultur*]."[137] Motorcycling, although a product of technological modernity, could simultaneously be situated discursively within an anti-modern and anti-civilizational rhetoric.

Non-contemporaneous motifs dominated the discourse of the motorcycle weekend, which often portrayed motorcycle campers in terms of "modern gypsies." "Those who search for the romantic in wandering and lingering ... Not like in the old days with a bundle tied to a stick, no, with the quick machine, wandering, hunting, climbing, looking and always just looking. That is the yearning of the sportsman in a leather jacket, helmet, and goggles." With his, presumably male, "wandering comrades," the motorcyclist set up camp: "What a singular appeal does the nightly campsite in the fresh air have, when the air smells so sweetly under a starry sky! Forest and meadow eavesdrop on a summer night's dream, when suddenly in the headlight a neat tent of bamboo and aluminum poles emerges from moss and grass between two towering trees."[138] The fetishization of nature went in hand with the fetishization of the technological object, and constructions of Weimar motorcycling masculinity

Image 3.8. "Motorcycle and Tent," in *Das Motorrad*, 1929 © DAS MOTORRAD / Motor Presse Stuttgart GmbH + Co KG.

embodied contradictory impulses of an unevenly industrialized society, seeking to obfuscate conflict over shifts in the political economy through a retreat into the timelessness of nature.

Thus, the coexistence of temporalities also allowed urban temporality to stand alongside the rural as experienced through a modern technological instrument. The motorcycle, if not necessarily the motorcyclist, was portrayed as being at ease in both the city and the country. For example, in 1924, F. Paul Fritsche described first the advantages of having a motorcycle in the city and its usefulness for the modern man in terms of practicing his profession. He then went on to describe the experience of the motorcyclist on the rural road. "Far away from the bustle of the city and the exciting trade rivalry, in the silence of sublime nature, a man with a motorcycle is a free person, dominator of all his yearnings and all of his desires … What delicious experience brings every such day of relaxation, and when he returns from such an escape to the great outdoors to his workplace, so is he strengthened in the feeling of experienced freedom, and goes back with joy to his workweek."[139] The motorcycle could not only help in overcoming the challenges of the hectic business world of the city, but could also provide a means of escaping that world. Instead of standing in contradiction to each other, the motorcycle offered a method to erase the tension between them.

While, as George Mosse argued, the trope of nature most often functioned to "direct attention away from the impersonality ... of modern technology ... toward preindustrial ideals of individualism, chivalry, and the conquest of time and space," some accounts of motorcycle weekends took a more utilitarian and consumerist approach.[140] In Ilse Lundberg's description of a "Motorcycle Radio Weekend," for example, Hilde and her male companion not only ride out on their motorcycle to a lake with their tent in tow, but they have a portable radio set along with them. When Hilde asks the male companion why he did not climb a tree to attach the radio antenna, he replies that he did not want to ruin his "new knickerbockers." After the radio is set up and she listens with earphones and starts dancing to a "Black Bottom," he "beats the rhythm with a teaspoon on an aluminum pan." Despite the thoroughly modern portrayal of Hilde and her companion, their experience of a "wild jumble of nature and technology" is nevertheless presented as an antidote to the harmful effects of a "dark parlor" in the city and to the monotony of everyday life with "a briefcase in hand."[141]

"Ideal Types" of Motorcyclists—Discursive Representations of the Variegated Habitus of Weimar Motorcycling Masculinity

Within the vast trove of motorcycling literature produced during the Weimar Republic, readers encountered a variety of models of masculine behavior. The different available variations of the motorcyclist reveal the possibilities and boundaries of enacting modern masculinity in 1920s and early 1930s Germany. Unlike the figure of the engineer, who was tied into the process of production, the historical ideal types discussed here are linked by their status as consumers. Drawn loosely from Max Weber's *Idealtyp*, my use of the concept of ideal types understands that while these types are abstractions, they nonetheless can provide a useful interpretive framework.[142] By employing multiple ideal types, I dispute the concept of a uniform, singular concept of German motorcyclist masculinity. The theoretical apparatus of the ideal type nevertheless allows me to trace constitutive and overarching elements articulated within sometimes competing varieties of German motorcycling masculinity. From the simultaneously self-disciplining and disciplined "Sportsman" to the rebellious *Halbstarke* to the conspicuously consuming "Motorcycle Apollo," these ideal types provide evidence of how the habitus of Weimar masculinity was constituted and contested through the practice of motorcycling and the act of consuming.[143]

The "Ideal Unadulterated Sportsman" versus the "Schbortzman" and the "Halbstarke"

Although the "Sportsman" was a hotly contested category, discerning an ideal type of "Sportsman" motorcyclist, based on analyzing both positive and negative discursive representations of "Sportsman" masculinity, is heuristically useful for arriving at an understanding of hegemonic masculinity during the Weimar Republic.[144] Alexander Büttner, the prominent Weimar sports journalist who also authored "A Motorcyclist's Development," contrasted the "Ideal, Unadulterated Sportsman" with the "Schbortzman" in his 1924 book, *My Motorcycle and I: A Book about Sports and Touring*.[145] His portrayal of the "Ideal, Unadulterated Sportsman" listed the "most important characteristics that motorcycle sport is able to awaken and steel in people" as follows: "Alongside bodily flexibility and tenacity are above all intellectual and spiritual values: guts and courage borne out of self-confidence and technical skill, control and consideration in harmonious union, this is what distinguishes an ideal, unadulterated [*in Reinkultur*] motorcycle sportsman."[146] Due to the increasing popularity of motorcycling and shifting demographics of motorcycle ownership, as well as the close association of the automobile with the upper classes during the Weimar Republic, the ideal type of "Sportsman" motorcyclist masculinity varied significantly from prewar conceptions of bourgeois masculinity. Although continuities persisted, for example in the ideals of "self-discipline" and "restraint," recurrent political and economic crises destabilized the smooth reproduction of the social order. The ideal of the "unadulterated Sportsman" adheres to a Weimar-era "code of conduct." Helmut Lethen argues that codes of conduct "draw certain elementary distinctions: between what is inner and outer, male and female." Through registering "separate spheres", "forms of expression" are regulated that "recommend and describe techniques of mimicry in the face of a violent world, subordinating everything to the protection of an individual's defenseless objectivity." Codes of conduct, Lethen argues, "promise to lessen vulnerability, suggesting measures that will immunize people against the shame to which the collective subjects them."[147]

Motorcyclists employed codes of conduct to regulate both individual motorcyclists' behaviors and to internally police the motorcycling community. Writing in to the public opinion column of *Das Motorrad*, one motorcyclist engineer, for example, castigated and wished to cast out those who did not comport themselves according to a "code of conduct" that befits the character of an "unadulterated Sportsman."[148] Associating youth with a lack of discipline, this engineer's conception of who belonged to the community of "Sportsmen" was exclusionary; any attempt to instill self-discipline in young motorcyclists was futile. The engineer begins by speaking of "human materiel," vocabulary George Mosse terms "dehumanizing" and an "abstraction that was at the core of depersonalization." Asserting that, "unfortunately, regarding human materiel, these times are thin," he continues by outlining "the difference between 'sportsmen' and 'riders'": "Let's first pick out among the masses the *Halbstarken*, also known to us Hamburg residents as 'Lions' ... Preaching morals to this category of riders would be to take on a Sisyphean struggle; let us leave the task of educating this illustrious group as energetically as possible to the police."[149] The figure of the *Halbstarke*, often translated as a "young hooligan," is most commonly associated with Germany in the 1950s, but it was already a pejorative referent to male youth in the 1920s.[150] Drawing a strong connection between war and a decline in morality, this author argued that the "brutalization of mores [*Verwilderung der Sitten*] that resulted from wartime must be curbed, and those who have a sense of decency will allow themselves to be steered in the right direction."[151] Pointing to a generational divide between males socialized before the war and those socialized during the war, the author's opinion reflected both a general anxiety about youth during the Weimar Republic and a trend towards drawing a "sharp distinction between enemy and friend." According to Mosse, this trend, amplified through the experience of World War I, "encouraged the homogenization of men ... into a coherent mass."[152]

The "Schbortzman," Büttner's term for a type of miscreant "Sportsman," also relied upon a divide drawn between pre– and post–World War I era morality.[153] Referring to "Schbortzmen" as "stinking heroes," he quoted a newspaper article that blamed the "new era" for their lack of discipline.[154] Sarcastically referring to this type of motorcyclist as "desiring to be admired as cannons," he derided these "heroes of the rural road" for racing "through the landscape as if all of nature was worth nothing more than to be covered in dust." Most of all, Büttner surmised, these types sought to create a spectacle. "If there are no admirers then the most wonderful spurts, the frightful racket of the motor, the dirty stink of castor-oil and the swashbuckling racing pose (with the nose to the front wheel) would also be of no value."[155] Having acquired his motorcycle "with his dear money," all he desires is to be "seen and heard." Büttner intended his "Schbortzman" to stimulate a sense of disgust with the form of showy masculinity that needed spectators in order to feel validated. In this worldview, "Sportsman" masculinity was to be restrained and self-disciplining. Youth and freedom, linked here to male consumption, were portrayed as a danger to the proper order of society, nonetheless, "the 'Schbortzman' just so happens to be a phenomenon of our times."[156] Although he judged the "Schbortzman" harshly, Büttner tacitly acknowledged that new configurations of masculinity centered around male consumption, and such as the "Schbortzman" were certain to be a feature of modern industrial life. Indeed, according to Büttner's own vocabulary, the "Schbortzman" was a figure who "we don't need, but will never be able to eradicate."[157] Such harsh language reflects the intensity of the conflicts over how to regulate practices and behaviors that defined and delimited appropriate masculinity.

Grease Monkey

Compared to the negative image of youth represented by the *Halbstarke* and the "Schbortzman," the *Schmier-Maxe* ("Grease Monkey"), the term for the technical assistant to a motorcycle racer, provided an ideal type that was a positive complement to the ideal type of the "Sportsman." In "The Grease Monkey: His Mores and Customs," an article first published in *Echo Continental*, the tire manufacturer-owned magazine, and republished in *Der Deutsche Motorfahrer*, the youthful character of the term was emphasized. By associating it with other "neo-German" words such as "*knorke*" (swell), "*dufte*" (smashing), and "*schnafte*" (cool), the *Schmier-Maxe* was marked as belonging to the growing urban youth culture: "It is well known that only a truly cool grease monkey is swell enough to guarantee a smashing race." The "Grease Monkey" also held a junior position vis-à-vis the racer; he is referred to in the context of "service to his master"; "his official title is 'assistant.'"

While the "Grease Monkey" moniker also included the figure of the mechanic in the pit at an automobile race, the author maintained that "the only real and true 'Grease Monkey' is the Motorcycle Monkey." The difference the author cited was in the relationship between the "Grease Monkey" and the racer: "The Monkey is as important as the rider, maybe even more important: there is camaraderie in sport, which you would expect under so many layers of grease.... What would a rider be without his 'Grease Monkey'?" While the relationship is hierarchical, with the racer as the "master" and the "Grease Monkey" as the "assistant," it is nonetheless presented as symbiotic—the racer was dependent upon the technical competence of his "Grease Monkey." Moreover he was also dependent on his camaraderie. For example, when "the champion is lifted off his machine, stiff as a rod after hours of racing; when he is supported and carried, his paralyzed bones helped to move again, then the 'Grease Monkey' is also at his side." The "Grease Monkey" also functioned as a moral support to the racer: "And when the rider, who believed himself to be in last place, then finds out that during the race half or even more of his opponents dropped out, then the pride of the 'Grease Monkey,' his friend and helper, is at least as great and as justified as the racer. Whether basking in the glory of triumph, or mourning bad luck, the close connection between the rider and the 'Grease Monkey' is always evident. And it couldn't be otherwise."[158] The relationship between the "Grease Monkey" and the racer echoed both the camaraderie of the battlefront and the brotherhood of the shop floor. In this portrayal, the bond was homosocial, allowing no space for the intrusion of a female.[159] By virtue of his technical skill, his "service," and camaraderie, the "Grease Monkey" represented an acceptable and even admirable ideal type of young motorcycling masculinity.[160] Through the association to technical skill and camaraderie, the "Grease Monkey" was firmly linked to masculine productivity instead of to feminized consumption. As in the case of the "Sportsman," the act of masculine consumption was rendered invisible or irrelevant through the enactment of practices perceived as being outside the realm of consumption.

The Leather Jacket

In contrast, the "Leather Jacket" was an ideal masculine type whose identity was inseparable from male consumption. Hans Natonek, in "The Second Saddle," took the saying "The Clothes Make the Man" to an extreme—the male motorcyclist is portrayed as a "Leather Jacket":[161]

Slowly, a strongly built, about 6-horsepower, new model motorcycle rat-a-tat-tats with restrained energy through the springtime street at the leisurely pace of a flaneur. It turns around and cruises the street again. The Leather Jacket on the motorcycle, a cigarette in the mouth, sizes up the pedestrians. Pedestrians size up the Leather Jacket. A few girls smile. These and those kinds of people. Also some nice respectable girls smile. And why shouldn't they; after all, the pillion seat is still unoccupied, as if it wanted to say: "Please take a seat, Fräulein, the springtime world is so vast and beautiful. You see, if you drive straight down this noisy, boring, big-city street, in just a few minutes you will be in the blue yonder, in the unknown . . .

Consumer commodities—the leather jacket and the motorcycle—are depicted as the most important markers of the man's modern masculinity.[162] Natonek provided the motorcycle, rather than the motorcyclist, with an almost irresistible magnetic quality for women. He implied that without the motorcycle or the leather jacket the man would not have been able to pick up a girl. The clothing and the vehicle he purchased were explicitly portrayed as endowing the man with sex appeal and a masculine identity. Inhabiting the space of the city with the attributes of the flaneur and the consumer, it was only through his possession of both a motorcycle and leather jacket that he was able to conquer the "unknown." The "unknown" referred to two forms of "nature" that were portrayed as "other" to the modern metropolitan man—the rural and the female.

In the ideal type of the "Leather Jacket," the motorcycle provides the man with the means to conquer time and space, but also to become "mighty" and to dominate women. "Enthroned on the front," he is the "leather-clad ruler of the handlebars, mighty man, master over six racing horses, at once exploding forth with a racket like a herd of mustangs." Moreover, "wherever he wants to go, she has to go too, whether she wants to or not. To wherever you ride, Lord, I shall ride there too. (What else can she do?)"[163] The colportage of images around the "Leather Jacket" jumbled class and status markers and performances. Aristocratic in his "enthronement," bourgeois in his "flaneurie" and working class in his accoutrements—the leather jacket and the cigarette dangling from his mouth, the ideal type of the "Leather Jacket" integrated divergent elements of hegemonic masculinity. Ownership of a motorcycle and leather jacket signaled both the ability to conquer nature and women, and the possession of an irrefutable, palpitating, and materially transcendent masculinity. Indeed, in echoing a biblical quote, Natonek presented the ideal type of the "Leather Jacket" as possessing godlike qualities.[164]

Precisely because his masculinity was defined through consumption and appearances, rather than production and physical strength, the ideal type of the "Leather Jacket" was vulnerable to attack. Fritz Kantor's rhyming poem, "The Leather Jacket," pokes fun at the idea of purchasable masculinity.[165]

If you don't have enough for the smallest *Muckepicke*,[166]
Bear it with humility—be a man
And don't quarrel with destiny—
Purchase a leather jacket!

Wearing it on pleasant days you can go
Walking with your "bride";[167]

If you encounter a high-class car,
Stop and stand a minute.

Tell her with a nonchalant countenance,
About your "powerful BMW."[168]
Say only: "It runs like a honeybee!"
And you will augment your reputation.

If the little one also wants to go for a ride
Then just tell her offhandedly:
"Since my win at Monza[169]
The piece of junk is still in the repair shop!"

But when she finally begins to doubt,
Regarding this and that and anyhow,
Then send her packing —
And find yourself a new one, who believes you![170]

In the poem, Kantor reiterated the hierarchical relationship between the sexes, with the male dominant over the female; never does he suggest that the female would be an active motorcyclist, but rather that she would serve as an accessory to him. The leather-jacketed character, however, lacks funds to purchase a motorcycle and is thus portrayed as lacking the necessary consumer item—the motorcycle—that possessed the power to endow a man with the "Leather Jacket" masculinity necessary to not only capture but to hold the interest of a female. While the leather jacket was enough to temporarily maintain the ruse of potent masculinity, without a motorcycle, the man would be suspect and insufficient.[171] In "Little Rules for Motorcyclists," Ilse Lundberg's humorous list of "twelve golden rules," the figure of the "Leather Jacket" resurfaced. Lundberg's eleventh rule addressed matters of a sartorial nature: "The less horsepower your motorcycle has, the more leather is needed in the production of your outfit. Thus the name '100-horsepower-outfit!'" Mirroring the ideal type of the "Leather Jacket," Lundberg linked masculinity to consumption: if the primary consumer object, the motorcycle, was not sufficiently powerful, then the secondary consumer object, clothing, could compensate for insufficient masculinity.[172]

Motorcycle People: Apollo, Venus, and the Enemy

Related to the ideal type of the "Leather Jacket" was the figure of the "Motorcycle Apollo," who was defined primarily through his role as a consumer. A short story by E. Best van Hoven,[173] "Motorcycle People" contrasted the "Motorcycle Apollo" with the "Motorcycle Venus" and the "Motor Enemy." A dynamic and powerful archetype of masculinity, the "Motorcycle Apollo" "can do everything better than everyone else": "One glance—and ten ladies have fallen for him. Two glances—and ten 'also-motorcyclists' won't dare to speak another word. Three glances—and even the most bold traffic policeman would flee, whimpering for mercy. That's the effect the 'Motorcycle Apollo' produces." The "Motorcycle Apollo" indeed embodies a godlike ideal type of masculinity, with both the capacity to attract female attention and to command male obedience authoritatively.

However, like the "Leather Jacket," his contours vary significantly from the ideal type of the "Sportsman" or the "Grease Monkey"—the primary practice that defines his Apollonian masculinity was consumption. His suits are "cut by the best tailor," because anything else would be "rubbish," equivalent to having a motorcycle with a low-powered engine. He would never been seen without a crash helmet or leather cap, except "when he's under the hair dryer. But even then he is breathtakingly beautiful, the 'Motorcycle Apollo,' and when he lights a cigarette on top of that—well!" Cosmetics are an important part of his beauty regimen, and unlike the "Sportsman," the "Motorcycle Apollo" seeks to avoid the effects of the elements on his skin: "Before every ride he anoints his visage with a strong smelling cosmetic, so that sun and dirt will have no effect. He never rides without gloves. Never without a shaving kit. Never without Chypre Extra from Houbigant."[174] While there is a definite satirical element to Best van Hoven's portrayal of the "Motorcycle Apollo," the fact that consumption defines his identity is presented as neither unthinkable nor as a specific problem. Above all, commanding the "appropriate motorcycle, a racing machine of the strongest caliber" that "makes noise enough for three, spews out enormous amounts of exhaust" and "howls like an East Asia steamer in the densest fog" is a requisite for being "Mr. Motorcycle Apollo." She portrayed him as a singular icon of modern masculinity, his masculinity defined by what and how he consumed. An "inimitable" character, he views: "Inclines of 30 percent: a bagatelle. Overtaking a 60-horsepower vehicle 500 meters ahead: a bagatelle. Cutting the most hellish curves at full throttle: a bagatelle. Running over an entire choral society: a bagatelle." A blasé attitude towards conquering space, regardless of danger to life and limb, is a characteristic of the condition of motorized modernity. While Best-van-Hoven took her portrayal of the "Motorcycle Apollo" to extremes, she also claimed that he was a "most charming fellow" and, in the negative comparison with the

"Motor Enemy," presented the "Motorcycle Apollo" as an archetype of modern masculinity.

Like the "Motorcycle Apollo," his female counterpart, the "Motorcycle Venus" is also presented in mythical terms, yet is also defined through her consumption: "She can do everything better than the others. No one can sit as regally on the pillion seat as she can. Her breeches are a poem, her leather jacket a thorn in the eye of all of her female acquaintances, her boyfriend, however … can even awaken the envy of the gods." In addition, she is "able to speak about everything, without her, nothing would work, no one else can understand as well as she can. What is a motorcycle without a female pillion seat rider? Exactly as much of an unviable creation as a man without a motorcycle." She also "knows no fear," "knows all the brands of motorcycles," and demands more speed. Her modernity is undeniable: "It's also pleasant when grandmas and grandpas or whatever other useless remnants from the nineteenth century have to jump quickly out of the way when one passes." Above all the "Motorcycle Venus" has a blasé attitude: just as the "Motorcycle Apollo" sees everything as "a bagatelle," she "couldn't care less" about anything. While the "Motorcycle Venus" represented an archetype of hypermodern femininity, her existence was contingent upon the "Motorcycle Apollo" and she was fated to be an accessory, with her role defined through his. Nonetheless, her presence on the motorcycle was integral to his godlike status—for without her, he too would be an "unviable creation."

The "Motor Enemy" is the negative caricature to both the "Motorcycle Apollo" and the "Motorcycle Venus." This anti-motoring masculine ideal type is presented as "always being from the last century." Portrayed as a crotchety old man, the "Motor Enemy" has an unkempt beard and a walking stick, and is particularly incensed about motorcycles: "The 'Motor Enemy' picks up the scent of the object of his hatred everywhere." Whenever the "Motor Enemy" saw a motorcycle, he was "ready to fight." He would publicly exclaim, "'This must come to an end!' or 'That such a thing is tolerated!' or simply, 'Bah!' He then looks around waiting for a sign of approval. Most of the time the applause doesn't come." Paranoid and spiteful, the "Motor Enemy" fears the modern world. For example, "if the maid is beating the carpet (God save him from the vacuum cleaner!), he will say: 'Naturally, there goes another one of those things backfiring through the streets in the early morning, so that a respectable citizen can't get any sleep.'" Most of all, in contrast to the "Motorcycle Apollo," the "Motor Enemy" is notable for his impotence. In a speech to his regular's table, the "Motor Enemy" proclaimed: "'But if the police themselves are riding motorcycles, which I have seen with my own eyes today, then we are powerless, totally powerless, my dear sirs. Only a flood of biblical proportions will be able to help us!!!'"[175] The antiquated views of the "Motor Enemy" were portrayed as out of synch with the modern era. Lost to the future, the enemies of motorization were resigned to the past. Although the "Motorcycle Apollo" was an exaggeration of an ideal type of modern motorcycling masculinity, Best-van-Hoven's transparent portrayal of his participation in consumer society was, in opposition to the "Motor Enemy," presented as the perhaps lamentable, but undoubtedly inexorable future.

Conclusion

Identifying ideal types of motorcycling masculinity reveals the deep schisms not only in which practices and behaviors were accepted as constituting appropriate masculinity within the motorcycling community internally, but also in general in the Weimar Republic. No "unique logic of meaning and identity" dominated motorcycling discourse during the 1920s.[176] While masculinity was not the only category undergoing intense negotiation, in concert with other social categories such as class, generation, geography, and femininity, masculinity provides a valuable lens for understanding the social landscape of the period. In the post–World War I era, structural upheavals in terms of politics, economy, and society were reflected in general anxiety about youth. In contrast to the figure of the "Ideal Unadulterated Sportsman," the figures of the "Schbortzman" and the *Halbstarke* provide evidence of an intergenerational struggle both within the motorcycling community and the community at large, and points to how the questions around youth and discipline were a major source of conflict during the Weimar Republic.

Modern masculine identities, like modern femininities, were increasingly enmeshed with practices of consumption. A mass industrial, mass consumer economy necessitated male participation in consumption. Yet German motorcyclists struggled over how to incorporate the act of male consumption into a repertoire of masculine practices and behaviors. Consumption, generally associated with a loss of masculine identity (and power), put male motorcyclists in need of a redefinition of the relationship between masculinity and modes of production, consumption, and leisure that would preserve and strengthen their privileged status. One alternative, embodied in the figures of the "Leather Jacket" and the "Motorcycle Apollo," was to embrace consumption as a new way to exert power over women, nature, and other men. Another alternative was to locate motorcycling masculinity within the field of sports, and that framed it as a set of practices situated discursively outside of the modern world of consumer goods.

Notes

1. The cover image of this book is also from the same campaign. The artist of this image, however, is not Hohlwein.
2. Merki, *Der holprige Siegeszug*, Table 9, 109; Table 11, 123.
3. Herbert Schmidt-Lamberg, "Verbreitung des Motorrades in den verschiedenen Berufsgruppen," *Motorrad-Sport, -Verkehr und-Technik*, no. 49, 1930, 4.
4. See endnote 3 of Introduction.
5. Mosse, *Fallen Soldiers*, 7; Kühne, *Kameradschaft*; Kühne, *Belonging and Genocide*.
6. On the "motorcycling milieu" in Britain, see Potter, "An Exploration of Social and Cultural Aspects of Motorcycling," especially 51–100 and 190–233.
7. Gijs Mom offers some comparative data on the spread of the car and the motorcycle in North Atlantic countries. See Mom, *Atlantic Automobilism*, 287–306.
8. Members not listing an occupation represent 6.1 percent of the total sample. Ten occupations listed were not clear or could not be grouped easily into one of these categories (1.7 percent of total sample). 1924 statistics are author's own, compiled from *Der Motorradsport; motorsportliche Mitteilungen bayrischer Motorradklubs*, VNFM, Verlag Druck A. Mayer [1924].
9. Dietmar Petzina, Werner Abelshauser, and Anselm Faust, *Sozialgeschichtliches Arbeitsbuch: Materialien zur Statistik des Deutschen Reiches 1914–1945*, vol. 3, in *Statistische Arbeitsbücher zur neueren deutschen Geschichte*, ed. Jürgen Kocka and Gerhard A. Ritter (Munich: C.H. Beck, 1978), 55.
10. While no women were listed with a professional designation, one was listed as "wife" and another as "wife of an engineer."
11. See Chapter 1, and Steinbeck, *Das Motorrad*, 132–70.
12. Stiftung Deutsches Technikmuseum Berlin, Historisches Archiv. FA Zündapp, 1.2.004 AK B0898: Zündapp-Verkaufsbüro Köln: Aufstellung der Verbraucher-Geschäfte in der Zeit vom 1.1.1929–31.7.1929 and FA Zündapp, 1.2.004 AK B0899: Zündapp-Verkaufsbüro München: Aufstellung der Verbraucher-Geschäfte in der Zeit vom 1.1.1929–31.7.1929.
13. Schmidt-Lamberg, "Verbreitung des Motorrades," 3.
14. Compilation of occupations based on motorcycle registrations from *Straße und Verkehr*, nos. 1–3, 1929.
15. Ibid. See also Table 9b "Erwerbspersonen nach Wirtschaftsbereichen (in percent)," Petzina, Abelshauser, and Faust, *Sozialgeschichtliches Arbeitsbuch*, 55.
16. Following his "economic-psychological" approach, Schmidt-Lamberg attributed the high number of unemployed to the "active drive of the Rhinelander to a self-employed occupation in times of unemployment." He asserted that these unemployed persons sought to create employment for themselves as couriers. Dr. Herbert Schmidt-Lamberg, "Die Motorisierung des Rheinlandes. Eine wirtschaftspsychologische Untersuchung," *Rheinische Heimatsblätter*, no. 4, 1932, 126–27.
17. Schmidt-Lamberg, "Verbreitung des Motorrades," 4.

18. *Straße und Verkehr*, no. 1, 7 January 1929. Siegfried Kracauer's exposé, *The Salaried Masses*, provides a vivid description of this new class of employee.
19. See Richard Biernacki, *The Fabrication of Labor: Britain and Germany, 1640–1914* (Berkeley: University of California Press, 1995).
20. "Arbeiter oder Mitarbeiter?," *Der Schlossermeister; Fachzeitschrift zur Förderung von Technik und Wirtschaft*, no. 41, 1927, 725–26.
21. Economic theorists such as Werner Sombart and Karl Schmoller employed conflicting characteristics to define "craft trades" and "industrial factories." See Konrad Kroeker, *Fabrik- oder Handwerksbetrieb; Ein Versuch zur Aufstellung leicht anwendbarer Unterscheidungsmerkmale der beiden Betriebsformen* (Berlin: Carl Heymanns Verlag, 1927), 5–6.
22. Alf Lüdtke, "The 'Honor of Labor': Industrial Workers and the Power of Symbols under National Socialism," in *Nazism and German Society, 1933–1945*, ed. David Crew (London and New York: Routledge, 1994), 72.
23. Lüdtke, "The 'Honor of Labor,'" 87, 77.
24. Seiler, *Republic of Drivers*, 17–35. Eric Jensen makes a similar argument in regard to the importance of sports during the Weimar Republic. See Jensen, *Body by Weimar*, 6–8.
25. Geiger invoked the term "social habitus" within this work. The question of *Mentalität* (mentality) was his central research problem. Geiger, *Die soziale Schichtung*, III–IV, 13, 77–82.
26. Here Geiger uses the term *Lebensduktus* (life-characteristic or life-flow) instead of social habitus. Geiger, *Die soziale Schichtung*, 80.
27. On the importance of clubs and journals for popularizing "mobility machines," see Möser, 59–60, 299–302; and Merki, *Der holprige Siegeszug*, 222–29, 303–16.
28. Weihe, "Das Kraftrad als Befreier," 13.
29. In 1925, Braunbeck's address book listed approximately seven hundred motoring clubs Germany-wide. See Braunbeck, *Braunbecks Addressbuch*.
30. For more on the ADAC and motorcycling during the Weimar Republic, see Steinbeck, *Das Motorrad*, 126–29.
31. See "Die Förderung des Motorradsports," *Rad-Welt*, no. 12, 1923, n.p.; "Motorradsport: Der A.D.A.C.-Hauptversammlung," *Rad-Welt*, no. 14, 1923, n.p.; "Die Krisis im Motorradsport: Vertiefung der Gegensätze," *Rad-Welt*, no. 24, 1923; F. Paul Fritsche, "Zusammenschluß der Motorradfahrer," *Rad-Welt*, no. 28, 1923.
32. "Deutscher Motorradfahrer-Verband," *Rad-Welt*, no. 32, 1923.
33. In 1925, another vitriolic exchange in the respective journals of the clubs took place. See Hugo Kalinowski, "Der verstorbene Sportgemeinschaft D.M.V.-A.D.A.C.," *Motorrad-Sport, -Verkehr und -Technik*, no. 16, 1925, 8–9; "Nochmals A.D.A.C.-Spiegel," *Motorrad-Sport, -Verkehr und -Technik*, no. 25, 1925, 7–8.
34. "Statistisches aus den deutschen Kraftfahrer-Verbände," *ADAC-Motorwelt*, no. 10, 1929, 6. See also Steinbeck, *Das Motorrad*, 129.
35. For example, Deutscher Motorradfahrer-Verband (DMV) an MInn, 17.3.25, MINN 66417 (1.11.1924–30.6.1925), Kraftfahrzeug allgemein, Ministerium des Innern, Bayerische Hauptstaatsarchiv; Dr. Rödel, "Der 'Fortschritt' in der steuerlichen und verkehrsgesetzlichen Behandlung des Kraftfahrers," *Motorrad-Sport, -Verkehr und -Technik*, no. 7, 1926, 8; Hugo Kalinowski, "Die Bemühungen des DMV zur Schonung der Motorräder bei der Erhöhung der Kraftfahrzeugsteuer," *Motorrad-Sport, -Verkehr und -Technik*, no. 10, 1926, 10–11; Dr. Luckow, "Mitteilungen unserer juristischen Abteilung, Maßnahmen gegen

verkehrsfeindlichen Anordnungen," *Motorrad-Sport, -Verkehr und -Technik*, no. 33, 1928, 16.

36. In 1924, the DMV held its annual meeting in Naumburg an der Saale; the 1925 meeting was in Nuremburg, and 1926 in Düsseldorf. These annual meetings were quite large; for example, over 240 motorcyclists took part in the rally and over 100 more attended the meeting in Nuremburg. "DMV-Hauptversammlung in Nürnberg," *Motorrad-Sport, -Verkehr und -Technik*, no. 12, 1925, 6. "Heil Euch in Düsseldorf!," *Motorrad-Sport, -Verkehr und -Technik*, no. 19, 1926, 11.

37. "Motorradfahrer, tretet dem DMV bei!," *Motorrad-Sport, -Verkehr und -Technik*, no. 1, 1924, 7.

38. Artur Vieregg, "Pflege des Klubsportes," *Motorrad-Sport, -Verkehr und -Technik*, no. 42, 1926, 8.

39. Kühne, *Kameradschaft*, 29, 62.

40. Ibid., 95.

41. The DMV organ, *Motorrad-Sport, -Verkehr und -Technik*, often published articles about women either as active or passive motorcyclists. See Chapter 6.

42. "Der große Münchener Motorsport-Tag und der Motor-Club 'Knatternde Gesell' (M.K.G.)," *Motorrad-Sport, -Verkehr und -Technik*, no. 28, 1925, 10–11.

43. For example, see the photo album, Mein Sport-Album, Photo-Haus Alb. Eichhorn, Plauen, Stiftung Deutsches Technikmuseum Berlin, Historisches Archiv.

44. Staatsarchiv München, Polizei-Direktion Sachakten 5899: Motorrad-Club-München 1910.

45. They reported having 127 members in 1927. Staatsarchiv München, Polizei-Direktion Sachakten 5892: Klub für Motorsport "Sturmvogel."

46. In contrast, the "Motorsport Club München," a non-DMV aligned club that claimed to be both apolitical and non-religious, explicitly allowed women who were in possession of their own motor vehicle to join as active members. Due to low female ownership levels, the fact that a club was potentially open to female membership would not have had much influence on the actual numbers of female members of motoring clubs. Nonetheless, it does demonstrate that, at least technically, overall the organized members of the motorcycling milieu did not foster an exclusively homosocial environment. Staatsarchiv München, Polizei-Direktion Sachakten, 5885: Motorsportklub München-Ost.

47. The DMV was loosely affiliated with the AvD. "Statistisches aus den deutschen Kraftfahrer-Verbände," 6. See also AvD, ed. *100 Jahre AvD; 100 Jahre Mobiliät* (Königswitter: Heel, 1999); *Motor-Tourist, Zeitschrift der Deutschen Touring-Clubs.*

48. Horst-Peter Schulz and Hermann Rösch, eds., *Der (Arbeiter) Rad und Kraftfahrbund "Solidarität": ein Verzeichnis seiner Bestände im Archiv der Sozialen Demokratie und in der Bibliothek der Friedrich-Ebert-Stiftung* (Bonn: Historisches Forschungszentrum, 1996). See also, Robert F. Wheeler, "Organized Sport and Organized Labour: The Workers' Sports Movement," *Journal of Contemporary History* 13, no. 2 (April 1978): 197–98.

49. "Der Motorradsport der 'Solidarität,'" *Sportpolitisches Rundschau*, no. 5, 1930, 115.

50. *Concordia, Organ des deutschen Rad- und Motorfahrer-Verbandes "Concordia" e.V.*, Bamberg.

51. "Der neue, nationale Automobilclub," *Der deutsche Motorfahrer*, no. 10, 1929, 12–13. After the National Socialist *Gleichschaltung* in the summer of 1933, Carl Eduard von Sachsen-Coburg und Gotha went on to become the Reichsbeauftragter für das Kraftfahrwesen [Reich Commissioner for Motor Vehicle Matters] and was honorary president of Der Deutsche Automobil Club [The German Automobile Club, DDAC]. See Dorothee Hochstetter, *Motorisierung und "Volksgemeinschaft", Das NSKK 1931–1945*, Institut für Zeitgeschichte 68, (Munich: C.H. Beck, 2005), 213; "Präsidium und Leitung des DDAC," *DDAC-Motorwelt*, no. 46–47, 1933, 3.

52. Pamela E. Swett, *Neighbors and Enemies: The Culture of Radicalism in Berlin, 1929–1932* (Cambridge: Cambridge University Press, 2004), 142; *Münchner Post*, no. 190, 20 August 1930, 2.

53. According to police reports from Munich, the SA-Motorsturm first appeared in the election campaign in April 1930. They understood themselves as an *Überfallkommando* (flying squad). They also claimed to have "nothing to do with the NS-Automobile Corps." Pol.-Dir-München Sachakten, 6833: SA-Motorsturm. The NSKK was a subordinate organization of the Nazi Sturmabteilung (SA). See Hochstetter, *Motorisierung und "Volksgemeinschaft,"* 25–35.

54. There were also motorized members of the Communist Party's *Rote Frontkämpferbund*, see Lützen, "Radfahren, Motorsport, Autobesitz," 371; *AIZ*, no. 23, 1930, 458; *AIZ*, no. 40, 1930, 795; Swett, *Neighbors and Enemies*, 184, footnote 151.

55. Hochstetter, *Motorisierung und "Volksgemeinschaft,"* 60–62.

56. "Sitten der Strasse," in *Das Motorad*, 1929: 1733.

57. "BMW Clubnachrichten," *BMW-Blätter*, no. 9, 1931, 6.

58. "Zündapp Club Berlin e.V.," *Motorrad-Sport, -Verkehr und -Technik*, no. 45, 1928, 33; "'Marken' Club oder unabhängiger Club?," *Der deutsche Motorfahrer*, no. 4, 1930, 13–14. See also Braunbeck, *Braunbecks Adressbuch*.

59. Kracauer, *The Salaried Masses*, 77.

60. "Halt! Werbt für Euern Verband!," *Motorrad-Sport, -Verkehr und -Technik*, no. 49, 1926, n.p.

61. "Aktuelles: DMV am Ende – Der Deutsche Motorradfahrer-Verband in schwerer finanzieller Bedrängnis," *Der Motorsportler*, no. 11, 1932, 9. It is, however, possible that some of the members decided to leave the DMV to join politically oriented motorcycle groups in the early 1930s as budgets grew tighter and the political situation in Germany became increasingly radicalized with the growing severity of the World Economic Crisis.

62. In comparison, Braunbeck's 1925 edition of the same book had listed only forty-five trade journals. Braunbeck, "Fachzeitschriften und Sportzeitschriften des Motorfahrzeugwesens," in *Braunbecks Adressbuch*.

63. Review of *College Girls*: " … especially women will read this description of one of the most incomprehensible problems in the land of unlimited possibilities: the morals of the American bourgeoisie and especially the women. Fabian, like Sinclair Lewis, dos Passos, and all others who dare to tell the truth, shows in *College Girls* the superficial morality under the social mask of America." "Bücherschau: Werrner Fabian, *College Girls*, Roman aus dem Leben amerikanischer Studentinnen," *Motorrad-Sport, -Verkehr und -Technik*, no. 32, 1930, 21. Review of *Die Schönheitspflege des Mannes* asserts: "The unkempt man does not get ahead in his occupation, he has no successes is society, he doesn't feel

accepted anywhere and is rejected everywhere … It is well known that men are more vain than the weaker sex." "Bücherschau: *Die Schönheitspflege des Mannes* von Dr. med. Rothe," *Das Auto*, no. 28, 1927, 784. The masculine ideal presented in Dr. med E. Rothe's beauty care manual puts forth a vision of masculinity that is based on physical health, mental faculties, and strength: "Before the war, intellectual education was popular. The professor controlled the era. Then it was pure strength. The boxer, the record-breaker was glorified. Maybe we now belong to an era where the holy trinity of spirit, strength, and health will be appreciated in man." E. Rothe, *Schönheitspflege des Mannes* (Berlin: Max Hesses Verlag, 1927), 23.

64. See Eric Weitz' chapter on "Bodies and Sex," in *Weimar Germany*, 297–330.
65. *Das Motorrad*, 1928: 2.
66. Friedmann, a German Jew, was taken to task for having an anti-nationalist standpoint; writing in his defense, he stated: "We do not act in a nationalist or an anti-nationalist manner." "Deutschland c/a Ausland," *Das Motorrad*, 1929: 1633. This became a particularly contentious point in the early 1930s—see Epilogue.
67. Another such debate in *Das Motorrad* focused on whether or not it was appropriate for dentists, because of their supposed need for a steady hand, to ride motorcycles, and was framed in terms of the potential physical harms and benefits, mirroring debates that focused on the potential harms and benefits of motorcycling on the female anatomy. The debate on dentists and motorcycles took place in 1929, with all of the respondents, four dentists and two doctors, agreeing that motorcycling posed no problem for dentists, as long as the dentist was "hygienic" and did not tinker on his motorcycle during office hours. "Öffentliche Meinung 301–307, Darf ein Zahnarzt Motorradfahren?," *Das Motorrad*, 1929: 1046–47.
68. Schmidt, *Sich hart machen, wenn es gilt*, 69–72, 84–86.
69. Schmidt, *Sich hart machen, wenn es gilt*; Lynn, "Contested Femininities"; Weinbaum et al., *The Modern Girl*.
70. See advertisements: "Schlanker ohne Qualen," *ADAC-Motorwelt*, no. 27, 1931, 29; "Nicht nur für Zwanzigjährige," *ADAC-Motorwelt*, no. 27, 1932, 38; "Dicksein ist nicht Schicksal," *ADAC-Motorwelt*, no. 29, 1932, 38; "Schlank ist jugendlich," *ADAC-Motorwelt*, no. 40/41, 1931, 26.
71. "Beide waren gleich Dick," *ADAC-Motorwelt*, no. 47, 1927, 44.
72. "Schlanke Figur," *ADAC-Motorwelt*, no. 11, 1926, 43.
73. See the collections at the John W. Hartman Center for Sales, Advertising, and Marketing in the David M. Rubenstein Rare Book and Manuscript Library at Duke University. Many of their collections are available online.
74. Modern Girl Research Collective (MGRC), "The Modern Girl Around the World: Cosmetics Advertising and the Politics of Race and Style," in Weinbaum et al., *The Modern Girl*, 25–54. See also, Poiger, "Fantasies of Universality?," 317–44.
75. "Mit Nivea in den Ferien," *ADAC-Motorwelt*, no. 30, 1933, 19.
76. For ads portraying the new woman, see "Die Frühling fordert sorgfältige Hautpflege mit Nivea Creme," *ADAC-Motorwelt*, no. 15, 1930, 13; "Freilicht, Freilut und Sonne!," *ADAC-Motorwelt*, no. 33, 1930, 9; "Auf jeder Fahrt!," *ADAC-Motorwelt*, no. 21, 1932, 11; "Nur Nivea Creme," *ADAC-Motorwelt*, no. 7, 1930, 15. For ads depicting men, see three different ads with the same title depict variations of new men: "Vor dem Rasieren," *ADAC-Motorwelt*, no. 48, 1928, 11; *ADAC-Motorwelt*, no. 32, 1932, 11; and *ADAC-Motorwelt*, no. 51/52, 1932,

21; two different ads titled "Angenehmes Rasieren" also portray different types of men. See *ADAC-Motorwelt*, no. 36, 1929, 17; and *ADAC-Motorwelt*, no. 39, 1930, 11.

77. "Jawohl!," *ADAC-Motorwelt*, no. 12, 1928, 13.
78. "Welche Handcreme soll man nehmen?," *ADAC-Motorwelt*, no. 28, 1928, 32; "Vorbeugung gegen Schnupfen," *ADAC-Motorwelt*, no. 50, 1928, 21; photo caption: "Die Fahrer beschmieren sich mit Nivea-Creme," in the article "Winterfahrt 1930 Garmisch-Partenkrichen," *ADAC-Motorwelt*, no. 7, 1930, 8.
79. MGRC, "Modern Girl," 50.
80. "Sexuelle Nervenschwäche (Impotenz) – Herbaria," *ADAC-Motorwelt*, no. 3/4, 1933, 27. See also Schmidt, *Sich hart machen*, 86–88.
81. "Achtung Männer," *ADAC-Motorwelt*, no. 32, 1928, 28.
82. Ad published in the working-class weekly, *AIZ*. On the same page there is an ad for Stock motorcycles that promises "the inevitable increase in performance." See "Neurasthenie," and "Die ganze Kreis," in *AIZ*, no. 15, 1927, 12.
83. "Nerven! Nerven!! Nerven!!! – Biomalz," in *AIZ*, no. 40, 1929, 795.
84. "Motorrad-Radio-Wochenende," *Das Motorrad*, 1928: 466–68; Marlice Hinz (Text and Drawings) "Die Eroberung des Weltalls," *Motor und Sport*, no. 18, 1927, 34; Gustavau, "General Opel ändert das Weltbild," *Das Motorrad*, 1929: 576.
85. Illustrations to article by Gerda Wunderlich: "Die Kleidung der Wanderfahrer: Brief einer erfahrenen Motorradwanderin an ihre Freundin," *Das Motorrad*, 1929: 1434–35; Ilse Lundberg, "Auto und Motorrad-Moden," *ADAC-Motorwelt*, no. 11, 1925, 29–30; Ilse Lundberg, "Wie kleide ich mich auf dem Motorrad?," *ADAC- Motorwelt*, no. 5, 1926, 20–22.
86. Sabine Hake, "In the Mirror of Fashion," in von Ankum, *Women in the Metropolis*, 185. See also Breward, *The Hidden Consumer*, 1–2.
87. Sophie Woodward, "Looking Good: Feeling Right – Aesthetics of Self," in *Clothing as Material Culture*, ed. Susanne Küchler and Daniel Miller (Oxford: Berg, 2005), 21.
88. For examples that deal with the British case, see Breward, *The Hidden Consumer*, and Laura Ugolini, *Men and Menswear: Sartorial Consumption in Britain, 1880–1939* (Aldershot, Ashgate: 2007).
89. Julia Bertschik, *Mode und Moderne: Kleidung als Spiegel des Zeitgeistes in der deutschsprachigen Literatur (1770–1945)* (Cologne: Böhlau Verlag, 2005), 186–87.
90. Bertschik, *Mode und Moderne*, 187–88.
91. Wunderlich, "Die Kleidung," 1434.
92. Franz Franziß, "Der knatternde Gesell," *Motor-Tourist*, no. 20, 1930, 11.
93. "Motorsport Moden der Saison," *Der deutsche Motorfahrer*, no. 5, 1928, 21.
94. Lundberg, "Wie kleide ich mich," 20.
95. "Die Mode im Herbst," *Der deutsche Motorfahrer*, no. 10, 1930, 16; "Die Mode im Herbst," *Der deutsche Motorfahrer*, no. 9, 1928, 17.
96. Möser, *Fahren und Fliegen*, 223–38, here 228–29.
97. Lundberg, "Wie kleide ich mich," 22.
98. Sutton, *The Masculine Woman*, 30.
99. Anita [Daniel], "Modernes Paar," *Berliner Illustrirte Zeitung*, 9 May 1926, 608; reproduced in Sutton, *The Masculine Woman*, 31.
100. Sutton, *The Masculine Woman*, 30; Ilse Lundberg, "Motor, Sport, Mode," *ADAC-Motorwelt*, no. 4, 1925, 20–21.

101. Alebü [Alexander Büttner],"Für den Gabentisch des Kraftfahrers," *Motorrad-Sport, -Verkehr und -Technik*, no. 51, 1930, 17; also published in *ADAC-Motorwelt*, no. 49, 1930, 14–15; Dr. Georg Schramm, "Winke für das Weihnachtsgeschäft," in *FKZ*, no. 48, 1927, 5–6.

102. "Sport und Photographie erschienen heute unzertrennbar . . . ." "Motorsport und Photographie," *Motorrad-Sport, -Verkehr und -Technik*, no. 48, 1930, 23–24. X.P. Anders, "Die Objektivsubjekt und die Tücke," *Motorrad-Sport, -Verkehr und -Technik*, no. 52, 1930, 6–7. Alexander Büttner published an entire book on motoring and sports: *Das Knipsbuch des Sportmanns* (Stuttgart: Dieck & Co., 1927).

103. "Motorsport und Kamera," *Motor und Sport*, no. 24, 1927, 14–19.

104. Mom, *Atlantic Automobilism*, 137–38.

105. Wajcman, *Feminism Confronts Technology*, 143. For a history of tinkering in the United States, see Franz, *Tinkering*. See, for example, articles: "Pflege des Motorrades, Wie beugt man Störungen vor?," *Motorrad-Sport, -Verkehr und -Technik*, no. 5, 1930, 4–5; Alexander Büttner, "Von Pannen, Hindernissen und andere Landstrassenabenteuern," *Das Motorrad*, 1925: 477–78; Hanno Losotta, "Der Bastler und sein Motorrad," *Motorrad-Sport, -Verkehr und -Technik*, no. 40, 1928, 26.

106. Möser, *Fahren und Fliegen*, 320–26.

107. Franz, *Tinkering*, 12, 8.

108. See the discussion of the motorcycle as "bride" in Chapter 7, "Sex and the Sidecar."

109. Möser, *Fahren und Fliegen*, 323.

110. These quotes are from a humorous book about motorization in a section entitled "Brahmanical Wisdom by Patindraht Aristodaagopel," published in 1933. J.W. Gräf, *Die Hupe* (Radolfzell am Bodensee: Hein Verlag, 1933); also, for example: Florestan, "Ein paar Gebote für den Motorradfahrer," *Der deutsche Motorfahrer*, no. 8, 1928, 14; Ilse Lundberg, "Kleine Regeln für Motorradfahrer," *Das Motorrad*, 1925: 307–8.

111. See "Briefkasten" in *Das Motorrad*, 1927–1932. An example of a 'diagnostic' question: "Briefkasten 2451, Es liegt am Vergaser", *Das Motorrad*, 1928: 702; examples of 'tuning' and self-built motorcycles: "Briefkasten 2438, Der Umbau einer Zweitakt-Maschine," *Das Motorrad*, 1928: 698, and "Briefkasten 2456, Zulassung eines selbstgebauten Rades," *Das Motorrad*, 1928: 705; and an example of a bicyclist who wanted to "upgrade" to a motorcycle: "Briefkasten 1726, Ruppe-Einbaumotor," *Das Motorrad*, 1927: 401.

112. See "Briefkasten" in *Das Motorrad*, 1927–1932. Examples of letters written by war invalids: "Briefkasten 1814, Der Schwerkriegsverletzter," *Das Motorrad*, 1927: 480; and "Briefkasten 1785, Führerschein für einäugige," *Das Motorrad*, 1927: 455.

113. Ryshka, who accompanied Köhler on an overland journey by motorcycle from Sri Lanka to Germany, stated "Hanni knows our machines inside and out." She was the person responsible for the maintenance of the Ardie Silberpfeil motorcycles they traveled on. Max Ryshka, "Hanni Koehlers Indienfahrt," *Das Motorrad*, 1931: 1151–53. For more on the exceptional female motorcyclist Hanni Köhler, see Chapter 6, "Motoring Amazons."

114. Wajcman, *Feminism*, 140–46.

115. See also Lützen, "Radfahren, Motorsport, Autobesitz," 369–77.

116. "Angewandte Relativitätstheorie," *Das Motorrad*, 1929: 534.
117. "'Der rasende Motorradfahrer' und der – ach so harmlose – Automobilist," *Motorrad-Sport, -Verkehr und -Technik*, no. 36, 1928, 3.
118. See also, for example, B. Lenstersok, "Reiseerlebnis eines 'Flohes,'" *Motorrad-Sport, -Verkehr und -Technik*, no. 28, 1925, 28; "Das 'Motor-Ekel,'" *Motorrad-Sport, -Verkehr- und Technik*, no. 17, 1929, 24.
119. Hugo Egert, *Der Kraftwagen im deutschen Verkehrswesen* (Halle a.d. Saale: Martin Boerner, Verlagsbuchhandlung, 1929), 18–19.
120. Lützen, "Radfahren, Motorsport, Autobesitz," 369–70.
121. Edelmann, *Vom Luxusgut zum Gebrauchsgegenstand*, 108.
122. See Chapter 4, "Is Motorcycling Even Sport?"
123. "Öffentlicher Meinung 219, 'Perlen vor die Säue werfen' ist ein Sprichwort," *Das Motorrad*, 1929: 163. See also "Öffentliche Meinung 216, Motorradfahren steigert das Allgemeinbefinden," *Das Motorrad*, 1929: 116.
124. On the importance of the bicycle as individualized transportation, see Möser, *Geschichte des Autos*, 208: "The most important 'people's vehicle' was still the bicycle. In 1932, there were fifteen million bicycles in Germany, whose yearly capacity was comparable to the Reich's railway system. The 2.2 million motor vehicles, and from that sum merely 490,000 automobiles, were in contrast hardly of consequence."
125. Weihe, "Kraftrad als Befreier," 13.
126. Ilse Lundberg, "Die Sozia: Wie sie sein soll und wie nicht," *ADAC-Motorwelt*, no. 1, 1926, 24.
127. See, for example, the short story "Duel" for a competition between the rider of a stronger machine versus a rider of a small-powered motorcycle: Ernst Ernst, "Zweikampf," *ADAC-Motorwelt*, no. 4, 1924, 20–23.
128. Weihe, "Kraftrad als Befreier," 13.
129. Heinrich Rippel, "Motorrad und Zelt," *Das Motorrad*, 1929: 1430–32, here 1432.
130. Theo Rockenfeller, "Das Wochenende des Motorsportlers: Aus der Praxis – Für die Praxis," *Motor und Sport*, no. 19, 1927, 19.
131. Rockenfeller, "Das Wochenende des Motorsportlers," 18.
132. Karl Vetter and K.A. Tramm, *Das Wochenende; Anregungen zur praktischen Durchführungen* (Berlin: Rudolf Mosse Buchverlag, 1928).
133. Rudy Koshar, *German Travel Cultures* (Oxford and New York: Berg, 2000), 73. See Paul Friedmann, "Motorwandern," *Das Motorrad*, 1929: 1419; "Vom Motorrad-Wandern," *Das Motorrad*, 1925: 40; "Wanderfahrten auf Gummi; Die Schönheiten des Motowandern," *Motorrad-Sport, -Verkehr und -Technik*, no. 42, 1926, 14; G.A. Mulach, "Wanderfahrt," *Motorrad-Sport, -Verkehr und -Technik*, no. 39, 1926, 12–13; Thyl Eulenspiegel [pseudonym of Alexander Büttner], "Sommerliche Wanderfahrt," *Motorrad-Sport, -Verkehr und -Technik*, no. 31, 1926, 6–7; Theo Rockenfeller, "Wochenend und Sonnenschein," *BMW-Blätter*, no. 19, 1932, 8–9.
134. Zündapp advertisement 1927, published in *Das Motorrad*, 1927: 16.
135. Here Weitz is describing the silent film, *Menschen am Sonntag*, shot by Robert Siodmak and "written" by Billy Wilder. As befitting a film that has documentary ambitions and that deals with Berlin on a Sunday, one shot shows a woman mounting the pillion seat of a motorcycle, and a number of long shots show motorcyclists driving out of the city. Weitz, *Weimar Germany*, 161–62; Siodmak, *Menschen am Sonntag*, Filmstudio 1929 (1929/2006).

136. Ernst Bloch, *Erbschaft dieser Zeit* (Frankfurt am Main: Suhrkamp Verlag, 1985), 56–57.
137. Vagabundus, "Durch die Fränkische Schweiz nach München," *Das Motorrad* 1925: 60–62.
138. Killian Koll [pseudo. Walter Julius Bloem], "Motorrad-Zigeunern," *BMW-Blätter*, no. 13, 1932, 16–17.
139. F. Paul Fritsche, "Motorrad-Industrie-Verkehr und -Sport," *Motorrad-Sport, -Verkehr und -Technik*, no. 33, 1924, 10.
140. Mosse, *Fallen Soldiers*, 107.
141. Lundberg, "Motorrad-Radio-Wochenende," 466–68.
142. Other scholars of masculinity have also employed ideal types. For example, in his study of historical forms of masculinity, J.A. Doyle identifies six ideal types of masculinity: the heroic man, spiritual man, chivalrous man, renaissance man, the hedonist, and the he-man. See J.A. Doyle, *The Male Experience* (Dubuque, IL: William C. Brown, 1989). See also John Beynon, *Masculinities and Culture* (Buckingham: Open University Press, 2002), 58–68.
143. My choice of the various types of masculinity to analyze was based both on prevalence within the motoring literature as well as for the exemplary quality that each type possesses in terms of its explanatory power for understanding the variegated habitus of motorcycling masculinity during the Weimar Republic.
144. The following chapter discusses sports in greater detail.
145. Büttner's book was clearly popular as by 1925 it was already in its 11th reprinting.
146. Alexander Büttner, *Mein Motorrad und Ich: Ein Buch von Sport und Wandern* (Stuttgart: Dieck & Co., 1924), 92.
147. Lethen, *Cool Conduct*, 18.
148. These aspects are discussed at greater length in the following two chapters.
149. "Öffentliche Meinung 225, Etwas über Motorradsport und Ethik," *Das Motorrad*, 1929: 212.
150. "In the 1950s, the press resurrected the term *Halbstarke* ('hooligans,' literally 'semistrong'), which had been used for young male working-class delinquents since the second decade of the twentieth century." Uta G. Poiger, *Jazz, Rock, and Rebels: Cold War Politics and American Culture in a Divided Germany* (Berkeley: University of California Press, 2000), 80.
151. "Öffentliche Meinung 225," 212.
152. Mosse, *Fallen Soldiers*, 179.
153. Büttner was born in 1897, making him 27 in the year of publication of *Mein Motorrad und Ich*, and in his early twenties when World War I ended.
154. The article Büttner cited at length was from the *Allgemeine Sportschau*, Nuremberg, 31 October 1923.
155. Büttner, *Mein Motorrad und Ich*, 94.
156. The noise of the motorcycle is compared to that of the machine gun and of a "fat Berta": "If he is capable of misfiring the engine, so that it explodes like a machine gun and like a *dicke Bertha* ["fat Bertha"; a 42-inch mortar and one of the best-known pieces of artillery in World War I], then he can be assured of attention." Büttner, *Mein Motorrad und Ich*, 95.
157. The German word Büttner used in this context was "*ausrotten*," which can be translated as either "eradicate" or "exterminate."

158. "Der Schmier-Maxe; seine Sitten und Gebräuche," *Der deutsche Motorfahrer*, no. 6, 1930, 10–11 (there is a note at the end of the article indicating it was originally published in the *Echo Continental*).

159. Nevertheless, the category of the "Grease Monkey" was not limited to men's self-identification. In 1929, a woman wrote a letter to the "Tourist Advice" column of *Das Motorrad*, identifying herself as a "Grease Monkey": "Although I only count as a 'Grease Monkey,' or as my husband says less respectfully as 'Sidecar Fat,' I read your magazine with great interest and have learned a lot from it even as an amateur." It is clear that the man does not identify his wife with the more technically inclined "Schmier-Maxe" although she herself does. "Schmier-Maxe" was also the colloquial term for the person in the sidecar during sidecar races, who helped the driver increase the angle when taking a curve. See Letter: Frau Herta M. in B, "Touristischer Ratgeber 462. Schmiermaxe und Spionage," *Das Motorrad*, 1929: 1396. See also Chapter 7, "Sex and the Sidecar," for the example of Gori, a female "Grease Monkey."

160. The many motorcycle races held during the Weimar Republic fed many youths' desires to become motorcycle racers. While wealthier motorcyclists and engineers dominated the first years of racing during the republic, by the end of it men from all classes were participating in Germany's top-class races. For example, Toni Bauhofer, Otto Ley, and Ernst Henne all began their motor sport careers when apprenticing as motor vehicle mechanics. Hans Soenius, one of the most popular racers during the Weimar Republic, was the son of a publican and hotelier. See Matthias Murko, *Motorrad Legenden* (Nuremberg: W. Tummels, 1994).

161. Natonek, a writer, theater critic, and editor of German-Jewish decent, was born in the Austro-Hungarian Empire in 1892. In 1917, he assumed the post of chief editor at the *Neue Leipziger Zeitung*. He won the Goethe award in 1932 for his novel *Kinder einer Stadt*. In 1933 he was forced into emigration, first to Prague and in 1938 to the United States. Natonek died in 1963. Werner Röder and Herbert A. Strauss, eds., *Biographisches Handbuch der deutschsprachigen Emigration nach 1933 / International Biographical Dictionary of Central European Emigrés 1933–1945*, Vol. 2 (Munich: Saur, 1983), 847.

162. In the 1950s, the "leather jacket" was again raised as the symbol of male youth: "Commentators increasingly identified *Halbstarke* by their fashions. Some simply referred to them as the 'leather jackets.'" Poiger, *Jazz, Rock, and Rebels*, 80.

163. Hans Natonek, "Der zweite Sattel," in *Motorrad-Sport, -Verkehr und -Technik*, no. 16, 1924, 22.

164. The passage rephrased by Natonek was "For wherever you go, I will go," from The Bible, Book of Ruth, Chapter 1.

165. Possibly a very early work by Friedrich Kantor (who later used the pseudonym Friedrich Torberg).

166. Literally "muscle axe," colloquial for a motorcycle.

167. For a discussion of the figure of the "bride," see Chapter 7, "Sex and the Sidecar."

168. Even in the 1920s, BMWs were status items of consumption.

169. An important motorcycle and automobile race held in Italy.

170. Fritz Kantor, "Die Lederjacke," *Motorrad-Sport, -Verkehr und -Technik*, no. 37, 1925, 17.

171. The ability to inhabit flexible identities through ruses, guises, or lies is a common trope in Weimar motoring literature. This is frequently the case in terms of stories about sexual relationships, in which a motoring encounter allows a woman or a man to assume an alternate identity, furthering the concept of motorization as an "escape from the everyday." See Chapter 7.

172. Ilse Lundberg, "Kleine Regeln für Motorradfahrer," *Das Motorrad*, 1925: 307–8.

173. Ernestine Best van Hoven, author of minor detective novels. Reinhard Oberschlep, ed., *Gesamtverzeichnis des deutsch sprachigen Schrifttums*, Vol. 13 (Munich: Saur, 1976), 158.

174. Chypre is a type of perfume (originally made by Coty), similar in status to Chanel No. 5, and Houbigant was a world famous perfume manufacturer.

175. E. Best van Hoven, "Motorradleute," *Das Motorrad*, 1929: 348–49.

176. Gartman, "Three Ages of the Automobile," 170.

CHAPTER 4

"Is Motorcycling Even Sport?"
Strength and the National Body

When *Das Motorrad* published a letter from a reader asking "Is Motorcycling even Sport?," it provoked an intense debate that ran its course over fourteen months in the magazine's public opinion section. In some ways the issue of whether or not motorcycling is a sport has not, even to this day, been resolved to the same extent as it has for cars. Cars, outside of the road trip and beyond the racing circuit, have long been viewed primarily as a mundane means of personal transportation. Motorcycling, however, has never completely lost the allure of its connection to sport, risk-taking, and the fantasy of adventure. Pierre Bourdieu connected this "endangerment to the body" to the "working classes" in his discussion of sports in *Distinction*: "The instrumental relation to their own bodies which the working classes express in all practices directed towards the body . . . is also manifested in choosing sports which demand a high investment of energy, effort or even pain (e.g., boxing) and which sometimes endanger the body itself (e.g., motorcycling, parachute jumping, and to some extent, all the 'contact sports')."[1] The debate in *Das Motorrad* illuminates how motorcyclists themselves understood the practice of motorcycling, and why defining 'sport' was so contentious.

Sport was a field of contestation for the newly emergent mass society. Motorcyclists' contributions to this debate reveal competing visions and articulations of the national body. In light of severe economic, political, and social ruptures, the debate over sports gave voice to both anxieties about and hopes for reformulating the nation through engineering the "new man" and "new woman."[2] Practicing motor sport involved using industrially produced technical commodities, and was thus particularly controversial. By defining motorcycling as a sport, a motorcyclist consciously self-identified being both masculine and modern. What, however, it meant to be a modern man remained contested.[3] Within this debate, different imaginations and expressions of masculinity during the Weimar Republic found articulation, ranging from the figure of the "true sportsman" to the "show-off dandy"; from the "technically savvy cosmopolitan" to the "conqueror over time and space." Building upon the "ideal types" explored in the previous chapter, I analyze the intersection between sports and motorcycling masculinity, and argue that the zeal with which the debate was conducted reflected the depth of social schisms within the Weimar Republic.

The "Age of Sports" — Social and Political Interpretations

The changing demographic of motorcycle dispersion discussed in the previous chapter provides an important key to understanding the intensity of the debate on whether motorcycling could be considered a sport. Prior to World War I, motorcycles were a luxury article for the "less wealthy of the wealthy sports fans."[4] By the end of the 1920s, the motorcycle was increasingly bought, sold, and used as an everyday transportation vehicle.[5] The percentage of motorcycles listed as being used as a sporting good only fell indirectly in proportion to the rising number of motorcycles on the streets.[6] Coinciding with the steep rise in the popularity of the motorcycle, the question arose as to whether motorcycles were still primarily sporting goods, or if they were merely an inexpensive, and potentially dangerous, means of personal transportation.[7]

A second crucial context is the history of the social and political role of sport in Germany and its relationship to the health of the nation. A strong political connection established in the nineteenth century between physical activity and imaginations of the German nation continued into the Weimar Republic. Taken to the utmost extremes under the National Socialists, the relationship of sport to the health of the nation resonates to this day. Prior to German Unification in 1871, efforts to promote physical education were largely framed in terms of fostering nationalist sentiment.[8] The widespread gymnastics movement, whose leading figure *"Turnvater* Jahn" was given the honorific of "father," demanded national unity and national strength.[9] As industrialization, nationalism, imperialism, and urbanization reshuffled the structure of society, new associational patterns began to supplant older forms of sociability. As historian Svenja Goltermann argued, "In an era of rapid social change and accelerated geographic and social mobility, the associations often filled a vacuum in the disintegrating system and changing social order."[10] Associational life blossomed during the years after the unification of Germany in 1871. Religious and political organization of all stripes began to coordinate physical activities in affiliated clubs, a feature of social and cultural life that persisted through the Weimar Republic.

From the nineteenth century onwards, the phrase "a healthy body in which a healthy spirit resides" was often engraved in Latin [*mens sane in corpore sano*] over the entrances of many *Gymnasium*, the German equivalent of High School. The name of the school itself shows the close connection between both physical and intellectual education in Germany, as well as the German educated class' understanding of the genealogy of their educational (physical and intellectual) system as originating in ancient Greek and Roman civilization.[11] In the context of urbanization and intensified industrialization during the Wilhelmine period, physical activities beyond the physical exercises and gymnastics began to find a broader audience. Self-organized youth groups, such as the Wandervogel [Birds of Passage], rebelled against both the harsh discipline of the Wilhelmine classroom as well as the lack of access to open spaces, leading to hikes and camping outings to the nearby countryside, during which they would sing songs praising the beauty of nature. Such "male virtue building" projects strengthened the linkage between the structure of the body and the structure of character. The Wandervogel's self-understanding of their purpose was strengthening masculine attributes and making "boys into men" by sublimating erotic desires through fostering camaraderie and love of the homeland.[12] Weimar-era critic Kurt Tucholsky later commented on the youth movement's ambitions: "If the youth movement has any purpose at all, it is this: to create men. New humans, totally differently minded, a reorganized *Geschlecht* [race/gender/sex]."[13] While signaling the increasing importance of "youth" as a category, the Wandervogel movement did not upset the hegemonic understanding of masculinity, sharing an ideological vocabulary of healthy minds and healthy bodies.

Alongside youth groups and gymnastic organizations, different types of sport, adopted and adapted from the sport movement in England, became increasingly popular in Germany in the years before World War I, even among the working classes. Women and girls, although to a far lesser extent and at a later date than their male counterparts, also began to participate in sport activities and associations. A large number of sport clubs were founded that offered a variety of specific sports, team and individual, to choose from—for example, soccer, cycling, swimming, ice skating, rowing, skiing, and tennis. The first automobile and motorcycling sporting associations were also founded before World War I.[14] The field of sport, like leisure, also offered the opportunity to experience modern mobility. Whether it involved taking a train to see a soccer match in a neighboring city, riding a bicycle to complete in a swim heat, or even reading a newspaper about the Olympic Games first held in Athens in 1896, sports provided opportunities to participate in new forms of sociability, impacting everyday rhythms and transgressing spatial and social constraints. While still primarily a bourgeois phenomenon, sports were evolving into a mass-based industry, both in numbers of participants and spectators.[15]

After the end of World War I, the sport movement in Germany exploded. As sport historian Christiane Eisenberg argues, sports were an "agent of modernization."[16] Sport became a central topic in newspapers, newsreels, books, radio programs, and conversations during the Weimar Republic. The number of sport institutions, associations, and events mushroomed. Sporting goods were increasingly produced according to standards that would appeal to a mass-consuming public, both in terms of affordability and ease of use. Soccer, winter sports, boxing, tennis, horseback riding, mountaineering, motorcycling, bicycling, track and field, and a plethora of other sporting activities commanded the attention of the masses and claimed portions of many paychecks. Increasingly popular throughout the republican era, sport was understood as capturing the "pulse of the times" and as an "attitude to life"; an evocative expression of youth, modernity, vitality, beauty, and strength. One journalist commented in 1928: "Sporting events are the only recurring events in which hundreds of thousands of the most diverse people find themselves with something in common: with the same forgetting of the everyday, in a collective state of euphoria. The single ego loses itself completely, and, of even greater importance today, even the political factions are lost."[17] During the Weimar Republic, sport represented a field in which social and political boundaries could be both transcended and reinforced. Indeed, as with most mass phenomena during the Weimar Republic, the discourse around sport was riddled with social and political ambiguities. Concerns about sports, bodies, and health were indicative of broader conflicts over defining social categories and norms. As historian Eric Weitz eloquently and succinctly commented, "bodies were organized and liberated in that curious mixture that characterizes so much of the Weimar experience."[18]

When the Weimar Republic was constituted in 1919, sport and physical culture, for both the elite and the masses, moved center stage. Edmund Neuendorff, a former leader in the pre–World War I youth movement and a great admirer of "*Turnvater* Jahn" (Gymnastics-Father Jahn), he headed the Prussian High School for Physical Education—an influential organization, founded in 1920, that organized mass events for youth.[19] In his four-volume history of German physical education, he likened the rise of sport during the 1920s to a "true triumphal procession," citing "powerful allies" who helped to make sport "impossible to think away": the mass public, the press, business, and the medical profession.[20] On the importance of the public and the press, Neuendorff was impressed with the fact that even those who were not sportsmen themselves "ran to every sporting event and followed the ups and downs of the contest with enthusiastic attendance." In jubilant terms, Neuendorff celebrated the rise of sport: "A new epochal feeling ruled the people who had been transformed through technology and industry. The meaningfulness of 'being there' that attending a premiere of a Wagner opera or an Ibsen drama once held for the educated public was now transferred to a far larger public of educated and uneducated—for example, when a soccer match between national teams was being played, or when Peltzer or Houben[21] were at the starting blocks and up against top foreign competitors, or wherever an old record was broken and a new one was made." Refusing to reduce mass spectatorship to "lascivious sensationalism," he instead claimed that their participation benefited the reputation and the development of sport. In addition to a proliferation of sports reporting in both metropolitan and provincial daily papers and newly founded specialized sports journals, programming directors for the new technology of the radio devoted extensive amounts of broadcast time to covering sporting events. Sports reporting began to influence the rhythm of everyday life: "Monday morning, men and youth scrambled to get their hands on the sports papers that reported about the Sunday contests."[22]

In the context of the rise of sport to the status of a mass phenomenon, sporting events became symbols of struggles of far greater significance than simply competition between teams or individuals.[23] Although during the imperial period sport was viewed as one instrument for fostering social cohesion, after World War I the social role of sport took on new dimensions. Under the conditions of the Versailles Treaty, mass conscription was forbidden and the size of the army severely restricted, eliminating the two years of compulsory physical training for males that was interpreted by many as endangering the physical material and social fabric of the Fatherland, a view that was widely circulated in the popular and the academic press.[24] Thus, widely propagated during the Weimar Republic, a substantial number of Germans came to view sport as the primary means for regaining bodily discipline and for guaranteeing a healthy population. Nevertheless, there were sports skeptics and, in the nascent German Republic, sport was a key field in which social contestations were played out. Anxieties over sport, health, and the nation spanned the political spectrum, from the far left to the far right.[25]

Motorcyclists Debate "Is Motorcycling Even Sport?"

The lively fourteen-month-long debate was sparked among the readership of *Das Motorrad* when a letter writer attacked motorcycling both for not conforming to the nineteenth-century bourgeois ideal of sports as providing a "healthy mind in a healthy body" and for its inability to provide "a harmonious training of the *entire* body and spirit."[26] He continued by criticizing the supposedly harmful effects of motorcycling, arguing that the popularity of motorcycling was solely due to Germany's relative postwar poverty.[27] A postscript inserted by the editorial board that called for "motorcycle 'sportsmen'" to defend themselves resulted in an outpouring of opinions weighing in on whether or not motorcycling qualified as a sport. Unlike the ideal type of the "sportsman" discussed in the previous chapter, the published responses show how opinions about sport were mobilized from disparate and sometimes contradictory positions, and reveal what was at stake in the competing definitions of sport.[28] The debate also provides ample material for investigating how, through associating motorcycling with sport, the relationship between masculinity and consumption was effectively effaced.

Of the letters published over the course of the debate, the large majority countered the accusation that motorcycling was not sport. A good many of these letters, however, expressed the view that motorcycling did not unconditionally qualify as a sport, although under certain conditions it could legitimately be claimed to be a sport. Only one letter agreed with the original letter writer's opinion that under no circumstances did motorcycling qualify as a sport. The question of how to define sport was central to most arguments both for and against motorcycling as a sport. While the definitions supplied by the authors differed considerably, the letters demonstrated a preoccupation with classification and definition that was common to Weimar discourse.[29] The three overarching concepts that structured this debate were: "presence of mind"/"training of the mind"; "training of the body"/"control over the body"; and "struggle against nature/machine." Secondary lines of argumentation responded to specific points raised in the initial letter about the effects of motorcycling on health, especially in regard to women, the "up-to-datedness" or "modernity" of motorcycling, and Olympians as the sporting ideal.[30] Looking in detail at this public debate provides insight into how sport, as a concept and to some extent as a practice and site for performing identity, was a field in which contestations over the definition of social categories were played out.

The one author who unconditionally agreed with the initial letter that motorcycling did not qualify as a legitimate sport claimed to be a "passionate motorcyclist" who "since 1908 has practiced physical exercises such as gymnastics, swimming, field athletics, ice skating, and hockey." His dismissive opinion of motorcycling as a sport was based on a view of physical culture that clearly derived from the pre–World War I gymnastics movement, in which he stressed that sports should be defined as "intensive bodily movement with as light weight clothing as possible, so that light, air, and sun can exercise their beneficial influence." Motorcycling, a sport that required heavy protective clothing, could thus not qualify as sport. His formulation of proper masculinity and sportsmanship furthermore adhered to the nineteenth-century concept of sport expressed in the adage "a healthy mind in a healthy body."[31] Appropriate sporting masculinity for the two opponents of defining motorcycling as a sport was at once restrained yet active and essentially bourgeois.

Alongside offering his opinion on what qualified as true sport, the author argued that motorcycling was harmful to the rider's health, because "the vibrations necessarily eliminate the harmonious cooperation of body and mind. Each and every vibration presents a small shock, and one's nerves are constantly agitated." Stressing the effect of motorcycling on the nerves, this anxiety over the ambivalent and possibly harmful effects of technology on health should be placed in the context of debates over what could best secure the health of the industrializing nation. He called on "those who would like to see themselves considered sportsmen" to "preserve your health through true sport and don't let envious motorcycle enemies reduce your enjoyment of the manifold pleasures that motorcycling has to offer. However, should someone still want to claim that motorcycling is a sport, let him, in the circle of his 'sporting brethren'—the bowlers, the stamp and curio collectors—feel like a 'cannon.'"[32] Both this letter as well as the initial letter point to ways in which the debate over the concept of motorcycling as sport was embedded in a larger contest over social status and social capital, and experienced and actualized in performances of masculinity.[33] Above all, the two letters that denied that motorcycling qualified as a sport indicated a pervasive unease with many aspects of the societal, physical, and emotional changes wrought by increased industrialization, urbanization, and rationalization, all concerns commonly expressed during the first decades of the twentieth century.

On the other side were numerous letter writers who defended motorcycling as a sport. Their definitions of sport reveal attempts to demarcate the boundaries of a community of motorcycling sportsmen. The caveats to classifying motorcycling as a sport thus provide insights into the relationship between sports and understandings of masculinity, especially in regard to consumption. Within the debate, pro-sport motorcyclists also drew distinctions that delimited proper from improper masculinity. In a letter that addressed the complicated relationship between industrial technologies and bodily health, the "anti-gymnast" tied sports to technology and the strength of a modern masculinity and modern nation. Asserting that what had previously been called gymnastics was now called sport, the author, a World War I veteran, subsequently questioned the value of gymnastics by casting doubt on its usefulness for the "health of the nation." He argued: "The cult of the body and glorification of sun-tanning musclemen won't bring about the kind of people that can endure strains. And you would know that if you had the advantage of going through the steel bath of 1914–1918." He argued that the strenuous activities involved with motorcycling, such as dirt-track racing and long cross-country rides, were more appropriately classified as sport than "Nivea skin cream, walking barefoot, and swimming trunks."[34] Gymnasts and sunbathers were depicted as pretty boys who would not have the wherewithal to defend the nation as opposed, presumably, to motorcyclists. Even the types of physical exercises held on barrack grounds were subject to his scorn. Increasingly coded as effeminate and soft, especially by those who were battle-tested or had suffered from the effects of the postwar economic instability, the ideal of bourgeois masculinity that had dominated the prewar era of sports was no longer deemed suitable for the new era. In suggesting that the appropriate name of the era was the "age of technology" rather than the "age of sport," this author captured the intensity of debates over the ramifications of industrialization on the health of the nation.

Demarcating distinctions was central to how motorcyclists sought to define masculinity in the debate about sports. Class-based distinctions were on display in the frequent mocking of automobile drivers in the motorcyclists' responses, and contained implicit or explicit definitions of manliness. Praised by one author because motorcycling "requires total control over the machine, the body and a presence of mind in every situation," "steeling the body and the mind." This author insisted that motorcycling required "a good dose of courage and sporting spirit, energy, and a firm belief in victory." In order to underscore this version of virile sportsmanship, the author established a hierarchy of masculinity in which motorcycle riders were more masculine than automobile drivers: "We passionate motorcyclists will gladly leave you your seat in your comfortable car. Or do you feel like a sportsman when your chauffeur brings you to your destination in your closed limousine?" Here the motorcyclist's conception of appropriate masculinity conflated sportsmanship with an anti-bourgeois stance.[35] Another letter writer derided automobile drivers with their "fancy gadgetry" and "pimped out" cars with "8-cylinder original sissy motors," blatantly showing his contempt for conspicuous consumption. Proper masculinity, for this author, was firmly tied to austerity; and a motorcycle, in comparison to a car, was an austere machine, stripped of unnecessary accessories and exposed to the elements. He constructed rigid and immobile distinctions that he framed in terms of a hierarchy of masculinities: "We who feel ourselves to be motorcycle sportsmen, we know what our sport is. Perhaps a third of all motorcycle owners are sportsmen by *our* definition." Again, mere ownership of a motor vehicle, even of a motorcycle, was not considered sufficient to claim ownership of the title "sportsman," and the virile masculinity associated with it.[36] Definitions of sports also served to differentiate between different types of motorcyclists, creating exclusion mechanisms based on improper masculinity. The author of yet another letter grouped motorcyclists into three categories: "true sportsmen," "posers" or "show-offs," and those who used a motorcycle as a "means of transportation." In his opinion, sport could be valued in two different ways: "either as enjoyment, entertainment, etc., or as *struggle*, in which ambition is trained." Struggle, in his view, was a necessary component of the right of motorcyclists to claim the title of "true sportsmen."

Tinged with angst, the unease around masculine consumption was explicitly expressed in the author's remarks on "posers" or "show-offs." In a derisive tone, the author scathingly assessed "so-called Sunday afternoon riders who want to impress with unnecessary noise." "First of all: the smaller the motor, the fancier the leatherwear, preferably with a crash helmet;" the author continued by attacking "the others with a huge engine, with creased pants, patent-leather shoes, and without a jacket or headgear. The reason: they want to stand out and are looking for a female passenger. Once they have found someone appropriately saucy, then the ruckus starts, full throttle with an idling engine, flames shooting out of the exhaust pipe." With echoes of the "Leather Jacket" and "Motorcycle Apollo" ideal types, the author did not consider dandy-like "show-offs" worthy of the title of "true sportsperson," and thus also put their masculinity into question; however, he tacitly acknowledged that consumption—be it of a large-engine motorcycle, of fancy leatherwear, or of patent leather shoes—was an important component for self-fashioning a modern identity. Material accessories alone could not confer the qualities of a "true sportsperson." Instead, he associated conspicuous consumption with insufficient masculinity. Arguing against classifying motorcyclists for whom motorcycling was a "means of transportation, for example for a vacation or a Sunday excursion," as sportsmen, he reasoned that, while they "ride most sensibly, for them ... riding is no longer enjoyment. They are, so-to-speak, chauffeurs." Practicing sport, in this author's view, was to be strictly separated from work; it was not, however, also leisure. Instead, the essential quality for a true sportsperson was their willingness to engage in struggle, not for daily bread, but struggle for struggle's sake, a point of view reiterated by other authors. Associating sports with struggle and control over the mind, the body, the machine, and nature was a common rhetorical strategy. The pervasive use of these keywords together signals how motorcyclists attempted to silence their role as consumer by pronouncing motorcycling as struggle. Thus, it was not the motorcycle as a material good that provided the basis for an identity as a sportsperson, but instead how and why the motorcyclist rode the motorcycle.[37]

Motorcyclists also gave expression to social anxieties over the restructuring of relations of production and consumption through invoking the category of labor.[38] Another author, who reported "consuming 20,000 km yearly," took a more inclusive approach by grouping "true sportspeople" into three categories: racers, touring riders, and traveling salesmen. Motorcycle racers possessed "the coldest blooded temperature and are completely entangled with the machine ... The racer has no nerves." On the other hand, the traveling salesmen had to balance the pressures of the "race for time and money, [and] professional annoyances," and so would "hardly be carried away by enthusiasm for nature or his fellow humans," whereas the touring motorcyclist can "let the film of life and nature pass by him peacefully." For the author, each of these types of rider qualified as sportsmen, despite different reasons and ways of motorcycling. In the case of both the motorcycle racer and the traveling salesman, the practice of labor was enwrapped in the performance of sport.

"Weekend motorcyclists," who he grouped together with the touring motorcyclists, were also analyzed within the context of work, although situated in a modified frame of reference. He argued that "the average petty bourgeois" did not believe that "relaxation means racing out into the weekend," claiming that "only those who are healthy and have bodily strength and yearn for light and sun but who are forced because of their occupation to spend six days between filing cabinets and desks understand what I am talking about." The workweek was the source of "dangerous tension" that needed to be released, and only after having "consumed at least 100 kilometers" would a "satisfactory diffusion" have taken place to permit "relaxation to set in." Directly connecting unsatisfying working conditions of white-collar labor to desires for new forms of leisure and consumption, the author proposed sport as compensation for the drudgery of everyday life, and a form of release.[39] Comments on the relationship between the transformation of labor and the importance of sport were tied to larger concerns about the implications of capitalist modernity.[40] Motorcyclists' attempts to negotiate the reorganization of the labor market found expression in the debate on motorcycling as sport.

Reflecting broader social concerns about sports, bodies, and health, most of the authors defended motorcycling as a means for gaining "robust health," claiming that, in contrast to driving a car, it exposed the rider to the elements and thus strengthened his physical constitution. One author went so far as to list concrete physiological improvements such as a "broadening of the shoulders and a strengthening of the arm and buttock muscles," as well as "an enhancement of a general sense of well-being."[41] Another line of argument was that motorcycling trained "strong nerves" or "nerves of steel"— a characteristic that was attributed to both a masculine and an anti-bourgeois attitude. Motorcycling masculinity certainly shared many attributes with boxing masculinity. Bertolt Brecht, for example, described the boxer as "essentially male: the genuine 'hard guy' … His sinewy body, stripped of fat through disciplined training, functioned like an anatomical suit of armor." The pugilist, so in Eric Jensen's reading of Brecht, "established an ideal for the Weimar man who had grown soft, and even decadent, in the modern metropolis."[42] Max Schmeling, Weimar Germany's most prominent boxer, even owned a Harley Davidson. In his memoirs, he recollected: "It was the times of the large motorcycles. Everyone dreamed of a Harley Davidson. The machines represented the intoxication of speed, which everyone back then was obsessed with, but also the experience of unbounded freedom played a role."[43] Both motorcycling and boxing "popularized an ideal of working-class toughness, the promise of upward mobility, and the allure of self-invention in modern society."[44]

After the bourgeois fixation with "neurasthenia" during the Wilhelmine era and following the "steel bath of 1914–1918," motorcycling discourse displayed an obsession with "nerves of steel," tied implicitly and explicitly to masculinity.[45] "[Motorcycling] demands nothing more than iron-hard masculine energy, when the rain pours down and the stomach rumbles—the unbendable will alone is the crucial factor."[46] Proclaiming "good nerves are more valuable than beautifully formed bodies," most saw themselves, in contrast to bourgeois car drivers, as real sportsmen, exposed to the elements: "In the fight with storm and weather—not sitting in a luxury limousine—we motorcyclists have hardened ourselves against climactic influences and through our sport have gained robust health."[47] Many of the letter writers viewed the "true motorcycle sportsman" as combining physical skill with both technical knowledge and psychic fortitude.[48] Emphasizing training both the body and the mind, these authors reworked the nineteenth-century bourgeois conception of manhood to argue that motorcycling as a sport represented a field in which man could struggle and overcome challenges posed by external and internal conditions. In the discursive representation of the Weimar-era "true sportsman" motorcyclist, the masculine act of consumption was obscured by attitudes, behaviors, and practices believed by the "sportsman" motorcyclist himself to transcend the crass materiality and pernicious feminization of the modern world.

Yet, like the prizefighter that Jensen argues "established flexible standards of masculinity for the postwar man," not all motorcyclists in the Weimar Republic adhered to an aggressively masculine interpretation of motorcycling. Within the letters published in *Das Motorrad*'s public opinion section, some stressed motorcycling as a means of training both "presence of mind" and an ability to navigate the modern world. Calling those who failed to recognize motorcycling as a legitimate sport "philistines," one letter writer, for example, presented a very broad definition of what qualified as sport, including aspects of the motorcycling experience such as "faultless technical knowledge," "reading maps," and "learning new languages on trips abroad" as indicators of the ability of motorcycling to develop the faculties necessary to become a technically savvy and cosmopolitan modern man. Deviating from interpretations that hearkened back to nineteenth-century ideals, he instead argued for a reformulated understanding of the value of sports, in which sports functioned as an individualized form for training the body and the mind appropriate to the conditions of modern society.[49] Regardless of how an author positioned himself in terms of motorcycling as a sport, the positive qualities that could be acquired by motorcycling were always linked to the role of sport in furthering the health of the people, indicating the varieties of imaginations for what qualified as a healthy practice for building a healthy nation.[50]

Byway I: "Too Much Sport"? Working-Class Attitudes to Motorcycling

In 1929, a shorter debate was held in the definitive working-class weekly, the *AIZ*, after a reader complained that it had devoted too much copy to sports in recent issues, although he also claimed to understand the importance of sport for the working-class movement.[51] The letter provoked so many responses that the editors could only print a handful of excerpts, but all disagreed that the *AIZ* was wasting space by filling three pages with sports reporting. Instead, the published replies indicate how important sport was to the working classes during the Weimar Republic.[52] Readers heaped praise on the editor's dedication to promoting working-class sport by showing "such classic images of the best performances of international working-class sport." "The worker looks for his sport, whether he practices it or not, in the *AIZ*." Expressing appreciation for being able to see his "brothers, from all around the world," compete against each other, a "red sportsman" from Thüringen maintained, "a steeled body is necessary to be prepared for the future struggle." His definition of struggle and the sporting body not only echoes the debate in *Das Motorrad*, but was also echoed in other readers' comments. For example, a reader from Ratibor commented that "in times of capitalistic rationalization," the body is "rapidly worn out." The "counterweight for this is working-class sport and its many sporting associations, which provide every worker with the possibility to maintain and steel his health, not least for the final battle of the proletariat."[53]

Although the readership of the *AIZ* clamored for sports, the *AIZ* towed a strict editorial line, condemning what it judged to be the "excrescences of bourgeois sport." A critique of the "rushed tempo of our times" argues that "the quest for continually increased performance is a contemporary phenomenon," which is "expressed in the rationalized production in factory and office ... This quest is a driving force in every sporting activity." The "madness for breaking records" led to the "breeding of sports 'canons'—particularly capable individuals," and was a symptom of the culture of bourgeois capitalism. "The 'canon,' the record-man, is hardly more than a much sought-after commodity." The motorcycle racer, "unthinkable without the direct support of a manufacturer," was an object in "this thoroughly contemporary capitalistic haggling over 'human' matter."[54]

An admixture between technology and sport, motorcycling thus often provoked an ambivalent response of whether or not it helped produce healthy bodies. As Adelheid von Saldern has argued in terms of the Eilenriede race in Hannover, motor sports did not sit easily within efforts to promote healthy activities.[55] The left, in particular, had the difficult task of simultaneously integrating a critique of motor sport into a critique of capitalism while coming to terms with the fact that, by the end of the Weimar Republic, motorcycling was no longer a sport for the wealthy. For example, in his 1931 treatise on *Sport and Working Class Sport*, Helmut Wagner addressed "machine sport" as an example of the "capitalist class" buying "'sport' for money like he sells other products on the commodity market ... Performance is still the dominant principle, but it becomes increasingly technically independent, it is rationalized and mechanized." Wagner compared motor sports with "gladiatorism arising anew, at a higher technical-social stage." Grounded in a concept of the progression of society in stages, Wagner viewed "machine sport" as a product of capitalist society. "Sport does not develop organically from life and labor of a people as it does in simple societies ... The focus of true sport activities—also in an increasingly technologized future—will be in the sport that trains the body, in the simple, corporeally appropriate and natural form of physical exercise."[56] Despite the socialist rhetoric, issues raised in the debate among motorcyclists in the pages of *Das Motorrad* resurfaced in Wagner's book. "It depends on the performance of the designing engineer and the mechanical engineer; it requires the necessary technical skills and the necessary 'calm' and cold-bloodedness of the 'sportsman.' Will and control of nerves are trained in machine sport." Wagner asserted that because the motorized sports did not "require physical strength or skill," "machine sport" was primarily a "sport of the nerves."[57]

Struggle and sport were, however, important themes in "revolutionary" socialist circles.[58] The *AIZ*'s sport section regularly covered the activities of working-class motorcycle associations, including competitive races. Reporting on the first Germany-wide communist sports meet in Erfurt, which attracted "thousands of red motorcyclists," the paper praised working-class athletes for their "revolutionary spirit, their invincible enthusiasm, their passionate willingness to sacrifice for the common goal of the revolutionary class struggle."[59] Indeed, the German communist movement mobilized motorized sport and struggle in the service of the socialist world revolution. *Kuhle Wampe*, the 1932 communist-produced early sound film, is a stridently political depiction of working-class life at the height of the World Economic Crisis. The screenplay, written by Bertolt Brecht, follows the Boenicke family, and in particular daughter Anni, through struggles with unemployment, suicide, eviction from a tenement, alternative living in a weekender community, an unplanned pregnancy, and a broken-off engagement to her fiancé Fritz. *Kuhle Wampe*, Berlin slang for "empty belly," also addresses problems in the world economy in its final scene, illustrated through a political debate that ensues during a local train ride over why coffee reserves were being burned in Brazil.

A sports festival organized by the Red Sports League that includes a motorcycle race is the setting of the turning point in the film. The motorcyclist-comrade protagonist, Kurt, played by Adolf Fischer, is the only clearly identifiable male hero in the film; he always has the best politically enlightened viewpoints and advice. For example, at the festival, a short scene involves Kurt and a vendor of political pamphlets.

Image 4.1. Still from *Kuhle Wampe oder: Wem gehört die Welt?*, in *Illustrierter Film-Kurier*, Literaturarchiv Marburg.

The vendor shows Kurt a pamphlet about contraception, to which he replies, "I already have one." He then decides to purchase a pamphlet about shop floor organizing. Despite the film's clear-cut political support of working-class internationalism, the lyrics of the song that accompanies the Red Sport League races employed a martial language, emphatically urging the youthful *Rote Sportler* (Red Sportspeople) to "Gather in Common Struggle; Learn to Win!" The song is synchronized to images of shapely, youthful bodies, both male and female, engaged in competition, including a motorcycle race, which Kurt, of course, wins. Through participating in mass sporting events, either actively or passively, the film sells the idea that it is possible to forge a solidary community through sports.[60] In the late Weimar era the socialist and communist view of physical exercise as bodily training was not far removed from nationalist assessments of sport.[61] Across political divides, iterations of discomfort with materialism reflected anxieties about Germany's transition to a consumer-driven industrial capitalism. Nonetheless, while communists and socialists, like nationalists, foregrounded the importance of the collective over the individual, the socialist collective was international and future-oriented. Regardless, however, of political leaning, in looking to sport as a way to reinvigorate the health of the social body, Germans often responded to massive economic and social disruptions by invoking the concept of struggle.

"Strengthening the Body of the Whole Race": Struggle and "German Sport"

A schoolteacher who responded to the debate in *Das Motorrad* claimed his purpose in life was to "observe the dictate of the harmonious training of humans and to help sport achieve its proper place in schools." By emphasizing struggle as the essential element of sport, he insisted that personal development required struggle. In his view, the body and the machine were comparable instruments that could be tuned to perfection, demonstrating an understanding of the body in mechanical terms as an infinitely improvable machine. The man's struggle is with "the machine, with the roads, with the weather, and with breakdowns." [62] Many motorcyclists viewed conquering nature, including one's own body and mind, as proof of their masculine strength and their right to call themselves sportsmen. As motorcycling was and is associated with risk-taking and the desire to overcome challenges posed by external and internal conditions, it is unsurprising that many Weimar motorcyclists invoked struggle to describe the value of motorcycling.

In the same way that neither the right nor the left dominated the concept of camaraderie during the Weimar Republic, no group controlled the meaning of struggle and all mass-based movements integrated a concept of struggle into their rhetorical repertoire. Specific viewpoints can nevertheless be mapped within the political landscape, and debates over the value of sport and motor sport reflect the available social and political imaginations. Despite differences in evaluating the importance of sport, the practice of cultivating the body was pervasively regarded as vital to securing the health of the population, whether understood in terms of the proletariat, Republican citizens, or a racially pure *Volksgemeinschaft*.[63] In the context of accelerated social and spatial mobility, the discussion on sport, leisure, and the gendered relationship of physical bodies furthermore recorded reactions to shifts in the political economy and the multiple and instable constructions of the "new man" and the "new woman."

The president of the DMV, Artur Vieregg, offered a definition of sport in his brochure *Sports and its Goals with Special Consideration for Questions of Today* that was echoed by many of the letter writers in *Das Motorrad*'s sports debate.[64] Sport was "a physical activity outside of one's job that, in utilizing all physical and mental capacities, results in top performance through a struggle to win without material compensation or the creation of material value."[65] His definition had much in common with pre–World War I bourgeois interpretations of sport, yet it was also an update in comparison with the mentality of the traditional bourgeoisie.[66] Thus, on the one hand, Vieregg believed in the principle of "general sports education" and "consistent bodily training in winter and summer," and opposed specialization at an early age, arguing for the training of the "entire body and mind."[67] On the other hand, Vieregg's views were also shaped by Germany's defeat in World War I and the subsequent political upheavals. Writing in 1924, he asserted that one "not to be underestimated" reason that sports had become a "cultural good" was that "sporting discipline" helped to "keep the masses under control [*das 'In der Hand haben' der Massen erleichtert*]" and that the creation of new groups through sports "offered the opportunity to maintain or revive the strength of the people [*Volkskraft*]."[68] The "questions of today" that Vieregg believed needed "special consideration" regarded, in the first instance, how to control and channel the energy of the masses into rebuilding the "strength of the people." Sports associations as "bearers of culture" were central to this task. By "bringing forth sportspeople, bridging differences between status and lineage, helping in building a moral life, and again strengthening the body of the whole race," sport associations thus, "gave new heart to the Fatherland."[69] The highest ideal of sport for Vieregg was "service to the Fatherland. The idea of the Fatherland can never be better advanced than through German sport." Local interests fade, "class differences are bridged, and the national feeling is fostered." For Vieregg, German sport was the "cornerstone" for "raising a free, strong, responsible race." It would "create leaders who, gifted with fresh resolve, sober faculty of judgment, and parliamentary and social instruction, would carry with them the honor of sport, which is not concerned with the gain of material goods, but in pursuing non-material goals."[70] While avowing to be in favor of parliamentary democracy, Vieregg, like many of his contemporaries, was anxious about the effects of industrial capitalism.

The tensions of a society in transition were also reflected in attempts to re-establish moral norms and delimit the bounds of Germanness. Vieregg's vision of sport revealed how, in popular discourse, sport was increasingly tied to an exclusive notion of belonging to the Fatherland. On the one hand, Vieregg argued that there was nothing more "sinful" against the "spirit of sports" than to organize sports clubs around politics or religion. "The 100 meters are not run differently if I am a German nationalist [*deutschvölkisch*] or a communist, or if I belong to a Protestant or Catholic church. Whoever brings domestic politics or religion into sport sins against the spirit of sport." On the other hand, Vieregg expressed sympathy for those who "as Germans do not want to join into a community with 'un-Germans': because our sport is first of all *German* sport."[71] In viewing "religious, political, or particular interests" as grounds to disqualify a person or association from inclusion in the German sporting community, Vieregg problematically linked sportsmanship to Germanness and a non-pluralistic understanding of the Fatherland.[72] As the head of the largest German motorcycling association during the Weimar Republic, his views on sport contained a dubious non-inclusive character, in which the concept of being a sportsperson was tied to being German, and vice-versa. Unwillingness to practice sports exclusively for the Fatherland was cause for expulsion from the collective.

During the Weimar Republic, sport was not only a question of popular concern, but also of intellectual interest. In *Body Culture: An Attempt at a Philosophy of Physical Education*, Robert Schulte, a psychologist and lecturer at the Deutsche Hygiene Museum [German Hygiene Museum] in Dresden, attempted to analyze sport in terms of its "immanent value and transcendental value."[73] On the one hand he presented a materialist argument that sport as a "performance value" created the possibility of "increasing the performance of the national economy." Citing the example of the "Anglo-Saxon peoples," Schulte considered sport as having the ability to "increase occupational performance and lengthen the time-span a worker is fit for work." In the twentieth century, all "civilized nations" had recognized "physical exercise as a standard method of maintaining and recouping the productive strength of the population." Although his assertion appears to provide a positive evaluation of "Anglo-Saxon" culture, at other points in the text he criticized both US and British societies. He derided both the "Americanized belittlement of sport" through the "sensational glorification of record breakers" and "fairness" as an expression of "English rationality" and as "convention, constraint, and profit considerations," which he judged as "pseudo values."[74]

For Schulte, the materialist "performance value" was secondary to the "hygienic" and the "pedagogic-psychic" value of sport. The "hygienic value" of sport applied to both the "physical" and "spiritual–mental" sides. He argued that the "weekend movement" was particularly important for improving the general "social hygiene" of the population, and represented an "infinite boon" as a "source of regeneration for humankind's physical and mental happiness." He argued that the "freedom of the modern civilized human during such a short but periodic span of his existence can make the deepest and highest strengths of the human personality blossom." "Ever faster and cheaper" technological methods for transporting "the broad masses out from the confines of the city and to the green ring of the forest areas" would hence make it "possible to redress the damages done by the age of industrialization. Relaxation, vacation, sport, games, and working in allotment gardens are vital for the health of the people—these are the matters that are most important in every possible human context: for health, joy of life, economy, and the common welfare."[75] Schulte's disquisition on sport points to how sport was increasingly interpreted as a necessary antipole to industrial labor. Many of the attendant effects of industrialization, including urbanization and proletarianization, were judged as negatively impacting the health and happiness of society. Technologies of motorization, through their imagined ability to provide greater mobility and easier access to nature, could thus—so Schulte and others argued—contribute to building a happier and healthier society.

Beyond promoting values rooted in material existence, according to Schulte, sport also fostered aesthetic, ethical, and metaphysical qualities. Gender and sexuality were two important aspects of Schulte's ruminations on the aesthetics and ethics of sports. Regarding aesthetics, he claimed that "the *deformation of the natural* psycho-physical and aesthetic *characters of both sexes*" was to be "unconditionally rejected." He cited "taut and strong male bodies" being "softened" through an "overly feminine conception of gymnastics" and more "graceful and soft female organisms" being "completely deformed through excessive sport performances."[76] On the one hand, Schulte positively evaluated some affects of sport on gender. He applauded, for example, the increased "interest in the human body, its beauty and our duties towards it" that had "fortunately eradicated many nonsensical phenomena, above all in terms of women's clothing."[77] On the other hand, he noted with concern a rise in the "occurrence of decadence" and "mirthless prurience, meaning the growth of anti-biological, unaesthetic, and amoral sources of excitement."[78] By invoking "complementary values of hard/soft," Schulte constructed a value system that stressed gender difference as indispensable for a healthy society.[79]

Yet Schulte's discussion on the "ethics" of sports reveals that during the Weimar Republic mainstream attitudes to the relationship between the body and questions of morality and sexuality no longer strictly conformed to nineteenth-century bourgeois mores. Claiming that "ethical pseudo-values that are nothing else than pedagogic-psychological developments of value," he argued that "apparently ethical values of physical culture" were "exceptionally limited by convention," "in the same way that human morality and true morality do not have to be consistent with each other, and the same as the case with morality and law, religion and theology, truth and science, love and marriage, all of which are supposed to belong to the other, but in reality do not appear to be linked." Questioning established social and moral conventions was common to modernity, in the Weimar Republic and elsewhere. Schulte adhered to the view that sexuality should be natural and unselfconscious, and that sport could increase "moral naturalness and responsibility," even when "youth of both sexes view the unclothed body."[80] Schulte's position shows how gender and sexuality during the Weimar Republic were discussed and experienced with increasing candor, as well as how this openness and flexibility was framed in terms of the morality and health of the social body.

Schulte's book on physical culture was accompanied by a series of photographic plates that aimed to illustrate the different social values of sport. Although Schulte's text did not address motorcycling or motor sports, the captions provided for two photos that depicted a motorcycle race indicate that Schulte viewed motorcycling as a form of both physical and mental training. One caption read, "The Start of a Motorcycle Race: Persistence, Agility, Presence of Mind"; while the other read, "Heavy Machines in a Race: Cold-Bloodedness, Calm Nerves; Perception of One's Own Body; Will to Win."[81] Both the photographs and the captions capture Schulte's investment in the "psychic-pedagogic" value of sport for producing a body politic. Another set of photographs, for example, visually represented the "philosophy of sports." Juxtaposed against each other, one portrayed neatly arranged formations of bodies—the caption read "Gymnastics Demonstration with a Tendency towards Uniformity"—and the other photo showed spectators in disarray at a soccer match—the caption for this photo read "The Surge of Sporting Enthusiasm at a Competition."[82] What was important for Schulte was the "formative character" of sports, one that he viewed as "more fruitful and more valuable" for the "design of the totality of the people" than the "breeding of downright super jocks."[83]

Carl Diem, the first director of the College of Physical Education and Germany's twentieth-century version of "*Turnvater* Jahn," articulated many of the themes in the debate on sport in *Das Motorrad* in a preface he provided for the 1925 nationalist-leaning book, *Deutscher Sport.*[84] His introductory words mirror many of the motorcyclists' responses, including the issues of mastery of external forces, physicality, materialism, spirituality, competition, and a return to nature.[85] Fraught with contradictions, Diem's thoughts on the definition of sport were as inconclusive as in the debate among the motorcyclists. Indeed, after all his consideration of the various qualifiers, Diem had to admit that there was no adequate definition for sport.

Diem's focus, however, was on the "German youth" who understood "what sport is and what it is worth." For Diem, "Sport is the methodical training of the body [*Körperzucht*] and bodily and spiritual devotion; it is where talent and affinity coincide in the individual. Sport is the school of character, the trial of the will, and the service of friendship." Like so many others, he was concerned with the effects of industrial modernity on the health of the nation: "The dust of civilization dissipates and the oppressiveness of the built environment of the city disappears in the shouts of joy over the pursuit of sporting ambitions. From enormous effort, the mastering of pain and risk, hardened humans are produced. Striving for the highest performance means satisfying the most ancient yearnings of mankind towards perfection; this is the truly aristocratic in democratic sport." Diem, perhaps the most respected living authority on sport of his day, abundantly mixed metaphors and metaphysical, anti-civilizational rhetoric, and offered a definition of sport that firmly linked its purpose to securing the health of the national body.[86]

Subservience to a higher order was the subject of another essay in *Deutscher Sport* that addressed the question of the "disposition of the sportsman." Rehearsing *völkisch* tropes, the author, Dr. J. Klein, believed sport was about "community building and acting within a community." Standing in contrast to the "German spirit," Klein presented "'pure' reason (ratio)" as the "the source of such powers that destroy the community." Criticizing "liberal-Manchesterian" rationalism and "the ruthless protection of personal advantage raised to the highest principle of life," Klein argued that "English 'business' and success, in which wealth replaces the old Prussian-German life ideal of occupation, responsibility, and status as the worthwhile purposes in life." Klein's nostalgia for "old Prussian-German" values based on a social order rank according to productive occupation reflected the pervasive anxieties about the social and economic restructuring of postwar German society. Indeed, the category of labor was central to Klein's critique of German society and his understanding of the value of sports. Wilhelmine society had fallen under the sway of "rationality and a materialistic spirit" that had led to "addiction to the total mechanization of life, in which, according to the English example, work is viewed as something burdensome, in contrast especially to the German-speaking peoples, who consider work a duty and an imperative." In Klein's analysis, shifts in the political economy had led to a degradation of the category and praxis of labor. He denounced a materialist worldview in which labor was understood as a "commodity" and not the "function of the spiritual-creative forces of humans." At the turn of the twentieth century, according to Klein, "German life was like a big cemetery, although still shining, brilliantly mechanized with machines and instruments." He furthermore blamed the imperial system for believing that "political power had enduringly been secured with the donning of military pants and the trampling of a once-beautiful meadow. We saw where this oppression, indeed partial negation of the spiritual forces . . . led to, through the horrific experience in the World War and afterward in Russian Bolshevism." Despite enduring all these calamities, the youth of Germany had, however, "remained healthy" and had understood the need to "resist the rationalization of time, the mechanization of life, and the formalization of all living conditions." Above all, Klein asserted, this resistance found its expression in the "disposition of the sportsman" and the "drive for the true German *Volksgemeinschaft*." Like Vieregg, Klein criticized sports associations that were organized on a confessional or political basis, naming the Catholic Deutsche Jugendkraft and the Socialist Arbeiter-Turn- und Sportbund as examples of organizations that "abuse the homegrown will for renewal of the German sporting youth." "Organic thought," instead, should replace the "conceit of rationality."[87] Citing Adolf Friedrich von Mecklenburg, a sport enthusiast, a high-ranking member of the AvD, and the last governor of Togo, Germany's colony until World War I, Klein concluded that sports should be "education in sense of the three pillars: German, Loyal, Diligent [*Teutsch, Treu, Tüchtig*]. To be a sportsman means to possess these characteristics."[88] *Völkisch* ideologies were socially acceptable within the upper echelons of the sports movement in Germany by the mid-1920s, perceptible in the racist and anti-Semitic undertone in Klein's essay.

Yet, despite Klein's distaste for the "mechanization of life," the second volume of *Deutscher Sport* included a tribute to the "German automotive industry" and "the German man," who "possesses spirit, energy, drive, and skill, and provides soul and life that make victory and performance possible in the first place." Accompanied by photos of German motorcyclists, including Ernst Henne, the text praised the record-breaking feats and claimed that a "new chapter in the glory of German sport and German performance" was being written by German motorcyclists. While the emphasis in *Deutscher Sport* was on the performance of the man, rather than the machine, even ardent supporters of a specifically and racially defined German form of physical education defined motoring as a valid sport.[89] Thus, the concept of struggle in sport during the Weimar Republic was largely conceived in terms of serving a greater purpose. German commentators on the "value of sports" situated it as a means of training that surpassed its benefits for the individual body, and thus markedly diverged from Anglo-American models of sport and competition.

Byway II: "German Sport" and "German Industry"

Accompanying the spread of industrialization, sport and sporting events became important symbols for judging a nation's strength, prosperity, and virility across the globe. As a modern means of measuring the might of both industry and sport, results of motorcycle and automobile races were understood as significant indicators of national power. Intrinsic to a nation's self-understanding as modern was the symbolic linkage between technology, industry, and material and moral progress.[90] After World War I, German motorcycle manufacturers and enthusiasts fretted over losses in international races and celebrated victories as a sign of a reawakened national power.[91] Moreover, motor sport associations such as the DMV argued that motor sports were important precisely because they could revitalize the German economy.[92]

When international motorcycle racers faced each other head to head, the German motoring press expressed both awe and anxieties, again linking national strength to sporting strength and to individual bodies. The Tourist Trophy (TT) on the Isle of Man was recognized as the most prestigious race, and the winning motorcycles and riders were seen as instantiations of both sporting and economic power. Although it was not until 1931 that Germany was represented in the TT race, competition between German and British racers was the subject of intense interest.[93] Fritz Pullig's novel of "love, motor, and sports," *Rennfieber (Racing Fever)*, serialized in the DMV journal *Motorrad-Sport, -Verkehr und -Technik* in 1929–1930, is anticipatory in nature, taking the TT-race as its starting point and describing the adventures and misadventures of a "famous German motorcyclist" on the Isle of Man.[94] Pullig's fictional TT-match-up aside, Germans indeed competed against British motorcyclists in numerous other races during the Weimar Republic. One of the most fiercely disputed races was the Grand Prix of Germany, held on the newly constructed Nürbergring in Saxony. After a British victory in the 1930 race, one commentator remarked: "Hats off to the English! But a compliment for NSU that performed better than the winners' list indicates, and a doubly hearty congratulations for Wiese, the 'up and coming German man'—or has he perhaps already arrived?"[95] Indeed, in questions of motorcycling, Germans had long looked to England as the "Motherland" of sports and, until 1931, the nation with the highest per capita ownership of motorcycles with a mixture of admiration and apprehension.

In regard to the sporting and industrial rivalry between Germany and Britain, the German motorcycle industry's confidence that it was rapidly gaining ground on the British motorcycle industry grew over the course of the Weimar Republic. Indeed, by 1930, voices within the German motorcycling community felt so certain of German progress vis-à-vis the British that they declared: "Germany is capable of building good and fast motorcycles, as the wins of BMW and DKW at many races demonstrate, as well as the world record of Henne on the BMW-compressor shows." Hence, the author maintained that the British industry "knows to respect the great significance of the German production—and also to fear it!"[96] And indeed, reviewing a "490 cc Ardie 'Silver Eagle': A Very Modern German Product Featuring an Interesting Duralumin Frame and Elaborate Equipment," a journalist for the British motorcycling press remarked: "It impressed the eye as something upon which nothing has been spared—something very, very modern. Its ultra-modernity was, perhaps, the strongest impression which the Ardie left behind it."[97] By the beginning of the 1930s, British observers of the German motorcycle industry conceded that "within the past few years the position has greatly changed; Germany has learned much about motorcycle building, and German machines have gained respect both in racing and in the field of commerce."[98]

Victories in the sport of motorcycling racing, through combining technological strength and endurance with physical prowess, were interpreted in both nations as representing a highly modern means of proving national strength. After the British motorcycling team performed poorly at the International Six Day races, the reporter from the British magazine *Motor Cycling* commented, "These results must be regarded as rather humbling to our national pride and damaging to our national prestige. We have always considered ourselves to be supreme in all branches of motorcycling sport, but here clearly is a branch of it in which we must for the meantime give other nations best."[99] Moreover, imaginations of national power were inscribed onto the bodies of the motorcycle racers who became symbols of modern masculinity. Marieluise Fleißer, a popular Weimar Germany novelist, listed the British TT star Cecil Ashby as one of the men she would "like to marry": "I saw his 20-second fueling time at the Bäderrennen from very close proximity, his cold-blooded calm and control over the material, as though a current flowed throughout his whole body that would have made others fly for years."[100] The combination of motors and sports resulted in a pastiche of the modern and archaic, melding traits such as heroism, technology, speed, and the ability of man to conquer nature.[101] Motorcycle racers, especially the elite who took part in international races, were understood as embodying twentieth-century masculinity, simultaneously virile and technical.

Germans celebrated Ernst Henne's spectacular record-breaking speedtrials for BMW as proof that Germany was rising again in the early 1930s. On hearing the news that Henne had again beaten the British and secured the fastest speed ever on a motorcycle, the ADAC sent a telegram of congratulations: "With pride and satisfaction we congratulate you most heartily for your fabulous success through achieving the absolute world record for motorcycles. Our whole Fatherland will celebrate this exceptional success with you."[102] Magda Amann-Binder, writing for the BMW journal *BMW-Blätter*, gushed over Henne's prowess: "Germany's best rider" possessed the "highest measure of human power to concentrate, the necessary presence of mind ... United with the machine, with which the man is intimately melted during such a performance," the racer does not "submit without restraint to the machine; instead the feeling of power, which originates from overcoming resistance, masters the machine and leads it to augmented performance."[103] Other prominent male motorcycle racers, such as Toni Bauhofer and Hans Soenius, were also cited as being examples of an ideal type of modern German masculinity. Soenius was described as "taut of body, brown of face," and popular with women.[104] Bauhofer, who had been a pilot in World War I, was lauded for his "fearlessness of death, and his great fighting heart."[105]

Motorcycling magazines sold the idea that "every motorcyclist has a little bit of motorcycle racer in him." Inevitably, even if the motorcyclist primarily used the vehicle for transportation or for business, he would accelerate down a straight stretch of road and "taste the enjoyment of full speed. For every motorcyclist, the moment also arises when he has to demonstrate courage, guts, and decisiveness, where possibly his or another human life is involved."[106] If every motorcyclist could potentially be a motorcycle sportsman, then every motorcyclist could potentially be of service to the German nation, as an article on "motor sport discipline" by Hugo Kalinowski, vice chairman of the DMV, argued: "Even the most die-hard pacifist would not be able to deny the successful effects of inculcating common thinking, feeling, and acting through general military service." Stripped of "this form of national education," he urged Germans "to dedicate ourselves to the preservation of sporting discipline with double the seriousness ... When our motorcyclists have fully comprehended the scope of this moment, then it will be easy for the individual to adjust his behavior accordingly." Perhaps, as Eric Jensen argues for track and field athletes, boxers, and tennis players, because the motorcycle racer "projected an individualism that stood in counterpoint to the communal approach of other strands of German physical culture," Kalinowski found it necessary to propose that the "highest leitmotif" of the motorcycle sportsman should be that he be "a part of a whole to which he must subordinate himself."[107]

Conclusion

Sport was an important field on which conflicts brought about by the upending of the political order were negotiated, and the discussion around motorcycling and sport provides ample evidence of Germans' unease with political and social change. Competing visions of what defined a sport or a sportsperson provide insight into how motorcyclists attempted to negotiate their identities during a period in which the primacy of production was giving way to the growing importance of consumption. Sport allowed men to shore up the boundaries of normative masculinity and to create distinctions within masculinity. Importantly, the post–World War I obsession with sport points to the widespread sense of an urgent need to rehabilitate the nation. As Eric Weitz noted, commentators from across the political spectrum believed that "active bodies would make individuals whole again and thereby repair the collective German body."[108] By emphasizing struggle as the pivotal moment in sport, motorcyclists veiled their participation in consumer society through hiding behind the idea of sports as the individual pursuit of a healthy modern body for the sake of a healthy collective social body. The contention that too few Germans were invested in the republic to allow it to develop into a durable and viable entity is a point that many historians have subsequently raised. While this argument remains persuasive, regardless of political affiliation, Germans on the whole were highly invested in sport, and the concepts of struggle, youth, and community resonated throughout society.

Notes

1. Bourdieu, *Distinction*, 212–13. What Bourdieu labels "working class," I would instead argue is an articulation of a particular masculinity.
2. Jensen's *Body by Weimar* focuses on the practices of tennis, boxing, and track and field. Christiane Eisenberg has explored the meaning of sport in terms of the "sociation" of the bourgeoisie in Germany from the nineteenth century to the mid-1930s. The main focus of her analysis of the bourgeois habitus of sports, however, is on the period before the Weimar Republic. See Christiane Eisenberg, *"English Sports" and deutsche Bürger: Eine Gesellschaftsgeschichte 1800–1939* (Paderborn: Schöningh, 1999). Jensen's analysis, unlike Eisenberg's, rightly stresses the open-endedness of sport in the Weimar Republic, with each type of sport as a site for negotiation, determining and policing boundaries.
3. Schmidt, *Sich hart machen, wenn es gilt*, 88–106.
4. Merki, *Der holprige Siegeszug*, 65–66.
5. See statistics in Appendix.

6. In 1927, only 1.2 percent of motorcycle owners possessed a license to participate in competitive motor sporting events, and these racing vehicles were,
   for the most part, also employed for occupational purposes beyond racing.
   Edelmann, *Vom Luxusgut zum Gebrauchsgegenstand*, 108.

7. On "de-sportification" and everyday use of new "mobility machines," Möser,
   Fahren und Fliegen, 133–35, 163.

8. The leader of the early nineteenth-century gymnastics movement, Friedrich
   Ludwig Jahn, better known as "Turnvater Jahn," was involved with the
   anti-Napoleonic "liberation" movement in Germany. Christiane Eisenberg
   claims that Jahn initiated the "gymnastics movement with the goal of recruiting a paramilitary reserve army" in the first decades of the nineteenth century."
   Eisenberg,*"English Sports" und deutsche Bürger*, 105–20, here 108.

9. Eisenberg, *"English Sports" und deutsche Bürger*, 105–20; Svenja Goltermann,
   Körper der Nation: Habitusformation und die Politik des Turnens 1860–1890
   (Göttingen: Vandenhoeck & Ruprecht, 1998), 61.

10. Goltermann, *Körper der Nation*, 62–63.

11. See Mosse, *The Image of Man*, 27.

12. Ibid., 95–97.

13. Ignaz Wrobel [pseud. Kurt Tucholsky], "Alte Wandervögel," *Die Weltbühne* 25
    (1926): 966. The problem with interpreting the last word lies in how the German
    concept of *Geschlecht* can denote race, sex, gender, lineage, or tribe.

14. Until the Weimar Republic, however, membership in motoring clubs remained
    confined to the upper classes. See Eisenberg, *"English Sports" und deutsche
    Bürger*, 162–214.

15. Despite the upper class hold on many of the sporting activities—many types of
    sports obviously required a significant investment in capital and leisure time,
    both of which were unavailable for workers in Wilhelmine Germany—by the
    beginning of World War I, there was also effectively an institutionalized system
    of Socialist "counter-cultural" sporting (and youth) organizations. For example,
    Socialist bicycle club "Solidarität" was established in the 1890s and had 150,000
    members by 1913. See Schulz and Rösch, *Der Arbeiter Rad und Kraftfahrbund
    "Solidarität"*, 8–9.

16. Eisenberg, *"English Sports" und deutsche Bürger*, 216–33, here, 233.

17. Herman Kasak, "Sport als Lebensgefühl," *Die Weltbühne*, no. 41, 1928,
    557–58.

18. Weitz, *Weimar Germany*, 312.

19. See Eisenberg, *"English Sports" und deutsche Bürger*, 376–77.

20. Edmund Neuendorff, *Geschichte der neueren deutschen Leibesübung vom
    Beginn des 18. Jahrhunderts bis zum Gegenwart*, vol. 4, *Die Zeit vom 1860 bis
    1932* (Dresden: 1932), 682.

21. Dr. Otto Peltzer and Hubert Houben were contemporary German Olympic
    track athletes. For more on the popularity athletes during the Weimar Republic
    such as Peltzer, see Eisenberg, *"English Sports" und deutsche Bürger*, 368–70;
    and Jensen, *Body by Weimar*, 99–132.

22. Neuendorff, *Geschichte der neueren deutschen Leibesübung*, 682.

23. The meteoric rise of sports following the end of World War I was hardly unique
    to Germany, playing an important role in constituting modern societies across
    the globe. See, for example, Wilson Chacko Jacob, *Working out Egypt: Effendi
    Masculinity and Subject Formation in Colonial Modernity, 1870—1940* (Durham,

NC: Duke University Press, 2011) on physical culture and sport in Egypt and the (un)making of modern colonial masculinity.

24. See, for example, the essay from the Prussian Welfare Office's statistical report on sports and sports associations from Prussia: Preussisches Ministerium für Volkswirtschaft, *Sport-Statistik; Amtliches Quellenwerk, Quellenwerk zur 1. amtlichen Statistik des Freistaates Preussen über Turnen, Sport, Wander Übungsstättenbau-Vereinswesen, nach dem Stande vom 1. Januar 1928*, ed. A. Mallwitz (Kassel: Rudolph'sche Verlagsanstalt, 1928), 3–4.

25. Jensen, *Body by Weimar*, 3–13.

26. According to George Mosse: "The Roman slogan 'a healthy mind in a healthy body,' eventually inscribed above gymnasium throughout Europe, sums up this linkage, which was to prove ready-made for the creation of a masculine stereotype." Mosse is referring to the pervasive Enlightenment view that "body structure" was related to "character." See Mosse, *The Image of Man*, 27.

27. Text of the letter that sparked the debate: "We live in the age of sports. There is an obsession with calling every physical activity 'sport', whereby it is totally misrecognized that true sport requires the harmonious training of the entire body and spirit [*die harmonische Ausbildung des ganzen Körpers und des Geistes*]. If we observe the physical builds of our Olympic contenders, we see the fruits of their training, namely beautifully formed, true sport-builds that are always the masters of their entire muscular system. Bodies trained to suppleness, bestowing them the proper conduct in every situation. Bodies that are hardened against climactic influences—that have paid for their replete health through sport. And how does it stand with you, my very honorable Messrs. Motorcyclists? I think a comparison would be catastrophic for you. I, myself, even know of "motor-sportsmen" that are not capable of getting their leg over their saddles without difficulty. And daily one sees people riding by that are everything else than sportspeople. We think further of the many "motorcycle sport-mates" who, through . . . their motorcycles, have acquired some kind of bodily defect. And yet sport should bring about healthfulness. Think of the many female occupants of the hospitals that as *Sozias* [female pillion-seat passengers] sustained such grave harm. This destructive enjoyment is supposed to be sport, when it is precisely the woman who should think about maintaining her health according to methods appropriate to her constitution. No, no, my honorable sirs! I am no enemy of the motorcycle, but I have to dispute the description "sport" in all respects, alone in the interest of public health [*Volksgesundheit*]. If, it is said, in the article (Issue 21), "1,000,000 Motor Vehicles" in Germany, that we can be proud of the colossal increase in motorcycles, so I would only want to point out there's absolutely no reason to be proud, because its exactly this increase in motorcycles that speaks for Germany's poverty. In the case that we still had the same national wealth [as before the war], then the highest percentage of today's motorcyclists would be sitting in a comfortable car. Am I right?" "Die Öffentliche Meinung 196, Ist Motorradfahren überhaupt Sport?," *Das Motorrad* (1928): 958.

28. Already during the Wilhelmine era, a conflict had erupted over the question of "English sports" versus "German gymnastics." See Eisenberg, *"English Sports" und deutsche Bürger*, 250–61.

29. Lethen, *Cool Conduct*, 22.

30. I deal with the question of health and women in Chapter 6.

31. See Mosse, *The Image of Man*, 27.

32. "Die Öffentliche Meinung 215, Motorradfahren ist nicht immer Sport," *Das Motorrad*, 1929: 116.
33. "Die Öffentliche Meinung 215," 116.
34. "Die Öffentliche Meinung 224, Geistesgegenwart kann man sich durch Motorradfahren anziehen," *Das Motorrad*, 1929: 166.
35. The author also indicated that he and his family experienced economic decline in the post–World War I years. "Die Öffentliche Meinung 212, Ich glaube, der Herr hat noch nie auf einem Motorrad gesessen," *Das Motorrad*, 1929: 114.
36. "Die Öffentliche Meinung 219, 'Perlen vor die Säue werfen' ist ein Sprichwort," *Das Motorrad*, 1929: 163.
37. "Die Öffentliche Meinung 201, Die richtige Einteilung der Motorradfahrer," *Das Motorrad*, 1928: 1000.
38. Also see Erik Jensen's analysis of "The Rationalization of the Track and Field Athlete," in Jensen, *Body by Weimar*, 101–14.
39. "Öffentliche Meinung 225, Etwas über Motorradsport und Ethik," *Das Motorrad*, 1929: 212.
40. Social commentaries by Kracauer, Bloch, and Tucholsky also address the relationship between sport and capitalist modernity; see, for example, Kurt Tucholsky (Theobald Tiger), "Week-end," *Die Weltbühne*, no. 18, 1927, 705.
41. "Die Öffentliche Meinung 216, Motorradfahren steigert das Allgemeinbefinden," *Das Motorrad*, 1929: 116.
42. Jensen, *Body by Weimar*, 50.
43. Max Schmeling, *Max Schmeling: An Autobiography*, trans. Georg B. von der Lippe (Chicago: Bonus Books, 1994), 22. For more on Schmeling, see Jensen, *Body by Weimar*, 50, 63–64, and 71–76.
44. Jensen, *Body by Weimar*, 50.
45. See Radkau, *Das Zeitalter der Nervösität*, 215–32, 389–407.
46. "Die Öffentliche Meinung 216," 116.
47. See "Die Öffentliche Meinung 224," 166; and "Die Öffentliche Meinung 213, Auch bei anderen Sportarten kommen Herzfehler, Muskelentzündungen usw. vor," *Das Motorrad*, 1929: 114–15.
48. See, for example, "Die Öffentliche Meinung 216," 116–17; and "Die Öffentliche Meinung 225," 212.
49. "Die Öffentliche Meinung 217, Was kümmert's den Mond, wenn ihn der Hund anbellt?," *Das Motorrad*, 1929: 117.
50. See, for examples of these various positions: "Die Öffentliche Meinung 212," 114; "Die Öffentliche Meinung 213," 114–15; "Die Öffentliche Meinung 217," 117; and "Die Öffentliche Meinung 225," 212.
51. *AIZ*, no. 20, 1930, 392.
52. The *AIZ* debate provides evidence that a modern concept of competitive sports was important to the Communist worldview, revising Christiane Eisenberg's thesis that competitive sports were anathema to the Socialist and Communist working classes. See Christiane Eisenberg, "Massensport in der Weimarer Republik," *Archiv für Sozialgeschichte* 33 (1993): 137–77.
53. *AIZ*, no. 25, 1930, 492.
54. "Hetz-Tempo der Zeit," in *AIZ*, no. 1, 1930, 18–19.
55. von Saldern, "Cultural Conflicts," 321–23.
56. Helmut Wagner, *Sport und Arbeitersport* (Berlin: Büchergilde Gutenberg, 1931), 112–16.

57. Wagner, *Sport und Arbeitersport*, 117.
58. Weitz, *Weimar Germany*, 318–21.
59. *AIZ*, no. 25, 1930, 498.
60. *Kuhle Wampe oder: Wem Gehört die Welt?* (1932). Director: Slatan Dudow; Screenplay: Bertolt Brecht; Music: Hans Eisler; Cinematography: Günther Krampf. British Film Institute, 1999.
61. See George Mosse's discussion of "warriors" and "Socialists," in *The Image of Man*, 107–32.
62. "Die Öffentliche Meinung 214. Houben, Dr. Peltzer, usw. sind mit hochgezüchtigten Rennmaschinen zu vergleichen," *Das Motorrad*, 1929: 115–16.
63. See Schmidt, *Sich hart machen, wenn es gilt*.
64. Dividing sports into different types, he located motorcycling within "technical sports," moving away from the nineteenth-century tradition of grouping motor sport together with bicycling under equestrian sports. Artur Vieregg, *Der Sport und seine Ziele: Unter besonderer Berücksichtigung der Gegenwartsfragen* (Berlin: Fischer Sport-Verlag, 1924), 10; see also, Eisenberg, *"English Sports" und deutsche Bürger*, 236–41.
65. Vieregg, *Der Sport und seine Ziele*, 5–6.
66. Eisenberg, *"English Sports" und deutsche Bürger*, 258–61.
67. Vieregg, *Der Sport und seine Ziele*, 11–12.
68. Ibid., 9.
69. Vieregg uses the term *Geschlecht* here, which I have translated as "lineage" and as "race" to fit the context of his quote. Vieregg, *Der Sport und seine Ziele*, 44.
70. Ibid., 49.
71. Emphasis in original. He does, however, add, "to turn a club into a romping place for political or religious conflicts is an absurdity." Vieregg, *Der Sport und seine Ziele*, 45.
72. Ibid.
73. Robert Schulte, *Körper-Kultur: Versuch einer Philosophie der Leibesübungen* (Munich: Ernst Reinhardt Verlag, 1928), 36–37. The Deutsches Hygiene Musuem was founded in 1912 and was very active throughout the Weimar Republic in promoting knowledge of anatomy, as well as hygiene, nutrition, and preventative health care.
74. Although "physical exercise could complement or replace military training," in his opinion, this was not the original purpose of physical education, therefore military training and training of the body were "best kept completely separate from each other." Schulte, *Körper-Kultur*, 39–40, 58–59.
75. Ibid., 44–45.
76. Ibid., 53.
77. Ibid., 52.
78. Ibid., 62.
79. Wajcman, *Feminism Confronts Technology*, 146.
80. Schulte, *Körper-Kultur*, 57, 59, 62.
81. Ibid., Plate 13.
82. Ibid., Plate 19.
83. Ibid., 37–38.
84. Diem also was involved in the planning of the 1916 Olympics in Berlin (cancelled due to World War I) as well as the 1936 Olympics. For a detailed biographical

sketch of Diem's early career, see Eisenberg, *"English Sports" und deutsche Bürger*, 223–25.

85. Original quote: "Is it physical exercise [*Leibesübungen*]? There are many different types of sport, for example, motorcycling, sailing, and also riding horses where it is about the mastery of external forces, where one's own physical power plays less of a role. Yes, chess playing and collecting stamps and other activities are grouped under the concept of sport, without being physical exercise. What unites these different types of sports? Is it that one does something for itself, for the sheer joy of it? Surely here is an important feature of the concept of sport, but still the boundary is not fixed, then all professional sport competitions are considered sport in both discourse and praxis. Competition? Sport is struggle, but this criterion, as much as it touches on the innermost core of the goal of sport, is not completely valid; because all tours, whether on foot or on water or in the air, the conquering of a mountain, ice or snow, are also possible without any competition or attempt to break a record, and also belong to the sport movement. Is it the return to nature? Here also, as much as we want to understand sport as an active experience that takes place in god's miracle, clear formulas are elusive. Some types of schooling of the body through sport can be found in indoor gymnasiums and on indoor tracks." Carl Diem, Preface, in Fritz Merz, ed., *Deutscher Sport*, vol. 1 (Berlin: Deutscher Sport-Verlag, 1926), 7–8.

86. Diem, *Deutscher Sport*, Vol. 1, 7–8. Nonetheless, according to Eisenberg, Diem supported an "apolitical" approach to sports, strictly refusing to allow racial, anti-Semitic or, by the end of the Weimar Republic, the increasingly popular National Socialist ideologies into the classroom of the German High School for Physical Activity. Eisenberg, *"English sport" und deutsche Bürger*, 363–66.

87. This is a play on words: instead of *Standesdünkel* (class conceit), he employed the neologism *Verstandesdünkel* (rational conceit).

88. *Deutscher Sport*, vol. 1, 17–24.

89. *Deutscher Sport*, vol. 2, 58–60.

90. See Rieger, *Technology and the Culture of Modernity*.

91. Parts of this section were discussed in Sasha Disko, "The Image of the 'Tourist Trophy' and British Motorcycling in the Weimar Republic," *The International Journal of Motorcycling Studies* 3, no. 3 (2007).

92. "Osterbetrachtungen über den deutschen Motorradsport," *Motorrad-Sport, -Verkehr und -Technik*, no. 14, 1926, 10–12.

93. See Disko, "The Image of the 'Tourist Trophy,'" 4–5. For the history of the TT-race from a British perspective, see Simon Vaukins, "The Isle of Man TT Races: Politics, Economics and National Identity," *International Journal of Motorcycle Studies* 3, no. 3 (2007).

94. Fritz Pullig, *Rennfieber*, in *Motorrad-Sport, -Verkehr und -Technik*; first installment was published in no. 39, 1929.

95. "Großer Preis von Deutschland, Sonntag 29. Juni 1930; Englischer Erfolg beim Großen Preis von Deutschland auf dem Nürburgring," *Motorrad-Sport, -Verkehr und -Technik*, no. 27, 1930, 3.

96. Eduard Voigt, "Schnitzel und Späne von der T.T.," *Motorrad-Sport, -Verkehr und -Technik*, no. 27, 1930, 17.

97. "490 cc Ardie 'Silver Eagle': A Very Modern German Product Featuring an Interesting Duralumin Frame and Elaborate Equipment," *Motor Cycling*, vol. XLIII, no. 1099, 1930, 217.

98. "What Germany is Doing," *Motor Cycling*, vol. XLIII, no. 1107, 1931. 502–4.

99. "We Suffer Defeat," *Motor Cycling*, vol. XLIV, no. 1137, 1931, 607.

100. Marieluise Fleißer, *Die List, Frühe Erzählungen* (Frankfurt am Main: Suhrkamp Verlag, 1995), 73. For an investigation of masculinity and the TT Race, see Alan Terry et al., "Spectators' Negotiations of Risk, Masculinity and Performative Mobilities at the TT Races," *Mobilities* (2014): 1–21.

101. Merki, *Der holprige Siegeszug*, 247–86.

102. "Ernst Henne wieder absoluter Weltrekordinhaber," *ADAC-Motorwelt*, no. 45/46, 1932, 4.

103. Magda Amann-Binder, "Interview mit Ernst Henne," *BMW-Blätter*, no. 10, 1931, 24–25.

104. "30 Minuten bei Hans Soenius," *Motorrad-Sport, -Verkehr und -Technik*, no. 14, 1930, 19–20.

105. "Deutsche Sportsleute," *Motor und Sport*, no. 14, 1927, 14–15.

106. Walter Dreher, "Die Eignung zum Motorradsport," *Das Motorrad*, 1929: 1750–51.

107. Jensen, *Body by Weimar*, 7. Hugo Kalinowski, "Motorradsportliche Disziplin," *Motorrad-Sport, -Verkehr und -Technik*, no. 20/21, 1924, 15–16.

108. Weitz, *Weimar Germany*, 318.

CHAPTER 5

Deviant Behaviors
Inclusion, Exclusion, and Community

Motorcycles reshaped the experiential landscape of Germany, for those who owned a motorcycle and those who did not. As the numbers of motorcycles on the streets steadily increased, the opprobrium towards motorcyclists increased. One particularly disquieting aspect was the noise produced by motorcycles. One article published in 1924 in the *Casseler Post* labeled motorcyclists "a public menace" and called motorcycles the greatest endangerment to "public security." The author asked when the police would "finally bring themselves to confront the malicious mischief," damning motorcycles as the "most obnoxious and abhorred of all modern means of transportation." Public space had been invaded by the noisome vehicles: "Even in the most remote parts of the city, one is not safe from the ear-deafening, nerve-shattering, putt-putting, and clattering that can be heard for kilometers." The author complained that "this outrageous state" could not be justified by claiming "the necessity of accelerating traffic as much as possible." Arguing that only a small number of motorcycles were used for business purposes and that "for short trips within the city a bicycle is fully adequate," the author bemoaned the police's lax attitude towards motorcyclists, and concluded by suggesting that "the majority of the population would welcome a decree in which, within city limits, motorcycles would only be allowed to be pushed by the hand."[1] During the Weimar Republic, public animosity against motor vehicles coalesced around disapproval of motorcycles in particular.

Public outrage at motorcyclists was not a phenomenon unique to Germany. As Steve Koerner has shown for the English case, motorcyclists there did not enjoy a positive reputation either. A confidential memorandum of the Royal Automobile Club's Motor Cycle Committee reported that, "in practically every part of the country, the general public is definitely antagonistic to motor cyclists; the press is prejudiced against them; the police harry them; the authorities regard them with disfavour. Outside of their ranks, motor cyclists can barely muster a friend."[2] Indeed, a 1926 article in the Evening Standard referred to the stereotypical motorcyclist as "a disagreeable young man who wore his cap the wrong way round and he transported himself by means of his horrible machine from the place where he belonged to places which [*sic*] did not want him."[3] Given the extent of spatial and social relations reordering involved with allowing motorized vehicles into everyday life and public space, motorization was necessarily a contentious process.[4]

Reflecting on the relationship between safety and risk in the United States, mobility scholar Jeremy Packer argues that "an increasing mobile population is perceived as a set of risks and threats. The means used to manage and control these disruptions tell us much about both the social order and the struggles against it."[5] Examining specific legal codes provides an inkling of how the process of motorization worked out on the ground; however, its discursive edges, published and reprinted in countless newspapers and magazines, prove more insightful for tracing everyday struggles between the motorized and the non-motorized. Through looking at deviant behaviors, such as violence, accidents, drunk driving, joyrides, and noise making, public attitudes towards motorcyclists and motorization gain substance and texture. Analyzing debates over emergent practices reveals contestations, both between non-motorized and motorized, as well as among the motorized—the car drivers versus the motorcyclists—over the right to define appropriate comportment in public spaces. Conflicts over mobility vividly illustrate the dynamics of inclusion and exclusion within the motoring community and society as a whole, and the fixing of formal and informal boundaries of acceptable behavior. Struggles over transgressive practices demonstrate the contentious nature of defining the acceptable boundaries of the community, and of defining normative modern masculinity.

This chapter also deals specifically with how the non-motorized were also subject to the changes wrought by motorized mobility, and looks at their oft hostile relationship to the intrusion of motorcycles into everyday life. It furthermore investigates attempts on the part of the state, the police, and intermediary organizations to mediate the conflict between the motorized and the non-motorized, as well as the motorcycle community's own attempts to regulate motorcyclists' behavior. While problems with motorization precipitated conflicts in an ever more industrialized, urbanized, and mobile mass society, specific conflicts between motorists and non-motorists also served as a pretext for expressing anxieties over the instable social, economic, and political conditions during the Weimar Republic.[6]

A Dog's Day: Road Rage in the Weimar Republic

In the 28 April 1928 issue of *Das Motorrad*, a curious article, "Dogs," appeared, authored by Hans Kater, written in a humoristic style.[7] He began his essay by describing an encounter with a dog, "which, out of inborn laziness, took no notice of my vehicle, more accurately, mischievously winking, calmly continued laying in the middle of the road. This dog will hardly deploy itself as an immobile traffic obstacle a second time, because as my 600 kg heavy *Muckepicke* ['muscle-axe,' 1920s colloquial for a motorcycle]—naturally, unavoidably—ran over his tail, he was suddenly very alive." Kater claimed that he was a dog lover and that "truly damn vicious dogs, that pose a danger to the calves of riders," were a rare occurrence, and that "most riders who, at every opportunity, grab for a whip, a pistol, or a 'dog-bomb'" were either "mediocre riders or natural-born enemies of dogs."

His advice to motorcyclists when confronted by "a four-legged beast" was to "keep your calm and not to attempt frantic dodging maneuvers or spastic kicking." He stated that honking would be understood by most dogs as a "call-to-arms" and that the best way for the rider to extricate himself from the situation was to either ride faster or to bring his motorcycle to a standstill, as "for most dogs, a stationary bike loses all appeal." In the case of "truly vicious dogs," Kater advocates that "the rider defend himself against the damn dogs through beating,

Ein Freund hatte sogar einen Spieß an seinem Rade angebracht und trainierte als spanischer Stierkämpfer . . .

Image 5.1. Illustration from Hans Kater, *"Hunde"* (Dogs), in *Das Motorrad*, 1928
© DAS MOTORRAD / Motor Presse Stuttgart GmbH + Co KG.

kicking, and firing warning shots, and if these methods are unsuccessful, through the running-over of the opponent in order to render him unfit for battle." He then weighed the relative merits of employing a pistol in defense against "two- and four-legged attackers." The remainder of Kater's essay continued in a similar vein; he related sadistic, yet humorous stories while assessing the advantages and disadvantages of the diverse anti-canine defense tactics, the most barbaric being a roasting spit mounted on the front wheel of a motorcycle.

While detailing such an absurd essay may seem dubious at first glance, this article sparked another fascinating debate among the readership of *Das Motorrad* that spanned almost a year's worth of issues. No less than thirty-five letters to the editor were published in the "Public Opinion" section during the course of the debates. The issues raised therein ran the gamut from pacifism to violence; from the general public's opinion about motorcyclists to who "owns" the streets; and from the envy of those who do not own motorcycles towards those that do to the ethics of motorcyclists and motorcycling. In the letters, readers addressed their relationship to private property, to law and order, to technology and nature, and to the decline of values through the collective violence of World War I, revealing class, status, and gender distinctions that at times disrupt standard historical interpretations while simultaneously underscoring others. The dog debate illustrates how an analysis of violence illuminates the range of attitudes towards motorized mobility and the variety of modes of negotiating the uneven and instable social terrain of modernity in Weimar Germany.

A letter submitted by a man with a doctorate, and of aristocratic heritage, opened the debate with a rousing call for all motorcyclists to "beat, kick and, as far as I'm concerned, shoot (for those who hold gun licenses) and even stab" these "plagues of the open road." He justified his opinion by stating that "the road belongs to us and not to the damn city or village dogs," and that every dog that he "temporarily or permanently maims" was one less dog that could cause injury to a fellow motorcyclist. Motorcyclists should be awarded more respect: "The times when motorcyclists, in the general public's opinion, were rated beneath bowwows are happily behind us, ever since a light went on in the heads of the rural 'Daddies' that motorcycles are also a form of transportation."[8] A touchstone for the subsequent debate, this letter, written by a member of the educated classes, addressed many of the issues that were important to motorcyclists: who owns the road, public opinion about motorcyclists, the rights of a dog owner vis-à-vis a motorcyclist, and the level of acceptable violence.

Proclaiming "Bravo! Herr Doctor!," a candidate for a law degree enthusiastically likewise supported a motorcyclist's right to run over dogs. He claimed that despite his more than 50,000 km riding experience, his only serious accidents were "caused by these miserable damn dogs and bastards." The student of law based his justification of a ruthless approach towards dogs in the domain of law and property rights, "Every forest ranger has the right to shoot any loose dog in his district because of the eventuality of the dog killing game!" He was particularly incensed that "motorists are to be denied the right to keep our domain of the streets, dearly financed through our taxes, free from this vermin that causes not only damage to our property but also life-threatening injuries to our sporting comrades!" He continued by asserting "that it is not only our right, but indeed our duty, to do away with the dogs," citing "paragraphs 823 and 828 of the civil law code." He insisted that, "in every instance of an accident," any offending dog owner should be "thoroughly prosecuted . . . so that these people, who, in their indifferent attitudes, represent the root of all evil, become conscious of the fact that a motor vehicle is not a toy and that the lives of the passengers and traffic safety are really important." Beyond legal measures, he presented violence as both a legally acceptable and ethically desirable method in the fight against dogs and in the schooling of their owners: "A boot is not as effective as a firm rubber truncheon! One blow to the snout of a Fido and the dog dentist has a new patient." He furthermore condoned the use of a pistol (although he too remarked on the necessity of having a license), and gave advice on the angle and distance that would be most effective—"fifteen degrees at a distance of thirty meters." With cowboy-like glee, he remarked: "And now that the weapons industry has bestowed upon us a superb one-handed six-caliber handgun that can be comfortably strapped in a holster for its immediate use, this manner of 'shooting down' is surely the simplest and best."[9]

Indeed, it was not uncommon for motorists in general to carry firearms. In a 1924 advertisement from a motorcycling magazine, the firm A.-G. Lignose advertised a "One-Hand Pistol: The Safe Utility Weapon [*Gebrauchswaffe*] for Motorcyclists. Because it can even be loaded, cocked, and made ready to shoot with one hand inside a bag. It is carried unloaded and therefore, even in a crash, is completely harmless for the carrier." In a review of the pistol, the editors of the magazine remarked that the "unfortunately still unsafe conditions mean that both automobilists and motorcyclists need to protect themselves from sudden assaults."[10] Not only the experience of World War I, but also the continuing violence during the Weimar Republic—from its inception in revolution to the almost civil war like qualities of the brutal suppression

of the revolution through the collusion between the SPD Reichswehr minister Gustav Noske and the *Freikorps*, and to putsch attempts and strike waves—left its mark upon Germany and an entire generation of Germans in a variety of ways, including the consequence of an abundance of weapons in circulation and a large portion of the male population with the necessary experience to deploy them effectively.

The law student ended his letter by calling upon the motoring clubs to "have no hesitations about unofficially organizing a dog-hunt instead of a foxhunt ... Thus! Once more unto the breach! Torero! Fiat justitia, pereat canis!"[11] Like the previous author, the author of this shockingly violent letter also belonged to the so-called educated classes, the *Bildungsbürgertum*. This law student grounded his right to willfully and without provocation kill any dog in terms of defending his private property. Due to the taxes he paid on his motorcycle, this author regarded himself as the rightful owner of the streets. Motorized modernity challenged the relationship between the ordering of property and the use of space.

Penned by another student of law calling himself Mr. "Bello" (both a play on the verb *"bellen,"* to bark, and a popular dog's name), the following letter published in the debate responded to the previous two letters by insisting that motorcyclists, when encountering stray dogs, were required by law to dismount, a law that he claimed "any student of law knows." Beginning his letter by chastising the first author's brutality, "Bello" argued that "as long as such elements continue to exist within our ranks, we should not be surprised if the rural population hate us, in the best scenario as 'plagues of the rural road.'" In his opinion, motorcyclists needed to be considerate of others: "Only the greatest of consideration for human and animal alike can win us sympathy. Up to this point, I have always managed to avoid hitting any dog, because I *wanted* to, and that's what it depends on." Again, such opinions show how motorization precipitated conflicts, in this case between rural and urban inhabitants, and the variety of strategies to resolve disputes. Indeed Bello's letter demonstrates that not all motorcyclists equated ownership of a motor vehicle with ownership of the road.

Bello's letter, however, then took a nastier turn; he expressed a wish that the next time the aristocratic doctor ran over a dog on purpose, "hopefully a tree or a stone will be able to look upon the insides of the precious doctor's head ... Then the dog can die at least with the knowledge that his death contributed to purging the area of one specimen of street vermin." Bello further stated that in the case that the doctor was successful at getting away with running over the dog without falling victim to a tree or a stone, Bello would council the doctor to accelerate rapidly, otherwise the "rural daddies" were likely to deal out the same treatment to the doctor that the doctor had dealt out to their dogs. "As experience shows," Bello maintained, the "treatment will be a brilliant success. The patient will become the most considerate person that one could imagine."[12] Bello's letter highlights the intense potential for conflict, and the presence of violence, or at least its threat, in forging the motorcycling community. Following his logic, in the interest of making motorcycling more acceptable to the general population, and especially to the rural public, draconian measures should be the appropriate punishment for those who trespass the norms of the imagined motorcycling community.[13]

As in the case of the sports debate, in a postscript to Bello's letter, the editorial staff of *Das Motorrad* called upon its readership to submit their views on this controversy. In a following issue, the heated debate about motorcycles and dogs was featured in the Public Opinion section. On the right side of the page, letters "For Dogs" were printed, on the left side of the page, letters "Against Dogs." The titles of the letters indicate the passion aroused by this subject: on the side "For Dogs"—"He Loves Running Away," "The Best Would Be to Push the Cycle," "I Reject the Right of Might," "And If an Elephant Were to Cross Our Path?," and "Calm and Caution and a Pop-Cork-Gun;" on the side "Against Dogs"—"Whip and Revolver Against Every Damn Dog!," "There's Only One Enemy – the Dog!," "Shoot Immediately!," "Bitter Fight Against the Bellos!," "Hold On Tight to the Handlebars, Give Gas with a Hurrah . . .," "When It Has to be, Beat and Kick, Stab and Shoot!," and "Let the Beasts Have It!"[14]

The most common themes in the letters "Against Dogs" were the dangers stray dogs pose to motorcyclists, the value of a human life over that of a dog, the streets belonging to motorists, the right of the motorcyclist to protect himself, his passengers, and his private property from attacking dogs, and the relative advantages of rubber truncheons, guns, and "running-over" as defense tactics.[15] The arguments "For Dogs" often stressed that such violent behavior served to damage the public's opinion of motorcyclists, especially in regard to the rural population. Their reasoning varied from asserting that such behavior did not befit a member of a *Kulturnation*, that the most dangerous menaces were motorists who claimed to own the street, that some four-legged creatures have more reason than some two-legged ones, and that either stopping or swerving were more effective and safer tactics to prevent an accident than beating, kicking, stabbing, shooting, or running over dogs.[16] Regarding the authorship of all these letters, none of them included an academic title with their signature, ostensibly indicating that unlike the authors of the first three letters, these readers/writers did not identify as *Bildungsbürger*. At least two of the authors had fought in World War I; one was on the side "Against Dogs," one on the side "For Dogs."[17] One of the authors "Against Dogs" stated that he used his "motorcycle primarily to practice his profession."[18] The authors of two of the letters "For Dogs" claimed to have more than twenty years riding experience (one since 1904, the other since 1906), while one author of a letter "Against Dogs" stated that "unfortunately" he was "only a bicyclist."[19] Many of the letter writers lived in urbanized areas, embarking on the weekends for rides in the countryside, where they encountered as traffic obstacles not only stray dogs, but geese, cows, goats, and sheep, as well as horse-carts, bicyclists, farmers, old women, and children.[20] Nevertheless, at least one author ("For Dogs") lived outside a major urban center, in a town that "on beautiful summer Sundays is traversed by many hundreds of motorcyclists."[21]

The juxtaposition of a few of the letters "For Dogs" and "Against Dogs" sheds light on conflicts over levels of violence and the appropriate comportment of motorcyclists on the road. The expression of violence present in the against-dogs letter "There is Only One Enemy – the Dog!," written by a World War I veteran, was intense. He found it "incomprehensible" that motorcyclists would try to protect such "vermin." Instead, he went to considerable lengths to arm himself against dogs: "[I modified] a rubber truncheon by affixing to the tip a jagged shell splinter that I brought back with me from the battlefield . . . One blow, and its innards and entrails decorate the road. [Yuck! The Eds.] My shell splinter that did so much damage on the battlefield seems to want to make amends by giving them damn dogs only what they deserve." The violence done upon his body on the battlefields of World War I continued to have deep reverberations after his return to civilian life. He followed other authors in justifying violence through ownership of the road: "Or is the life of a motorcyclist worth less than that of a dog? Isn't it already enough that motorcyclists are endangered by other traffic obstacles? The road belongs to us! . . . For what our money's worth, we motorcyclists don't need to stop for every damn dog and wait until 'sweet Bello' decides to move out of the way."[22]

However, as in the case of Bello's letter, expressions of this level of violence were not unique to those on the "Against Dogs" side. For example, in the letter "It Would Be Best to Push the Cycle," the author tied in his loathing of motorcyclists who behaved violently and disregarded the value of life with the defense of Germany as a *Kulturnation*.[23] "It is deeply saddening and shameful for us as a *Kulturnation* that among the so-called educated classes there are still those who hold these sorts of views. I only wish that on the avenues I would catch one of these beasts of a human being in the act, as he wouldn't slip through my fingers; then I would teach him culture in my way, so that he wouldn't yearn for it a second time." He saw the other side as ineducable, "bringing a lawsuit against these types won't help anything because these people are not only a danger to animals; no, they are a danger to all of us sporting comrades." His approach to dealing with motorcyclists who brought shame upon the *Kulturnation* mirrored the violence found among those who find it acceptable to "beat and kick, stab and shoot" stray dogs: "I only wish that, when such beasts [motorcyclists] race through the towns, that there is someone among the rural population who would throw a stick in the spokes, so that he falls and immediately breaks his neck. [Please, please! The Eds.] Then we would be rid of at least one of these street vermin."[24] What is particularly fascinating about this response was the way in which he turned the rhetoric used by those "Against Dogs" into rhetoric against motorcyclists who did not comport themselves in a way supposedly befitting of a member of a *Kulturnation*.[25]

Expressions of weariness with violence, however, can also be found. The most articulate expression was written in a letter "For Dogs." The author, also a World War I veteran, who for "four years heard the sounds of bullets whistling," firmly rejected "the right of might": "A motorcycle club under the leadership of a prospective lawyer (perhaps later to be the district attorney) armed to the teeth organizing a dog-hunt through villages—beating, stabbing, shooting—I would alarm the riot squad in the capital, the provincial administration, and the D.A.'s office." He censured those who would perpetuate a cycle of violence: "All in all, this does not get us any further . . . We should be thankful that the times of armed mobbing are over. Let us exercise every possible consideration, because truthfully the streets and the rest of those who use the streets were there before us . . . I reject the right of might."

Publishing a full range of positions, the editors at *Das Motorrad* closed the debate on dogs by allowing "The Neutral" to "Have Their Say!"[26] One "neutral" author urged motorcyclists to take up the "subject rationally and exercise a just critique." While acknowledging the problems stray dogs could present to motorcyclists, he favored the legal route of bringing a lawsuit against those dog owners who let their dogs run loose. "All in all, it can't be denied that the dog is a living being like humans are. They also have their good sides: think about dogs for the blind, firedogs, watchdogs, etc. It's all a question of upbringing. To want to exterminate all dogs is a utopian dream." Moreover, the author remarked that other participants in traffic, such as bicyclists, pedestrians, and the elderly, could present a greater danger to the motorcyclist, "besides the fact that there are potholes, slippery streets, etc. The doctor [in reference to the author of the first letter published in the debate] could go after them with the same kind of pluck as against dogs." Having offered a "reasonable suggestion" as to how to deal with dogs, the author concluded: "One must not be dragged into any kind of action out of spitefulness that one, as an educated person, would perhaps later regret. What would the doctor say if the general public beat all motorcyclists (often not unjustly called street vermin) to a pulp if this person, whether in the right or in the wrong, ran someone over?"[27] The debate on dogs provides insights into how acceptable levels of violence were worked out, and patterns between ownership and violence are discernible. The motorcycling community did not present a unified front when dealing with conflicts between the motorized and the non-motorized; this was still in the process of negotiation, in everyday encounters on the open road.

Despite the plurality of opinions and the evidence of a lively debate culture about dogs, the motorcycling community was keen to create internal cohesion through delimiting the bounds of acceptable behavior. Reacting to the debate on dogs, a letter on "The Ethics of Motorcycle Sport" expressed anxiety about the reputation of motorcyclists: "How does a true sportsman behave on a motorcycle? Outside of the circles of motorcyclists and those who wish to be motorcyclists, the sport of motorcycling is not recognized as such. Why not? Why is the motorcyclist so commonly referred to as 'a rowdy', rejected as a sportsman, and referred to as 'the motor*cyclist*' with a half-mocking, half-indignant aftertaste? Because—unfortunately—it is an accurate description of 80 percent of my dear sporting colleagues. The proof? The topic 'The Dog'!"[28]

In order to be a true sportsman, and hence, in the author's view to be someone worthy of belonging to the motorcycling community, a motorcyclist needed to possess "strictest self-discipline, cold-blooded calm, and consideration of others."[29] While all motorcyclists could potentially be included within the community of the "true sportsman," to belong, they had to abide by the rules. "The first and foremost law is: Never bring another in danger! The strong are always considerate; inconsideration and rudeness is always a sign of weakness and insecurity ... Refinement of mind marks the true sportsman, helpfulness and kindness towards others, modesty and unobtrusiveness."[30] The traditional masculine quality of strength is thus explicitly linked to consideration, kindness, modesty, and unobtrusiveness, whereas weakness is linked to inconsideration and rudeness, and no contradiction existed in his mind between being simultaneously cold-blooded and kind-hearted. He attributed animosity towards motorcyclists to a lack of proper education and manners among many motorcyclists. As Jeremy Packer noted regarding the post–World War II motorcycling community in the United

States: "The rider must be trained, educated, regimented, and ultimately outfitted... Much like an athlete or a soldier, it is said that in order to survive one must be disciplined, and much of this discipline is to come from within."[31] The motorcycling milieu attempted to bound itself by creating self-disciplining mechanisms within the motorcycling community and establishing a set of "rules for the road," etiquette designed to "tame the rowdies" that were giving motorcyclists a "bad name."

While motorcycling journals and clubs saw themselves at the forefront of establishing the boundaries of acceptable behavior, members of the motorcycling community at large also contributed their opinions on how to deal with delinquency and deviant behaviors. One author of a letter to the public opinion section of *Das Motorrad* claimed "the police cannot be tough enough on the noise-makers and wild riders."[32] Other members of *Das Motorrad*'s readership similarly lamented the lack of proper manners of many motorcyclists: "The Zeitgeist, lacking common sentiment and consideration of others, can be witnessed on the rural roads." This author believed that the responsibility for providing a remedy for "firecrackers" and "other such ingrates" would fall to trade journals, like *Das Motorrad*. "Through continual guidance," their influence could have a "great traffic-moralistic [*verkehrs-moralisch*] effect." He proposed four rules of motorcycling to "again take to heart":

1. Drive as you wish your comrades would.
2. Always reckon with traffic amateurs, especially in city traffic.
3. Preserve your nerves and always enjoy yourself while riding, thus never race at an inappropriate place.
4. Remember, the police are always in the right when they issue you a citation![33]

To the twenty-first-century reader these rules may seem like pat aphorisms for driving behavior that should be second nature to all drivers. However, as Peter Norton has shown for the United States, during this period, driving was not yet second nature, either for the motorized or the non-motorized: "During the 1910s and 1920s competitors fought to retain, or establish, legitimate title to the streets."[34] The legal code that governed different types of traffic was still in the making. Thus, instead of using the language of legal standards, these rules mimic the biblical Golden Rule, "Do unto others as you would have them do unto you," and so were perhaps more easily assimilable to existing ethical frameworks.

German cultural theorist Helmut Lethen identified a resurgence of "shame cultures" during the Weimar Republic, in which "external compulsions regulating behavior are visible."[35] The DMV, the umbrella organization of the motorcycling community, participated in such shame-based behavioral regulation by regularly publishing "blacklists" of motorcyclists who had transgressed the boundaries of appropriate motorcycling behavior.[36] In an article published in the organ of the DMV about "Traffic Discipline," the author maintained: "Good-natured cajoling alone helps nothing. Nothing remains but coercion. It is truly a pitiful sign that it is not possible to instill discipline in the users of the streets that is in their own interest, except through the threat of the rod, like children in school. But apparently it can't be done differently." Lethen tied the increasing power of shame to a proliferation of "codes of conduct": "Amid the unmanageable complexity of postwar society, in situations of economic insecurity and uncertain social status, the rules inscribed in codes of conduct operate to draw certain elementary distinctions between what is inner and outer, male and female. They mark separate spheres; they regulate forms of expression and realize the self's equilibrium."[37] Weimar "codes of conduct" that bounded the "habitus of objectivity" were marked by a dual paradox: "an acceptance of the individual's status as an object" while simultaneously holding out "the possibility of making that same individual the master of his or her fate."[38]

Accidents, Joyriding, and Drunk Driving: Risk and its Regulation during the Weimar Republic

As the "dog debate" above illustrates and as Peter Norton explored in terms of the urban figures of the jaywalker and the joyrider in the United States, the process of motorization produced struggles over uses of public space and private property, between the motorized and the non-motorized.[39] With increased mobility, both spatial and social, insecurity was perceived more acutely, generating new configurations of social conflict over private rights and the public order.[40] In this section, I explore three further aspects of motorization categorized as social threats: accidents, joyriding, and drunk driving, which took on greater importance as the numbers of drivers increased after World War I. The ability of everyday individuals to possess things with the potential power to kill arbitrarily bred social strife and provoked calls for containment. Exploring the "darker" sides of motorization reveals how regulating private property and managing social risk during the 1920s and early 1930s became particularly urgent in the context of the fractured social, political, and economic space of newly republican Germany. Efforts to criminalize joyriding and drunk driving reveal how new technologies, on the one hand, held out the potential to stimulate new social freedoms and, on the other hand, simultaneously precipitated social anxieties and created increased impetus for implementing instruments of social control. In the process of motorization, as Jeremy Packer argues, safety and risk stand in a relationship of "productive tension."[41]

Accompanying the increase of personal motorized transportation, provisions, laws, policing tactics, and industries were developed to manage the risk the technology presented. In 1927, according to the legal advisor of a motorcycling magazine, it was necessary to submit the following papers to the authorities in order to apply for a driver's license:

1. Birth certificate.
2. Certificate from a state-appointed doctor that the applicant has no bodily defect that would impede his capability to operate a motor vehicle.
3. Photograph.
4. Proof that driving was learned at a driving school or by a person approved as a driving instructor.[42]

The legal advisor also noted that "a certificate from the police attesting that the bearer has no previous criminal record is not necessary," but rather it was up to "local police authorities to examine whether there were facts that would demonstrate that the applicant was not suited to driving a motor vehicle; for example, serious crimes against property, the proclivity to drunkenness or rowdiness, [and] especially brutality."[43] Motorization increased the reach of the state, augmenting its potential to regulate and control the population. Alongside creating a register of drivers, the various arms of the state also participated in organizing property relations by implementing measures to more fairly distribute risk and criminalize aberrant behavior. The need to regulate the process of motorization produced both normative social categories and practices, and expanded the legislative and police apparatus needed to enforce the new codes.

The political and social impulse behind regulating motorization during the Weimar Republic was neither uniform nor directed, and to describe the vehicular code as static or monolithic would be misguided to say the least. While not entirely haphazardly contingent, devising systems for regulating traffic and drivers often proceeded by trial and error. However, analyzing the establishment of a "highway code," as Henri Lefevre called it, exposes struggles and compromises over how to organize society and the economy in the newly created Republic.[44] The legal authority's final advice to the magazine's readers about the new licensing requirements regarded the scope of applicability: "These legal requirements apply for all of Germany, and we recommend that you make your police authorities aware of these paragraphs."[45] Motorization was still, in the terminology of Raymond Williams, an "emergent culture," and examining the legislation and policing of motorization reveals the extent to which the relatively new nation-state of Germany remained a fractured space in the process of being made.[46]

Accidents

One of many letters to the legal column of *Das Motorrad* about the consequences of accidents, the writer detailed a crash that had killed his female passenger and, as a result, had the potential of putting severe economic strain on the motorcyclist. According to his account of the incident, the "young lady," whom the author claimed not to have known before, had insisted on taking a ride on the back of the motorcycle to another city, despite supposedly having been "warned of the dangers." Due to a defective tire, they crashed. His female passenger was pinned under the motorcycle and, on the way to the hospital, died from a fractured skull, despite the letter writer's claims to have "done every-thing humanly possible" to save her. He subsequently informed her parents about the death, and offered to pay for the funeral. The parents informed him that the local gymnastics association would pay for the funeral and that he would not incur any financial obligations. Three months later, however, the parents of the female passenger had sent him a notice that he was to pay 1,000 RM or be faced with a civil lawsuit. The letter writer claimed he had "no cash assets" and sought an answer to what his responsibilities were in this case.[47] The question of "guilt" functioned on a legal as well as a moral level.

As the letter above shows, the process of motorization brought with it not only the promise of a quick ride to another city, but also incalcu-lable dangers, thus precipitating social conflicts between the motor-ized and the non-motorized.[48] According to an analysis of incidents reported in motoring magazines, accidents were the primary motivator behind forms of protest against drivers, including violent attacks that, especially during the Wilhelmine era, sometimes had lethal outcomes. With the gradual increase of motorized transportation and the imperial state's active promotion of the new technology, public squares, streets, and sidewalks were reorganized to facilitate motorized transportation, subjecting non-motorized forms of transport—horse carts, bicyclists, and pedestrians—to subordinate positions vis-à-vis motor vehicles.[49] The question of who should bear responsibility for accidents, however, provides an example of how the state, both Wilhelmine and Weimar, sought to distribute the social risk and to reduce the potential of social conflict by legislating that the burden of proof was on the motor vehicle owner. Nonetheless, the fines imposed by the courts were relatively insignificant in contrast to the damage inflicted on third parties and to the wealth possessed by most motorists before World War I.

After World War I, with a wider dispersion of motorized technologies over a broader range of the population, the question of the equitable distribution of risk shifted again.[50] While insurance was not mandatory, as more and more motorists came from less wealthy segments of society, insuring motor vehicles and motorists became an increasingly important branch for the insurance industry.[51] For example, during the 1920s, many motoring clubs contracted insurance companies to provide cheaper insurance for members. In general, motorcyclists were less wealthy and also far less likely to cause property damage or fatal injuries to third parties than their automobile-driving counterparts.[52] The disparity between automobiles and motorcycles in terms of wealth and incidences of third-party accident injuries was reflected in the number of insurance policies held by each: by the end of the Weimar Republic, 80 percent of car drivers had taken out an insurance policy in contrast to only 10 to 15 percent of motorcyclists.[53]

With an increase in the degree of motorized transportation, the number of accidents involving motor vehicles also increased. Data on types of motor vehicle accidents became part of the annual statistical yearbook of Berlin in the early 1920s, and by the mid-1920s included statistics on the cause of accidents such as speeding, drunkenness, and wrong turns. In addition, the yearbook compiled information on the numbers and types of violations of the traffic code. Berlin's 1928 statistical yearbook recorded a doubling in the number of accidents from 1926 to 1927, from about thirteen thousand to over twenty-one thousand; by 1929, however, the number of recorded accidents had stabilized at approximately twenty-seven thousand.[54] Daily newspapers printed excerpts from the police blotter in which traffic accidents were featured regularly, making motor vehicles appear particularly threatening. In the opinion of the non-motorcycling public, motorcycles were often portrayed as particularly dangerous vehicles and motorcyclists as the most inconsiderate and reckless participants in modern traffic. This was an image that the motorcycling press often attempted to counter by seeking to place the primary blame for the increase in accidents with other road users, especially automobiles, pedestrians, bicyclists, trams, and horse carts.[55] One motorcyclist proclaimed, "The days of pedestrian imperialism are over!"[56]

Motorcycling accidents were prominent enough to have an entire book devoted to them. The handbook, *Motorcycle Accidents*, published in 1929 by Dr. Albert Sachs, systematically detailed possible risk factors for motorcyclists from "driving too fast" to "too thin tires." Interspersed with quotes from classical authors, for example Goethe's aphorism, "Whoever seeks to hide a secret is an enemy," the handbook claimed to "uncover causes of accidents and provide means to prevent them."[57] Sachs' approach to the dangers of motorcycling was measured. In his introductory chapters he focused on the reputation of motorcycling and the changing reality: "It is totally undeniable that once upon a time motorcycling had something 'ballsy' about it, and in the circles of thoughtful people was thoroughly discredited. But somehow in a strange way this *prejudice* has stayed with us until today, even though the motorcycle has changed completely." Sachs believed, however, that "new dangers" had emerged: "Above all . . . the dangers of greater speeds, which 'thanks' to further innovations on the machine have increased more and more . . . Low taxes and the low purchase price . . . have contributed to its rapid and broad distribution, and therefore unfortunately also to its dark side that is constantly in our minds in the form of the accident chronicles in the daily papers."[58] He stressed the vulnerability of the motorcyclist as a road user: "In relatively minor incidents the motorcyclist must pay with his skin, whereas the automobile driver would perhaps accrue a small amount of material damage." Sachs chastised motoring magazines and motorcycle dealers "who would rather silently ignore the question of motorcycle accidents, posing them as flukes or as a nasty side effect of motorcycling."[59] For Sachs, educating motorcyclists about the possible sources of danger was the best means in terms of preventative measures, as well as increasing the standing of motorcycling as a form of transportation and sport.

Public outcry over the human cost of motorcycle accidents also bled into debates over the utility of motorcycle racing. In a lead editorial on the accidental deaths of motorcycle racers, the author lamented that motorcycle sport was unfairly targeted as being particularly dangerous in comparison to horse racing, boxing, fencing, football, and even tennis. "How great is the number of sportspeople who have suffered massive injury, who have even been crippled, by supposedly completely harmless types of sports. There is a known instance in which a young lady lost an eye through a tennis ball." Arguing against a ban on motorcycle racing, the author continued: "And wouldn't anyone who suggested a ban on competitions in riding, fencing, boxing, football, tennis, etc. be generally subjected to laughter? Why then this severity towards the

sport of *man and machine*? Against this grand and bold sport that is
still so necessary—even now!—to popularize motor vehicles for our
industry!"[60] Nevertheless, the author of the editorial did have to admit
that "in the past three years" at least forty-five racers or their team-
mates had died—"a large number indeed."[61] Rather than acknowledging
the destructive potential, and sometimes fatal outcome, of motorcycle
racing, the concluding remarks offered up a fatalistic analysis of death
as the great equalizer: "At the strong and weak, famous and unknown,
Thanatos throws his spear. He is the great conqueror that no mortal
can resist. And whose lot has been cast falls as his prey. Crashing in
the middle of the course, he is taken away in the middle of his life."[62]
Crashes, however destructive to life and limb, took on an almost fatal
allure in the emergent culture of motorcycling.

Despite the high rate of accident fatalities among motorcycle racers,
the association between crashes and the masculine attributes of bravado and toughness was thus widespread in motorcycling rhetoric.
Crash, an expressionistic poem, illustrates how accidents and masculine
tenacity were discursively intertwined:

> . . . I cower deeply in my saddle,
> In my arms and legs streams
> A vortex of explosions.
> The wind, my cold opponent,
> Blusters around my limbs.
>
> . . .
>
> Time is forgotten,
> Like a meteor I cut
> Through the night.
>
> . . .
>
> Then a sudden jolt
> In my joints,
> I clamp on tight, endure.
> The machine springs sideways,
> Like a horse bolting,
> My arms pull in the reins,
> Yet I am thrown from the saddle
> By the momentum of my body.
> I sink—eternally and deeply—
> Into shimmering white fog.
>
> . . .

From deep unconsciousness
I get back up.

. . .

The motor thunders all worries
From my mind,
All the painful heaviness
From my limbs.
We ride on.[63]

This poem, reminiscent of futurist literature, glorified both the magically animated relationship between the modern knight-like rider and his machine transformed into a horse, as well as the experience of the crash. The crash was portrayed as an inevitable and important rite of passage in the life, and perhaps death, of a motorcyclist. Accidents were, so Kurt Möser argues, the price of riding a motorcycle.[64]

The contribution of the motoring press to the formation of a bounded community based on a conception of masculinity that emphasized bravery can be seen in a series of articles "Crash Dangers, Crashes, and Crash 'Technique'," written by Hans Kater, the same author as of the "Dogs" article: "That our sport is not made for trembling old men or sissies, but rather demands a hefty dose of bodily strength and resistance, presence of mind, and a sense of responsibility, merely serves to increase its allure."[65] In the course of the article, Kater recounts his many crashes, each time escaping relatively unscathed. To his reader he recommended that in the case of "impending danger, my dear sporting comrades, do not immediately think this time it will all go wrong." Instead Kater asserted that they should "grit their teeth and as quick as a flash consider the possibilities to evade and block," emphasizing courage and quick-thinking as indispensable traits. Kater saw a "true motorist" not as "overconfident, arrogant, or a daredevil," but rather as "sober-minded, cold-blooded, and having guts."[66] Through discourse on crashes, the ideal-type motorcyclist was increasingly circumscribed in terms of masculine attributes that brought together a technically oriented, sober-minded rationality with physical cold-bloodedness.

While motoring magazines simultaneously upheld the allure of the crash, they also attempted to play down the risks of motorization by asserting that increased technical perfection, easier handling, better brakes, better streets, as well as increased education about traffic laws, had and would further diminish the number of accidents.[67] Generally speaking, education, especially for novices and youth, about the dangers of motor vehicle accidents and how to avoid them was the most commonly cited intervention in terms of accident prevention. Educational tactics, however, could take on a more exclusionary tone. For example, one suggested examining drivers' psychological fitness as a means of reducing the number of motor vehicle accidents. According to proponents of so-called "psychotechnics," good driving skills could not necessarily be learned, but were determined by the driver's "psyche"—"the quality of his 'senses' and his natural ability." An author of a 1929 article on "psychotechnics" called for "abnormally harmful and unsuited elements to be excluded from qualifying for a driver's license."[68] Applied to motorization, as well as many other spheres of life, "psychotechnics" and the language of inclusion and exclusion shows the push toward systematizing and biologizing social norms during the Weimar Republic.[69] As the example of accidents and accident prevention makes clear, what was promoted as a neutral technology had significant social consequences. Motor vehicle accidents increasingly threatened the lives and limbs of both the motorized and the non-motorized, and strategies were developed that sought to curtail the damage and to distribute the social risk involved with motorization.

Joyriding

The introduction of motor vehicles presented new problems in terms of regulating private ownership. The illegitimate appropriation of modes of transportation was not criminalized in Germany on the basis of *furtum usus*. This law, dating back to the Lombard Edict, determined temporary possession of a movable object, such as a horse, as not necessarily subject to criminal punishment. Upon the initial introduction of the motor vehicle in the late nineteenth century, *furtum usus* was carried over and applied to the new technology.[70] Although the unauthorized use of a motor vehicle by anyone who did not hold the proper driving license was an act punishable by law, in many instances there was no legal basis for reprimand. If the "intent" was only to use the vehicle "temporarily" and not to "take it into his possession," under the legal code no criminal act had occurred.[71] As motor vehicles became more widely dispersed and easier to operate, the legal misappropriation of motor vehicles became an everyday event during the Weimar Republic.

The fact that these *Schwarzfahrer*, literally "black-riders," were not subject to punishment created problems in a mass society that was increasingly, although incompletely, ordered through the regulation of private property. A comic that appeared in a 1929 issue of the leading motorcycling magazine in Germany depicts the ubiquity of the threat of theft. The title of the joke is *Vertrauensperson*—"The Trusted Third Party." A motorcycle owner asks a random man on the street:

> "You, young man, do you know how to ride a motorcycle?"
> "I have no idea," the young man replies.
> "Very good, then watch my motorcycle for five minutes!"[72]

Employing humor to address motorcycle theft demonstrates that it was a commonplace occurrence, as a joke, in order to be found funny, has to contain some amount of self-evident understanding to be readily comprehensible to its intended audience. Joyriding opened up the possibility to partake in motorized modernity for those normally excluded, and to enjoy a privilege ordinarily restricted to a relatively small minority during most of the Weimar Republic. Joyriders subverted economic hierarchies by seizing control of coveted status symbols that, according to much of the discourse surrounding joyriding, cunningly appropriated not only a higher social status, but one that was tied to enhanced sexuality.[73] The joyride facilitated fluid identities and opened up possibilities for experiences outside the everyday.

As joyriding became more commonplace and increasingly posed a problem for ordering the incipient political economy, it was concomitantly perceived and framed as a threat to public safety. Many who proposed toughening the law against joyriders did so on the basis that the condoned practice of *furtum usus* was anachronistic and presented real problems for motor vehicle owners who had often invested not insignificant amounts of capital during a period of chronic economic instability. Other opponents of joyriding consciously connected other areas of social conflict, such as youth and drunk driving, to the risks that unauthorized riders posed for society as a whole.[74] Although the German legal code did not provide concrete guidelines for dealing with joyriding, courts often sided with the owners of motor vehicles; cases against chauffeurs, who without the knowledge of their employers engaged in joyriding, were particularly contested.[75] Despite the increased criminalization of the practice of joyriding during the Weimar Republic, the motorists' lobby continued to persistently petition the government to classify joyriding as a criminally punishable category of theft or larceny, and thus to remove the automobile from the status of *furtum usus*, a natural law, and to inscribe it as private property in positive law. Only in October 1932, however, was the practice of joyriding incontestably criminalized in Germany through a legal ordinance, indicating the *longue durée* of processes of motorization, the halting consolidation of the regime of private property, and the persistence of everyday efforts to contest the capitalist social order.[76]

Drunk Driving

Drunk driving represented a further precipitant of social conflict in an increasingly motorized society. Driving under the influence of a mind-and-behavior-altering substance was viewed as a growing threat to public welfare that demanded containment and management through implementing a variety of strategies of social control, from education to social humiliation and legal punishment. Although awareness of the severe social implications of drunk driving grew during the first decades of the twentieth century, as with joyriding, it was only in the closing year of the Weimar Republic, 1932, that the Verordnung über Kraftfahrzeugverkehr [Motor Vehicle Traffic Code] was revised to include the explicit criminalization of driving while intoxicated.[77]

In 1929, approximately seventeen out of every one hundred motorcyclists arrested by the police were reported to be drunk, according to the German Association Against Alcoholism's traffic division, a percentage they cited as being higher than in a number of other European countries.[78] In an effort to discourage drunk driving, the association published a journal, *Der Pionier*, whose stated mission was the "promotion of sobriety and safety in the transport sector." Articles such as "The Dangers of Alcohol and Motorcycling," and reprints of the most gruesome accounts of traffic accidents caused by intoxicated drivers culled from the German daily press, were geared towards educating the public about how alcohol impairs the ability to operate motor vehicles, and the shaming of those who indulge in such behavior. The motor vehicle trade press also published articles on the problem of drunk driving, reminding their readership not only of the dangers that it presented to life and limb of the motorist and the public, but also of the legal potential of their license being revoked or their vehicle being confiscated, both threats that were framed in terms of a loss of freedom of mobility and diminished social status.[79]

Drunk driving was widely understood as standing in a causal relationship to the increased likelihood of injury and fatality accidents, and was thus portrayed as a socially unacceptable behavior that posed a grave threat to the integrity of the collective social body. Morality and sobriety formed a constellation in the perception of both outspoken teetotalers and the motor vehicle trade press in general. A short rhyming poem published in *Der Pionier*, "Man at the Wheel," both consciously linked drunk driving with unnecessary risk to life and property, and exercising restraint to inhabiting proper masculinity. The last stanza sums up the general gist of the poem: "In short, evil temptations I do forsake; that none has cause to become irate." Another poem called alcoholics "members of a cowardly breed," and shamed them as "destroyers of the public good."[80] And although the discourse against drunk driving attempted to shame men from driving under the influence by connecting sobriety with proper masculinity, an aura of masculine virility continued to adhere to the ability to drink large quantities of alcohol. An article published in a motorcycling journal by an author of sports novels, Walter Julius Bloem, called motorcyclists "strong types," "chaps typically able to handle their alcohol." Bloem, however, condemned drunk driving, asserting that, in the hands of those under the influence of alcohol, motor vehicles became "murder weapons" and asserted that drunk drivers had earned "the gallows"—wording that stresses an outlaw image of both motorcycling and drunk driving.[81]

During the Weimar Republic, the motoring community took concrete steps to regulate its members' behavior, so as not to increase the potential for conflict with society at large.[82] One rather novel educational approach adopted by many clubs across Germany was the gymkhana, where riders would consume alcoholic drinks successively in between driving rounds of an obstacle course.[83] These events were designed with the intention of demonstrating the deleterious effects of alcohol on motor skills and judgment to motorcyclists and the wider public. Other strategies suggested by members of the motoring community to curb the practice of driving under the influence included restricting the amount of alcohol motorists were allowed to consume at tourist cafes and rest-stops, and in convincing restaurants not to serve "known motorists" alcohol.[84] The legal-bureaucratic system in Weimar Germany recognized the threat of drunk driving through penalizing intoxicated drivers, especially those who caused accidents, and through codifying alcoholism as a medical reason for denying a driver's license application.[85]

With private individuals propelling masses of metal at velocity into public spaces, motorization represented a profound incursion of modernity into everyday life. As forms of "social delinquency," to cite Michel de Certeau, joyriding and drunk driving were "alternately playful and threatening."[86] The unease around accidents, drunk driving, and joyriding in the Weimar Republic reflected emergent social conflicts over the right to define private property and the public good. These "deviant behaviors" contained and produced struggles over defining both the integrity and moral order of society, signaling, in terms of both criminalization and patterns of prosecution, the halting and incomplete transformation of space, time, and the political economy during the Weimar Republic.

Noise and Nerves in the "Roaring" Twenties: Class, Gender, and Generational Conflicts

By the summer of 1928, with the number of motorcycles on German roads having increased fourfold since 1924 from under a hundred thousand to almost half a million, the press and the police launched a vigorous and vociferous campaign to combat motorcycle noise.[87] The editors of *Concordia*, the newspaper of the Union of German Bicyclists, welcomed the renewed official crackdown on noise pollution caused by motorcyclists:

> The battle against the noisemakers and other reckless motorcyclists seems finally to be taken up energetically and with justification! At a roadside control of the main roads leading out of Munich, no less than thirty-six motorcyclists were 'caught in the act,' having undertaken modifications on their exhaust pipes (naturally after registration), *making a terrible racket* … At a second control seventy motorcycles were examined, out of which *20 percent* (!) had modified exhaust pipes and thus were causing a huge spectacle. The motorcycles were confiscated and referred to the official expert for examination.[88]

Noise nuisances, unlike joyriding, fell under the general nuisance laws, and producing what was perceived of as excessive noise could thus be subject to punishment of a fine. Although the noise produced by motor vehicles had been a point of contention for as long as they existed, by the late 1920s motorcycles in particular were officially targeted as noise nuisances by communal governments, and local and state police agencies.[89]

Noise: A Technical or a Social Problem?

While noise pollution, and street noise in particular, was not a new point of conflict, rapid industrialization and urbanization in Germany from the 1860s onwards aggravated the potential for discord.[90] In 1908, the doctor, educator, and philosopher Theodor Lessing published a polemical piece "against the noises in our lives," in which he emphasized the noise pollution caused by motor vehicles as "a new kind of noise," "incomparably more terrible" than any other kind of noise humanity previously had to endure.[91] In the same year, Lessing founded an "Anti-Noise Association," modeled after the New Yorker "Society for the Suppression of Unnecessary Noise."[92] Motor vehicles, however, were not the primary target of the prewar anti-noise association's efforts: "While the second goal listed by the association was the eradication of children's noises from the streets, there was no mention of automobile noise, and the eighth goal merely encourages the improvement of electro- and automobiles."[93] Nonetheless, the automobile industry, press, and clubs viewed Lessing and the anti-noise association as a threat to Germany's nascent motor vehicle industry, and insistently sounded alarm against the "tyranny of the nervous," branding the anti-noise activists as "neurasthenics" and "unworldly intellectuals," and attacked them for supposedly impeding the progress of building a modern society.[94] While anxieties and conflicts over the social implications of modernization and motorization were evident in pre–World War I society, the heightened sense of social instability during the Weimar Republic increased the potential for clashes between different social actors and groups.

By the beginning of the Weimar Republic, improvements to automobile exhaust systems and new legislation requiring adherence to technical norms had greatly diffused the noise problems caused by cars. Motorcycles, however, continued to produce significant noise pollution and, with growing ownership numbers among a broader spectrum of society, were increasingly perceived as a serious public nuisance.[95] In the spring of 1926, following numerous complaints about the noise produced by motorcycles, the Reich Transportation Ministry issued a clarification statement in which, according to Paragraph 3, Section 1 of the Verordnung über Kraftfahrzeugverkehr [Motor Vehicle Traffic Code], from 5 December 1925, "*all* motor vehicles are required to be constructed in such a manner that precludes the possibility of any irritation of persons or endangerment of horse carts through the noise caused by motor vehicles." Further, as of 1 March 1926, it was officially stipulated that all internal combustion engines, including motorcycles, must be equipped with a sufficient muffler to absorb noise, and any modifications to the muffler or exhaust system were forbidden. Among other issues regarding motor vehicles, the Reich Transportation Ministry also stated that it planned to discuss the question of whether further measures were necessary to control the noise specifically caused by motorcycles in their consultation scheduled for the end of 1926.[96] This official stance had far-reaching implications for the everyday experience of motorcyclists.

Noise pollution was more of a social problem than a technical problem. The DMV took up the issue of the new regulations on motorcycles.

In an article in the umbrella organization's journal, the author agreed with critics that "certain types of motorcycles with highly compressed engines make too much noise." He nevertheless found it "incomprehensible that just because of a small minority of vehicles on the road, a formerly common piece of equipment [the exhaust valve] should be forbidden." He went on to blame highly compressed motors on the German motor-vehicle tax formula, as the amount of tax due on a motor vehicle was levied according to cylinder volume: "The engine designer is forced to keep the cylinder volume as low as possible, but nonetheless the same kind of performance is demanded of these engines that in other countries is expected of engines with double or triple the cylinder volume." The author asserted that "it is a fact, proven thorough testing," that mufflers designed to eliminate all noise often considerably reduced engine performance and furthermore cause the motor to overheat on difficult terrain. In a nod to the relationship between economic strength and motor strength, he stated: "The resulting damage is known to all drivers and owners of small-powered cars and motorcycles who are especially affected, as naturally, in the case of these vehicles, diminished performance makes itself much more felt than in the case of a strong engine with the corresponding energy reserves."[97] Although motorcycle engineers were aware that highly compressed motors increased noise emissions, the motor vehicle tax code and high operating and maintenance costs encouraged engineers to develop highly compressed motors, often two-stroke engines, well known to produce far more noise than larger cylinder volume four-stroke engines. While a political decision prompted a technical decision that resulted in increased social conflict, the social conflict was latent in the very terms of the debate about technology.

In the reformulated law, the word "unavoidable" was struck from the phrasing of Paragraph 3, Section 1—"the law regarding the reduction of noise, smoke, steam, or bad smells." Critics of the revised law intimated that the unreasonable legal formulations would lead to unequal and unfair treatment of motorists under the law and by the authorities: "It is the opinion of the law makers that such nuisances are to be ascribed to the 'ill will' of the motorists, who must then be punished through the pocket-book." Critics also pointed to the potential for arbitrary and unfair policing. On the one hand, he lauded the urban police for being "more understanding . . . than one would expect from the wording of the law." In contrast, he argued, "the motorist in the provinces is completely at the mercy of the 'subjective' opinion of the officer, who mostly lacks technical education and insists on the exact wording of the law, often adding his own two-cents in order to fill the town coffer."[98] Interpreting the legislative measures and police actions to curtail noise, opponents criticized the revised Traffic Code as hampering the innovative ability of the inventors and designers of motor vehicles, and hence as impeding the overall growth of the German economy. Motorization thus gave rise to a further source of conflict between the public and the state.

Policing Noise: Motorcyclists and the State

A cartoon titled "The Police Arm" provides a humorous perspective on the measures taken by the police: a telescope arm extends itself to apprehend the wayward motorcyclist. This cartoon highlights not only the problem of smoke and noise pollution, and conflicts between motorists and the police, but also the fascination of Weimar society with technical solutions to social problems.

1. Max roars with much noise and smoke through a quiet town. Because he has yet to get the traffic morals down.
2. My dear Max, please take care. The guardian of the law is aware.
3. With the mechanical arm invented by me, lightning-fast you will be snapped by the gendarmerie.
4. He reels you in, there's no way to flee. Hand over your papers, as quick as can be.[99]

While motorists in general were subject to the arbitrary nature of the early motor-vehicle laws and the policing of them, the specific issues of noise and smoke pollution brought motorcyclists in particular into the sights of police action, and thus into conflict with the state, on an everyday basis.

After the passing of the 1926 Verordnung über Kraftfahrzeugverkehr, police officials throughout Germany, and especially in the larger cities, intensified their actions against street noise caused by motorists, and motorcycles in particular. The police campaign against motorcyclists so lauded by *Concordia* included setting up roadside controls on the major roads leading out of cities and towns, and implementing controls inside the cities on major arteries: "Police controls stop motorcyclists on the open road and make them show their papers. Official experts examine the machines. Exactly and precisely. They examine the mufflers and pipes, they finger around on the throttle, etc. They turn their attention to the brakes … every motorcycle not finding grace in the eyes of the strict officials is—confiscated."[100] Although all motorists and vehicles were officially subject to these roadside inspections, motorcycle owners complained of being unfairly penalized by these police actions.

DIE MOTORISIERUNG
DER POLIZEI

Im klassischen Lande der höchstentwickelten Schmuggel- und Verbrechergilden, der Banksprengungen mit Dynamit und der Mordkolonnen — also in USA —, wo auch der Kraftfahrzeugverkehr gigantische Zahlen erreicht hat, besitzt die gesamte Polizei in Stadt und Land ein aus der Erfahrung heraus zweckdienlichst erkanntes Instrument, das starke Motorrad.

Auch die europäischen Staaten haben diese Erkenntnisse sich zu eigen gemacht und wertvolle Ergebnisse im Kampf gegen Verbrecher- und Rowdytum eben durch die Hilfe des Motorrades erreicht. In Deutschland selbst ist in Bayern die Landespolizei und -gendarmerie sozusagen selbstverständlich mit starken BMW-Jagdmaschinen neuester Konstruktion ausgerüstet. Desgleichen die Landes- und Schutzpolizeistellen in Baden, Sachsen usw. Selbst das kleine Oesterreich hat mit BMW-Maschinen die Motorradpolizei geschaffen, desgleichen die Motorradbundesgendarmerie. Ja, selbst die Republik Columbien schafft sich eine schnelle Motorradpolizei. (Und zwar mit starken deutschen BMW-Maschinen gegen die schärfste englische Konkurrenz).

Preußens Polizei und Landjäger müssen bis heute noch vergeblich auf eine durchgreifende Schaffung von starken Polizei - Motorradkorps warten. Damit haben sie sich einer besonders starken Waffe begeben. Abgesehen von der gerade in unserer Zeit besonders schwer ins Gewicht fallenden Frage der Anschaffungskosten,

Westfälische Polizei

2

Image 5.2. Motorcycle Police Policing Motorcyclists. In *BMW-Blätter*, 1932, BMW Group Archive.

Nonetheless, in 1928 and 1929, as complaints in the press and from the general public grew louder, the police intensified their actions to abate the noise pollution caused by motorcyclists.

While officially approving of the policing of errant motorists, motorcycle organizations were wary of possible discrimination of motorcyclists by the authorities. On several occasions, the DMV issued letters to ministers of the interior and the Reich transportation minister criticizing the unduly harsh treatment of motorists, and motorcyclists in particular.[101] A 1926 letter began by first welcoming the general order issued by the Prussian interior minister in the summer of 1926 to police authorities to "use utmost care in applying the Verordnung über Kraftfahrzeugverkehr, to only issue a warning as a rule, and only in the most extreme cases to impose a minimal fine, so that in all cases the impression is avoided that the pursuance of such infractions could serve the purpose of securing revenue."[102] The organization stated its interest in "educating" motorists, in order to avoid "an easily incurred and understandable embitterment" on the side of the general public against motorized traffic. However, pointing to the fact that motorcyclists generally belonged to a lower social class than automobile drivers during the Weimar Republic, the letter insisted that, "the imposed fines are often not at all in proportion to the economic situation of the person affected." The letter also claimed, based on reports from its members and other affected motorists, that "fines in considerable amounts are imposed on a massive scale daily." The DMV asserted that it would vigorously defend the interests of its members, and demanded that the Interior Ministry regularly control everyday police praxis regarding the fair application of laws directed towards motorcyclists.

Responding to complaints made by individuals and automotive organizations about unfair police actions, the Prussian interior minister regularly issued orders to local police authorities to exercise restraint when reprimanding motorists: "Warnings are to proceed properly and tactfully according to the circumstances of the situation and the persons involved ... If punishment is necessary, then the penalty is to be determined according to person and action." Indeed the minister argued that the police "overlook that the same penalty affects the poor and the well off completely differently." The minister urged the police forces to take "the economic conditions of the violator, which in general should be known well enough, into consideration ... I forbid that the number of reports made by the police and the country police is taken as the measure for judging their performance."[103] This order indicates that the Prussian minister of the interior did not equate ownership or use of a motor vehicle with wealth, and that he acknowledged that police fines could pose undue economic hardship, especially on motorcyclists. However, the DMV saw these directives as falling on deaf ears. In a 1928 letter to the Reich Transportation Ministry, the DMV again complained that, "in praxis all of these appreciated directives [to ensure the fair application of the new law] have died away without having any effect." The organization reiterated their protest that local police authorities were implementing traffic laws arbitrarily, and that "the impression cannot be avoided that the police are simultaneously attempting to increase revenue." The organization viewed local police authorities in particular as "thwarting the requirements of modern traffic with amazing stubbornness."[104]

During the course of 1929, in an effort to reconcile the perspective of the police with that of motorcyclists, *Das Motorrad* published a series of eight articles. In the series "From the Praxis of a Policeman," Police First Lieutenant Arno Brösicke from Barmen, himself a self-described motorcycling enthusiast, addressed the most salient legal issues for motorists and motorcyclists in particular from the perspective of "an experienced traffic policeman."[105] In one of his articles, Brösicke dealt with the question of the policing of noise nuisances: "The wrath of our dear fellow citizens directs itself solely against the misfiring and roaring noises caused by the exhaust fumes. We all know they don't belong to the most pleasant of noises, at least not for innocent bystanders. For a few years now, the authorities' fight against such noise has been in full force." While Brösicke pointed to the fact that the impression of exhaust noise as a nuisance is "totally subjective," he saw police measures to abate the noise caused by misfiring motorcycles as being in the interest of the general public.[106] Commenting on the reaction of motorcyclists to the intensification of roadside police controls and the "lively protest against the actions of the police authorities," he argued that it was undeniable that these measures were justified and were "primarily directed against the inconsiderate rider." On the other hand, he stated: "If the one or the other person believes himself to have been unjustly reprimanded, then I would ask that it should be taken into consideration that it is in no way the intention of the police authorities to harass motorcyclists, but simply that, out of consideration for fellow citizens, it was necessary to take action against excessive behavior."[107] While simultaneously adamantly defending measures taken in the name of "our dear fellow citizens," Brösicke suggested that better technology and more "noiselessness contests" were possible remedies for the problem of noise pollution.[108]

With the conflict between motorcyclists and the police heating up, *Das Motorrad* published an editorial lead piece that specifically addressed the issue.[109] In an open letter to Police Lieutenant Brösicke, the editor of *Das Motorrad*, Paul Friedmann, stated that Brösicke's portrayal in his articles of the "modern police officer" as "strict and just, yet with the smiling benevolence a father has for his ill-mannered yet not evil-natured children" was a "wonderful and strange fairy tale" for the vast majority of German motorcyclists. Friedmann asked why there was such a great discrepancy between "theory and praxis" in policing, citing two instances in which the editorial staff of *Das Motorrad* had unwittingly come into direct conflict with the police authorities. In an "Open Answer to an Open Letter," Brösicke responded to Friedmann's accusations regarding the unfair treatment of motorcyclists by police authorities.[110] In Brösicke's opinion, the question of the "'Motorcyclist and Police' is only one chapter of a great problem, 'Citizen and Police,'" which he believed was more aptly described under the rubric of "People's Police." "Do we already have this 'People's Police?' No! Are we on the way to having one? Yes! ... It's only been a few years since we began trying *to make a friendly, always-ready helper out of an ill-mannered, unchecked, power-heady [Machtdünkel] encumbered police force*. We have to break with an entire system in the conception of police activity." Referring to the opaque and arbitrary nature of policing practices during the pre-republic era, Brösicke stressed postwar attempts at restructuring of the policing system. The state apparatus was a complicated patchwork affair during the Weimar Republic, and Brösicke's comments reflected the ambiguity and instability of the relationship between post-imperial society and the state.[111]

According to the "modern" policeman Brösicke, the title of "People's Police" must be bestowed by the people themselves, as they would have to feel that the police were acting in the interest of the "people." However, Brösicke also promoted the idea that citizens had as great a responsibility as the police in this process. The police represented an "unavoidable state-necessity, as long as there are wrongdoers that step out of line to the detriment of their fellow citizens." The highest priority for the police, according to Brösicke, was to protect "the general well-being ... all individual or group interests must be subordinated. It is in this spirit that laws are passed. Whoever breaks the law and is called to account for this, should not see this as police harassment, but should examine whether or not he is not actually in the wrong." Furthermore, Brösicke complained that the majority of police officers had to deal with rude outbursts and ignorance on a daily basis. On the other hand, he admitted that some officers also lacked proper manners and that "in the majority of cases, officers do not have to deal with evil-natured wrongdoers." "Rubber truncheons and pistols are the weapons of the police only in the most serious circumstances. His daily weapon is politeness; politeness disarms. Politeness is, however, also a virtue that does not appeal to every type of character, in which case serious and adamant training is required to remedy this flaw." During the Weimar period, contemporaries often commented on the "rough tone" of discussion, and lamented the general "brutalization of manners."[112] Despite Brösicke's own conciliatory tone, it is clear from the phrasing of this article that the conflict between motorcyclists and the police had become nasty on both sides. Brösicke saw "bitter gall" in Friedmann's reproaches, and viewed the relationship between the police and motorcyclists as "unfortunate."

The discussion in *Das Motorrad*, as well as from articles and letters to the editor that appeared in other trade journals and in the general press, makes clear that motorcyclists did indeed perceive themselves to be unjustly harassed by the police.[113] Riders of the smaller, tax- and license-free motorcycles were especially resentful towards police actions against noise pollution. A letter published in the legal advice column of *Das Motorrad* described how one particular policeman, who had "the reputation of instituting all kinds of legal proceedings," subjected the author on numerous occasions to inspections regarding noise emissions.[114] Although the author claimed that he had consulted three policemen with expertise in motor vehicle issues who had determined his motorcycle to be within the range of acceptable noise levels, the policeman nonetheless served him a ticket for 3,30 RM.[115] This motorcyclist was not unique in his perception of being the target of unjustly harsh treatment by the police.[116] Not only were motorcyclists subject to random roadside inspections, but in many instances, if the responsible policeman, who motorcyclists often complained lacked the necessary technical competence, suspected the motorcycle of not conforming to the stipulations, the motorcycle would be confiscated and the owner subject to fines and the sum necessary for the repairs. The police practice of confiscating motorcycles particularly upset motorcyclists, not only because of pecuniary penalties, but because confiscation often prohibited them from carrying out their professional obligations, inhibiting them from taking part in the promises of motorized mobility.[117]

The Social Implications of Policing Noise

"Street Noise," a 1929 article by Heinz Peters, identified both the actors and the issues involved in everyday conflicts over uses of the road. He also attempted to identify why motorcycles in particular were targeted.

For Peters, responsibility for the problem lay less in the construction of motorcycles "delivered with their pretty, state-stipulated exhaust systems," but rather within the motorcycling community, with "those among us, the 'also-riders' and sport heroes who cannot do without clouds of oil and thunderous crashing." Peters identified young motorcyclists as particularly egregious transgressors of appropriate behavior. In his mind, their behavior legitimized their exclusion from the motorcycle community. "If a young motorcyclist has the ambition to make a machine gun out of his state-licensed motorcycle—out of pure mischief, unrecognized sport mania, or in the honest wish to increase the performance of his motorcycle 10 percent so that he can achieve 120 km/h in the city—then we, the moderate people, can only be in favor if the police painstakingly pursue them."[118] The association of reckless, rowdy, and noisy motorcyclists with youth was a theme that runs throughout the discussion on noise pollution, both in the trade journals and in the general press.[119]

Engineer and chief editor of *Das Motorrad*, Paul Friedmann, underscored the correlation between youth and noise in his 1928 article "Unnecessary Noise": "It certainly does not serve the cause of promoting motoring sports, when time and again we see young people revving their engines when the motor is idle, and perhaps also opening and closing the throttle in order to create the impression of being an experienced motorcycle racer within their crowd of admirers."[120] "Confused by the Sides of Grace and Hate, his Character wavers," a 1928 editorial in the DMV journal, provides another example of how, within the motorcycling community, youth were seen as the primary noisemakers. The author lamented that there were "still far too many motorcyclists that lack consideration for their fellow humans, without thinking that they are unnecessarily intensifying the opposition of the authorities and the public against motorcycles—and their users." The author's description of these "inconsiderate" riders echoed many of the characteristics of the "Schbortzman," the anti-ideal of appropriate motorcycling behavior. "With a roar they 'start their engines,' in a nighttime race. They roar through the quiet streets, no holds barred. It's almost always young riders that act so imprudently." He claims that their aim is to "show off as 'sportsmen' in a heroic pose. They feel the brazen sound of the racing machine ought to awaken amazed admiration in passers-by, yet it arouses only annoyance and hate against the innocent motorcycle."[121] The fact that admonishments of the motorcycle press and clubs were targeted at "youth" reflects a general concern about youth, as a category, during the Weimar Republic. While on the one hand they were sometimes held up as repositories of the "uncorrupted German spirit," especially in terms of sports, on the other hand "youth" were also often conceived of as a "problem," with discussions revolving around lack of fathers, parental supervision, consumption habits, sports, and morals.[122] Akin to anxieties about the "new woman," the preoccupation with the "youth problem" in the Weimar Republic was a further expression of unease over the transformed social order.

Due to the prominence of the issue, it is hardly surprising that the debate about noise and youth spilled over into *Das Motorrad*'s public opinion section. One thread was expressed in terms of youth's opposite, maturity. One author maintained: "Situated, mature people, who are able to stand by their man in every life situation, are just good enough to drive a motorcycle. All others should first learn to control themselves, before wanting to control a motorcycle."[123] Alongside "maturity," the reaction of motorcyclists to legal measures and police action was often couched in the language of respectability: "respectable" motorcyclists fear they will be lumped together with the "inconsiderate," and thus be subject to unfair treatment by the authorities. Within motorcycling journals, numerous editorials and letters to the editor condemned the "unsports-manlike" and "inconsiderate behavior" of reckless and noisy motorcy-clists as contributing to, if not responsible for, public animosity towards motorcyclists.[124] "Respectable" motorcyclists claimed the reputation of motorcycling was suffering more damage from "sport comrades who feel they are the sole rulers of the streets and who stomp on the rights of their fellow citizens than from anything else." In order to firmly bound the community and regulate behavior, it was necessary to severely dis-cipline the delinquents: "The police cannot be harsh enough against the noisemakers and the wild riders, and the police will be of more use for our wonderful sport than all those who cuss about and warn against traffic traps."[125] The singling out of youth sheds light on the dynamics of inclusion and exclusion that operated in the forging of the male-domi-nated community of motorcyclists. The language of "respectability" cul-tivated in the motorcycling milieu during the Weimar Republic contained strong undertones of compliance to class, gender, and generational norms, primarily connoting an unquestioned acceptance of order. In the repeated lectures that "motorcyclists … exercise consideration towards the nerves of their fellow human beings," the underlying reproach was against nonconformity. Obedience to authority and the acceptance of order, however, did not necessitate a stance of tolerance or universal-istic humanism. On the one hand, motorcyclists often criticized police profiling. On the other hand, the desire to differentiate between "respect-able" and "inconsiderate" shows that mechanisms of inclusion and exclusion served to bind and bound the motorcycling community.

In the context of policing of noise, motorcyclists also often expressed anger at being unfairly targeted in relation to other vehicles. Although many took the position that the police had the right and duty to intervene in traffic in order to ensure safety and to regulate its flow, they nonetheless took issue with the fact that the police seem to be making no attempt to reduce the noise created by other vehicles, above all public transport vehicles. Painting an image filled with mutual animosity on the part of all participants in traffic, Peters suggested the police were less than efficient at regulating conflicts of interest: "At the present moment, mutual incitement to violence and abuse reigns. Every class of road user attempts in less than flattering essays and articles to place the blame on the other; so that bicyclists curse at the trams, motorists at pedestrians, pedestrians at horse-carts, and everyone together at the police on high." Peters argued that motorcycles were not at fault for excessive street noise, but that many other types of vehicles—such as streetcars, horse-carts, trucks, and buses—were much louder, without being targeted by the police or the judicial system. Describing the "modern automobile as quiet as its shadow," he claimed the motorcycle was perceived as the "enfant terrible," and the public's outrage over noise pollution was thus specifically directed against motorcyclists.[126]

In "Check [as in "checkmate"] the Street Noise," an article published in 1928, the author compared the police actions against street noise to a chess game or to a battle: "With the attack against the motorcycles, the campaign against street noise has been opened. Let's hope that after the first successful battles the officials put their well-tested combat patrols into action against other disturbers of the peace." Railing against the noise created by public transportation, the author demanded that the police take action against them: "The next advance should be directed against the streetcar that, bound to the rails, can be called one of the worst traffic obstacles in the modern cosmopolitan city. And it would also be a commendable assignment to quiet the terrible noise of the Leviathans of the streets, the autobuses and the trains, in the interest of the peace-seeking residents."[127] Motorcyclists felt unfairly targeted by police in their fight against street noise, particularly in contrast to the equally noisy, if not noisier, means of public transportation. In this case the private individual saw himself in conflict and subject to unfair treatment vis-à-vis the state and the state's own purported interest of abating noise.

While the non-motorized majority had indeed long since been incensed over the noise and smoke pollution caused by motor vehicles, the public's growing hostility towards motorcyclists in particular was certainly in part due to the rapid increase in the sheer numbers of motorcycles on German streets. In 1924, there were 97,965 motorcycles registered in Germany, but by 1929 the number had increased sixfold, with noisier and noisome small-powered motorcycles making up more than a third of the registered motorcycles. By the end of the Weimar Republic, there were over 800,000 registered motorcycles in Germany, and more than half of them fell under the category of small-powered motorcycle. In comparison, the number of automobiles in Germany had increased less than fourfold in the same period, from 132,179 to 497,275. The increase of absolute numbers of motorcycles during the latter years of the Weimar Republic can nonetheless only partially account for these attacks against motorcyclists.

Descriptions of Sunday mornings on roads leading out of major cities in the late 1920s depicted veritable motorcycle convoys. Alongside privately organized excursions, clubs and trade magazines also organized mass rides on weekends. For example, 135 motorcyclists of both sexes took part in the second "weekend ride" hosted by *Das Motorrad* in August 1927, which the magazine reported was a "great success."[128] Celebrating the "array of roaring machines," "the astonished Berlin day-trippers stopped in their tracks and formed cordons" to watch "an impressive parade" of seventy motorcycles "disappear at a brisk pace." In towns on the outskirts of Berlin, the motorcycles were "greeted" by "waiting crowds" and "so it happened that walls of people lined the streets, looking enviously on the shining faces riding the 'roaring devil's things.' The weather god meant well with us, and seventy motorcycles stir up a lot of dust when it hasn't rained for three weeks, and half of the dust covered our faces." This report, while seemingly optimistic, nonetheless reveals the latent conflict between motorcyclists and the rest of the population. The description given by Paul Friedmann, who, as both a motorcyclist and editor of the leading independent motorcycling magazine, was highly invested in motorcycling, evoked a sense that the non-motoring public was enthusiastic about their ride. The reality of the noise made and the dust kicked up by seventy motorcycles, however, is strong evidence that the motorcycle convoy annoyed many of the non-motorized, disrupting the quiet and calm of a summer Sunday. Despite the spectacle appeal of masses of motorcycles, the everyday nuisances of noise, dust, and exhaust fumes that accompanied the growing numbers of motorcyclists resulted in increased hostility towards them.[129] The non-motorized complained that for them the only "benefits" of the process of motorization were "a lot of noise, stink, splashing with dust or puddle-mud, and a threateningly high mortal risk."[130]

By the late 1920s, anti-automobile sentiments in Germany had generally diminished; however, despite the general trend towards traffic and hence conflict regulation, public protest against motorcyclists increased during this period.[131] Many cities, towns, and villages took concrete measures against the motorized Sunday invaders by enacting Sunday driving bans. For example, as *Motorrad-Sport- Verkehr und -Technik* reported in 1926, in Saxony, "as in numerous other areas of Germany," a driving ban on all motor vehicles was in place on numerous streets.[132] While many restrictions affected all types of motorized traffic, in certain cases, motorcyclists were singled out. The City Council of Heidelberg, for example, sought to enact a law forbidding all motorcycle traffic on the main street of Heidelberg.[133] The article, "A Medieval City Council," published in response to the council's attempt, pointed to the failure of the "glorious German revolution" to cast off antiquated customs. "Despite the knowledge-disseminating alma mater in this beautiful little city, it seems to be completely dark in the high chambers of the city council." The author upbraided the city government for being backward looking and imposing arbitrary restrictions on mobility. The lines of the conflict were drawn along who was modern and who was not.

Communal government action against motorcyclists was not, of course, limited to Heidelberg. Many tourist and spa towns enacted city ordinances prohibiting motorcycles, and the Allgemeiner Deutscher Bäderverband [General German Spa Association] specifically targeted motorcyclists as unwanted public nuisances.[134] In 1930, Dr. Friedrich Uhde, the mayor of Bad Pyrmont, a spa resort in Lower Saxony and a member of the Spa Association, attacked motorcycles as an "infernal devil's invention that should be exterminated."[135] In the summer of 1929, Uhde enacted a law according to which all riders of two-stroke motorcycles had to push their motorcycles within the town limits, or else be subject to a fine. During the 1920s, even as motorized traffic in general became increasingly regular and regulated, motorcyclists were picked out, amongst all motorists, "to be exterminated", "eradicated," or subject to the harshest discipline.[136]

Noise and Nerves of Steel

It rattles, roars, hoots and screams,
"Motorcycle – Look Out!" Everyone to the side,
Though the smallest on the road,
It makes as much of a din as a double-wide![137]

For many motorcyclists, part of the allure of a motorcycle was undeniably connected to the noise it makes. *Knatternde Gesell*, roughly translatable as roaring, put-put, or rat-a-tat fellow, for example, was popular as a club name. It was also the title of a short story from 1930 that explicitly associated the modern with the romantic, and noise with nature in the experience of motorcycling. Many recurrent themes regarding the experience of motorcycling are revisited in this piece: technology and nature, timelessness and modernity, risk and relaxation. "I've seen all of them, motorcycle sportsmen of all grades and shades ... Here they still fight and wrestle over the advantages of the rural road, over the weal and woe of the weather, over the up and down of endless kilometers ... Subtly and indefinably, the aura of distance flows, bringing experience from near and far away." The noise of the motorcycle was inextricably linked to the promises of freedom and mobility: "I like nothing more than to sit far above the wide, well-kept mountain road in the high summer grass, and alongside the chirping of the crickets and the buzzing of the bees to hear the powerful droning and throbbing of the motors, uphill, downhill."

> Here they come, flying, one after the other in an almost uninterrupted chain, everyone in a world of his own ... One almost recognizes the brand and the model from how they lay on the street, how they take the curves, switch gears, in the roaring, in the desire to leave behind the wide band of the shimmering street, or quietly and pensively to go on their way, to enjoy in a measured tempo being surrounded in the wonders of the flying-by environment.
>
> Free and unbound, the modern vagabond goes his way, alone, as a couple, with or without sidecar, the guessing game is fun: where to, where from ... The motors drone, the valves hammer, technology sings her song in the solitude of the mountains, in the shadows of the forest and in the jaws of the trees streaking by.[138]

This short ode to motorcycling illustrates how noise constituted an inseparable element that amplified the sensations of a particularly modern experience. Rather than a nuisance, the external noise of the motorcycle emphasized, on the one hand, a feeling of carefree adventure, and on the other hand, provided an inner sense of quietude and contemplation.[139] Describing motorcyclists as "modern vagabonds," the author summoned up romantic notions of motorcycling masculinity. The pastoral was contemporaneous with the industrial. Nature and technology, increased tempo and relaxation, noise and solitude were not construed as irreconcilable opposites, but rather as necessary complements.

Although a major selling point of the motorcycle was that it allowed the rider to "experience the joys of nature independently of train schedules," public opposition to motorcyclists stemmed in part from a rejection of motorcyclists' attitudes towards nature, time, technology, and risk.[140] One central critique of motorized mobility was based on the how it supplanted quietude and diminished the collective right to tranquility. In an ambivalent portrayal of motorized modernity, one motorcyclist argued, "In the time of post horns, hoop skirts, and Biedermeier tail-coats, the world and its colorful hustle and bustle was accepted; one acted with more sensitivity, more sentimentality." In the era of motor-ization, "the overly sensitive among us curse at the roaring motors and the hustle and bustle. Certainly some things have changed in terms of how life is viewed. Time has become more bustling." Rather than criticize the new age, the author argued that "today, the environment is a different one and the human has become more decided and more spirited. Technology or no technology, whoever thinks that with the appearance of motorists the joy of contentment has disappeared, or that the 'German' disposition rolled away with the last mail coach, is mis-taken."[141] While motorcyclists attempted to diffuse the conflict by ren-dering motorcycling a natural part of German development, the social conflict over motorcycle noise stemmed from aversions to changes in the physical and perceptual landscapes during the Weimar Republic. For much of the non-motorized population, the auditory accompaniment underscored the sense of an inescapable invasion and conquering of public and private space. Unease with shifts in the relationship between time and space produced by processes such as mechanization and motorization was at times expressed in hostility towards motorcyclists.

Beyond the promise of motorcycles providing access to freedom and nature, part of the appeal of motorcycles was tied to the racetrack and the association between noise and strength. Hermann Homann employed both the technique of photomontage and descriptions of noise in order to convey the strength of the machines and the excite-ment of the race in his poem "Start." The fourth stanza describes the moment the race starts:

The flag falls: like a mad pack
Suddenly racing motors howl
And lunge after the swift victor's spoils –
A bath for the nerves, music to the ears.[142]

For those with noise-steeled nerves, the ruckus of the start of a race is a salubrious experience.

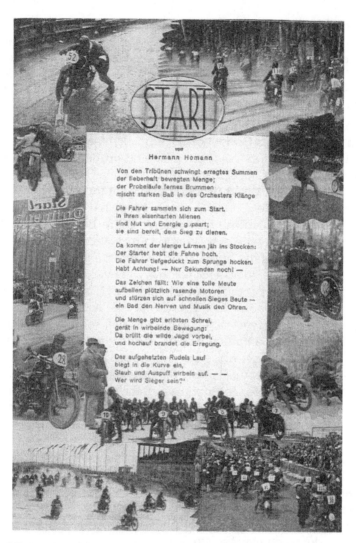

Image 5.3. Hermann Homann's Poem "Start," in *Das Motorrad*, 1929 © DAS
MOTORRAD / Motor Presse Stuttgart GmbH + Co KG.

The noise produced by the motorcycles was an essential element of
the overall attraction of attending such an event. "On the racetrack we
should let the roaring monsters be in peace. They belong there. The
extraordinary performance of the racing machines cannot be achieved
without the ear-deafening noise; and it gives the spectator, especially
the inexperienced spectator, joy, because not only the eye but also the
ear conveys the image of breakneck speed."[143] Photographic images

portraying the start of a motorcycle race could capture a sense of the smoke and the chaos of the event. The image, nonetheless, was silent. The speed and power of the engine was in part conveyed by the noise the motorcycle made, and an essential ingredient of the sensory experience of motorcycling was noise.[144]

Outside the arena of the racetrack, noise also continued to be a welcomed constituent component of the experience of motorcycling for many motorcyclists. In a book on "manners for the industrial employee," Acutus, the pseudonym of Kurt Lubowsky, provided comical suggestions for mastering modern life.[145] Point eight in his suggestions for motorcyclists loosely followed a "Cartesian logic": "Exhaust valve and horn are indications of your terrestrial existence. Demonstrate that you are there. 'Look out! We're alive.' Only rogues are modest."[146] The noise made by the motorcycle announced the presence of the motorcyclist.[147] Countless technical articles advised readers to listen carefully to the sound of the engine as the best way to detect problems, and motorcyclists trained their ears as diagnostic tools.[148] The sounds made by the pistons and valves in a motorcycle engine were often compared to a living organism's heartbeat: "Not only the eye and the nose perceive her expressions of life: but also the feeling . . . One feels something: alongside the hot breath of the engine, the beats of her heart. They let us experience our connection to her, when her heart skips a beat we are thrown out of every train of thought. Let us become one with her. Her pulse and ours determine to equal extents the ride, the camaraderie."[149] For motorcyclists, noise was a necessary and constitutive element of the motorcycling experience, and was linked to modern masculinity.[150]

Conclusion

Motorization sparked anxieties and struggles over ways of regulating accelerated mobility.[151] A 1926 story, "My New Motorcycle," by Kurt Schwitters, a prominent representative of literary modernism, provides a humoristic example of the fear of technology becoming unmanageable. A man, tired of expending energy pedaling a bicycle, decides to buy a motorcycle. The dealer sells him a motorcycle, he learns how to start it, jumps on, but forgets to ask how to bring it to a stop. In his ignorance, he thumbs the throttle and, instead of stopping, the motorcycle speeds up. "You should have seen the tempo with which the nag suddenly tore off. A fast train couldn't have kept up. The thing began speeding, I was forced to spasmodically grip the handlebars, it shook my hands, and I had an indescribable fear." Trapped on this out of control motorcycle, he mood swings between mortal fear and exquisite pleasure. At one point the rider imagines "every tree is my gravestone," yet as cars "avoided me timidly" and "I whizzed by," he found the experience "swell" [*knorke*]. As it grows dark and he has no lights, he is convinced he will die. Pondering his last will and testament, he decides, "I will bequeath the motorcycle to my nemesis." Eventually he speeds into a city, where policemen struggle unsuccessfully to stop him. Then the gas runs out and the motorcycle slows to a stop, "gasping its last breaths." He greets an approaching policeman as his "savior," calling him a "lovely angel, but this love was not requited. He dragged me to the station and locked me up for fourteen days. But, still, I had amused myself like a king."[152] Schwitters, a modernist who tried, "through language and material, to find out the reality of his time," provides a reading of Weimar modernity in "My New Motorcycle" that combines the fear and excitement that motorized mobility could simultaneously induce, and illuminates how technology was framed in terms of a precarious social order teetering on chaos.[153]

Debates over the regulation of motorization and its by-products, such as accidents, drunk driving, joyriding and noise, reveal struggles between different social actors: between the state and the citizen; the "rowdy" and the "respectable"; the urban and rural; the motorized and the non-motorized. Negotiations over violence, ethics, and the public nuisance of loud exhaust pipes further demonstrate how motorcyclists sought to establish a bounded community based on a mutual understanding of appropriate motoring behavior. The process of motorization, particularly rife with both contradictions and the potential for sparking social conflict during the Weimar Republic, heightened the sense that intense instability and crisis were perpetual. Motorcyclists appeared to embody the disorder of spatial and social relations. As economic unevenness triggered struggles around ownership and belonging, dynamics of inclusion and exclusion became increasingly relevant in a society that confronted democracy and consumerism with ambivalence.

Notes

1. "Der Landplage der Motorräder," *Das Motorrad*, 1924: 220.
2. As cited in Koerner, "Four Wheels Good," in Thoms, Holden, Claydon, *The Motorcar and Popular Culture*, 161.

3. Ibid.
4. For regulation in England, see Potter, "An Exploration of Social and Cultural Aspects of Motorcycling," 147–89.
5. Packer, *Mobility without Mayhem*, 13.
6. Peter Norton has discussed the contested nature of the adoption of the automobile in the United States; see Norton, *Fighting Traffic*. Mom also looked at the process of normalizing motor vehicle traffic in the North Atlantic zone; see Mom, *Atlantic Automobilism*, 565–619. Möser also offers insights on violence and motorization; see Möser, *Fahren und Fliegen*, 337–44.
7. Hans Kater, "Hunde," *Das Motorrad*, 1928: 268–71.
8. "Öffentliche Meinung 149, Hunde," *Das Motorrad*, 1928: 443. The very complex question of how the non-motoring public, both rural and urban, viewed motorcyclists, and whether or not motorcyclists ever became acceptable to the public, is addressed at greater length below in the debate on noise. For a discussion of the resistance towards and eventual acceptance of the motor vehicle in Germany, from its inception through to the early 1930s, see Uwe Fraunholz's *Motorphobia*. Fraunholz provides a thorough analysis of the causes and manifestations of anti-motoring protest, both qualitatively and quantitatively. He also discusses the steps the state undertook to regulate the conflict between the general public and motorists, such as the development of traffic rules, obligatory insurance, and a tax code. For a comparative European perspective on resistance to motorization, see Merki, *Der holprige Siegeszug*, 143–98.
9. "Die Öffentliche Meinung 154, Noch einmal: 'Hunde!'" *Das Motorrad*, 1928: 485.
10. *Motorrad-Sport, -Verkehr und -Technik*, no. 9, 1924, 29. Further evidence of the ubiquity of the gun-toting motorcyclist is Kater's short story, "Autoverfolgung mit dem Motorrad," in *Motorrad-Sport, -Verkehr und -Technik*, no. 43, 1924, 23–24. In this car chase story, the hero motorcyclist takes up a chase after an automobile had run over a small girl in a village in a hit-and-run accident. After a series of failed attempts, at the end of the account the motorcyclist is finally successful, by stopping the car at a railway crossing: "We hurry towards the car's occupants, I hold my Browning in my bag ready, just in case, and the crossing guard swings his club threateningly. But both driver and passenger are half-numbed by the collision and do not think of resistance."
11. "Öffentliche Meinung 154," 485.
12. "Öffentliche Meinung 164, Noch eine Meinung zu 'Hunde'" *Das Motorrad*, 1928: 568–69.
13. Another letter took a similar, yet less radical stance to "Bello." The author, "one Herr Wolff," a traveling salesman, claimed that, despite having lost no love for dogs and therefore no reason to defend their existence, "the mastery of the motorcycle" would render every "potentially bothersome" dog harmless and that most of his "sporting comrades" would reject the method recommended by the aristocratic doctor. "But putting aside all the risks involved for the rider if v. B's method were employed (nervousness, uncertainty in steering, attack of the irritated dog, ending in the rider falling), it makes us so unpopular with the population that the 'good old times' of the generally raging hatred towards motorists would soon be resuscitated." This letter indicates that, by 1928, there was less resistance to motorists by the general public than there had been previously; however, it also indicated that tolerance remained tenuous. "Öffentliche Meinung 162, Noch einmal Hunde," *Das Motorrad*, 1928: 568.

14. "Öffentliche Meinung 167–179, Für Hunde und Gegen Hunde," *Das Motorrad*, 1928: 689–92.
15. "Öffentliche Meinung 172–179, Gegen Hunde," *Das Motorrad*, 1928: 689–92.
16. "Öffentliche Meinung 167–171, Für Hunde," *Das Motorrad*, 1928: 689–92.
17. "Öffentliche Meinung 169, Ich lehne das Faustrecht ab," and "Öffentliche Meinung 173, Es gibt nur einen Feind – den Hund!," *Das Motorrad*, 1928: 690–92.
18. "Öffentliche Meinung 178, Drauf, auf die Bestien!," *Das Motorrad*, 1928: 692.
19. "Öffentliche Meinung 174, Gleich erschießen!," *Das Motorrad*, 1928: 690.
20. "Öffentliche Meinung 172, Peitsche und Revolver gegen jeden Köter," *Das Motorrad*, 1928: 689; "Öffentliche Meinung 176, "Den Lenker festgefaßt – Gas und mit Hurra ...," *Das Motorrad*, 1928: 691; "Öffentliche Meinung 174," *Das Motorrad*, 1928: 690; "Öffentliche Meinung 178," *Das Motorrad*, 1928: 692.
21. "Öffentliche Meinung 169," *Das Motorrad*, 1928: 691–92.
22. "Öffentliche Meinung 173," *Das Motorrad*, 1928: 690.
23. *Kulturnation* is in itself a thorny term, often analyzed as a community based on a bounded concept of *Volk* (defined by *völkisch* ideologists as a community of blood, race, and cultural tradition), in contrast to "civilization." The concept of *Kulturnation* was also employed by Nazi ideologues as the fruition of a unification of *Geist* and *Technik*. See also Herf, *Reactionary Modernism*, 22–23, 35, 168–69.
24. "Öffentliche Meinung 168, Am besten ist es, das Rad zu schieben," *Das Motorrad*, 1928: 691.
25. Historicizing the particular usages of *Kulturnation*, forcing it to conform to a particular telos, and, thus, denying the concept its inherent malleability, which, like the open-ended term *Heimat*, in my opinion, made it so easily appropriable by the National Socialists and other proponents of a *völkisch* conception of the German nation, is both tricky and potentially rewarding. Norbert Elias, writing in 1939, problematizes this very point by stating: "Whereas the concept of civilization has the function of giving expression to the continually expansionist tendency of colonizing groups, the concept of *Kultur* mirrors the self-consciousness of a nation [that] constantly had to seek out and constitute boundaries anew, in a political as well as a spiritual sense, and again and again had to ask itself: 'What is really our identity?' The orientation of the German concept of culture, with its tendency toward demarcation and detailing of differences between groups, corresponds to this historical process. The questions 'What is really French? What is really English?' have long ceased to be a matter of much discussion for the French and the English. But for centuries the question 'What is really German?' has not been laid to rest." Norbert Elias, *The Civilizing Process. Vol. 2. State Formation and Civilization* (Oxford: Blackwell, 1982), 5.
26. "Öffentliche Meinung 180, Wie man im England denkt," and "Öffentlicher Meinung 181, Ein vernünftiger Voschlag," *Das Motorrad*, 1928: 732–34. A letter written by a German man residing in London compared the German situation to the English: "The English are very considerate riders and we can only learn from them ... You should make yourself conspicuous through your utmost consideration and politeness on the open road, and then perhaps motorcyclists will be as highly thought of in Germany as they are here in England." "Öffentliche Meinung 180," 732.
27. "Öffentliche Meinung 181," 732–34.

28. "Öffentliche Meinung 184, Die Ethik des Motorradsports," *Das Motorrad*, 1928: 778. The author's emphasis on "cyclists" hints at his implicit desire to distance motorcycles from bicycles.

29. Ibid.

30. Ibid.

31. Packer, *Mobility without Mayhem*, 139.

32. "Öffentliche Meinung 184," 778.

33. "Öffentliche Meinung 199, Die Ethik des Motorradsports," *Das Motorrad*, 1928: 959.

34. Peter D. Norton, "Street rivals: Jaywalking and the invention of the motor age street," *Technology and Culture* 48, no. 2 (2007): 332.

35. Lethen, *Cool Conduct*, 15.

36. "Schwarze Liste," *Motorrad-Sport, -Verkehr und -Technik*, no. 40, 1926, 6.

37. Lethen, *Cool Conduct*, 18.

38. Ibid.

39. Peter D. Norton, "Street rivals," 331–59.

40. Wolfgang Bonß, Joachim Hohl, and Alexander Jakob, "Die Konstruktion von Sicherheit in der reflexiven Moderne," in *Die Modernisierung der Moderne*, ed. Ulrich Beck and Wolfgang Bonß (Frankfurt am Main: Surkamp, 2001), 147–59.

41. Packer, *Mobility without Mayhem*, 15.

42. "Briefkasten 1846, Polizeiliches Führungsattest," *Das Motorrad*, 1927: 531.

43. "Briefkasten 1846," 531.

44. The process of motorization also contributed to the intensified collection of personal information by the state. Lefebvre, *Everyday Life*, 100–103.

45. "Briefkasten 1846," 531.

46. Williams, *Marxism and Literature*, 121–27.

47. "Rechtsauskunft 298 Todessturz der Sozia," *Das Motorrad*, 1929: 1446.

48. Steinbeck, *Das Motorrad*, 170–73.

49. Fraunholz, *Motorphobia*, 55–81. A similar process was taking place in the United States and in other countries; see Norton, *Fighting Traffic* and Mom, *Atlantic Automobilism*.

50. Fraunholz, *Motorphobia*, 217–23; Steinbeck, *Das Motorrad*, 171–72.

51. "Warum muss der Kraftfahrer versichert sein?," *Das Motorrad*, 1928: 1696.

52. Nevertheless, due to the vulnerability of motorcycle riders, some insurance agencies charged motorcyclists double if they used their motorcycle to transport passengers. Walter Ostwald, "Motorradbenutzung oder Soziusfahren: Doppelte Unfallprämie!," *Motor und Sport*, no. 32, 1927, 12.

53. Merki, Der holprige Siegeszug, 356–58.

54. Compare: "Table: 204. Zusammenstöße im Straßenverkehr 1927," in Statistisches Amt der Stadt Berlin, *Statistisches Taschenbuch der Stadt Berlin, 1929*, vol. 5 (Berlin: Verlag Otto Stollberg, Verlag für Politik und Wirtschaft, 1929) and "Table 222. Zusammenstöße im Straßenverkehr 1928", Statistisches Amt der Stadt Berlin, *Statistisches Taschenbuch der Stadt Berlin, 1930*, vol. 6. (Berlin: Verlag Otto Stollberg, Verlag für Politik und Wirtschaft, 1930).

55. See, for example, Otto Köster, "Ist das Verkehrsproblem der Großstadt gelöst?," *Der deutsche Motorfahrer*, no. 5, 1930, 3–5. W. Hering, "Verkehrsdisziplin: Motorradfahrer – Fußgänger und … Radfahrer," *Das Motorrad*, 1928: 294–95. In this article, Hering placed particular blame on bicyclists and their "special status" in terms of traffic laws.

56. "Eine Reichs-Verkehr-Ordnung? Verkehrs-technische Betrachtungen und Anregungen," *Motorrad-Sport, -Verkehr und -Technik*, no. 44, 1925, 5–6.
57. Albert Sachs, *Motorradunfälle* (Berlin: R.C. Schmidt & Co., 1929), 5.
58. Sachs, *Motorradunfälle*, 15–16.
59. Ibid., 16.
60. "Zum Gedächtnis," *Motorrad-Sport, -Verkehr und -Technik*, no. 50, 1930, 1.
61. Ibid., 1.
62. Ibid., 2.
63. "Sturz," *Das Motorrad*, 1929: 299.
64. Möser, *Fahren und Fliegen*, 456–58.
65. Hans Kater, "Sturzgefahr, Stürze und Sturz-'Technik'; Beobachtungen und Erlebnisse eines Unetwegten," *Motorrad-Sport, -Verkehr und -Technik*, no. 49, 1928, 3.
66. Hans Kater, "Sturzgefahr, Stürze und Sturz-'Technik,'" 6.
67. See, for example: "Vorsicht ist besser als Nachsicht," *Dixi-Magazin*, May 1930, n.p.; Dr. Roedel, "Das deutsche Straßennetz und der Kraftverkehr von heute und morgen," *Motorrad-Sport, -Verkehr und -Technik*, no. 37, 1925, 9–11; "Bücherschau: Unfälle im Straßenverkehr," *Motorrad-Sport, -Verkehr und -Technik*, no. 43, 1925, 16; Hugo Kalinowski, "Das Motorrad in der modernen Verkehrs-Entwicklung," *Motorrad-Sport, -Verkehr und -Technik*, no. 17, 1926, 10–12; "Eisenbahnübergänge und Kraftfahrzeug-Unfälle," *Motorrad-Sport, -Verkehr und -Technik*, no. 51, 1926, 11; "Mehr Recht – und mehr Rücksicht," *Der deutsche Motorfahrer*, no. 10, 1929, 1–3.
68. H. Eichhorn, "Psychotechnik und Unfallverhütung im Kraftverkehr," *Motor und Sport*, no. 32, 1927, 10–11; also, Alexander Büttner, "Lerne Geschwindigkeit schätzen; Ein Beitrag zur Psychologie des Kraftfahrers," *Motor-Tourist*, no. 20, 1929, 8–9.
69. See Kracauer's discussion of "psychotechnics" in the sphere of employee selection practices and employee aptitude testing. Kracauer, *The Salaried Masses*, 33–39.
70. "Schwarzfahren soll strafbar werden," *Der deutsche Motorfahrer*, no. 1, 1930, 16; "Schwarzfahrt," *Motorschau*, no. 1, 1932. The law regarding "joyriding" in England was similarly vague until 1930. See O'Connell, *The Car and British Society*, 103.
71. "Schwarzfahren soll strafbar werden," 16.
72. "Das lachende Motorrad: Vertrauensperson," *Das Motorrad*, 1929: 27.
73. See, for example, the joke: "Joyriding: When a man commits a folly, there is mostly a woman behind it." Gräf, *Die Hupe*, 43. See also the humorous short story: "Klemmke stellt sich dumm und wird freigesprochen," *Motor und Sport*, no. 1, 1927, 35–36.
74. Dr. J. Rauschmayr, "Rechtsfolgen der Schwarzfahrt," *Motor-Tourist*, no. 21–22, 1929, 15–16; "Der Schwarzfahrer," *Das Motorrad*, 1929: 555; M. Heim, "Schwarzfahrten," *Der deutsche Motorfahrer*, no. 6, 1929, 5–6.
75. Fraunholz, *Motorphobia*, 71–72.
76. "Die Bestrafung des Autodiebstahls; Zur Verordnung gegen unbefugten Gebrauch von Kraftfahrzeugen und Fahrrädern vom 20.10.1932," *Der deutsche Motorfahrer*, no. 12, 1932, 233–35.
77. "Aus der Kraftfahrer-Arbeit," *Der Pioneer; Zeitschrift zur Förderung der Nüchternheit und Sicherheit im Verkehr*. Mitteilung der Abteilung

Verkehrswesen des Deutschen Vereins gegen den Alkoholismus e.V., nos. 6–8, 1932, 56.

78. Dr. Th. Thomas, "Alkohol und Motorradfahrt," *Der Pionier*, nos. 6–8, 1932, 18.

79. "Was geht das mich an!," *Der Pionier*, nos. 6–8, 1932, 58–61; "Ist das wirklich nötig?," *Der Pionier*, nos. 6–8, 1932, 78–79; "Und die Folgen," *Der Pionier*, nos. 6–8, 1932, 79–80.

80. Kurt Stolle, "Mann am Steuer," *Der Pionier*, nos. 6–8, 1932, 89. "Reich ihm die Hand," *Der Pionier*, nos. 6–8, 1932, 18.

81. Walter Julius Bloem, "Alkohol und Sport; Kleine Anregungen," *Motorrad-Sport, -Verkehr und -Technik*, no. 41, 1929, 25.

82. See also, Möser, *Fahren und Fliegen*, 332–37.

83. "Gymkhana," in *Concordia*, no. 6, 1929, 96; Bloem, "Alkohol und Sport," 25.

84. Thomas, "Alkohol und Motorradfahrt," 19.

85. "Kraftfahrwesen und Alkohol," *Der Pionier*, nos. 6–8, 1932, 78.

86. de Certeau, The Practice of Everyday Life, 130.

87. Fraunholz, *Motorphobia*, 41–42.

88. "Rund um den Motor," *Concordia*, no. 17, 1928, 342. Emphasis in original.

89. For an early article on the noise pollution caused by motorcycles, see "Die Landplage der Motorräder," *Das Motorrad*, 1924: 220.

90. See Hans-Joachim Braun, "Lärmbelästigung und Lärmbekämpfung in der Zwischenkriegszeit," in *Sozialgeschichte der Technik, Festschrift für Ulrich Troitzsch*, ed. Günter Bayerl and Wolfhard Weber (Münster: Waxman, 1998), 251–59; and Richard Birkefeld and Martina Jung, eds., *Die Stadt, der Lärm und das Licht: Die Veränderung des öffentlichen Raumes durch Motorisierung und Elektrifizierung* (Seelze: Kallmeyer, 1994).

91. Theodor Lessing, Der Lärm: Eine Kampfschrift gegen die Geräusche unseres Lebens (Wiesbaden, 1908), as quoted in Radkau, Das Zeitalter der Nervösität, 210.

92. The German anti-noise association was disbanded in 1911. Radkau, *Das Zeitalter der Nervösität*, 210. See also: Fraunholz, *Motorphobia*, 89; and Braun, "Lärmbelästigung," 252.

93. Radkau, Das Zeitalter der Nervösität, 211.

94. Fraunholz, *Motorphobia*, 90.

95. Fraunholz, *Motorphobia*, 87–92; Merki, *Der holprige Siegeszug*, 174–76. Steinbeck, *Das Motorrad*, 175–78.

96. "Autorecht: Belästigung durch das Geräusch von Krafträdern," *Das Auto*, no. 29, 1926, 683.

97. "Streiflichter auf die neue Kraftfahrzeug-Verordnung," *Motorrad-Sport, -Verkehr und -Technik*, no. 25, 1926, 9–10.

98. Ibid., 10.

99. This is a non-literal translation of the verses in order to keep the rhyming scheme. "Der Polizeiarm – D.R.P.," *Das Motorrad*, 1929: 1590.

100. "Schach dem Straßenlärm," *Motorrad-Sport, -Verkehr und -Technik*, no. 35, 1928, 7.

101. Dr. Luckow, "Stellungnahme des D.M.V. gegen zu strenge Handhabung der polizeilichen Strafverfolgung," *Motorrad-Sport, -Verkehr und -Technik*, no. 48, 1926, 4; Dr. Luckow, "Mitteilungen unserer juristischen Abteilung, Maßnahmen gegen verkehrsfeindlichen Anordnungen," *Motorrad-Sport, -Verkehr und -Technik*, no. 33, 1928, 16.

102. The letter discussed here was written in November 1926 by the lawyer of the DMV, Dr. Luckow, and was republished in "Stellungnahme des D.M.V.," 4.
103. "Preussische Ministerialblatt für innere Verwaltung 1929: Runderlass des Ministers des Inneren vom 28.12.1928," *Motorrad-Sport, -Verkehr und -Technik*, no. 24, 1929, 12.
104. Dr. Luckow, "Mitteilungen unserer juristischen Abteilung," 16.
105. The articles appeared in eight issues of *Das Motorrad* over the course of 1929: Arno Brösicke, "Aus der Praxis des Polizisten," *Das Motorrad*, 1929: 580–81, 627–28, 685–86, 885–86, 938–39, 1040–42, 1323–24, and 1538–39.
106. The relationship of the police vis-à-vis motorcyclists and the general public is addressed below in a discussion of the Volkspolizei [People's Police] in Brösicke's article "Polizei ca. Motorradfahrer; Eine offene Antwort auf ein offenen Brief," *Das Motorrad*, 1929: 1591–93.
107. Brösicke, "Aus der Praxis," 886.
108. "Noiselessness contests" were indeed organized by many clubs in the second-half of the 1920s. Even the Munich-based club Knatternde Gesell—ironically, the name means "roaring fellow"—held a "noiselessness contest" in 1925. Sixty motorcyclists took part; first prize went to Engineer Müller on a Zündapp, and second prize went to Miss Else Distler on a four-stroke Henderson. See "Der große Münchener Motorsport-Tag und der Motor-Club 'Knatternder Gesell,'" *Motorrad-Sport, -Verkehr und -Technik*, no. 28, 1925, 10–12.
109. Paul Friedmann, "Der Motorradfahrer und die Polizei; Ein offener Brief and Herrn Polizei-Oberltn Brösicke/Barmen," *Das Motorrad*, 1929: 919.
110. Brösicke, "Polizei ca. Motorradfahrer," 1591–93. All italics in the original.
111. See Belinda Davis, "Police and Patterns of Street Conflict in Berlin in the Nineteenth and Twentieth Centuries," in Alf Lüdtke, Heinrich Reinke, and Michael Sturm, *Polizei, Staat, Gewalt im 20. Jahrhundert* (Wiesbaden: VS-Verlag für Sozialwissenschaften, 2011), 81–103; and Peter Leßmann, *Die preussische Schutzpolizei in der Weimarer Republik: Streifendienst und Strassenkampf* (Düsseldorf: Droste, 1989).
112. Fraunholz, *Motorphobia*, 77.
113. The motoring press reported on the bans. One article proclaimed, "The Motorcycle is Not a Means of Transportation! That's the opinion of the Nationwide German Spa Association! – Spas and Motorcyclists – Spas make their own laws – Extermination of the "International [sic] Devil's Inventions." The author argued: "What we motorists cannot agree to is a fight against motor vehicles in general and the motorcycle in particular that is being preached by the spa association, and in part has been put into action." Wilhelm Hoepfner, "Das Motorrad ist kein Beförderungsmittel! Das behaupet der Allgemeine Deutsche Bäderverband! – Bäder, Kurorte und Motorradfahrer – Kurorte schaffen sich eigene Gesetze – Ausrottung der 'Internationalen [sic] Teufelserfindungen,'" *Motorrad-Sport, -Technik und -Verkehr*, no. 30, 1930, 5.
114. "Rechtsauskunft 303, Das knatternde Kleinkraftrad," *Das Motorrad*, 1929: 1502.
115. The legal advisors to *Das Motorrad*, however, cautioned him not to initiate legal proceedings, as "the police are currently engaged in a bitter fight to abate street noise."
116. Pertaining to the conflict between automobilists and bicyclists, see also "Fourth Class Citizen with Baggage." In this article, an automobile driver complains of two instances of harassment and unequal treatment vis-à-vis bicyclists:

"In both cases, we are dealing with German citizens with the same rights and the same obligations. The one, however, because he uses gasoline, is treated totally different than the other." "Staatsbürger 4. Klasse mit Traglasten," *Klein-Motor-Sport*, no. 10, 1928, 199–201.

117. "Mitteilungen unserer jurist. Abteilung, Zur Frage der polizeiliche Beschlagnahme von Motorrädern" *Motorrad-Sport, -Verkehr und -Technik*, no. 42, 1928, 2; "Schach dem Straßenlärm," 7.

118. Heinz W. Peters, "Der Strassenlärm," *Das Motorrad*, 1929: 734–35.

119. See, for example, in regard to young motorcyclists in particular, "Öffentliche Meinung 289, Junger Mann verteidigt sich!," *Das Motorrad*, 1929: 859–60, also regarding the question of tax and license unrestricted motorcyclists.

120. Paul Freidmann, "Unnötiger Lärm," *Das Motorrad*, 1928: 671.

121. The title is a quote taken from Friedrich Schiller's play, *Wallerstein*: "Von die Parteien Gunst und Haß verwirrt, schwankt sein Charackterbild," *Motorrad-Sport, -Verkehr und -Technik*, no. 25, 1928, 3.

122. Peukert, *The Weimar Republic*, 89–95.

123. "Briefkasten 279: Ein Schlußstrich unter die Führerscheinfreien," *Das Motorrad*, 1929: 694.

124. For example, in 1926 a motorcycle dealer published a letter to the editor in *Fahrrad und Kraftfahrzeug Zeitschrift (FKZ)*, the trade journal of dealers in bicycle and motorcycle parts, applauding the newly enacted law stipulating the forbidding of exhaust valves on motorcycles. The author, a motorcycle dealer, viewed the new stipulations as favorable to his own economic interests: "While I'm no friend of police decrees, I greet the action being taken against the roaring motorcycles, not only as a citizen, but also as a motorcycle dealer, because I expect these measures will lead to greater popularity of the motorcycle." "Unser Leser hat das Wort: Das Verbot von Auspuffklappen," in *FKZ*, no. 14, 1926, 14.

125. "Briefkasten 198: Eine Fachzeitschrift muß erzieherisch wirken," *Das Motorrad*, 1928: 959.

126. Peters, "Der Strassenlärm," 734–35.

127. "Schach dem Straßenlärm," 7.

128. Paul Friedmann, "Zweite Wochenendfahrt des 'Motorrades,'" *Das Motorrad*, 1927: 418–20.

129. As discussed in Chapter 3, during the last years of the Weimar Republic, mass political parties, such as the SPD, KPD, and the NSDAP had affiliated motorized divisions, which were activated in part for propaganda purposes. The Motor-SA, Motor-SS, and the NSKK [Nationalsozialistische Kraftfahrer Korps], were the NSDAP's motorized divisions. According to Dorothee Hochstetter's account, the Nazi propaganda rides were often described as unpopular due to noise and dust. See Hochstetter, *Motorisierung und "Volksgemeinschaft,"* 45.

130. Paul Zipperling, "Nachts auf der Landstrasse eine Entgegnung," *Klein-Motor-Sport*, no. 8, 1928, 166–68.

131. See Frauenholz, *Motorphobia*.

132. "Zur Sonntagssperre des Kraftfahrzeugverkehrs in Sachsen," *Motorrad-Sport, -Verkehr und -Technik*, no. 23, 1926, 7.

133. "Ein mittelalterlicher Stadtrat," *Das Motorrad*, 1924: 307.

134. "Straßensperrung für Motorräder," *Motorrad-Sport, -Verkehr und -Technik*, no. 6, 1928, 10.

135. Hoepfner, "Das Motorrad ist kein Beförderungsmittel!," 4–5.

136. Not only did non-motorists and automobile drivers use the language of "exter-
     mination" and "eradication" in regard to so-called "motorcycle rowdies," this
     language was also used by motorcyclists against other motorcyclists. See
     below, "Briefkasten 198," 959. Also Büttner, *Mein Motorrad und Ich*, 92–95.
137. Das rattert und knattert und tutet und schreit –
     „Motorrad – Achtung!" rennt alles beiseit.
     Ist's schier das Kleinste vom allem Gefährt –
     Und lärmt, als ob ein Lastauto fährt!
     A rhyme from a children's book introducing new technologies such as the
     automobile, radio, and motorcycle. In comparison to other technologies, the
     motorcycle fairs poorly, as the above verse demonstrates. Republished in "Der
     knatternde Dichter," in *FKZ*, no. 1, 1926, 11.
138. Franz Franziß, "Der knatternde Gesell," *Motor-Tourist*, no. 20, 1930, 11.
139. Mom, "Encapsulating Culture," 289–307, here 305–6.
140. "Wanderfahren und – Wanderfahren," *Motorrad-Sport, -Verkehr und -Technik*,
     no. 34, 1928, 6.
141. G.A. Mulach, "Wanderfahrt", *Motorrad-Sport, -Verkehr und -Technik*, no. 39,
     1926, 12.
142. Hermann Homann, "Start," *Das Motorrad*, 1929: 1525.
143. "Geräuschlosigkeitswettbewerb in England," *Das Motorrad*, 1927: 464–65.
144. However, whether every "inexperienced spectator" actually enjoyed the noise
     is open to debate. In the social democratic sport journal *Sportpolitisches
     Rundschau*, the article "Horsepower at the Race Track" provides the following
     description of a (rainy) day at the races: "The most notable thing about this
     motorcycle race is the racket of the machines, where in contrast it is known
     that at the horse race track quiet reigns—only when the favorites are behind
     and the underdog takes the lead, does the man who bets forget his good
     manners and make noise. At the motorcycle races, the motors take care of this
     quite thoroughly; it bangs and explodes, whereby the layperson doesn't know
     if such noise is actually necessary to such an extent." "PS auf der Rennbahn,"
     Sportpolitisches Rundschau, no. 11, 1930, n.p.
145. This slim book captures much of the Zeitgeist of the Weimar Republic. For
     example, on "rationalization," he writes: "It used to be 'in the name of the Father'
     or 'in the name of the People.' Today it is 'in the name of rationalization.'" See
     Acutus (Kurt Lubowsky), *Knigge für industrielle Beamte: Zeitstudien von Acutus,
     eine lustige Darstellung bitterer Erfahrungen gewidmet allen Berufsfreunden
     zum Verständnis ohne Brille* (Berlin: Verlag Walter Fiebig & Co., 1931), 11.
146. Acutus, *Knigge*, 23.
147. An article suggesting "a few rules for motorcyclists," applies the same kind of
     logic: "When buying a motorcycle, you shouldn't pay attention to its strength,
     but you should place value on the amount of noise that the motorcycle can
     make, so that the public delightedly stares at you as you race through the
     streets. For this purpose it seems advantageous when you enter a city to drive
     with an open exhaust valve and to use your Bosch horn as often as possible.
     You can be sure that attention and admiration will not be denied." Florestan,
     "Ein paar Gebote für den Motorradfahrer," *Der deutsche Motorfahrer*, no. 8,
     1928, 14.
148. For example: "Streiflichter auf die neue Kraftfahrzeug-Verordnung" *Motorrad-
     Sport, -Verkehr und -Technik*, no. 25, 1926, 9–10.

149 In German, "machine" is a noun that carries a feminine article. As the author wrote of the motorcycle as his "Comrade and Darling," using the possessive "her" instead of "it" conveys the sense of the article better. Georg Wilhelm Rapp, "Motorradfahrten; Allerlei Eindrücke," *Der Motorsportler*, no. 4, 1932, 4.

150 Mom, "Encapsulating Culture," 306.

151 Packer, Mobility without Mayhem, 12.

152 Kurt Schwitters, "Mein neues Motorrad," in *Das literarische Werk, vol. 2, Prosa 1918–1930*, ed. Friedhelm Lach (Cologne: Verlag M. Dumont, 1974), 269–70.

153 Friedhelm Lach, "Vorwort," in Schwitters, *Das literarische Werk*, 7. See also Möser, *Fahren und Fliegen*, 360–61.

CHAPTER 6

Motoring Amazons?
Women and Motorcycling

"The Girl and her Machine," a 1931 poem by Fritz Kantor, captures how twentieth-century concepts of femininity were imagined to have cast off the previous century's corseted norms. He begins the poem by describing "Babett," who "back in grandfather's day" was both a "doll and an industrious bee." Her thoughts revolved around her trousseau, as she sat, "her eyes lowered to her work, at the humming sewing machine." "Little" Babett's "purpose in life" was to be a housewife, caring for "a home and children, many in number." Standing in stark contrast to Babett, Kantor introduces the figure of Lu, who, "as soon as the sky begins to smile," readies her machine to "race into the sunny expanse":

> What does she care for man or child,
> When the motor's song and the spring wind
> Accompany her on a whizzing ride.
> And if a wild fellow [*ein wilder Gesell*] passes her –
> Ho, ho – she doesn't give in so fast.
> She fights with a defiant demeanor,
> There's only one love she knows,
> Only one joy she calls her own.
> The girl and her machine![1]

Contrary to the drastic difference Kantor portrays between "back then" and "now," women's lives during the Weimar Republic continued to be largely conscribed by traditionally anchored norms of femininity and womanhood. The image of the emancipated woman with the bobbed hair on a motorcycle who was in charge of her own purse and sexuality, one iteration of the globally circulating image of the "modern girl," was to a large extent just that—an image. Dominating debates on the boundaries of proper femininity, "she" received extensive media attention and "raised both hopes and fears about forces of modernity."[2] Already during the last decades of the imperial era, socially acceptable norms had been challenged by a first generation of feminists, and women's expanded roles during World War I provided a basis for arguing for equality under the law. However, despite these shifts, women during the Weimar Republic continued to encounter discrimination in their everyday lives, reflected not only in the unequal wage differential and the low numbers of female parliamentarians and industrialists, but also in daily discouragements from pursuing technical interests, such as studying engineering or taking up motorcycling. Women's often-subordinate economic positions constrained their chances of gaining hands-on technical and motorcycling experience. Still, by asserting themselves in new ways within the modern world some women bore a greater resemblance to Kantor's Lu than to his Babett, and, as more than just contested symbols of global modernity, these "Modern Girls" and "New Women" engendered both aspirations for and heightened anxieties about social and sexual mobility.[3]

Looking first at the lives of "active" female motorcyclists and female motorcycling authors, this chapter pays attention to their relatively scant voices in the pervasively masculine world of motorcycle discourse. Following Georgine Clarsen's lead, I hope to show that women's passion for motorcycling was "more than just a pale imitation" of men's through exploring the strategies women employed in order to participate in the modern activity of motorization, as well as the challenges they faced in their attempts.[4] The difficulties they faced were also repeatedly a topic in the predominantly male-generated discourse around women and motorcycling, Couched in terms of debates on women's health and women's technological aptitude, women encountered skepticism, if not hostility, when they attempted to enter the masculine world of motorcycling. Often labeled "motoring amazons," women motorists were not only socially suspect, but they also faced very real institutional obstacles when attempting to actively participate in the male-dominated practice of motorization. However, as Virginia Scharff, Georgine Clarsen, and others have argued in terms of early twentieth-century female automobile drivers, despite men's dominance in the world of motorcycling and the world at large, women did find ways to assert their needs and desires, and "in their words and actions they consciously located themselves as part of a progressive project of inventing and articulating new versions of what it meant to be a modern woman."[5]

Köhler, Körner, and Co.: Possibilities and Problems of Female Participation in a Male-Dominated World of Motorcycling

In 1931, Dr. Herbert Schmidt-Lamberg reported that the winter of 1930/31 had brought a "proliferation of women motorcyclists." From October 1930 to February 1931, no less than 216 motorcycles were registered to women. While Schmidt-Lamberg claimed that in previous years "the women's enthusiasm for motorcycling" during the winter months witnessed a "strong cooling-off," the "development of women in sports" had since led to the "rapid hardening of women" and their increased wintertime motorcycling activity.[6] Towards the end of the Weimar Republic, women increasingly took up motorcycling. Indeed, despite barriers and biases, during the early days of motorization women were not entirely excluded from the male-dominated worlds of motorcycling and motorcycle racing.[7] Even prior to World War I, there were active women motorcyclists. For example, Gertrude Eisenmann rode in a number of motorcycle races and became somewhat of a media star.[8] During the Weimar Republic, two exceptional and exemplary women, Hanni Köhler and Susanne Körner, broke through on the racing circuit. Motorcycling magazines often featured tales of their exploits, and they served as role models for other women who sought to become motorcyclists. Less spectacular travelogues and stories contributed by other female motorcyclists also helped women's voices become audible within the predominantly masculine world of motorcycling. Despite facing numerous obstacles, women thus penetrated the male-dominated world of motorcycling, and female motorcyclists contributed to reshaping gender relations.

In 1927, a journalist for the motoring magazine, *Motor und Sport*, Lotte Zielesch, wrote a short exposé celebrating Hanni Köhler as "one of our most successful female motorcyclists." Zielesch began with an exoticized description of Köhler's countenance: "Two big doe-eyes look at me from an Indian-brown face," her disposition as "humble and agreeable as a well-raised daughter of the house." Expressing surprise that "this young owner of world records sits in front of me and looks so different than I would have thought she would look like," the journalist bewondered Köhler's cool comportment: "She speaks about her amazing performances without the slightest trace of pride, indeed with a referee-like dispassion. She honors her successes with the sangfroid of an experienced sportsperson who takes all individual factors into account. Her being expresses masculine-active objectivity [*männlich-rührige Sachlichkeit*], which nonetheless has very little in common with the type of the 'masculinized woman' [*vermännlichte Frau*]."[9] Zielesch's description of Köhler was replete with the ambiguities and tensions around motorcycling and femininity during the Weimar Republic; the exoticism of female motorcyclists was matched in the exoticism of Zielesch's description of Köhler. With bobbed hair and "fresh face" she appeared as a living icon of the modern woman, yet "dispassionate" and possessing "sangfroid," Köhler's personality exuded "masculine-active objectivity." While attempting to defuse the notion that women motorcyclists were "masculinized she-men," the author, herself a woman, chose wording—"[she] looks so different than I would have thought she would look like"—that indicates the strong and pervasive tendency to associate active female motorcycling with a suspect form of femininity situated outside the norm.

Indeed, Hanni Köhler's biography and her own words demonstrate the difficulties involved with negotiating the rocky terrain of a world

Image 6.1. Cover Girl Hanni Köhler. *ADAC-Motorwelt*, 6 April 1928.

dominated by men, and offer strategies for gaining and holding ground in a masculine sphere of interest and activity. Born in Berlin in 1907 to Otto Köhler and Caroline Riedl, Hanni Köhler first rode a motorcycle at the age of fifteen.[10] A friend, Kurt Birnholz, who also became a prominent motorcyclist, initiated Köhler into the world of motorcycling. "He proudly showed me his Evans machine (acquired through borrowed money). Its newness excited me and I had to sit in the saddle." Because she was a "veteran bicyclist, riding was not difficult. Only an old man got terribly wound up and called a policeman and asked him to arrest me, because it was so irresponsible to let such a small girl ride a motorcycle. That could only result in catastrophe." A "wild hunt" ensued and, despite her lack of motorcycling experience, she was able to evade the policeman and return the motorcycle to Birnholz. Following this "debut," Köhler's father bought her an Evans motorcycle and she and her father joined a motor-cycle club.[11] A subordinate economic position meant that many women only gained access to motor vehicles through a male relative or friends.

Only a year later, Köhler participated in what she described as her most important motorcycle race, the 1924 North–South Race, a 420 km overnight race from Leipzig to Frankfurt/M that took her seventeen and a half hours. She was the only female to take part in her racing class among a field of six motorcyclists. During the race, she encoun-tered a series of difficulties, including having her headlight fail, "getting lost in swampy terrain," and having to push her motorcycle for six hours.[12] These were hardships that men often pointed to as evidence of their masculine strength. She described being at a point when she almost wanted to give up, however Kurt Birnholz, her motorcycling friend, gave her a pep talk. Later along the way she lost contact with Birnholz, and continued on her own. During the course of the race she described feeling as though she was specifically being targeted for abuse: "Suddenly a stone fell on my head. Right after that another fell on my hand. 'Dirty trick!,' I thought furiously and kept on riding. It didn't take long, and again something rushed past my ears. Now I was fed up, thought that someone was systematically bombarding me from the ambuscade, and dismounted." While it turned out that the "stones" were really apples falling from trees that lined the street, her sense of being "systematically bombarded" stands as an indication of the vulnerable position she felt herself to be in, either by virtue of her gender or of simply being a motorcyclist, or both. According to Köhler's recounting, further memorable highlights include her license plate becoming loose and "making an unnerving racket." She then encountered "three drunks, who, when they heard the sound of the motor, waved around sticks and tried to block the road," but she was able to "make a clean escape."

When she arrived at the first control station, she "asked meekly how many hours ahead the rest of the participants were." She was informed that she was the first to arrive and this gave her "an incentive. At once I was awake and raced on, and when I arrived [in Frankfurt am Main], I felt completely blessed. All of Frankfurt welcomed me. It rained flowers from all sides." Köhler was the only one within her racing class to even complete the strenuous nighttime race, and she was awarded the first prize as the winner in her class and also the first prize for the condition of her motorcycle.

The story that Köhler narrated was filled with adventure, and it was clear from the tone she intended to serve as a positive example to encourage other women to take up motorcycle racing. Köhler became an icon of "active" female motorcycling, taking part in innumerable races, including, in 1926, being the first woman to race on the AVUS Racetrack in Berlin. In 1927, on the Opel Racetrack in Rüsselsheim, she set a new world record on a 119 ccm-engine motorcycle over a period of both 12 and 24 hours.[13] She took part in the 1928 Länderfahrt and the cover of the *ADAC-Motorwelt* featured her alone with her motorcycle, with a sassy expression on her face (see Image 6.1). The caption declares, "Hanni Köhler, the penalty-free darling of the Länderfahrt."[14]

Even when she did not win, motoring magazines featured her, often smiling, as "the steadfast female sportsperson [*die tapfere Sportlerin*]."[15] In addition, in 1931, she undertook a nine-month 20,000 km overland motorcycle expedition from Sri Lanka to Germany, a remarkable feat for a person of either gender to undertake at that time.[16] Upon her return, she opened a motorcycle shop, "Johanna Koehler, Kraftfahrzeug- und Teilevertrieb," with twenty-one employees, on the Köpenickerstraße in Berlin.[17] Indeed, Köhler's status was so iconic that mass-distribution fashion magazines also chose her to represent the "modern sporting lady."[18] She was a model "new woman," with all of the contradictions such a label entails.

In an interview, "Hanni Köhler speaks," published in a special issue of *Das Motorrad* dedicated to "women and motorcycling," Köhler took a very adamant position on female motorcycle riders:

Interviewer: "You stress the word 'active,' Miss Köhler. What do you mean by this?"

Köhler: "In terms of active motorcycle sport, I mean that the woman herself sits in the saddle and has grown together [*verwachsen*] with her motorcycle. Nothing is worse than having to be dandled around as a 'clinging ape' [*Klammeraffe*] (and suddenly Miss Köhler's entire sporting temperament breaks through): There is nothing I hate more than this pillion-seat riding; the police should ban it."

In her own behavior as well in her clear statement against "pillion-seat riding," Köhler publicly contested the hegemonic motorcycling order of "active male" and "passive female." When asked if motorcycling had an "influence on the psyche," Köhler replied: "Without a doubt! Especially on the character. It trains women to be independent." Actively pursuing the sport required self-reliance: "You have to be able to control the machine, to repair flat tires on the rural roads; you have to be able to stand up to farmers and horse-cart drivers, and sometimes be very inventive in order to be able to help yourself out of a tough spot."[19] Köhler was distinctively outspoken, insisting that motorcycling allowed women to gain independence and become self-reliant. However, she was an exceptional figure in the world of Weimar motorcycling, and as such remained exotic. While her achievements were often celebrated within the trade journals, her insistence on "active" female motorcycling made her vulnerable to claims of not being properly feminine and upsetting the gender norm, and motorcycle magazines often labeled her a "Motorcycle Amazon."[20] While invoking the image of an "Amazon" sometimes served to celebrate female emancipation, it also carried with it a critique of defeminization.[21]

Perhaps in order to counter claims of being insufficiently feminine, Köhler took part in the 1927 contest "Who will be Germany's Motorcycle Queen?" sponsored by *Motor und Sport*. According to the rules of this contest: "Every man can vote once ... for the lady that you like best—this time it's just about beauty, as the motor-sporting capabilities will be honored in a special competition at the end of the sporting season ... The lady that has received the most votes will be crowned and presented to our readers as soon as possible, wearing her crown."[22] Hanni Köhler won this beauty competition and was crowned "German Motorcycle Queen 1927."[23] The fact that Köhler, with her bobbed hair and youthful vigor, was selected by the presumably largely male readership, is indicative not only of her celebrity status as an "active" female motorcyclist, but also of the shifting aesthetics and discursive understandings of beauty.[24] Through Köhler's biography, it becomes clear that women motorcyclists contested the association of "proper" femininity with passivity, and contributed to reconfiguring the discursive relationship between the genders through both their words and their actions.[25]

Susanne Körner was another active female motorcycling enthusiast who publicly asserted her opinions on women taking up motorcycling. Although she did not take as radical a standpoint as Köhler, Körner nonetheless asserted a woman's right to be treated as equal, if different, within the community of motorcyclists. When asked by an interviewer for *Motor und Sport* why she chose "the 'dangerous' sport of motorcycling over all the other sports, in which women have achieved successes," she replied: "I may presume that from your review of my riding skills you feel more goodwill than objection towards lady's motorcycle sport. Through your own experiences, I'm sure you share my opinion that ... the precisely controlled way of action—through intensive study of theory and practice—is capable of shutting out all types of inhibitions." She encouraged women to overcome their irrational and "superstitious" feelings and to engage in the learning and practice needed to master any skill. Körner's language, like that of many of her male colleagues, reflects a conviction in the ability to master both self and nature through "rationality" and science.

Like Köhler, Körner also began motorcycling at a young age. Körner's father, like Köhler's, also played an instrumental role in his daughter's decision to pursue motorcycling. Comparing herself to a "child of the theater," she described herself as "a child of motorcycling sport," speaking of her "father's occupational and sporting identity" as playing a "decisive role" in her becoming a motorcyclist: "In 1919, as a fifteen-year-old, I was 'taken along' for the first time on the pillion seat of a 'Mars' motorcycle. I wasn't the only member of the family who was allowed to augment the way that heavy motorcycle laid, but soon it was clear that I had a special talent for this service. I wasn't nervous, and was always on my toes. I leaned into the curves, gave hand signals before the police ordinances made them strictly mandated, never overlooked an opportunity to get gas or breakfast, and took care of the maps." As a "reward" for her services, she was given a pair of "high leather boots with a wide, masculine heel, white-gray breeches and matching jacket, and a cap that I could fasten under my chin." She implied that the first stage of her initiation into the male-dominated world was completed when she received her "masculine" outfit. In the early 1920s, while not unheard of, it was nonetheless uncommon for women in Weimar Germany to wear such attire, and she clearly remembers it as being an important step in having gained acceptance in the male world of motorcycling. For example, in a 1928 article on motor sports and fashion, the author lamented: "women wearing breeches or knickerbockers is still a bit daring and is seen as objectionable in many places." Thus, Körner and other female motorcyclists challenged gender norms through the sartorial practices associated with motorcycling.[26]

Addressing the "dangers" of motorcycling, Körner maintained "vis-à-vis the energetic life-sounds [*energischen Lebenstönen*] of the motorcycle," she "knew no fear, only childish trust and the fulfillment of my desires to travel. Trust, love, and wanting to get to know each other."

In the early 1920s she learned to ride a small-powered motorcycle by herself that she claims: "I didn't become unfaithful to for a long time, and I still value it today as a substitute for a bicycle and even more." In describing her growing and deepening relationship to motorcycling she moved away from an objective description, and instead employed the language of love and courtship. Despite the fact that her attribution of anthropomorphic characteristics to her motorcycle mirrored the language of male motorcyclists, she adopted strategies that indicate how the way she practiced motorcycle sports differed from typically male behavior. Her first "long ride" was a day-ride to Naumberg an der Saale. She then took part in the 1922 ADAC Belzig Classic and the *Reichsfahrt*, and claimed that she rode "a five-digit number of kilometers on a tax-free motorcycle" before switching to a more powerful 250 ccm motorcycle. She also described how she "gained practice in riding on rural roads" and competed against "experienced riders." "I never let myself get into dicey situations—one often rides faster when one avoids obstacles than to trying to 'take' them too cleverly." Körner asserted that her "behavior always found recognition among my male sports comrades," who, as "glad as they are to be helpful, don't want to be the victim of female moods and indiscretion." Female motorcyclists were subject to sex-based biases, as Körner's description reveals, however they also succeeded in adopting strategies, both on and off the motorcycle, that allowed them to gain at least partial acceptance within the male-dominated world of motorcycling.

Körner was perhaps best known for her multiple motorcycling expeditions throughout Europe and especially to England.[27] She made acquaintances with the British "Ladies' Motorcycle Clubs," serving as a representative of the German motoring clubs, including the Deutschen Damen-Automobilklub [German Ladies' Automobile Club], the DMV, and a number of other clubs. In the interview Körner expressed her "confident hope" that "a club for motorcycling ladies" would be established in Germany, "so that we can then speak in the real sense of a ladies' motorcycling sport." Rooting gender in difference, she argued it was wrong to include women "within the ranks of male competitors," because women, "(except for exceptional cases) do not want to compete against top male performances." She believed that "mixed-sex participation" was only appropriate in the case of "reliability trials," which she saw as "primarily a test of the machine materiel." Körner's call for separate motorcycling competitions for women was premised on a notion of sexual difference that served to reinforce notions of innate inequality between the sexes.[28] As Georgine Clarsen has argued, automotive technology was particularly productive in shoring up sexual difference.[29]

As a variant of the "masculine woman," the female motorcycle racer embodied the radical social changes in gender relations. Her presence as discourse and reality provoked both hopes for greater freedom and anxieties about the unhinging of a "natural" social and sexual order. As Katie Sutton argues, the masculine woman was "positioned at the juncture between fascination and rejection, tradition and modernity, heterosexual erotic appeal and the threat of sexual perversion," and, as such, she was "at the center of popular discourse about gender and social change."[30] Beyond Köhler and Körner, numerous other women contributed in various ways to shaping the discourse of motoring in general and motorcycling in particular. Countless females appeared in the pages of motoring magazines on motorcycles, most often as pillion-seat passengers, but sometimes as active riders, and even in racing situations. Female movie stars, such as Maria West, were featured on covers of motorcycling magazines, riding motorcycles in full motorcycle gear. DMV member Lilian Harvey, film star of both the silent and the talkie eras, was photographed in a leather jacket, knee-length skirt, and high heels, perched coquettishly on the edge of a motorcycle studying the "new traffic laws," with Theo Rockenfeller, a regular contributor to the club's journal. These celebrities were "self-fashioned 'new women,'" and by associating themselves with motorcycling, they embodied the increased spatial, social, and sexual mobility of the era.[31] Reading how women on motorcycles were perceived shows not only the possibilities for social change in the Weimar Republic, but also the attempts to tame and reframe the masculine woman as the "good comrade" and the "true *Sozia.*"[32]

A motorcyclist herself, Ilse Lundberg stands out as the woman with the most prolific publishing record in popular motoring magazines during the Weimar Republic. She not only wrote about motorcycling, but during the later years of the republic she increasingly wrote about women and automobiles. When writing about women and motorcycling, however, unlike Köhler and Körner, she mainly focused on the joys of "motorcycle wandering," rather than competitive racing or long-distance expeditions. The editors of *Das Motorrad* describe Lundberg as "loving the dreamy regions and the life of the gypsy in the outdoors."[33] In addition to short stories, she published numerous articles on ways in which women could share in making the experience of motoring more enjoyable for both sexes.[34] Although certainly an active proponent of women's rights to partake in motorization and modern society, she nonetheless generally framed "modern femininity" within a naturalized gender hierarchy in which women's proper role was at best that of a servile comrade to men.

Lundberg also penned abundant "advice" articles directed explicitly towards a female readership. These articles provide ample evidence of the shaping of an understanding of femininity in which women were encouraged to participate in the modern world of motoring, on the condition of accepting a subordinate role in terms of access to technology and economic resources. For example, in "How Do We Equip Ourselves for a Trip?," she advises women to ready themselves for motorcycling excursions by making sure they are well prepared with all the necessary supplies to enjoy a meal outdoors, including linens and a "string with which to tie a posy of handpicked meadow flowers."[35] In "The Art of Weekend Cooking," a man and his female pillion-seat rider embark on an overnight adventure by motorcycle: "We want to leave behind this noisy area for a whole one and a half days; we want to relax, recuperate fully, and be completely alone, as a twosome. We are independent, and we don't need a hotel or a restaurant." In this scenario, both the man and the woman enjoyed the liberation, both sexual and social, that the mobility of a motorcycle affords. While the legal status of the couple remained ambiguous, the language Lundberg employed in addressing this motorcycle excursion, however, demonstrates that her conception of gender roles was clearly delineated. The man, referred to as the "Führer," was in charge of the motorcycle and setting up the tent. The woman was responsible for creating a feeling of outdoorsy domesticity: making the coffee, setting the table "that will most often consist of a nice tablecloth spread out and a few flowers strewn about." Lundberg's conception of femininity, while modern in its form, was firmly grounded in traditional gender roles.[36]

In Lundberg's writings, the tensions within the relationship between women, motorcycling, and modernity are palpable. In the piece, "The *Sozia*: How She Should Be and How She Should Not Be," Lundberg trumpeted the *Sozia*, the feminine gendered occupant of a pillion seat, as "a modern concept, a new female characteristic." A *Sozia* should make herself a "useful assistant to the motorcycle owner." As a "first step to independence," she should be able to orient herself spatially and inform him of points of interest along the way, and, "if necessary, to stop passing cars with a pleading glance" to ask for extra gas or assistance. She should also be able to assist him with inevitable repairs. If she succeeds in acquiring these skills, then, according to Lundberg, "she too will be able to discover the world through the motorcycle, she will gather new impressions, and will make it further out into nature than all the other big city girls." Despite enjoying the benefits of modern mobility, Lundberg's *Sozia* was subservient to and still dependent on the male motorcyclist.[37]

In contrast, in "When a Lady Rides a Motorcycle," a short story published in a special issue of *Das Motorrad* dedicated to women and motorcycling, Lundberg's protagonist was an active female motorcyclist. Written in a style between a firsthand report and a fictional short story, Lundberg vividly described the wild and chaotic experience of riding in a metropolis: "When a lady rides a motorcycle—rides a motorcycle alone—she can without a doubt experience all sorts of things. If she rides in the big city, in the middle of the thickest melee of autobuses, streetcars, taxis, trucks, bicyclists, pedestrians, and horse carts, so is the experience that much more intense." While the opening sentences merely indicated the challenges of navigating through the traffic of the city, Lundberg went on to describe how and why motorcycling is especially difficult for a "young lady" and the characteristics she must possess in order to master the situation. While "strictly taken it's not exactly ideal for a young lady to scoot about in between the progressive signal system of green lights, past traffic towers and traffic police during the liveliest hours of the day," she argued that "if there is some kind of compelling reason to justify such a ride through the city, then it means demonstrating a clear head, calm nerves, and prompt decisiveness, in order to tame the 'forward storming power' of the motorcycle in the middle of the traffic chaos."

The story imagined an inexperienced young female motorcyclist "inadvertently getting caught up in the chaotic conditions of city traffic" with its "honking, ringing, and scampering." She is "often not a match for it," especially in comparison to an experienced *Sozia*, familiar with the "turbulence of the big city," who can "anticipate indecisive pedestrians and reckless drivers." Although Lundberg encouraged women to motorcycle to gain the experience needed to master the modern metropolis, her writings often reflect persistent stereotypes that women naturally had weak constitutions—physically, and, particularly, mentally. Active women motorcyclists, however, were subject to a specific form of harassment and ridicule. The story continues with the inexperienced motorcyclist losing her bearings and pulling over to the sidewalk to consult a map of Berlin. Immediately, "a horde of children storm out—girls and boys, they hoot and holler when they recognize that it is not a male rider. 'Look over here, a virago in pants!,' or 'Gee, fatso, shouldn't you rather be at home with your pots and pans?,' or 'Missy, make sure that you don't lose a stitch of your puttees'—and these are just harmless howlers of the Berlin big-city jargon." While women motorists in general were viewed with a suspicious and mocking eye, women motorcyclists embodied a liminal position in the signifying of gender, symbolizing a transgression obvious even for children.

The young lady's "adventure" continued when she almost ran over a "poor little purebred dachshund" that had strayed into the street. But would a "lady" run over a "harmless sweet little animal?—Of course not." Thus, the inexperienced female rider braked sharply, and the motorcycle came to a stop a few centimeters shy of the animal. Although the animal was spared by the goodness of womanly compassion, what ensued, however, was "crashing and clanking, shards falling to the ground, people badmouthing." A taxicab driver who had not anticipated her sharp braking maneuver skidded forward on the wet pavement and "landed rather un-gently on the left taillight of the motorcycle." Again, a crowd immediately gathered. "Four people gather—eight people gather—out of the eight it becomes sixteen, and out of the sixteen, vast masses. The Berliner always has time when something happens, even if it's just a broken lamp." The trope of the mass spectator is intrinsically linked to the trope of the modern metropolis. The woman motorcyclist becomes a modern spectacle, a subject of the gaze, if not ridicule, of the masses. As in the case of the taunts of the children, such a fender-bender constituted another moment of public shaming for the female motorcyclist. A policeman "with a severe countenance and readied pencil" then turned up and dispersed the crowd. He also collected and recorded the requisite information on the two parties—"Addresses are written down, birthdates and immunization data are noted, business cards and driver's licenses details exchanged."

Although the minor crash signified a moment of public humiliation for the female motorcyclist, the "young lady" was also portrayed as being endowed with a secret weapon specific to her gender. "The chauffeur grouses—and the lady smiles half-regretfully, half-conciliatorily. She smiles so enchantingly that the furious man is transformed into a tender gentleman—they both take comfort in each others' insurance policies and part with a comradely handshake." Lundberg portrayed the "young lady" as having the ability to charm her way out of an uncomfortable situation. This strategy had more rhetorical than practical force, as the reality of being a female motorist was often harsher, and women were often warned not to rely on their sex to extricate themselves from unpleasant encounters. Nevertheless, although ambivalent in both its emancipatory potential as well as its potential to challenge the hegemonic gender order, female charm, at least discursively, represented a gendered tactic that women could deploy to their advantage in the masculine world of motorization.

At the end of the anecdote, the once-inexperienced "young lady" motorcyclist has gained both experience and confidence, and learned how to hold her own in the "chaos of city traffic." "Yes—she's even

almost become fond of exerting her power of judgment and strain-
ing her nerves to the extreme." As she learns to "cross the wide Berlin
intersections in the slipstream of another vehicle," the public is both
"interested and amazed" at her capabilities, and "even in the thickest of
traffic she gets on very well with her male colleagues." In Lundberg's
portrayal of the "young lady" motorcyclists' development, nineteenth-
century gender norms persist alongside signs of change. Through
learning how to properly maneuver through city traffic on a motorcycle, the fact of being the source of a spectacle was transformed from
a cause of embarrassment to a reason for pride. Lundberg's depiction
conceded the right of women to acquire the skills in order to partake
in motorized modernity, while at the same time it demonstrated how
modern motorcycling femininity could be both socially liberating and
subject to particular public scrutiny.[38]

Other female motorcycle enthusiasts contributed their voices in
the form of travelogues. Gerda Wunderlich, for example, published a
piece in *Das Motorrad* titled " . . . And Pentecost on the Baltic Sea."[39]
Wunderlich, who traveled with two male companions on a Victoria
motorcycle with sidecar, wrote of passing by pleasant landscapes on
the journey from Berlin to the Baltic Sea: "The whole world seemed
green and blue and golden, and only every now and then was there
a house or two, as if by accident." However, she also reported not-so-
pleasant breakdowns: "The chain had broken—not so terrible in and of
itself, only if you do not have the appropriate chain-link and nobody
passes by, then you become perplexed; that is to say, in reality, you
curse." This was only the first of many breakdowns and flat tires on
their journey. After one flat tire, the male pillion-seat rider, Paul, was
forced to join her in the sidecar in order to reduce the load on the flat
back tire. "Paul 'sat' down, that is to say he squatted unhappily half on
my back and half on the luggage rack . . . In these moments we lacked
the rightful appreciation for the wonderful, strong salty air that was
blowing from the sea." Wunderlich, however, acknowledged breakdowns as a necessary evil of enjoying the pleasures of motoring, and
as part of the adventure.

Women, like male motorcyclists, were also astute observers of social
cues of motoring, and well versed in differentiating between status
symbols. For example, along the way, Wunderlich and her companions
met up with another group of friends traveling on a D-Rad, as well as
four people traveling on a BMW motorcycle with sidecar: "Those were
real gents—in elegant leather vests and leather breeches, the young
women with red rubber coats, you see!" Wunderlich's description of
their experiences the next day included more beautiful landscapes and

breakdowns, and, at seven in the evening, their departure back to Berlin. Driving through the night—"in the sidecar you can sleep well, despite the early morning chill"—they arrived in Berlin in the early morning: "A quick breakfast with hot coffee and then off to the office. It was a wonderful Pentecost—and we are very thankful to you, our Victoria!" Thus, despite all the breakdowns and "the hardships suffered," Wunderlich praised the motorcycle for the experiences it facilitated. Wunderlich's travelogue did not differ greatly from those written by men; for both male and female authors, descriptions of landscapes, motorcycle brands, and mechanical breakdowns made up the bulk of the reportage.[40]

A less typical female motorcyclist travelogue, "With BMW to Dalmatia," submitted by Sophia Skorphil, was published in *BMW-Blätter* in 1930. Unlike Hoffman and Wunderlich, Skorphil did not occupy the position of *Sozia*; rather, like Köhler and Körner, Skorphil was an "active" female motorcyclist.[41] Her trip took her 2,013 km in six days, from Vienna to the Adriatic coast at Tijesno and back. She spoke of the trip in terms of her and her sister "breaking free" [*durchgerissen*]: "Yes, as two married ladies taking a trip alone without marital appendages, and furthermore on a motorcycle, did not suit our strict husbands. But I'm like that, when I've decided to do something, especially something that I imagine to be so pleasurable, as the owner of my dear BMW R 63, well then, who is capable of being stronger-willed than I? My sister, well, I just packed her up with me and—we drove off happily." A long-distance motorcycle trip undertaken by two married women on a heavy 750 ccm-engine motorcycle without their husbands would have been an oddity.

Nonetheless, Skorphil's account generally follows the pattern of most early motoring travelogues. She leaves the congested city for the bucolic countryside, embarking on a journey that held in store both the pleasures of scenic landscapes and the hazards posed by livestock, breakdowns, inclement weather, and treacherously pothole-riddled roads. At one point, when describing how her front wheel broke loose, she remarked with amazement at her own capabilities of mastering a dangerous situation: "(I'm no coward and confess that this split second was the only time I said to myself: You shouldn't have taken this ride.) Today it seems to me as if it was someone else and not me who had jerked the bike at full throttle to the left side so that we were able to escape uninjured." At the end of her piece, Skorphil again asserts her independence of opinion: "And how often I was discouraged from taking this ride to the 'Wild Ones,' and I have to honestly admit that I enjoyed Dalmatia so much that I have the intention of riding there next year and staying for longer than fourteen days; that is to say, hopefully I can take such a long 'marriage vacation.'"[42] For Skorphil, there was "nothing more pleasurable than, on a whim, with or without destination, to view the beautiful world," and she openly portrayed her marriage as a constraint on her freedom, and the motorcycle as the means to escape.[43] Her motorcycle journey, although certainly uncommon, is remarkable for its emancipated point of view. In publishing this account, Skorphil actively contributed to reshaping and reconfiguring the realm of what was thinkable and possible for married women motorcyclists during the late Weimar Republic.[44]

Thus, female motorcyclists during the Weimar Republic both challenged and reproduced gendered stereotypes. Their voices and positions were not unanimous; they held a wide range of views on the appropriate roles of women vis-à-vis motorcycling—from Köhler and Skorphil's adamantly independent view of women's equality to Körner's position of women as different but equal, to Wunderlich and Lundberg's tacit acceptance of a subordinate role for women. The diversity of opinions represented by these female authors reflects the contested meaning of femininity during the Weimar Republic. One attitude they all shared, however, was that motorized mobility was a path to greater personal freedom and empowerment. Georgine Clarsen argued for the case of early U.S., British, and Australian female motorists, who "were also forced to grapple with elusive and fraught questions of how to participate in a technological world that had been gendered male—a world in which their female bodies were too readily deemed to be out of place."[45] Likewise, women motorcyclists during the Weimar Republic, above all those who refused to be *Sozias*, occupied a precarious and liminal position that challenged normative gender roles.

"Motorcycle Sport—Women's Sport"? Health and Technology in Debates about Women and Motorcycling

Women's accounts, however, represent only one side of how the discourse and practice of motorcycling was gendered. Statements by men outnumbered female voices about women's appropriate roles in a modernizing and motorizing society. In articles, editorials, and letters to the editor, men provided their opinions on whether or not motorcycling was an appropriate activity for women. Debate centered on the "dangers" of motorcycling for women's health in particular, as well as women's technological aptitude. While the majority of sources were written by men about women for a largely male audience, I also discuss the few and far-between voices of women who contributed to these debates.

The opinions ranged from almost entirely dismissive and restricting to almost unconditionally supportive and encouraging; however, most displayed a profound ambivalence to the idea and practice of women motorcycling. Some only accepted women as passive participants on a pillion seat or in a sidecar, while others encouraged women to learn to ride independently. The questions of if and how men envisioned women as motorists point to how femininity and masculinity were shaped through the distinctly modern practice of motoring.[46]

In a 1926 article, Alfred Nauck, an engineer and prominent author of numerous technical articles and books, proclaimed motorcycling a "women's sport."[47] Yet despite according women a place in the modern motorized world, Nauck's attitude also captures the ambivalent relationship of men to women and motorcycling. Due to increased "technical perfection, reliability and economy," Nauck asserted that motorcycling had "gripped broad circles from all sections of society, who also see motoring as a way to their own sporting activity." Positing the comparative advantages of the motorcycle as both a motor vehicle for transportation and an instrument to practice sports, he then asked: "If we develop these observations further, so the question will arise: Is the motorcycle also appropriate for women's sport, or do difficulties arise here, in which it would be prudent to advise women against using a motorcycle?" As long as the woman "possesses the necessary physical and psychological attributes," a motorcycle was "not necessarily an inappropriate sport instrument" for women. Judgments about women's technological savvy and their physical strength were at the heart of whether or not men believed motorcycling was an appropriate activity for women.

Despite Nauck's guarded approval, when addressing the question of why motorcycle sports would fail to attract women he drew upon the common association of women with irrational fashionable consumption, as "during long overland rides (depending on the weather), considerable dirtying or dusting can often occur ... With silk stockings, patent-leather shoes, and other fashionable things, motorcycle sports cannot be practiced!" Women's supposed vanity allegedly hindered their ability to participate in male-dominated spheres of motorcycling. However, this type of sartorial commentary was prevalent among both male and female authors and was not uniquely directed towards women. "After all," as Nauck remarked, "every sport requires a certain sacrifice and also the proper clothing. That is just as true for the practice of tennis, as well as for sports on the green fields like handball, as it is for motorcycling."

Nauck's positive appraisal of women motorcyclists was tied directly to postwar shifts in femininity. "The motorcycle is, to an exceeding extent, also suited for the woman who is a child of the times, who possesses energy and a certain derring-do. It lends the beautiful lady rider today's much sought after manly briskness and moxie." Nauck made a clear connection between motorcycling and a "modern" persona—dynamism and risk taking were presented as inseparable from inhabiting the modern Zeitgeist. He decoupled the masculine characteristics of "briskness and moxie" from a biologized concept of gender. Furthermore, Nauck's view of appropriate femininity included women being technologically proficient active motorcyclists: "There is hardly anything more attractive to imagine than a sports lady who steers her own motorcycle on a long touring ride and who possesses the valuable knowledge and capability of fixing the small malfunctions on her motorbike." Judging technical competency as a valuable skill for women to possess, and presenting the notion of technologically savvy women in a highly positive, sexually attractive light, Nauck's vision of the female motorcyclist underscored the heterosexual appeal of the masculine woman. Nauck even went so far in his imagination as to propose that the active woman rider could have a male pillion-seat rider as a companion.

In conclusion, Nauck lauded the achievements of "the array of brave women who have shown themselves to be courageous motorcycle racers," like Hanni Köhler and Susanne Körner, and praised the increased popularity of motorcycling among women. Reiterating common tropes of the appeal of motorcycling, he argued that the sport of motorcycling should also be considered an appropriate sport for women. "This sport is especially beautiful, satisfying for both spirit and soul, and also our highly developed industry delivers motor vehicles that, besides being completely reliable, are also highly economical and well designed. It is perhaps because of the last of these characteristics that motorcycling finds such an extraordinary approval with the modern sportswoman." Nauck's conclusion indicates that the industry perceived women as a potential market for motor vehicles, and motorcycles in particular. His conclusion, however, points back to the naturalized relationship between women and consumption: in Nauck's view, women found motorcycles attractive above all because of their appealing design.[48] Georgine Clarsen has argued for the U.S. case that "such gendered understandings bolstered a comforting investment in traditional ideals of masculinity placed in opposition to the commodification of mass culture, by suggesting that women were easily duped by fripperies of styling and fashion in automobiles, in contrast to men's rational adherence to solid engineering values."[49] Indeed, while Nauck's article contains abundant diction and content that challenged inherited gender roles, the association of femininity and consumption was nonetheless upheld throughout.

The Medicalized Debate on Women and Motorcycling

The question of women and motorcycling, however, is even more complex than Nauck's short article suggests. As was the case with many other contentious questions such as sport, violence, and youth, another debate took place in response to the proposition of "women on motorcycles." In the form of letters to the editor of *Das Motorrad*, contributed to by "experts" and "laypersons" (including husbands, boyfriends, and one woman) over the years 1927–1928, the debate reveals a variety of positions on women motorcycling. The letters suggest that the issue of women on motorcycles, as either passive or active riders, was fraught with tensions, as both an idea and as praxis.

Social hygiene and reproductive health surface as central concerns among both the doctors and the laymen who responded. All of the doctors who responded held some reservations about women motorcycling due to the damage that could be sustained by female reproductive organs. Providing a cautious and conservative view of whether motorcycling presented a threat to women's health, one doctor addressed the question solely in terms of the woman as a *Sozia*: "Pillion-seat riding is, for an organically healthy woman, not harmful, provided that the motorcycle has proper suspension and that the seat also has the necessary comfort, good cushioning, etc." He pointed to a number of technical measures to minimize the shock and vibrations for the *Sozia*, including riding only on "flawless streets" at speeds above 60 km/h, using "balloon tires," as well as adjusting the pillion seat to be closer to that of the driver's seat. Furthermore, "a woman should be enjoined from riding motorcycles directly before and during her period; however, there is considerable individual variation, so that in this moment it can only be judged on the basis of the constitution of the woman in question."[50] The general social taboo around women during menses appears to have had a continued influence on many medical professionals' opinions on when motorcycling is suitable for women. Moreover, with the authoritative stance, the doctor maintained that "Women with an illness of the lower abdomen (internal and external sexual organs, intestine, bladder, liver, spleen, kidneys, and stomach) should not ride motorcycles; the same goes for women who lean towards any kind of hysteria." Although particularly widespread in the pre–World War I era, the medical establishment's belief that vibrations negatively affect a woman's health, both mental and sexual, remained common in medical discourse during the 1920s. Indeed, the trope of linking hysteria to the womb dates back to Hippocrates; and the Hippocratic tradition, while especially prevalent in the nineteenth century, dominated the German medical sciences during the 1920s.[51] Another doctor, himself a motor-cyclist, was also highly skeptical of women on motorcycles, maintaining that riding on a "pillion seat requires continuously sitting in the spread-legged position—and it is exactly in this position that a woman's abdominal/reproductive organs [*Unterleibsorgane*] are extremely sensitive." He "urgently discouraged the use of a motorcycle pillion seat for longer and more frequent tours with a female escort," and recommended that male motorcyclists who wished to take their wives along should buy a sidecar.

Through spreading assumptions about the damage that could be sustained to female reproductive organs by riding on a motorcycle, the medical establishment contributed to limiting women's opportunities to participate in motorized mobility. A medical recommendation that women belonged in cars or in sidecars could also present an economic barrier. While automobiles were out of reach for most middle-class households, even sidecar motorcycles were a good deal more expensive, not only because of the extra cost of the sidecar, but also because the motorcycle itself had to have a stronger horsepower engine in order to carry the extra weight. Thus, the affordable, tax-free, moped-like small-powered motorcycles would not have been an available option if the advice of the doctor were heeded. Indeed the doctor's recommendations precluded women as "active motorcyclists," and relegated them to the relatively private and safe space of a sidecar, a more enclosed vehicle.[52]

While all the doctors who contributed their opinions to the debate expressed reservations regarding the effects of motorcycling on women's reproductive health, not all doctors took such a strong a stance against it. In 1927, for example, one medical doctor contended: "I believe, by and large, that the question [of whether a woman should ride a motorcycle] has already in praxis been answered with a yes. I believe it is more important to pose the question of when a woman should not ride a motorcycle." This doctor's reservations were also framed in terms of reproductive health. Menstruating woman, in his opinion, should avoid long rides and "pregnant women" were cautioned against riding a motorcycle during the first months of pregnancy as "experience shows that the danger of early termination is increased." Nonetheless the doctor held a generally positive opinion on the effects of motorcycling on women's health: "Motorcycle sport is a tasty and easily digestible medicine against anemia and a certain kind of frailty, and can only be recommended. Motorcycle touring ... is a perfect way for women to throw off all the oppressive ballast that has accumulated through everyday worries, in order to begin the new week fresh and in

a happy mood." Although the doctor reproduced the common association of women with nervous weakness, he recognized the "oppressive
ballast" that "accumulates" in the everyday lives of women.[53] His letter
shows that, at least in part, the German medical profession had adopted
the belief that sport and leisure were important aspects of balancing the
exigencies and pressures of modern life, for both men and women.[54]
A self-ascribed "modern doctor," on the other hand, focused specifically on "modernity" and "sports": "Modern doctors have broken with
the old notion that sports could be harmful." Despite generally support-
ing female motorcycling, he, like the other doctors, cautioned against
women riding motorcycles if they are pregnant or if they suffer from
"complaints of the female reproductive system." However, in a nod to
sex equity, the doctors also advised "those [men] suffering from cardiac
or other disorders" to seek medical advice, as a "prohibition on driving
cannot be ruled out." In conclusion, the doctor supported motorcycling
by both sexes, as "the medical profession is not aware of any disease
that is caused by motorcycling."[55] Thus, although trepidation remained
regarding women's reproductive health, by the 1920s, following the
general acceptance of women on bicycles, the medical discourse on
women and motorcycling had shifted their view towards seeing sport
as appropriate and even desirable for females.[56]

Laypersons also chimed in on the debate about women's health and
motorcycling.[57] The commentaries from these men at times reiterated
the medical discourse, but more often they presented a positive assessment of women on motorcycles. They held varying views on how active
a role a woman should have when motorcycling. For example, based
on "seven years of motorcycling" experience, in which he had "become
acquainted with almost all types of *Sozius* brides [*Soziusbräute*] and pillion seats," an "enthusiastic *Sozius* groom [*Soziusbräutigam*]" employed
normative categories of health alongside according a woman a semi-
active role while motorcycling. In his opinion motorcycling posed no
harm for "healthy women," who were above all to be "free from vertigo,
trusting in the driver, having a few grams of courage and humor in all
motorcycle situations, and a normal condition of the internal organs."
What he believed constituted a "healthy woman" certainly diverged from
nineteenth-century bourgeois conceptions of proper femininity. At the
same time, by referring to "normal" internal organs, the question of reproductive health was again a criterion for excluding females from motorcycling. His stance, nonetheless, supported the position that women
could enjoy motorcycling and, holding a definition of a "true *Sozia*" was
not far from the position Lundberg held—he maintained that all the
other traits required to be a "true *Sozia*" could be acquired while riding

on the "second seat." Experience would allow the woman to "really enjoy herself." "And then [riding] is no longer a boring, fearful, tense cowering behind the back of the man." Instead, motorcycling "becomes a fond activity and matter of course to support her driver." For example, "pressure on the hips, and he immediately knows that there is a car behind us. Two hearty strikes in his sides tell him that another motorcycle with *Sozia* wants to pass." Citing examples of *Sozias* who "immediately spot beautiful idyllic forest areas ... motifs for the camera ... cozy corners of nature for the hours of rest," the gendered division of activity was clearly defined. Despite the fact that the woman was relegated to a subordinate position on the pillion seat, the author provided the *Sozia* with an active role, not just in terms of safety, but also in terms of enjoyment for both participants.[58] Furthermore, rather than being innate, the traits required to enjoy motorcycling could be learned. Nevertheless, the motorcyclist who commanded the machine was gendered male.

Another letter from a man claiming to speak for "The Cautious Ones," spanned a semiotic bridge between the woman and the motorcycle by stressing potential "mechanical and physical types of damages." For the author, the "decisive factors" were the vibrations and the jolts that could be harmful for female reproductive organs. Again, this author's opinion reflected the prevalent male anxiety and unease about the effects of vibrations on female reproductive health.[59] In his opinion, however, "even sensitive women need not be denied the pleasure of pillion-seat riding." The female pillion-seat ride, however, was described in objectifying terms: "It is the duty of the driver, as with his machine, to carefully 'break in' his *Sozia*, and not immediately, at a tempo of 80 km/h, to race over rough pavement." Although he supported female participation in motorcycling and believed that women could gain pleasure through it, by associating the process of "breaking in" a new motorcycle with "breaking in" a new *Sozia*, he provides a clear example of the objectification of the woman and the correlation of women and motorcycles as objects men control.[60]

Husbands also contributed a number of letters to the debate. One letter from an "enthusiastic husband" was strongly supportive of his wife's and, in general, women's enjoyment of motorcycling. After issuing the typical caveats that a woman should not ride during "that time of the month" and especially not during pregnancy, he stated: "My wife likes to ride with me as often as she can when she has the time and she has already given me two very lively little girls." His statement demonstrates how supporters of women's sports increasingly sought to align female athleticism with motherhood.[61] Furthermore, arguing that the "good influence" on "the lungs as a result of the deepened breath and the free fresh air" were well-known benefits of motorcycling, the "enthusiastic husband" concluded: "And if she regains any energy through deeper sleep and, as a result, has more joie de vivre and creative power, isn't that the most valuable benefit that we can give our health?" In general, the "enthusiastic husband" equated motorcycling with corporeal regeneration and rejuvenation that was equally important for women, as wives and mothers, to brave the new world.[62] On the other hand, while rearticulating the prevalent fear of harmful effects of vibrations on the female anatomy, the "sportsman and husband" defended women motorcycling by comparing it to other sports, for example, bicycling or horseback riding, "two sports that are often practiced by ladies, during which the body is subject to decisively harder shocks and vibrations than on a well-suspended motorcycle seat or pillion seat." Lauding his wife for having attained a "driving license" and for being an "eager motor sportswoman," the author believed that there was no reason for concern about a "bride's physical well-being" when "placing her on the pillion seat." Still, while the "sportsman and husband" supported his wife's choice to be an active motorist, his language reflected the position of the male as possessive, active, and in control.[63] The sole published contribution written by a woman argued, given "certain requirements" were fulfilled, motorcycling was not harmful for women. A pillion-seat rider for seven years, she said: "I very often accompanied my husband on longer and shorter tours and I have, to date, never suffered even the slightest of harm." She advised wearing appropriate clothing—either coveralls for shorter trips or a leather jacket and knickerbockers for longer rides—to "protect against any inclement weather." She also viewed "a good pillion seat" as the "prerequisite for a pleasant ride."[64] The editorial staff of *Das Motorrad* closed the debate on the effects of motorcycling on women's health with an open and conciliatory tone, by stating that "the medical profession is not of one opinion" and that "one can summarize all the judgments in the following sentence: 'Don't be frightened, but be cautious, especially on poorly paved roads.'"[65] The preoccupation with the effects of motorcycling on women's health suggests that the medicalization of the debate in part contributed to reinforcing gender inequalities and male dominance in the field of motorization by solidly placing the responsibility for bearing and raising healthy children on women.

The debate, however, did not only take place within the pages of *Das Motorrad*. In 1930, Ilse Lundberg published an article in the *ADAC-Motorwelt*, where she maintained that the "topicality" of the issue of "housewife, child-rearing, and motor sports" could be seen in "countless debates" in women's magazines as well. Remaining conspicuously silent on issues of women's reproductive health, Lundberg asks: "Why should a woman who faithfully spends the whole week taking care of her children and household not find the time on Sunday to accompany her husband on a motorcycle tour as his '*Sozius* bride?'" Arguing that "sports girls" should not have to give up the pleasure of motorcycling merely because they are married, Lundberg furthermore maintained that the "'modern man' does not *only* want a housewife—he wants a true comrade and she should and must pursue his interests." While not contesting the role of the woman in the house, Lundberg nevertheless asserted a role for women outside of the house.[66] Women thus contributed to challenging the prevailing gendered norms for appropriate behavior by demanding to be active participants in modern society.

Women and Technological Aptitude

Almost a century after Köhler and Körner took part in their first motorcycle races, women's innate technological aptitude stubbornly remains a topic of debate. Consistently drowned out by a vocal chorus of male doubters and competitors, women have historically faced difficulties in gaining access to technology and technological education.[67] Confronted by an association of technological aptitude, rationality, and scientific praxis with improper femininity, women in many societies have struggled and continue to struggle in overcoming gender-based prejudices to claim rights to significant features of modern life. Women's partial exclusion from access to technology was and is predicated on a discursive reaffirmation of masculine dominance in the spheres of technology and industry. Although less prominent than the debate on whether motorcycling was harmful for women's health, discussions about women's capacity to acquire technological skills surfaced within the motorcycling magazines of the Weimar Republic. The commentaries show that women were restricted in terms of access to technology and technical education, and show how women were placed at a disadvantage in the emergent culture of mass motorization due to received and perceived notions of inborn technological ineptitude.

"Why are there so few female motorcyclists?," asked an article published in 1924 in the DMV journal. In an attempt to answer why there were so few female motorcyclists in Germany in comparison to the situation in England, despite design innovations that improved the reliability of small-powered motorcycles and the existence of a notable numbers of female automobile drivers, the male author located the "reason for the neglect of the two-wheeled vehicle among the daughters of Eve" in "prejudice." The author's explication, however, belied his own prejudices. By naturalizing the association of women as non-technical beings, he reiterated both the relationship of women to irrational consumption and a "common-sense" understanding of women's biological inferiority. Viewing women as physically weaker, he stated that the appropriate strength of a motorcycle for a woman is "350 ccm or less." He also asserted that a hand-operated starter "is more appropriate for women than a kick-starter, as it is easier to handle." In addition, he portrayed women as softer and in need of more comfort, for example in terms of the motorcycle seat. Following the logic of this piece, women were implicitly coded as technologically inferior: "It is, for example, not at all necessary to have a perfect mastery of mechanics in order to ride a motorcycle, nor to have a special training as a 'driving artist' ['*Fahrkünstler*']." The implication of this statement is that women were inherently incapable of acquiring "a perfect mastery of mechanics," or, in comparison to men, that women would be less successful at becoming "driving artists." Like Nauck, this author naturalizes the association of women with irrational consumption by assuming that women would not take up motorcycling because they would not want to be seen in unshapely garments:

> Many motorcycles, including those that are advertised by manufacturers as 'ladies' motorcycles,' do not sufficiently provide for protecting the rider against the dirtying of clothing. Oil and dirt have free play … except in the case that the female motorcyclist wraps herself in an entire coverall and outfits herself in a way that is not acceptable for many ladies because of 'beauty factors.' And—this can't be changed—vis-à-vis women's vanity, all rational arguments turn to dust!

Although physical appearance was an important element of modern masculine identities, almost invariably vanity and women's clothing were portrayed as essential for femininity. Women's "irrational" concern for clothing was thus tied to an inability to grasp "rational"—read "male"—arguments. Yet, despite equivocating on the gendering of technology, the author nonetheless encouraged women taking up motorcycling. His difficulties locating an appropriate place for women in the masculine-dominated world of motorcycling lie in part with his unquestioning acceptance of gendered stereotypes, and the liminal position of women motorcyclists.[68]

The male author of "The Lady at the Steering Wheel and the Handlebars" also questioned why, in 1925, the idea of a "motor sports lady" remained a social oddity, "despite all the reassessments of concepts and perspectives we have experienced in the last years, despite the general ascendancy of sports and technology, despite the emancipation of the woman, despite her outspoken 'masculinization' [*Verherrlichung*, sic] with page-boy haircut and men's clothing." Women motorcyclists continued to elicit amazement and disbelief, because, he claimed, "a woman and a machine are simply two things that do not at all seem compatible."[69] Indeed, while a "sports lady" playing tennis or swimming no longer provoked raised eyebrows, the idea of a woman mastering a machine was difficult to assimilate. The author believed that this was unlikely to change as motor vehicles would "in the foreseeable future" remain "complicated" and "require physical strength," and thus necessitate "presence of mind" and "physical agility." A "true motor sportsperson" was "instinctually and intellectually connected to the machine," qualities that the author identified as masculine by nature.[70] As Georgine Clarsen notes, "Privileged men could assume an identity of technically competent consumers, should they want to, with a minimum of fuss."[71] However, women motorists, due to their presumed physical and mental weakness, would, according to the author, remain exceptional figures: "It is certainly not pure and unmitigated joy for a representative of the weaker sex to have to change a tire on a glowing hot, dusty road by herself, or even to draw in a new inner tube and pump it up, or to repair a broken motorcycle chain by replacing a link."[72] Thus, rather than point to a lack of economic access or technical education, he reinforced and naturalized the association of feminine with weakness, as well as with inborn technical ineptitude, and elided the issue that it is highly unlikely that anyone would experience "pure and unmitigated joy" changing "a tire on a glowing hot, dusty road."

Nonetheless, the author, like Nauck, celebrated the sporting achievements of female motorists, including Köhler and Körner, recalling in detail women's "considerable successes" in motor sports, and predicted that women's participation in motorization would increase with improvements in motor vehicle engineering. "The time will come when the fairer sex will be found more often at the steering wheel or handlebars, and will dispute the prerogative of victory of the 'lords of creation.'" While women's eventual participation as equals in motor sports was accepted as a fact, it was simultaneously predicated on male achievements in engineering. Even if women were capable of competing as equals with men in a sporting environment, the author maintained that women were naturally inferior to men due to their lack of technological aptitude.[73] Motoring, as Kathleen Franz argues, became a site for men to "practice automotive authority and to portray women as technologically illiterate."[74]

The short story "Lu Learns to Ride a Motorcycle" rehearsed the trope of women's supposed disinterest in technology, and their inclination to conspicuous and irrational consumption. Narrated by a man with a sexual interest in Lu, the story relates how he tried to teach Lu how to ride a motorcycle. Whenever he attempts to explain technical details to her, she changes the subject to ask about a modern dance step or about what she should wear to a party they are to attend. On the day of their first practical lesson, she insists that he photograph her first in a variety of poses, and "three packages of film are wasted." Then, when he asks her to show him where the carburetor is located, she points to the magneto. This supposedly "unfortunately true story" persistently professes women's technological inferiority and fixation on surface appearances.[75]

However, some women who lent their voices to debates on technological aptitude also echoed the presumption that women were technically disinclined. In the article "Do Women Have an Understanding of Mechanics?" the female author first answered with a decisive "no." Comparing men and women, she asserted that only a minority of men lacked a mechanical understanding, "especially among the motorists. They either possessed an inborn love of their tools or destiny's hardships have taught them that the 'stuff' has to be in order for it to be useful in the decisive moment."[76] The author saw evidence of this naturalized masculine affinity for the tools of technology in the "joy" that a man experiences when he looks at a well-ordered toolbox, or when an chauffeur looks with "satisfaction" at his orderly garage, or when a husband calls his wife over to look at a dismantled motor in appreciation for the "pretty gearbox" or the "excellently ground pistons." She remarked that it was somewhat of a "puzzle" that men, who she judged as generally "raw and impatient," executed mechanical tasks "with caution and sheer inexhaustible patience." She then addressed women directly: "Can we be as enthusiastic as a man about technical improvements on the machine? Can we be so excited about the question of air or water cooling, chain or belt drive? Do we wait with impatience for the automobile or motorcycle show to see the newest innovations? Do we pay attention to technical, not fashionable, novelties?" She presents both a naturalized gender difference regarding technological skills, and, by evaluating a man's passion for the automotive and for tinkering in the same register as a woman's passion for fashion, she positioned both activities as complementary correlates.

Indeed, she concluded, "it is not too much to maintain that a small piece of our brain is missing, the piece where the man's special technical ability resides!" Citing the differences in mentality between boys and girls in terms of technical curiosity, she then offered an example of a woman's innate inability to succeed at gaining technical competency.

"An advanced female student at a renowned technical university," despite being a diligent student, "was not able to draw the cross section of a bicycle bearing." She then asked, "Do you think there is a male student at a technical university who would have even the slightest troubles with such a small thing?" Yet, in her opinion, women were not entirely to blame for their lack of skills: "Men don't help us out one bit. Not as long as they continuously usurp us with a despising: 'Oh, you'll never be able to do that.' On the contrary, if they were to let us tinker a bit more often and stand by our side and provide simple directions or good practical advice, we soon would be more proficient." She advanced the cause of "obligatory courses in how to use mechanics tools," which she saw as "indispensable knowledge for any lady motorcyclist or automobile driver." Pointing to women's lack of assertiveness in seeking out technical knowledge, she stressed that learning more about the mechanical aspects of motoring would allow women to gain "an understanding for the machine." In this female author's view, love of the object could only really come from knowing the object.

She also criticized how sexist stereotypes hampered women's access to technical knowledge, for example, on the showroom floor. During a sales pitch, she argued, males were designated responsible for judging the "mechanics," and females for judging the "design." "I have always been annoyed that men seem to find explaining the motor to us women totally unnecessary. Usually the sales representative points out the beauties and the comforts of the bodywork to us; it is believed that the inner workings are unfathomable to the lady." Connecting women's thwarted potential to acquire technical intelligence to their being consistently undermined by male behavior, she reveals how men's attitudes towards women's capacities shaped the modern world of motoring.

While overall the author presented a view in which capacity for technical abilities was clearly gendered, she based her reasoning for the difference in technological aptitude and skill between the sexes not only on the discrepancy in access to technical knowledge and training but also on how men relate to women. Like early US and British female motorists and tinkerers whom Georgine Clarsen and Kathleen Franz describe, women active in the motoring scene in the Weimar Republic did not perceive the idea of a woman gaining technical skills as inimical; instead they duly noted the considerable internal and external obstacles to women's access and attitudes towards technology.[77] Although the views in "Do Women Have an Understanding of Mechanics?" hardly represented a radical feminist stance, the female author nonetheless asserted the possibility of women being able to gain technical competencies, and that women would benefit from gaining these skills.[78]

Der Schlossermeister, the trade journal for metalworkers, many of whom were motorcyclists during the Weimar Republic, more generally addressed the need for "preparing for a modern society through educating towards technology." The article asserted the preeminence of technology in the modern world and the necessity of providing technical education for all of the population. While the article was primarily focused on technological education for males, in its conclusion it also addressed the same for children (teaching through play) and for women. "Not only youth require technical education, and not alone the masculine sex—just in the last years technology has had a lasting effect on the household and therefore on the woman—and so it is also mandatory that she gets to know about technology and to experience technology as a benefactress for humanity." Technical knowledge, the author argued, would "raise the prosperity of a nation ... and increase culture to ever-higher development. Technology deserves, therefore, to be known and loved by every person, because it is the basic element of good." Technology was seen as the key to forging a modern society, and women, as members of society, should be provided with technological education so that they could understand and thus appreciate and profit from the benefits of technology, and in order to increase the productivity and wealth of the modern nation. Nonetheless, by pointing to the importance of advancements of household technologies for women, the home, and especially the kitchen, was naturalized as the appropriate space for the woman. Indeed, while the author predicated a flourishing modern German nation on women partaking in technological advancements, their roles were apparently best confined to private and domestic spaces.[79]

Yet many women were keen on technologies that would carry them outside of the home. Margret Boveri, a motoring enthusiast, recollected how, as a young woman during the Weimar Republic, she trained her ear to recognize the sounds of different types of engines: "Back then we were all geared only towards motors. When you sat in a room and something drove by on the street, you had to be able to say whether it was a two-stroke of a four-stroke engine; a four-cylinder or a six-cylinder; and all that by ear alone."[80] Listening was one of the skills that motoring trained and, as Georgine Clarsen has argued, "driving required an active, whole-body engagement."[81] A commentary on the Weimar obsession with new mobility technologies, Boveri's description also demonstrates the degree to which females were invested in participating in the new motorized world. As a young woman during the Weimar Republic, she spent a considerable portion of her inheritance on purchasing a car; she recalled: "The driving examination was very difficult.

You had to be able to describe the entire mechanics . . . You had to know all of the innards and learn all their functions—differential, drive shaft, the rhythm of the pistons, and the construction of the muffler."[82] Despite the pervasive, sometimes internalized, stereotype that females lacked technical aptitude, women did actively seek out access to technology and technological knowledge during the Weimar Republic. In attempts to come to terms with the realignment of social traits such as femininity and masculinity, men expressed ambivalence to women's participation in motorization and held contradictory positions regarding a woman's place in the world. However, even as definitions of behaviors and spaces appropriate for females and males shifted, women faced considerable barriers to fully participating in modern, technological society.

Institutional Obstacles to Women's Participation in Motorization

Beyond the biases women encountered regarding their supposed deficiencies in physical constitution, rational thought, and technological aptitude, women were also subject to institutional obstacles and even police profiling based on their gender. Juridical and anecdotal evidence suggests that during the Weimar Republic women drivers of both motorcycles and cars faced intense scrutiny during examinations for driving licenses, as well as police harassment on the road. For example, Alfred Nauck cautioned women motorcyclists to always carry their identification papers and driver's license, because "a strict policeman will not make exceptions to the regulations just because she is a woman."[83] Indeed, law authorities often singled out women drivers on the basis of their sex. Even more so than for female automobile drivers, who were "welcomed as consumers," public reputations were at stake for the women who chose to participate in motorcycling—a liminal activity that placed them on the edge of femininity.[84] Although some in industry and in government administration attempted to counter the prevailing public opinion that women's constitutions made them ill suited for operating a motor vehicle, women nonetheless were regularly presumed to be inferior motorists.[85]

Indeed, women motorists, motorcyclists and car drivers alike, faced prejudice and very real institutional hurdles as they attempted to actively stake a claim to modern motorized mobility. The minister of the interior of the socially conservative state of Bavaria dispatched the following order to the Chambers of the Interior on 26 November 1926 regarding driver's license examinations. According the "perceptions" of the minister, "more and more women have of late been acquiring driver's licenses." As a response to "various doubts about the aptitude of women as drivers," the minister requested that, "during driving license examinations, female persons be handled with special diligence and during the practical part of the examination that attention is above all directed at whether or not the female examinee possesses the necessary calm and presence of mind, even in difficult traffic situations."[86] Such a decree from one the highest state officials was certain to have had a profound impact on the lives of women seeking to participate in motorization. The already acrimonious environment women faced as they attempted to exercise their legal equal rights to actively take part in modernity could have only become more hostile after the authorization of gender-specific profiling.

The extent of obstruction, however, at least from the official position, differed significantly between regions. The Reich minister of transportation felt behooved to admonish the Bavarian authorities after they submitted a request to the district minister of Hanover for information regarding a female driver of an automobile. The local gendarme in Miesbach, a small Bavarian town at the foot of the Alps, spotted a female driving a vehicle with a license plate registered in Hanover. A request for further information regarding the female motorist was answered as follows by the *Landrat* [District Administrator] of Nienburg at the end of August 1926: "The wife, Leonore von Eickhof-Reitzenstein, nee von Mosch, who has been in possession of a driver's license since 1913, was driving the automobile of her husband, Retired Major von Eickhof-Reitzenstein of Liebenau at the specified time."[87] The woman whose driving was deemed questionable by the Bavarian authorities was the aristocratic wife of a high-ranking member of the army, evidence that class and social ranking were less important than gender when it came to driving motor vehicles.

In response to the Bavarian authority's request, however, on November 9, 1926, the Reich minister of transportation sent the following dispatch to the Bavarian minister of the interior referring to "investigations of ladies, who are in possession of driving licenses." Remarking on the "fact that today a great number of women possess driving licenses," the minister concurred with his Prussian colleagues that "in the case where no punishable act has been committed, such investigations only burden state agencies ... The fact alone that a woman is driving a motor vehicle does not in itself justify an investigation."[88] While this document provides further evidence that women drivers were indeed widely targeted for scrutiny by the police authorities on the basis of their sex, it more surprisingly shows that a number of prominent ministers were willing to actively countervail against prejudices women encountered while driving. It also demonstrates the regional differences in the appraisal of female drivers during the Weimar Republic; the authorities in predominantly Catholic and socially conservative Bavaria pursued a more hostile approach to women drivers, while the authorities in predominantly Protestant and more socially liberal Prussia staked out less gender-biased positions.

The widespread institutional sexism in Bavaria against female motorists was also documented in the "Fortnightly Report of the District President of Upper Bavaria" from May 1927. The report contained the following misogynist comment: "The racing of automobiles on the winding mountain roads will demand ever more victims, even more so because the number of people chauffeuring members of the female sex has markedly increased."[89] Likewise, the general public's attitude that women were naturally inferior drivers persisted despite evidence to the contrary.[90] However, even in Bavaria, profiling of women was no longer acceptable from an official standpoint. In 1927, either as a consequence of the pressure from the Reich ministry of transport, or the increasing statistical evidence that women were not naturally ill-equipped to drive motor vehicles, or pressure from another source, the Bavarian minister of the interior felt inclined to send out a dispatch to all district offices and local police stations. Its subject was the "surveillance of motor traffic on rural roads," and it advised local gendarmes to "avoid petty and harassing complaints" and to approach motorists in a "cautionary and educational" manner. Among behaviors judged as "harassment" was targeting women motorists.[91]

In part, the press also sought to counteract the prejudices against female drivers. *Concordia*, the trade journal of the sports and former worker's welfare organization, wrote in 1928 that, "contrary to the long-held opinion, German and US statistics from authorities and driving schools show that **women** are really **good drivers** [bold in original]." Women "drive carefully and don't drink alcohol." "Lady drivers ... don't have ambition to race around with their vehicles like 'racing Rolands,' but rather treat driving more like a comfortable 'digestive stroll.'"[92] Although statistics demonstrated that women were not inferior drivers, and indeed, were safer drivers than their male counterparts, women still faced institutional and societal biases to participation in motorized mobility, and were subjected to public and official scrutiny.

Conclusion

Representations of, and attitudes towards, female motorcyclists were shot through with ambivalences. "The True *Sozia*," a poem published in a New Year issue of the NSU's journal on the eve of the Nazi's ascendency to power, exhibits a particularly apposite example of the shifts in conceptions of femininity. The attributes that a female motor-cycling passenger should have were described as "a flapper skirt and bobbed hair," bearing the markers of a "modern girl."[93] In comparison to the "'Sunshine-Good-Weather-Girl/' in her lace train dress/ that would fit better in a ballroom," the "true *Sozia*" would not "complain or cry when the sun won't shine." The male author asserted, "We need women, who don't tremble/ when it rains and storms, who/ stand by our sides, in word and deed/ in our gutsy sport." When mechanical problems arise, the "true *Sozia*" would "in the horrors of night and rain," help the male motorcyclist "take apart the back wheel/ Not caring about dirty hands/ Not complaining if her stocking gets smudged."[94] This poem, like much of the literature during the Weimar Republic that deals with women and motorization, and motorcycling in particular, contains ambiguities as to what constitutes proper femininity. Post–World War I social and politi-cal changes expanded possibilities for women from a greater range of classes to participate in the public sphere, even if often framed in terms of consumption and generally the subject of intense critique. By the end of the Weimar Republic the concept of "proper femininity" had been reconfigured. While decidedly subordinate to men, "aspects of women's 'masculinization' had successfully entered the mainstream and become part of a larger, modernized ideal of German womanhood," although the shape of femininity remained circumscribed within a larger set of social norms.[95]

Motoring was one important field on which these battles were played out. Women who motorcycled were seen as suspect, constantly on the verge of overstepping boundaries and disturbing gender norms. Motorcycles, rather than automobiles, were generally regarded as particularly inappropriate vehicles for "the fairer sex." Although some men contributed to furthering the rights of women as motorists, others remained anxious about what motorized mobility meant for social and sexual relations. Women faced societal censure when choosing to par-ticipate in activities that transgressed gender norms, regardless of class and status. Indeed, women motorists, and motorcyclists in particular, faced obstacles to participating in motorization during the Weimar Republic. Nevertheless, although a small minority, some women, as illustrated in the examples of Köhler and Körner, crossed the thresh-old and even participated in the almost exclusively male domain of competitive motorcycling. Women also contributed to shaping motor-cycling discourse, bringing in their voices, and staking a claim in motor-ized modernity. Through venturing into the male-dominated world of motorcycling, women motorcyclists thus subverted gender norms and were living embodiments of a reformulated "proper femininity." As definitions of what it meant to be a proper woman shifted, so did definitions of what it meant to be a proper man.

Notes

1. Fritz Kantor, "Das Mädel und seine Maschine!," *Das Motorrad*, 1931: 1345.
2. Poiger, "Fantasies of Universality?," 320.
3. Much work has been done on variations of the "new woman" and the "modern girl" in recent years. Sutton, *The Masculine Woman*; Sylvester, "Das Girl"; Lynn, "Contested Femininities."
4. Clarsen, *Eat My Dust*, 2.
5. Clarsen, *Eat My Dust*, 5. Clarsen also points out that motoring was "incorporated into twentieth-centry women's aspirations for major social change—for independence, mobility, meaningful work, and pleasurable lives." Clarsen, *Eat My Dust*, 3. See also Scharff, *Taking the Wheel*. For a comparison with women motorcyclists in England, see Potter, "An Exploration of Social and Cultural Aspects of Motorcycling," 101–46; and Koerner, "Whatever Happened to the Girl on the Motorbike?"
6. Herbert Schmidt-Lamberg, "Neueste Mitteilungen aus dem Motorradverkehr des Winters 1930/31," *Das Motorrad* (Vienna), no. 143, 1931, 6–7.
7. A 1922 article on the ADAC-*Länderfahrt*, in which Susanne Körner took part, mentions two women who rode motorcycles competitively before World War I. See Richard Koehlich, "Die Reichsfahrt der ADAC," *Der Motorfahrer*, no. 34, 1922, 505.
8. Berit Horenburg, "Frauen im Rennsport – Über frühe Rennfahrerinnen und Sozias," *Das Motorrad*, no. 17, 29 July 2013. http://www.motorradonline.de/szene-und-motorsport/frauen-im-rennsport-ueber-fruehe-rennfahrerinnen-und-sozias/466476
9. Lotte Zielesch, "Hanni Köhler, eine unserer erfolgreichsten Motorradfahrerinnen," *Motor und Sport*, no. 47, 1927, 31.
10. Hanni Köhler, later married Freiherr Ottokar von Skal und Gross-Ellguth on 5 January 1933 in Jeltsch, Lower Silesia, and ended her active motorcycling career. At the end of World War II, the von Skal und Gross-Ellguth family was stripped of its aristocratic titles, and expelled from Silesia, a region that was integrated into Poland following Germany's defeat in World War II. After expulsion, Ottokar and Hanni emigrated to Alaska. She died in Alaska in 1982. Bernd Tesch collects information on long-distance motorcycle travelers, including women; see www.tukutuku.de
11. "Was Hanni Koehler erzählt," *Das Motorrad*, 1927: 300–301.
12. Her finishing time gave her an average speed of approximately 40 km/h (25 mph); however, subtracting the six hours she spent pushing her motorcycle means that her average driving speed was approximately 61 km/h (38 mph). Considering the state of the roads during the Weimar Republic, this was indeed quite a feat.
13. Zielesch, "Hanni Köhler," 31.
14. *ADAC-Motorwelt*, no. 14, 1928, 1.
15. "ADAC-Bildnachrichten," *ADAC-Motorwelt*, no. 22, 1929, 6.

16. Max Ryshka, "Hanni Koehlers Indienfahrt," *Das Motorrad*, 1931: 1151–53; also Ryshka, "800 Kilometer ohne Signal," *ADAC-Motorwelt*, no. 40/41, 1931, 15–17.
17. *Tempo*, 4 June 1931.
18. See the description of the article published in *Die Dame* on "Die moderne Sportsdame," in Sutton, *The Masculine Woman*, 75–76.
19. "Was Hanni Koehler erzählt," *Das Motorrad*, 1927: 301.
20. For example: "Motorcycle Amazons – photo of Miss Hanni Köhler, the brave Stock Motorcycle Rider, at the finishing line of the Zurich–Berlin long-distance ride, in which she performed excellently." "Motorrad-Amazon," in *FKZ*, no. 2, 1926, 4.
21. Sutton, *The Masculine Woman*, 95.
22. An "Automobile Queen" competition was also held. In comparison to the thirteen women who were in the running for the title of "Motorcycle Queen 1927," over forty females participated in the contest for the title of "Automobile Queen 1927." See: "Königinnen-Wettbewerb von *Motor und Sport*" and "Wer Wird deutsche Motorrad-Königin und Wer Wird deutsche Automobil-Königin?," *Motor und Sport*, no. 22, 1927, 26–30.
23. The results were announced in *Motor und Sport*, no. 9, 1927, 28. Beauty competitions were commonplace in the motorized and non-motorized milieu. Also, numerous motoring clubs put on so-called *Schönheitswettberb* (beauty contests) in which members would decorate their cars and motorcycles, and the "most beautiful" would win a prize. These competitions increasingly came under fire as being "frivolous."
24. The woman crowned "Automobile Queen" had more of a nineteenth-century, bourgeois allure, underscoring the differences in habitus between motorcyclists and automobile drivers.
25. Sutton, *The Masculine Woman*, 75–77.
26. Anonymous, "Motorsport und Mode," *Der deutsche Motorfahrer*, no. 7, 1928, 20. The author continues by connecting motorcycling to a non-prude attitude: "Female motorcyclists and passengers will not be talked out of this comfortable and practical piece of clothing. The 'world' will say what it wants. Ultimately it could be that the 'mounting' of the lady behind the motorcyclist is as embarrassing as the dress in which she does it. If you look for a negative, you'll find one if you think too prudishly about our ladies' motor sport." See also Katie Sutton's chapter on the "masculinization of women's fashions," in Sutton, *The Masculine Woman*, 25–65.
27. Steven Koerner (no relation to Susanne Körner) mentions a 1927 ride Körner took to England in "What Ever Happened to the Girl on the Motorbike?"
28. All above quotes from Körner are taken from "Suzanne Körner, Ein Interview," *Motor und Sport*, no. 3, 1927, 12.
29. Clarsen, *Eat My Dust*, 4–5.
30. Sutton, *The Masculine Woman*, 8.
31. Photo: "Der Filmstar Lilian Harvey," *Motorrad-Sport, -Verkehr und -Technik*, no. 16, 1926, 4; *Der deutsche Motorfahrer*, no. 7, 1928, 1; Sutton, *The Masculine Woman*, 68–70.
32. Kühne, *Kameradschaft*, 92–96.
33. "Frauen auf dem Motorrad," *Das Motorrad*, 1927: 299.
34. An example of the advice articles penned by Lundberg: "What Should We Do in Winter?," "How Do We Equip Ourselves For a Trip?," "The Art of Weekend

Cooking," "How Can We Travel Well and Cheaply?," "Washing our Motorcycle," "When Someone Sells Their Motorcycle," "On Motor Sports and Radio Listening," "The Art of Open Air Cooking" and "Motorcycle Radio Weekend," among others.

35. Ilse Lundberg, "Wie rüsten wir uns zur Reise?," *Das Motorrad*, 1929: 736–37.
36. Ilse Lundberg, "Wochenend-Kochkünste," *Das Motorrad*, 1929: 1436–37.
37. Ilse Lundberg, "Die Sozia, Wie sie sein soll, und wie nicht," *ADAC-Motorwelt*, no. 1, 1926, 24.
38. Ilse Lundberg, "Wenn eine Dame Motorrad fährt," *Das Motorrad*, 1927: 527.
39. What is particularly interesting about the title and the description of the motorcycle trip is that it is completely secular. On their holiday, the mixed-sex group (with no indication of their relationship status) sunbathes, goes dancing, etc., enjoying avowedly secular activities on a high Christian holiday. Thus, this strongly indicates that one of the major Christian holidays, Pentecost, was understood more as an opportunity for leisure rather than as an important date for religious observance. Wunderlich also published "Die Kleidung der Wanderfahrer; Brief einer erfahrenen Motorradwanderin an ihre Freundin," on the sartorial practices of motorcyclists of both sexes in *Das Motorrad*: 1929: 1434–35, discussed in Chapter 3.
40. Gerda Wunderlich, "Und Pfingsten an der Ostsee," *Das Motorrad*, 1929: 1382–83.
41. Skorphil was married to an owner of a motorcycle repair shop in Vienna.
42. In this account, Skorphil debunks the idea of the people of the Balkans as "wild ones," rejecting a stereotype of the "Oriental" bestial exotic, and portrays them as "peaceful, friendly, and helpful" to the independent female motorist.
43. Sophia Skorphil, "Mit der BMW nach Dalmatien," *BMW-Blätter*, no. 8, 1930, n.p.
44. For an analysis of early long-distance trips undertaken by U.S., British, and Australian women motorists, see Clarsen, *Eat My Dust*, 64–85, 120–39, 140–57.
45. Clarsen, *Eat My Dust*, 158.
46. On motoring as a "site" of practicing modernity, see Geisthovel, "Das Auto," 37–46.
47. During the Weimar Republic, Nauck authored a number of books on the organization of repair shops, for example *Die Reparatur Werkstatt* (1930) and *Der wirtschaftliche Schlossereibetrieb* (1926), and contributed articles to motorcycling magazines on a variety of subjects from motorized weekend excursions to breakdowns; see, for example, "Mit Auto und Motorrad zum Wochenend," *Dixi-Magazin*, no. 8, 1930, n.p.; and "Pannen. Eine Sportliche Betrachtung über einen unangenehmen Begriff," *Klein-Motor-Sport*, no. 6, 1928, 110–11. During the Nazi era he published a number of pamphlets for the *Deutsche Arbeiter Front* on "replacing foreign resources with domestic resources" [*Ablösung fremdländischer Rohstoffe durch heimische Stoffe* (1937)] as well as the popular science book *Wunderland Technik* (1938, 1st edn). He continued to publish popular scientific books after the end of World War II, including a revised reprint of *Wunderland Technik* (1949) and *Die bedeutendsten Erfindungen* [The Most Important Inventions] (1950) in the BRD.
48. Alfred Nauck, "Motorradsport—Frauensport," *Der deutsche Motorfahrer*, no. 3, 1926, 5–6.
49. Clarsen, *Eat My Dust*, 84.
50. "Öffentliche Meinung 150, Der Arzt spricht," *Das Motorrad*, 1928: 397.

51. Lana Thompson, *The Wandering Womb: A Cultural History of Outrageous Beliefs about Women* (Amherst, NY: Prometheus, 1999), 23.
52. "Öffentliche Meinung 153, Noch Einmal: Ist meiner Braut das Motorradfahren schädlich?," *Das Motorrad*, 1928: 485.
53. On the "problem" of "hysterical men" in Germany, see Paul Lerner's excellent study, *Hysterical Men: War, Psychiatry, and the Politics of Trauma in Germany, 1890–1930* (Ithaca, NY: Cornell University Press, 2003).
54. "Öffentliche Meinung 63, Was sagt der Arzt dazu," *Das Motorrad*, 1927: 315.
55. "Öffentliche Meinung 151: Der moderne Arzt," *Das Motorrad*, 1928: 397.
56. Sutton, *The Masculine Woman*, 71–72.
57. This fact could be due to the editor's selection process as well as the fact that the readership of *Das Motorrad* was highly interested in, and supportive of, motorcycling; however, two letters do present a less positive view of women riding motorcycles.
58. "Öffentliche Meinung 65, Der begeisterte Soziusbräutigam," *Das Motorrad*, 1927: 315–16.
59. Also see Möser, *Fahren und Fliegen*, 361–62.
60. "Öffentliche Meinung 66, Der Vorsichtige spricht," *Das Motorrad*, 1927: 316–17.
61. Sutton, *The Masculine Woman*, 81.
62. "Öffentliche Meinung 64, Der begeisterte Ehemann," *Das Motorrad*, 1927: 315.
63. "Öffentliche Meinung 152, Der Sports- und Ehemann," *Das Motorrad*, 1928: 397.
64. Her phrasing implied that women have a certain constitutional weakness in comparison to men. In addition, her letter indicates that women were, for years on end, whether by choice or imposition, relegated to the backseat of the motorcycle. "Öffentliche Meinung 153, Zum Schluß die Motorradfahrerin selbst," *Das Motorrad*, 1928: 397.
65. "Öffentliche Meinung, Noch einmal," *Das Motorrad*, 1928: 485.
66. Ilse Lundberg, "Hausfrau, Kindererziehung und Motorsport," *ADAC-Motorwelt*, no. 2/3, 1930, 29. Emphasis in original
67. See Wajcman, *Feminism Confronts Technology*; Horowitz and Mohun, *His and Hers*; Horowitz, *Boys and Their Toys?*; Clarsen, *Eat My Dust*; Franz, *Tinkering*.
68. "Weshalb gibt es so wenig Fahrerinnen?," *Motorrad-Sport, -Verkehr und Technik*, no. 16, 1924, 25.
69. Thyl Ulenspiegel [pseudonym of Alexander Büttner], "Die Dame am Lenker und Steuer," *Motor-Magazin für Automobil-, Motorboot- und Flugwesen*, no. 30, 1925, 19. The article was reprinted in a slightly altered form in *ADAC-Motorwelt*, no. 1, 1926, 13–16.
70. Ulenspiegel, "Die Dame am Lenker und Steuer," 19–20.
71. Clarsen, *East My Dust*, 18.
72. Ulenspiegel, "Die Dame am Lenker und Steuer," 20.
73. Ibid., 21–25.
74. Franz, *Tinkering*, 69.
75. "Lu lernt Motorradfahren," *Das Motorrad*, 1929: 204–5.
76. "Hat die Frau Verständnis für Mechanik?," *Motorrad-Sport, -Verkehr und -Technik*, no. 13, 1925, 12.
77. Clarsen, *Eat My Dust*; Franz, *Tinkering*.
78. "Hat die Frau Verständnis für Mechanik?," 13.
79. "Die Erziehung zur Technik," *Der Schlossermeister*, 1927, 509–10.

80. Margret Boveri, *Verzweigungen, Eine Autobiographie*, ed. Uwe Johnson (Munich: R. Piper & Co. Verlag, 1977), 155–57. Bovari, who was born in 1900 and was later a prominent female journalist during the BRD, described her experience with motorization in her autobiography. During the Nazi era she undertook numerous trips to the Near East by automobile.

81. Clarsen, *Eat My Dust*, 14.

82. Boveri, *Verzweigungen*, 155–57.

83. Nauck, "Motorradsport – Frauensport," 6.

84. Clarsen, *Eat My Dust*, 158.

85. Another article that demonstrates the social bias against women motorcyclists describes a new sidecar contraption for use in driver training classes: "As ladies and older gentlemen, who as student drivers until now posed a certain risk to themselves and their fellow beings, can now be free of this worry, because the device allows the driving instructor who sits in the sidecar to take over complete control of the motorcycle from the sidecar." "Die neue Schulmaschine DRGM," *Motor*, no. 6, 1928, 72–73.

86. MInn (gezeichnet Stützel) an Regierungs Kammern der Inneren 26.11.1926 Betreff: Kraftfahrprüfungen, in MInn 66420 (1.9.1926–30.6.1927), Kraftfahrzeug allgemein, Bayerisches Hauptstaatsarchiv.

87. Landrat Nienburg an das Regierungspräsident Hannover, August 31, 1926, MInn 66420 (1.9.1926–30.6.1927), Kraftfahrzeug allgemein, Bayerisches Hauptstaatsarchiv.

88. Reichsverkehrsminister an MInn (K2461/26) gezeichnet: Rocholl, 9 November 1926, "Betreff: Nachforschungen nach Damen, die im Besitze des Führerscheins für Kraftfahrzeuge sind," MInn 66420 (1.9.1926–30.6.1927), Kraftfahrzeug allgemein, Bayerisches Hauptstaatsarchiv.

89. Auszug auf dem Halbmonatsbericht des Regierungspräsidenten von Oberbayern (1.15.1927) von 19.5.1927, Nr. 1044, MInn 66420 (1.9.1926–30.6.1927), Kraftfahrzeug allgemein, Bayerisches Hauptstaatsarchiv.

90. "Rund um den Motor," *Concordia*, no. 15, 1928, 300.

91. MInn an Regierungen, Kammern des Innern und Bezirksämter, 3.11.1927, Betreff: Überwachung des Verkehr auf Landstraßen, Minn 66421 (1.7.1927–31.3.1928), Kraftfahrzeug allgemein, Bayerisches Hauptstaatsarchiv.

92. "Rund um den Motor," 300.

93. See the Introduction in Weinbaum et al., *The Modern Girl around the World*, 1–24.

94. Hildebrandt Heinecke, "Die wahre Sozia," *NSU Mitteilungen*, 1933, 2831. In German, the poem follows a strict rhyming scheme.

95. Sutton, *The Masculine Woman*, 182.

CHAPTER 7

Sex and the Sidecar
Sexuality, Courtship, Marriage, and Motorization

"Gori in the Sidecar," an illustrated account of a motorcycle trip to the countryside, begins with the author and narrator, Wolf Albrecht Doernhöffer, a senior engineer for DKW, proclaiming Gori "the most darling girl to have warmed my sidecar cushion in recent times. Alongside many other good character traits, Gori knows that the female pillion-seat rider is a subordinate being, but she also must possess independent abilities to control the vehicle!" Picking her up for a ride in the countryside, Doernhöffer gushes over Gori's clothing: "She documents her sympathy with my machine" by wearing colors (a red jacket with yellow accents) that matched the motorcycle, a skirt the color of the sidecar, and stockings and shoes the color of the Continental-brand tires. "Thus, she belongs entirely to the machine!" When describing Gori's method of entering the sidecar—"The most charming way ... is simply to let yourself 'fall into the machine,' so that all passers-by of both sexes stop to watch in amazement"—Doernhöffer was clearly enjoying the spectacle himself. He also rehearsed tropes of women's technical ineptitude, calling Gori "a true help in the case of breakdowns of all kinds. Her area of specialty is changing the sparkplugs, even if she almost always forgets the gaskets!" He described their picnic as "so genuinely gypsy-like, and that is the most beautiful." Towards the evening, there is a rain shower—"Gori retracts like a snail in her sidecar house and sits warm and dry," while Doernhöffer gets thoroughly soaked, but all in all, he was "satisfied with the 'happy end' [in English in original]."

Doernhöffer's story of Gori and the sidecar, published in *Das Motorrad* in 1929, provides insights into how material objects, the sidecar and the motorcycle, mediated social and sexual experiences. The gendered aspects of motorcycling are blatant in Doernhöffer's account. The ideal sidecar passenger was to be well dressed, and have long legs to show off when falling into the sidecar, and she was to know how to cook. She was, however, also to be knowledgeable about motorcycles and a "Schmiermaxl"—a grease monkey, willing to get her hands dirty. As a

Ihr Spezialgebiet ist das Auswechseln von Zündkerzen — aber sie vergißt meistens die Dichtungen.

Eine treue Hilfe finde ich an ihr bei Pannen aller Art.

Mit Gori im Beiwagen!
In der Sommerzeit

Die charmanteste Art ist sich einfach in den Beiwagen fallen zu lassen.

Image 7.1. Gori in the Sidecar. In *Das Motorrad*, 1929 © DAS MOTORRAD / Motor Presse Stuttgart GmbH + Co KG.

"new woman" her sexual openness was presumed. Nonetheless, if she possessed all the desired characteristics, then she passed muster and qualified as "wife" material. Awash in sexual innuendo, Doernhöffer's account of Gori in the sidecar touches on numerous facets of the relationship between motorcycling, mobility, and sexuality during the Weimar Republic.[1]

The tricky terrain of gender, sexuality, motorization, and consumption produced conflicts that are more complex than standard historical interpretations of femininity, masculinity, and consumption during the Weimar Republic propose. Motorcycles were often portrayed as machines that immanently possessed sexual potency, and were perceived, at times with great anxiety, as precipitously accelerating sexual relations, and (by critics) as promoting promiscuity. Motorized mobility thus stirred up fear in some over the integrity of a social fabric already under duress. Others, however, described the motor vehicle's potential offer of (sexual) liberation as one of its greatest assets. Although the promise of being able to evade moral conventions held for both men and women, men enjoyed privileged access to commodities that increased their sexual capital. Looking at the intricate webs of male–female sexual intimacy on and off the road, from mere voyeurism to tentative selection (trying it on for size), from the rituals of purchase to trading in the old for the new, this chapter traces the various perceptions and responses to the increased circulation of the currency of sex and the acceleration of physical and social mobility.

By exploring a variety of mostly fictional sources, including poems, short stories, and novels, this chapter highlights attitudes toward the perceived impact of motorization on sexual relationships. Within the sources, the motorcycle generally functions symbolically as an instrument that encourages sexual liberation. Usually following a plot line that begins with a motoring encounter, a woman is brought into a situation in which sexual intimacy becomes a possibility, when it otherwise would not necessarily have been the case. More rarely, motorization is depicted as facilitating an inexperienced man to accumulate sexual experience. With few exceptions, motorcycles and automobiles are portrayed as catapulting both men and women headlong into precipitous sexual intimacy. The trajectory of these fictional accounts of motorized courtship was often marriage and family, circumscribing to a certain degree the limits of permissible relationships. Nonetheless, motorization also provided moments for escaping the confines of the home for both men and women, and for exploring the world and one's sexuality.[2]

"Love that Smells Like Gasoline": Courtship and the Commodity

The central love story in the pulp novel by Julius Donny, *Garage 13*, serialized in *Das Motorrad*, was propelled by a motorcycle ride. On one single afternoon, Cläre Braun, the daughter of a prominent banker, hitches a ride on the back of a motorcycle with two different male strangers.[3] First she accepts a ride to the "Swedish Pavilion" at the Halensee with the legal assessor Dr. Kurt Lamotte; then she and another man, "Wolf," take off on the same motorcycle for a joyride through the countryside around Berlin. During the second encounter, "new woman" Cläre—dressed in "silver-gray silk stockings"—calls herself "Karl" and pretends to be someone else, not divulging her identity as a daughter from a "good" house to Wolf, who likewise pretends to be a small-time crook, when he is actually the director of a factory that manufactures motors and motorcycles: "Only one topic did they, as if in silent agreement, avoid talking about: their personal circumstances."[4] The tensions in *Garage 13* are driven by small deceptions and subversions—one being the joyride on Lamotte's motorcycle, the other the feigning of false identities. Donny presents a world in flux, with the motorcycle joyride facilitating alternate personalities and increasing the fluidity of identity, opening up possibilities for experiences outside of the everyday.[5]

More than just allowing Cläre the opportunity to escape from her life of domestic propriety, the motorcycle ride exposes this "proper" young woman to the sexual gazes and advances of strange men on more than one occasion. Her body is first bared when Wolf accelerates the motorcycle, in order to test out its speed: "Only one [of a group of agricultural laborers] noticed with pleasure that even the silky white undergarments of the slender young girl whizzing-by on the pillion seat had slid up indecently high." After Wolf brings the motorcycle to a halt, "Karl"/Cläre was again exposed to a sexual gaze: "With a jubilant sigh, she let go of him and began to bring her toilette into order. Wolf turned around and, with pleasure, made the same observation as the quick-glancing agricultural laborer."[6] While motorcycling twice renders the young woman's body an object of a sexual gaze by strange men, Cläre takes pleasure in the ride, and her "jubilant sigh" may be an oblique reference to orgasm. As they continue on their ride, Cläre thinks to herself, "this is almost like a honeymoon," giving the encounter a hint of romantic propriety; and surely enough, soon thereafter she is locked in a steamy embrace with Wolf, a man whom she had only known for a few hours and whom she suspected of being a thief. "They then embraced each other and stood still in the middle of the dance and looked at each other blissfully and kissed. And then they lay down on the soft grass of the meadow that had been warmed by the sun and closed their eyes, and then slyly blinking, kissed again and again until they grew tired of this sweet game." In *Garage 13*, the motorcycle ride functions as a kind of mechanical aphrodisiac, facilitating a sexual encounter that would have been less likely, if not impossible, under other circumstances.[7]

Advertisements, poems, short stories, and comics all lent currency to the idea that a motorcycle facilitated sexual conquest. In the poem, "The 'Breakdown'" ["*Die 'Panne'*"], the motorcycle again serves as the agent facilitating the liberalization of sexual relations. Seven four-line verses describe "Fritz" and "Ruth" on their return trip from an outing on a Mars motorcycle. Fritz, however, would like to prolong their date:

With one swoop, the back-stabbing bad man –
Oh reader, silently shake your head,
Who would have thought Fritz capable of it –
Shut off the gas!

When the motorcycle comes to a halt, Ruth, who is also characterized as regretting the end of the outing,

. . . hops down graciously from the pillion seat,
And looks at him, rather interestedly,
As he tinkers around on the "Mars":
"What's the matter, Fritz?"

He sits down in the green moss,
"The motor is a little hot!"
He asserts – and gently pulls the little blond
On to his lap . . .

Apparently Fritz's strategy is successful, as "night had long since fallen" when the two return to town. Ruth's apparent technical ignorance is presented as allowing Fritz to feign a mechanical problem and accelerate the sexual relationship.[8]

A 1926 comic presents the relationship between motorcycling and sexuality by playing on the Roman emperor Julius Caesar's famous phrase: "I came, I saw, I conquered." (See Image 7.2). The motorcycle is the all-powerful weapon capable of seducing and subjugating any female, and a procurable enhancer of male sexual prowess. Only by virtue of possessing a motorcycle is the stout youth, dressed in modern attire but lacking the svelte body of a modern man, able to capture the attractive blonde, portrayed as a "modern girl."[9]

Image 7.2. Cartoon: "Cajus Jul. Cäsar," in *Motorrad-Sport, -Verkehr und -Technik*, 1926.

In the short story "Love in Four-Strokes," courtships, sexual relationships, and marriage are interpreted through different types of motor vehicle, again linking accelerated motoring mobility with accelerated sexual mobility. The story recounts observations supposedly made on a Sunday in springtime in Berlin, "the best time and place to witness 'love in four-strokes'" in all of its "forms, shapes and stages." "Sunday with seven suns in the heavens (the violins not included). It rattles and hisses and sputters [*muckepickt*] from all corners and directions." Counting the number of passengers, the author begins with "the number one."

> One? Simply a motorcycle without a 'with [*Sozia*]' ... That has nothing to do with love! Really? ... You think? ... Then you are mistaken: one only needs to strap a folded blanket onto the back rack and the female partner will be picked up along the way ... Watch: in the afternoon you will never see a motorcycle without a 'with [*Sozia*]' returning ... all are 'with.' You can even say with relative certainty: these two left together ... these two found each other along the way.

The motorcycle, with its promise of adventure and mobility, is portrayed as the primary object of desire in this story, and not the man. The author advances the claim that access to a motorcycle is a near guarantee for a man's success in initiating a sexual relationship or a courtship.

Modern love, meaning "love that smells like gasoline," is organized according to "classes and differentiations"—motorcycles with *Sozia* and those with sidecars, expensive two-seater sport cars and cheap three-seat Hanomags, a "highly elegant cabriolet," four-seat sedans and a seven-seat Buick, and even an omnibus. Each vehicle is portrayed as producing its own sexual surplus value. While monogamous hetero-sexual relationships are the norm, the author introduces the idea of simultaneous multiple sexual partners, for example when describing a vehicle and its occupants as "orgies of refinement," and proclaims that "two is the sacred number of love, even when three or four are accepted, it's still only two. At least four is two times two." Through exploring the relationships of the occupants, the author provides exam-ples of how the question of formal legitimacy is increasingly rendered less relevant in the modern motor age. For example, sketching an image of the passengers of the Hanomag, a relatively inexpensive German-built car the 1920s, he comments: "One sees: two completely happy creatures—beautiful, elegant creatures. Legitimate? Dear me, as if it mattered. Perhaps first the hors d'oeuvres of legitimacy, maybe already illegitimate legitimacy . . . what does it matter to us: they are happy and both look appetizing in their delicious little Hanomag.[10] And if they want to, they can go far distances . . . and the world is indeed so . . . beautiful." Through the offhanded dismissal of the need for legitimacy, the author hints that, as new technologies made indulging in sexual and personal liberation from place-bound constraints easier, the meaning of sexual propriety had paled for modern men and women.

A description of two occupants of a sports car goes even further in blurring the lines of appropriate gender and sexual norms. The sports car, a "small monster" with the "front high, back tapered," roared "with an open muffler, hugging the road in a hellish tempo." Two passengers, "reclined in their seats," enjoy the "purest culture of sport." Wearing the same attire—"the same golden-brown berets, the same sand-gray gaberdine outfits, the same suede gloves"—the author asks, "Are they two men?" However, "an indiscrete curl of a page-boy haircut betrays the gender of the passenger . . . Legitimate or half-legitimate or illegit-imate—in any case their love smells strongly of gasoline! . . . non Olex . . ."[11] The two motorists had "found each other in the love of sport, of the sleekness, of the total separation from 'usefulness' and 'practical.' The intoxication of speed is their most beloved '*Sakuska*'[12] to accom-pany love, and their children will then inherit a collection of sporting prizes, medals, and insignia, trophies . . . that is of course depending . . . naturally . . .!" The casual sexual relationship between the passengers is again made possible by the motor vehicle. Indeed, the sports car obvi-ates the necessity for formal or legal obligations. The pleasures of speed associated with the consumption of the motor vehicle are linked both to visceral consumption and to sexual appetites.

"Love in Four-Strokes" concludes with the author stressing the health benefits of motorized travel for a modern society. Motorization should, in the author's opinion, not only be linked to "the quest for purely functional health ... Otherwise we will become Americans with their standard weekend equipment—first, second, and third class, with their normal weekend mass places, with their flat-materialist joy about the purely practical and sober." Instead, the author invokes nineteenth-century romantic ideals: "Through centuries-long traditions and culture of the spirit we have retained something of the unreal Romantic, the rudimentary self-wallowing in a certain symbolism ... we are proud of our old culture and we love the sun, the sky, springtime, wandering for the sake of itself ... not because it is healthy, good for the skin, or builds muscles." Linking the mentality and metaphysical connection of German motorists to a less mechanized "old world," Germanic and romantic spirit embodied in anti-materialist symbolism, the author contributed to the sense of non-contemporaneity that was so characteristic of Weimar modernity. Spatial freedoms are associated with motorized mobility, social rejuvenation, and health, while at the same time they are framed in contrast to a crassly practical, pragmatic, and materialistic modern United States. "Endlessly the row [of motor vehicles] passes us by ... Always new visions ... Always new people ... Always new forms of the ancient story of the joy of life, of love, of nature, of the sun ... The old beloved and volatile roving spirit, a little bit of the gypsy life and the romance of the noble savage ... and a whole lot of fresh air and health!" Through rehearsing the standard trope of the motor vehicle as a means for escaping the monotony of everyday modern life, the author links an anti-materialist stance with the pleasures of motorization, and above all with enhanced opportunities for sexual adventure. Indeed, beyond merely connecting motorization with the healthful consumption of nature, the author stresses sexual liberation as the hallmark of Weimar modernity.

Juxtaposing alternate and competing models of modernity was a common mode of reflecting on social change during the Weimar Republic. Germans often critiqued US culture for its supposed prudishness and false morality. Raising the theme of sexuality and the difference between Americans and Europeans, "Love in Four-Strokes" concludes by urging Europeans not to become "Americanized": "Or do we also want to shed crocodile tears of outraged morality about the depraved, sinful youth of today? Do we want to exclaim, "Shocking!" [in English in original] about every illegitimate motorized couple ...? ... No, no, no ... let us remain Europeans ... and take pleasure in the sight of happiness on wheels—four-stroke love—that best likes to sputter and rumble out into the beautiful world without official permits, without the knowledge or permission of old hags." The author of "Love in Four-Strokes" cele-brates motorization for its capacity to loosen constraining conventions, framing a distinctly European alternate model of liberated sexuality and modernity as an antidote to the hypocritical, "flat-materialist," and mechanized US model.[13]

While motorcycles were often depicted as tools of seduction, enhancing attractiveness and facilitating casual sexual activity, without implying a deeper commitment, in the literature on love and courtship, the motorcycle could also be employed as a device to screen the qual-ifications of a potential marriage partner. For example, one magazine article provided advice to men on both how to use the pillion seat as a "love trap" and how to make use of a motorcycle to "test" the desirabil-ity of a woman as a life partner. Five photographs illustrated the piece, from the photographs depicting the "First Stage: The Invitation" to the final photograph "Happily Engaged!!!" In both the text and the pho-tographic depictions of courtship rituals on a motorcycle, the female never assumed an obviously active position. Nonetheless, the success of a union rested on the woman's ability to "prove" herself both on and off the motorcycle as a "good comrade for life."

In order to determine her suitability for marriage, the author suggested a motorcyclist should take the "apple of his eye" on a trial ride and artifi-cially punctuate the chosen route with seemingly unpredictable, trying situations explicitly in order to test the nerves of the female love interest. "Under conditions of the most oppressive heat," the author suggested the suitor should take his prospective bride to a "rural road with no trees" and pretend to "have a small problem with the motor. The motor hick-ups, thumps – stands still; now you've gotten yourselves into a fine mess." In the author's imagined scenario, both dismount and "you take off your jacket and work, sweating in her view. You try and try but can't find the problem. You become nervous, complain and sweat like a fishwife – you get it?" Through feigning technical difficulties, the author asserted that the man would be able to understand "a lot about the bigness or the littleness of her soul." If she is ready to help, she is a good match; but if she "sits down on the side of the road in a bad mood and makes things more difficult for you in your already difficult situation through all kinds of moods and barbs, or moreover if she is impatient or nervous, then put this in the minus column." Employing an accountant-like tabular approach to the question of compatibility, the author reinforced the con-nection between sexual and economic relations.

Beyond being willing to take a mechanical breakdown in good humor, a female's marriage suitability is also portrayed as hinged upon her recognizing the difference between the failures of the man and the failures of the machine. The author recommended that men immediately dump the woman if she is not able to make such a distinction: "Woe betide you, sports confrere, if you find yourself in the clutches of such an 'angel.' You'll never be able to do anything right, you'll always be at fault for every misunderstanding. Protect yourself and be careful! You should rather invent a reason to get rid of her; it will only be to your advantage." A woman who is able to maintain her good humor despite a mechanical mishap, who "banishes your bad mood with jokes and laughter, and who finds the breakdown 'heavenly,' is one you can easily commit to, and you will have a good comrade for life." The author portrayed an appropriate bride for a motorcyclist as one who willingly accepts the challenges of early motorized travel and the physical hardships of motorcycling, "without considering her manicured nails or being afraid of blackened, oil-stained hands." The author claimed that his own wife had to "withstand such endurance tests," and "not only in motorcycling, but also in life, she confirmed my theories."

While expressing approval of a form of companionate marriage, the woman, relegated to her position on the pillion seat, was nonetheless the passive, subservient partner. In the author's view of marriage, a suitable bride completely subsumed her own ego and ambition to the man's. In his final anecdote about how to find a suitable wife, he revealed that in the early days he had flown planes "when it was still an event." His female love interest was a schoolteacher, and she had arranged for a field trip to the airstrip for the entire school, including all the other teachers, where the man was scheduled to give a lecture about flying. Arriving a little early, and due to boredom and hunger, instead of waiting for the school group to arrive at the airstrip, he decided to "pay a visit to a hotel for a good drop of wine and some good food." When he returned to the airstrip, no one was there. He took off in his plane and "from a bird's-eye perspective I could see the endless line of people heading back to the city. And the outcome? Not a word of reproach, she was not huffy or offended, but instead her golden sense of humor disarmed me." In this anecdote directed towards advising men on the criteria on which to judge the suitability of a potential wife, the man's bodily needs and desires were accorded more importance than the woman's professional reputation. Although the author claimed he was "ashamed to this day" of his behavior, his tone belied his belief that a woman's proper role was not to assert herself within the relationship, even when the man caused her public and professional humiliation. The technological trappings of the relationship—the airplane and the motorcycle—were certainly distinctly modern artifacts, yet the author's insistent naturalization of a gender hierarchy, in which the male was the dominant partner, was no more than an updated version of patriarchy.[14]

Marriage and Motorcycles: A Close Reading of Three Short Stories

Although less frequent than male tales of conquest, a married woman's desire to own and ride a motorcycle was another recurring storyline that combined motorcycles, sexuality, and gender. In the short stories "She Rides a Motorcycle," "Susi Wins a Motorcycle," and "Darling Wife Practices Motorized Sports," a woman's desire for mobility disrupted the established spatial norms of middle-class marriage. Confronted by a wife's desire to be an active motorcyclist, each of these stories provides a different perspective on how motorcycling was perceived as a potential source of marital friction. While they all bear similarities, each offers a distinct reading of the appropriate relationship between a husband, a wife, and a motorcycle.

"She Rides a Motorcycle," penned by Lothar Sachs, a prolific author of operettas, presents the wife as emotionally manipulative and scheming, yet ultimately successful in her quest to own a motorcycle. The story contains theatrical elements, with the opening scene portraying the wife, Kitty, begging her husband to buy her a motorcycle and his adamant refusal.

> "Please, please, my darling treasure," the wife pleads, "give me that sweet little motorcycle that we saw at the exposition! You know how long it's been my most desperate desire to own a motorcycle." The arms of a pretty woman wrap themselves coaxingly around the neck of the spouse. He fends her off, determined and energetically. "That's the last thing I needed. Banish this thought right now! I have already sacrificed enough patience and money on your sporting extravagances, and that's the end of it."

The wife's desire is framed as pure extravagance; her wish for a motorcycle as irrational. The husband threatens her with "divorce, if you persist." While certainly adding a dramatic element to the story, the fact that divorce is presented as an easy out indicates the instability of the institution of marriage during the Weimar Republic. The narrative structure of the story clearly establishes the wife as completely financially dependent on her husband, and presents this circumstance as the ultimate, yet not uncontested, source of power in the relationship.

Nonetheless, the wife is eventually able to assert herself and gain control over the money needed to fulfill her desire for a motorcycle.

Following the initial altercation that ends with "slamming doors," the husband retreats to his study and the wife, Kitty, leaves the house. An hour later, the telephone rings:

> As the husband picks up the phone, a voice sounds as if from another world, foreign and disturbed. "For God's sake, Kitty, is that you? I almost didn't recognize your voice. What's the matter? Speak, darling." "I ... I ... just wanted to say goodbye to you. I'm not coming home again. I can't stand it ..." "But little Kitty, tell me what's happened? Don't torture me any longer!" "Oh, there's no sense in it anymore. You will certainly get divorced from me and I wouldn't survive that!" "Oh you silly head, who's talking about divorce? That's all nonsense. Come home at once!" "No, no, I don't trust the situation ... look, I will confess ... You gave me the household money for the whole month today ... and ... I happened upon the exposition hall again ... and there temptation took hold of my senses and ... I took the household money and ... spent it on a MOTORCYCLE. I am already terribly sorry about it, but ..." "But darling, how can you scare me so? I thought that something terrible had happened. It wasn't right of you, but paid for is paid for and we can't change that anymore. So please don't excite yourself any further and come home at once! You've already caused me such a fright!"

The husband's continuous use of diminutives in responding to his wife reflects the patriarchal ordering of their marital relations. Lacking autonomy and access to the purse strings, during this marital conflict the wife's only option is to emotionally manipulate the man into accepting her misappropriation of household funds. Her financial dependency is a constitutive dynamic in their marital relations. Yet through the division of domestic labor and resources, she controlled the money to run the household, opening up a space for her to fulfill her desire. In the end, although the wife is able to acquire the object of her desire, the freedom associated with consumption and possession was predicated solely on the wife's mastering the skill of being a "convincing actress." Despite Sachs' disempowering portrayal of a wife's limited options for negotiating marital conflict, he also paints the husband as an unwitting dupe, emotionally dependent on his wife. "She Rides a Motorcycle" illustrates why melodrama was such a popular discursive genre for exploring male–female emotional relationships during the Weimar Republic: through the use of exaggerated characters it could express the heightened sense of tension around power and sexuality within marriage.[15]

"Susi Wins a Motorcycle," Carl G.P. Henze's 1930 short story, also probes the relationship between motorization, consumption, and marriage. "Freshly married," the protagonists "lived in a small villa in the Tiergarten district of Berlin." The husband, Emil, is a "well-situated wholesaler who can provide his small, thin Susi with everything; thus their days flow by in calm, reputable harmony." The marriage is neatly ordered and contained within the bounds of bourgeois morality, including owning an automobile. However, an excursion Susi takes to the AVUS racetrack on the outskirts of Berlin sows the seeds of discontent, thereby initiating this story of marital struggle: "But one day this radiant marital heaven began to cloud over. While Emil was busy on business in Hamburg, Susi went to see a motorcycle race with her sport-enthusiast friend Ruth at the AVUS. Filled with excitement, she followed the interesting happenings, and her enthusiasm reached a climax when Hanni Köhler, gutsy as ever, rode her race." Referring to the AVUS, Hanni Köhler, and a motorcycling magazine, *Motorradsport*, the story evokes the experiential possibilities offered by the modern metropolis: "Susi had purchased the latest issue of *Motorradsport* on her way back from the racetrack. Sitting in her cozy corner under the large, softly radiating floor lamp, and with glowing cheeks, she immersed herself in the magazine. And during the night, while dreaming, she saw herself whizzing over the AVUS on a sleek machine." The imagery that Henze draws on is replete with unfulfilled female desire; the world in which Susi is turned on to motorcycling borders on the Sapphic—her friend Ruth plays the instigator and Hanni Köhler functions as the role model. The fantasy of escape offered by the motorcycle is paralleled in the possibilities for breaking out of the constraints of bourgeois marriage, and both are rhetorically linked, with her husband's absence allowing her the space to explore this unknown and seemingly forbidden world.

In contrast to the dynamic nineteen-year-old Susi, her husband Emil is portrayed as a bit too comfortable, complacent, and soft to be properly masculine. "Very much in love with his cute wife," he generally "fulfills her every desire." Emil, however, "is a strong opponent of motorcycles," and "feels quite good when lying back on the soft cushions of his elegant limousine." Instead of driving himself, "he leaves that to Franz, the gardener." Henze emphasizes the husband's lack of virility in comparison with Susi's nineteen-year-old "fervency" for motorcycles: "She's absolutely crazy about motorcycling and has a burning desire for the sleek machine that she dreams about the whole night." As an object of sexual desire, the character of Emil, with his love of creature comforts, pales in comparison to the motorcycle, which assumes the place of the coveted being.

Susi brings up the desire to own a motorcycle during a dinnertime conversation with Emil. Like the husband in Sach's story, Henze's Emil is shocked. He rejects her request, responding: "'No, darling, that is out of the question. You can't seriously think I would allow you to make yourself unhappy with such a work of the devil [*Teufelsding*]. And in any case this is not appropriate for my wife. When we want to drive, we'll take the eight-cylinder and not tootle about like every Tom, Dick, and Harry on such a gas-ass [*Benzinesel*].'" "With tears in her eyes," Susi attempts, without success, to "explain the beauties and the uniqueness of motorcycling to her beloved husband." Susi's subordinate position in the relationship is obvious: she is dependent on her husband's approval to acquire the object of her desire. Henze underscores Emil's social position as a conservative, not only in details about how he consumes, but also through Emil's perspective that motorcycling is an inappropriate activity for his wife. His demonstrative use of "we" obviates the wife's voice.

Nonetheless, another encounter with her friend Ruth, who Susi meets again outside a motorcycle dealership, helps Susi devise an alternate plan to gain possession of the object of her desire. Ruth tells Susi that she has just purchased a motorcycle and that although her "husband wasn't so enthusiastic at first, I was able to turn him around." Although Ruth is also dependent on her husband's approval, her character demonstrates that not all men judged their wives' motorcycling as threatening the balance of sexual-marital relations. Susi in turn tells Ruth how Emil would not indulge her desire: "He is very single-minded in his views." Again the modern metropolis is presented as the space for female liberation. As Ruth and Susi stroll through the Bismarckstrasse in the then fashionable Charlottenburg district of Berlin, they happen upon a poster offering a motorcycle as the first prize in a charity raffle. Susi purchases a ticket, landing the ticket with the "auspiciously inauspicious number 131313," and, despite thinking that it "would not be easy to overcome Emil's resistance, when the motorcycle is there then everything else will work out in the end." Back at home, Susi does not mention "the motorcycle business, and so [Emil] believes that the whole matter is settled, that it was just a silly whim of his little wifey. But Susi continues to wait impatiently for the day that the winning raffle ticket will be drawn." Again the language Henze employs expresses both Emil's association of female desire with irrational consumption, and Susi's tenacious and temerarious approach to achieving her goal of owning a motorcycle.

Of course, as revealed already in the story's title, Susi has purchased the winning ticket. As soon as she learns that she won, she rushes out of the house to behold and take possession of the long-sought-after object of desire. Susi bounds out of the house: "In a few moments, she is standing before her motorcycle, beaming with happiness. It is a magnificent 'Penta' machine, the bright red gas tank shines out colorfully from the black frame; the nickel-plated parts gleam brilliantly. In her joyous pride of ownership, Susi's little face competes with the color of the tank." The motorcycle frees Susi from the confines of the home. As a means to mobility and as an aesthetically pleasing object, the motorcycle is the source of pride and happiness, and represents the fulfillment of her desire.

Without her husband's knowledge, Susi then arranges to take motorcycle lessons. Here, Henze provided his female protagonist with an assertive and active character, seizing the initiative to partake in motorized modernity. Spending "every day with her driving instructor," Susi "becomes initiated into the secrets of riding a motorcycle." She is easily able to grasp its functions and "is soon throwing around technical terms like an old mechanic. . . . She also learns the dark sides of motorcycling—how to fix breakdowns, how to repair tires, greasing, and oiling. She sometimes has to scrub for a long time to remove the traces of oil and grease from her delicate hands." A "studious, eager student," Susi learns to "command the machine," epitomizing the self-confident new woman: intelligent, hardworking, and mechanically inclined.[16] Neither afraid of rolling up her sleeves and getting her hands dirty nor of moving outside the confines of bourgeois propriety in order to interact with strangers such as the motorcycle instructor, Susi is a hybrid of the "modern girl" and the "new woman." With moxie and perseverance, she snatches at the chance a motorcycle offers for expanding social and spatial horizons. By portraying Susi in an unambiguously positive light, Henze's characterization demonstrates shifts in the definition of "proper femininity." The vivacious new woman exudes both strength and self-confidence. The "modern girl," even if she is married, is prepared to stake her place in the modern world.

However, although Susi passes her exam "with splendid success," the potential for marital conflict over the motorcycle persists, as Emil is still unaware of her new motorcycle and her new skills. The remainder of the story depicts how the husband and wife negotiate this situation. The day following the exam, Emil returns home at the usual time for lunch, but Susi is not there as he expects her to be. He decides to wait on lunch for her, and "in the meantime hides behind his newspaper":

Suddenly his ears pricked up. Outside the door a rat-a-tattering motorcycle drove up and then a Bosch horn sounded off persistently. Irritated, Emil rose to find out who was the cause of the racket, but stopped at the window as if rooted on the spot. In front of the entrance: a motorcycle and a young lady in breeches and a red leather jacket sitting on it—his

Susi. Now she sees him, releases the horn button and waves to him with an attractive smile. Emil shakes his head without comprehension; for him the whole thing is mystifying. How did Susi get a motorcycle, and since when can she ride?

Emil is portrayed not only as the less active and less clever partner in the marriage, with a reversal of spatial roles, the husband is inside the domestic sphere of the house, while the wife is out conquering public spaces. In addition, his aversion to motorcycles and their noise alongside his shock at the sight of Susi motorcycling hints at his insufficiencies, both of being properly modern and properly masculine, while her modernity is on full display, with the motorcycle augmenting her social and sexual capital.

The potential marital conflict over the wife's choice to take up motorcycling is finally resolved on the one hand by reaffirming more conservative understandings of femininity and masculinity, while on the other hand pointing towards new ways of conceptualizing male and female roles within marriage. Susi, "with a hangdog expression on her face," but nonetheless "grinning mischievously," throws her arms around his neck when Emil begins to protest about "this rubbish." As she excitedly tells him "how it all happened," he decides "he can't be angry at his little wife and secretly he concedes to himself that in the nice sports clothes that fit her boyish, slender figure perfectly, she cuts a good form on the sleek machine." "Disarmed," Emil is defenseless against his wife's charms: "Franz had the next Sunday off and the eight-cylinder [limousine] was parked in the garage. But Emil trusted his little wife and rode out with her into the 'green.' Yes, when beautiful women ask, even the most solid principles melt into air." While Henze ultimately reverts to shoring up traditional gender norms by basing the husband's acceptance of his wife's nontraditional behavior on her physical beauty, the fact that the story ends with the husband riding pillion seat provides an image of a reversal of traditional gender roles in terms of the practice of motorcycling and its relationship to sexual hierarchy. Although "Susi Wins a Motorcycle" does not present a radical break from typical depictions of marriage with wives as objects of beauty and sexual ornaments and husbands as breadwinners, the character of the young wife along with the other female characters, Ruth and the real-life Hanni Köhler, with their dynamism and active presence, nevertheless conjure up a vision of modern femininity and marriage, in which women fulfill their desires and stake out a place in the world outside the home.[17]

Spousal strife around a wife's desire to own and ride a motorcycle is likewise the plot of Georg Oswald Bayer's short story "Darling Wife

Practices Motorized Sports." An author of expressionist poems and short stories, Bayer depicts the characters of both the husband and the wife with ambivalence in terms of their roles within the marriage, and thus provides a further scenario for evaluating how motorization precipitated conflicts that shifted the terms of heterosexual marriage and relationships between the sexes. This couple, as reflected the situation of most motorcyclists by the end of the 1920s, is not as wealthy as the characters of Emil and Susi. Instead of living in a luxury villa in the Tiergarten district of Berlin, they rent an apartment, do not have servants or own an automobile, and they have children. Yet, despite the differences between the characters, the narratives contain similar structural elements. As in "Susi Wins a Motorcycle," it is a female friend of the wife who introduces her to motorcycling. Told from the perspective of the husband, he recounts: "It began when one day a female friend of my wife sat in front of the house on a motorcycle with the exhaust pipe making a hellish racket, and waved up to the window: 'Don't you want to take a little ride?'" His wife grabbed his breeches from the dresser and his "shell-rimmed glasses" from the desk, kissing him as he tried "to give her a number of good tips about how to behave when motorcycling, and hasty like never before, she darted like a young girl down the stairs, sat down behind her friend and waved happily back to me." The husband, left behind, can only watch as the motorcycle carrying his wife, "drove off with such a speed that I would have been uneasy if I hadn't been convinced that my wife's friend possessed total control over the machine and had proven herself at racing events as a not-innocuous rival to male competitors hell-bent on victory." In marriage, propriety and property are presented as complementary. The female friend and her "complete control" over a machine, as well as her ability to challenge males in the masculine-dominated world of motorcycle racing, adds another layer of ambiguity to the relationship between the sexes. Thus, when the wife embarks on her female friend's motorcycle, Bayer calls the moral economy of marriage into question. Despite the husband's attempt to "mansplain," motorcycling allows the wife to literally put on the pants in the family, upending traditional bourgeois conjugal roles.[18]

This motorcycle ride has drastic and irreversible consequences for the marriage and for the husband's attitude towards motorization. The author's use of pointed and deliberate irony augments the ambiguity and uncertainty of the effects of motorization on the marriage: "If I had had a premonition about what consequences would accompany this ride, I would never have given my permission. It was extremely regrettable, and you can believe me that, with my innate good nature,

I would never have been seized by such a profound aversion to every type of motor sports that has now gripped my soul if this ride and its consequences hadn't forced me into such a position." While Bayer portrays the husband's privilege to grant "permission" as a natural right, the motorcycle in particular upsets the "natural" order of the marriage, and the husband loses control over his wife. The motorcycle and the female motorcyclist friend plunge the stability of the marriage and the relationship between the sexes into uncertainty and crisis.

Upon returning from the ride, the wife, like both the wives in the previous stories, "throws her arms" around her husband's neck, and, "still breathless with excitement," proclaims: "It was wonderful! You have to buy me such a bike! You know, when you see the street flying underneath you, when the trees dance by, and when the wind sings in your ears … oh, you can't describe it! If you only love me a little bit, then you have to give me such a motorcycle!" Through the motorcycle trip, the woman fully experienced the speed of modernity. Perceived as an exhilarating adventure, motorcycling allows her to escape the everyday routine of the household. Nonetheless, as in the case with the other two stories about motorcycling and marital conflict, the wife's financial dependency on her husband prevents her from fulfilling her desire to own a motorcycle. And again, money, marriage, and motorcycling provide the point of conflict within the relationship between the sexes. The man's response to the woman's desire for a motorcycle underscores her subservient position within the marriage. He asked her what she had made for dinner. Her disappointment with his reaction was evident: "She looked at me seriously and sadly, and spent the whole evening entirely in the company of our little ones, so that I saw myself prompted to flee to the friendly round of beers at my regular's table, where I would be safe from motorcycle pipe dreams and other irrational desires." Female passion for motorcycling is yet again associated with irrational desire. While the author certainly intends to inject humor into this story with the idea that men would not be interested in motorcycling, nonetheless the ideal the author conveys is that a wife's proper place was in the home, not on a motorcycle, and that above all she could only conform to her role as wife and mother by inhabiting her proper place. While the wife's possibilities for protesting her husband's attitude are circumscribed by her role as a mother, the safe space of escape for the husband is the homosocial space of his regular's table at the pub.

Although the husband at first refuses to engage with the wife's desires, the story alludes to a process of negotiation within the marriage, in which the husband convinces the wife that she needs to take

motorcycling lessons before it would make sense to purchase a motorcycle. The husband then contacts a male friend of his, Süßbruch, who
"for years had been paying homage to the sport of motoring" and who
agreed to give the wife lessons three days later. Until the day of her first
lesson, the "wife was so busy with making her sports wardrobe that she
asked me to take my meals at the tavern. With the help of a seamstress,
she turned my study into a somewhat colorful atelier for modern sports
clothing, so that the landlord called on us and filed a protest against the
establishment of a business enterprise." The wife's newfound passion
for motorcycling disrupts the normal and natural divisions and workings of the domestic space of the bourgeois home—the man is forced
to take his meals in the tavern, and his study space is converted into a
sewing room. Although the wife's space is normally limited largely to
the home, in this scenario the woman stakes out claims to new spaces
as well as new activities in the home, all of which, for the husband, are
unrelated to her role as wife and mother.

The husband increasingly takes a back seat to his wife's desires and
newfound passion for motorcycling. The day of the wife's first lesson
provides a good example of the subordination of the husband's interests
to those of the wife:

> An hour later Süßbruch drove up. He honked in front of our window with
> such vehemence that the landlord again appeared at my door ... He
> didn't look very friendly, and it cost me some trouble to induce him to
> step closer and taste some of my most recent shipment of wine, while my
> darling wife climbed onto Süßbruch's pillion seat and rat-a-tatted away,
> flying between the dancing-by trees, out into the lusciousness of a sunny,
> blooming landscape.

While the author does not directly insinuate that the wife is having
an extramarital affair, the situation nonetheless blurs the conventional
picture of bourgeois marital propriety that was contingent on a faithful
wife who remains in the safe space of the home. Partner swapping and
extramarital affairs, however, appeared as an element of modern marriage in motoring magazines. For example, a pair of photographs titled
"Motorbride," shows a woman riding with two different men (see Image
7.3). It is captioned: "The motor bride lets her husband instruct her, and
rides out with a male 'friend of the house.'"[19] Such images and stories
documented the emergence of a new sexual morality tied to motorized
mobility.[20]

As in the other two stories, the husband is left at home while the
woman ventures out into the world in the pursuit of motorization—a
reversal of the normal bourgeois gendering of the spheres of public

and private. Indeed, this husband also lacks many attributes of modern masculinity. For example, on the day that his wife was "first to master the machine on her own," he demonstrates weak nerves, a hallmark of insufficient masculinity: "I was requested to come along, but I declined. I shouldn't stress my nerves too much." In addition, he tries to convince his wife not to undertake her first solo ride. Süßbruch, the motorcycle teacher, turns this weakness against the husband.

> Süßbruch showed me sympathy in that he made a statement to my wife that I am a bundle of nerves and therefore unsuited to every sport; this is a regrettable circumstance considering the markedly sporty nature of my companion in life. I found him less sympathetic than usual, and I buried myself, as soon as they had left, in my work; however, I didn't succeed in getting a grip on the hallucinations that tormented me with confused, and in no way friendly, visions.

Bayer directly and negatively contrasted the frailty of the husband's character with the wife's sporty character as well as Süßbruch's modern sportsman masculinity.

The husband, so incapable of dealing with the stresses of modernity, suffered from hallucinations: "My unease increased so far that I threw down my pen, left the house, hired a car and raced down the rural road to where my wife was completing her first solo ride." The wife, however, has an accident during the ride, and the husband "found the woman who once promised obedience in front of the altar in a pitiable condition." The couple return to the house in an ambulance, which causes a public spectacle: "In front of our house a group of people had assembled who were indulging in adventurous speculations in unsuitable and totally inappropriate language as my wife was lifted out of the ambulance and carefully carried into our apartment." The wife's passion for motorcycling not only puts her family's reputation in jeopardy, but also endangers her bodily integrity. Bayer thus portrays the practice of motorcycling by the wife as so destructive to the moral economy of the family that the woman's body was literally broken.

The accident marks the fork in the road of the narrative, and through a convoluted set of twists and turns, including money problems, legal issues, and theft, the order of the bourgeois marriage is ultimately restored through the wife's decision to eschew the motorcycle in favor of her husband's promise to purchase her an automobile—a gender appropriate vehicle. At the end of the story, through the wife's lack of technical knowledge combined with her trust in a complete stranger, the motorcycle is stolen: "'Thank god!' said my wife, and as

Image 7.3. "Motorbride," in *Auto Magazin*, 1928.

I looked at her in wonder, she curled up close to me, wrapped her arms around my neck and said happily: 'It's better that the motorcycle is gone; it could have been the automobile, isn't that true?'" With the theft of the motorcycle, the normative roles within the marriage were re-established. The story portrayed motorcycling as disruptive and corrosive for the institution of marriage. It was capable of upending the normative and naturalized positions of wife and husband in terms of public and private, active and passive, *nervenstark* (strong-nerved) and *nervenschwach* (neurasthenic). Nevertheless, Bayer leaves open a possibility for women to participate in motorization without destabilizing marital roles. The automobile is an enclosed space—in Gijs Mom's terms, it is a "cocoon" that envelops the passengers, removing the threat of unwanted encounters. Thus Bayer's story ultimately promotes the automobile as a less dangerous form of mobility than the motorcycle, not only to the body but also to the stability of marital relations.[21]

In each of these stories, it is the wife's relationship to the motorcycle that determines the narrative arc. The motorcycle creates the situation in which the tenets of middle-class marriage are questioned, above all in its ability to provide the wife with the opportunity to enjoy spatial liberation from the confines of the bourgeois home. In Bayer's story, the female is eventually sequestered into the safe space of an enclosed vehicle, while Henze's Susi finally both steers the handlebars and wears the pants in the marriage. Unlike an automobile, which could be compatible with bourgeois propriety, the motorcycle gave rise to marital discord and transgressed the traditional bounds of marriage. Nonetheless, in each of the three stories, the wife's financial dependence on her husband reflects how the power structure within marriage was largely determined by economic factors.

Byway I: "He, She, It"—Two Perspectives on a Three-Way Relationship

"He–She–It," and "He, She, and the Motorcycle," two short stories bearing similar titles, respectively explore heterosexual relationships and motoring through the lens of the woman/wife and through the lens of the man/husband. The husband and wife authors, Ilse Lundberg and Theo Rockenfeller, were both prolific journalists who contributed articles and books on a wide range of topics that document the culture of motoring in Germany from the 1920s to the 1950s.[22] Both of the stories address the ordering of the triangulated relationship between the male, the female, and the motor vehicle. Juxtaposing the two stories demonstrates how consumption practices influenced modern relationships and the shape of modern femininity and modern masculinity.

In "He–She–It," a short piece written for BMW's customer magazine, Lundberg appraised gender and marital relations for the motorized of the Weimar Republic. She first sets up a comparison between "modern marriage" and marriage "back then." "'He–She–It', that is to say: 'He', the driver, 'She', the sweetest of all *Sozias*, and 'It', the motor vehicle. That's the way it is today." In days of "grandmother and grandfather, the influence of the automobile on marriage was not known."[23] Back then, Lundberg asserts, "the highest happiness for a young wife meant possessing a big cupboard full of linens, an apartment full of figurines and kitsch, and a sewing table with a dozen projects. The husband of those days looked forward to his leisure time in front of the fire, his robe, slippers, and long pipe." Describing the past as a model of (petit) bourgeois domesticity, men and women were imagined as belonging to different spaces, separated by gender. In contrast, Lundberg described the modern (auto)mobile marriage as based on "camaraderie and a feeling of belonging together," gained through shared "experiences on the rural roads." The young husband and young wife are no longer interested in conventional, housebound domesticity, but instead look forward to "exploring the smiling world" together. In the service of selling motorization, Lundberg paints acquisition of individual (family) motorized mobility as bringing a welcome transformation in the relationship between husband and wife.[24]

In "He–She–It," it is an automobile that alters the dynamic within marriage. Regardless of the type of vehicle discussed, Lundberg's portrayal of the relationship between husband, wife, and motor vehicle, as the pivotal object in the constellation, follows a similar trajectory. Lundberg articulates a concept of modern marriage based on a companionate relationship. The roles the partners inhabit, however, are hierarchically ordered and clearly divided, even when Lundberg places the woman behind the wheel or handlebars.[25] The young female driver and modern wife in "He–She–It" is the type of woman who "cannot wait patiently for her husband to return from work; a day can often be very long." During her daytime drives, she gets "a gleam in her eye" when the motor vehicle "behaves like a well-trained dog." The motor vehicle, in this case a car, fills her with pride and joy. "Very happy that she is in possession of her youth and her joie de vivre—and she is proud too. Proud of the fabulous automobile, of her capabilities, and of her husband, who, without envy begrudges her nothing and always eggs her on to new deeds." To reward him for his generosity, the young modern wife washes the car, checks the oil, air, and coolant levels, and awaits her husband out front of his bank building at 5 p.m. sharp. Interestingly, there is almost a utilitarian element to Lundberg's portrayal of "modern motorized marriage"; the wife's spatial freedom is contingent on her service of the motor vehicle for the husband's benefit. As the wife punctually awaits him outside his office in the freshly washed car, he races down the stairs in leaps and bounds: "A quick, comradely hand-shake—then she moves from the place behind the wheel, so that he can also savor the joys of driving. And when pulling away, he remarks gleefully, 'It's so nice to have a little chauffeur at home.'" Indeed, it is ambiguous enough whether the man's excitement when she picks him up is more about seeing his wife or his car. In Lundberg's concep-tion of a "modern marriage," the woman clearly enjoys the freedom of mobility that exploring the city and countryside in a motor vehicle affords. Yet, through virtue of his ownership of a motor vehicle, he is the true "master." Responsible for helping to care for the car, as well as for preparing snacks for the journey, Lundberg's wife-passenger is a subordinate yet necessary pole in the three-way relationship. Lundberg thus concluded the article: "He, she, and the motor vehicle. All three must be inseparable. Comrades of the rural road." Despite her talk of comradeship, Lundberg's version of happy modern marriage is a com-munion based on a shared enjoyment of consumption, in which it is nonetheless the woman's duty to serve the man.[26]

Rockenfeller's "He, She, and the Motorcycle" also begins with a sort of historical tableau: a retelling of the biblical story of creation. "In the beginning, naturally, there was 'he' and nothing else for a long time; then 'she' came out of his ribs, a 'branch office' [*Filliale*] of him, in a sense; and only their togetherness creates the desire for a motorcycle." She is depicted as a product of his ribs and she is relegated to the pillion seat: "But the affair has a catch. Who sits on the pillion seat 99 times out of 100? A female being." Rockenfeller does not mince words about the possibilities a motorcycle can offer in terms of sexual adventure. Indeed, he chastises the advertising industry for supposedly neglecting the most persuasive selling point of the motorcycle: Why do brochures and catalogues of motorcycle companies always speak in such a high-brow manner, so soberly and objectively, of saving time, saving money, of business travel, etc.? Why do the ad bosses beat around the bush like cats around hot porridge? Why do they not write: 'After working and rushing about during the week, it is glorious to ride out into the quietude of nature with a lovely being on your pillion seat. The two of you are so alone, left to your own devices, and hours of delicious delights are granted both.'" Indeed, the "Leather Man" [*Ledermann*] and the "Clinging Ape" [*Klammeraffe*] both enjoy the sexual liberation of a motorized trip.

"He, she, and it – the man, the *Sozia*, and the motorcycle! Today you can find the unity of this trinity everywhere." Rockenfeller extols the triangulated relationship between the man, the woman, and the motorcycle, yet the trinity is predicated on the man being in control through his possessive relationship to both the motorcycle and the woman. Concluding the story, Rockenfeller claims that "if he starts to have a wandering eye, or she suddenly wants a bigger engine motorcycle, then soon enough you will see the following classified ad in the local paper: 'Motorcycle—elegant and reliable machine with all chicaneries—and passenger for sale at a good price.'"[27] For both Lundberg and Rockenfeller, a consumer commodity—a motor vehicle—is the linchpin of the heterosexual relationship. Both the woman and the machine are objects of exchange over which the man possesses a natural right to command. He is in the saddle and holds the purse strings.

Possessing the Bride? Sexual Economy, Motorcycles, and Motorization

Gilgi, One of Us, a best-selling novel authored by Marieluise Fleißer, describes a conversation between two mothers hoping to marry off their daughters: "'A heavenly automobile' raves Mrs. Becker stubbornly, she is in her own way an ultramodern mother: *Auto, Auto über alles* . . . 'If a man only has a good character,' says Aunt Hetty. 'If he has a first-class car, then his character is good enough, one would think . . . And even if it's just a motorcycle with a sidecar.'"[28] In the sexual economy of motorization during the Weimar Republic, ownership of a motor vehicle was an important marker of sexual and marital desirability in a world of consumer goods. The man was less important than his wheels. A motorcycle was better than nothing, but not nearly as desirable as a luxury sedan. Women and men become sets of objects in a world of objects, each with their price tag.

Isle Lundberg's description of the three-way relationship in "He–She–It" likewise does not mince words about the role of the motor vehicle in the field of sexual economy in 1920s Germany: "Today, love goes through the automobile. Men, for example, who own a BMW automobile or motorcycle, belong to the most sought-after matches. Such a motor vehicle works like magical lenses. He, the master and owner, shines in the most rose-tinted light—and if he is acceptable enough in other regards, then often there are no more barriers to marriage."[29]

The commodity, with its ability to bedazzle, "works like magic glasses," allowing the "master and owner" to "shine in the most rose-tinted light," providing substance to Karl Marx's famous portrayal of the secret of the commodity fetish.[30] "Does the Motorcycle Have a Soul?" probes exactly this unification of object–subject that the commodity personified. Most motorcyclists who owned a motorcycle for a while, the author muses, "only occasionally verbalize" the "peculiar belief" they hold, that could be summed up as follows:

> "She" is a fun old wreck, but I can rely on "her"! These words grant the bike personal characteristics that would be nonsensical when speaking of a dead machine. And then notice the "she"! When considering purchasing a new motorcycle it is at first only an "it," but after it is transferred into proprietary possession and has been used for a while, the neuter sex [*sachliche Geschlecht*] disappears and the dead commodity [*totes Ding*] turns into a "she."

Emphasizing the emotional capital invested by male owners in the machine, the author also links the act of taking proprietary possession to feminizing the object of consumption.[31]

A short piece penned by long-time president of the DMV, Artur Vieregg, "The Springtime of the Motorcyclist" takes this line of argument further. He opens the article with a sexually imbued image of spring with "buds swelling" and "the sun lovingly caressing our cheeks." The motorcyclist "rushes to his beloved machine in order to busy himself with her spring toilette." Vieregg used his authority to give advice to those motorcyclists for whom the "warmth of springtime awakens longings to zoom out to the rhythm of the motor strokes": "First of all, at night, when you are lying in your soft and pleasant bed, dream of your machine. She is for you, like the rifle for the infantryman, your bride. Lift yourself up in the morning after pleasant dreams, and before officially getting up, observe your machine with a loving gaze." Through feminization and sexualization, mass-produced technologies, such as the motorcycle or the infantry rifle, are transformed, losing their depersonalized materiality and taking on attributes of animate beings. "With the softest rags and best brushes you should caress all visible parts," because "your bride should stand flecklessly before you." Following the initial caresses, the motorcyclist is then advised: "Lubricate all her delicate limbs and joints with oil, immerse yourself in all her intricacies and see to the frictionless motility of all of her limbs and joints." After performing "this work with grace and dignity, then bring out your manly side: arm yourself with all your screwdrivers and wrenches, and have a go at her body [*geh ihr zu Leibe*]. Your bride wants to feel your

strength." By describing the motorcycle as "the bride," Vieregg feminized and rendered the motorcycle as an object of sexualized desire
and conquest. Motorcycling as an act of masculine consumption was
thus discursively naturalized as an act of sexualized possession and
male domination.[32]

Yet during the Weimar Republic the sexual-economic relationship
between the sexes and motorcycling was more complicated than a
simple homology between the bride and the motorcycle would indicate. A senior engineer from Berlin, Engelbert Zaschka, connected
female desire for motorcycles to healthy, modern sexuality. Recalling
an advertisement he had seen in the daily papers from an "'Au pair,
21 years old, music and nature lover, seeks an established man with a
motorcycle for the potential purpose of marriage. Offers (with photo)
can be sent to 'Motor-Girl,'" he remarked: "It would be better if young
ladies would . . . also ask for a disclosure on the brand of motorcycle and
the strength of the motor, if the machine has at least two gears, if they
desire a sidecar, all that's worth knowing!! It could happen that instead
of the expected 'heavy cannon' the suitor arrives on a droning bicycle
with an auxiliary motor." Again, the sexual economy of motorcycles, in
terms of the attractiveness of a large engine versus a small engine, is
transparent. Zaschka's tone implies that women were actively seeking
out motorcyclists for the motorcycle, and not for the man. "Actually us
men should feel a little insulted that a girl, like in the announcement
above, wants to marry the motorcycle; the man is to a certain extent the
'necessary evil.'" The author thus purports that it was unreasonable for a
man to assume he could compete with a motorcycle. "But because all of
us motorcyclists are reasonable fellows, we absolutely cannot be jeal-
ous of our more powerful rivals; on the contrary, we are happy when
the gentle sex also feels love towards the apple of our eye and therefore
gladly takes our comrade into marriage with us—as a harmless friend
of the family." Zaschka described the motorcycle as a bonding element
between the man and the woman; as an object of desire for both the
man and the woman.

Where did men locate women's passion for motorcycling? Zaschka
argued, "Women love the power of motorcycling and the speed with which
the bike climbs the mountain." Even more attractive for women was the
intensity of "the feeling of balancing when riding around curves and the
feelings of joy called forth by speed . . . It appears to us directly paradoxical
that a highly sensitive 'little soul' would rave about a heavy, cannon-like
motorcycle, but it is psychologically understandable." Zaschka turned the
notion of the bride on its head and presented a psychosexual explanation
of women's attraction to motorcycles, especially large-powered motor-

cycles.[33] Zaschka's account portrayed both human desire and motor-cycling as healthy for men and women alike.[34] Yet, whether portrayed as a bride or as a heavy cannon, in the sexual economy of motorcycling, the man was always clearly in possession of the coveted object.

Conclusion

Motorization altered patterns of courtship and sexuality. Sexual experiences were accelerated as the motor vehicle allowed for an escape from the everyday. These developments were not viewed without apprehension on the part of many contemporary observers. Some viewed the pillion seat as an instrument for fulfilling natural sexual desires, while others saw it as a path straight to hell. An article in the SPD journal *Sport-Politische Rundschau*, "Young Happiness and the Pillion Seat," addressed the thorniness of the process of motorization for the moral and sexual landscape of a fragmented society:

> My dear motorcyclist and my dear nice girls on the pillion seat: YOU ARE ALL SINNERS! And the pillion seat is the most devil-like invention . . . In Schussenried in Württemburg there is a sign at a Catholic church that doesn't present the motorcycle or its pillion seat in a favorable light. [The sign reads:] "We want to call attention to something we see so often today: *A girl on the pillion seat of a motorcycle*. It hangs there in an ugly pose like a *deformed ape* on the back on the ratter box, at every moment in danger of being thrown off. That is perhaps not the greatest evil. Experienced doctors point out another danger: namely that the *sensual feeling* of the girl is *powerfully aroused*. In the quiet of a distant rural guesthouse this feeling can be *increased* to the extreme. After the refreshment *a short walk is taken together in the close-by forest*. And the misfortune is quick and certain to occur, if the lady has as much moral feeling as to interpret the misfortune as a misfortune. How much young happiness is destroyed by the pillion seat! There are *motorcycling wives* that have the worst heartache when they see a motorcycle pass by, because they have to *think of all the misery that the motorcycle has brought to their family!*

The Social Democratic commentator remarked that the priest, who "composed this masterpiece of sexual research," must have known well the "devilish effects and consequences of the pillion seat." Moreover, "with or without a motorcycle, with or without pillion seat, men and girls in the blossoming of May . . . have the strong need to be alone. And even if it's in the shady dusk in the forest."[35] The effect of motorization and motorcycles in particular was a subject of debate during the Weimar Republic, the one side seeing it as a danger to the moral fabric of society and another seeing it as simply a new technology that produced new forms of age-old behaviors. Nonetheless, in an age of mass-produced commodities, social relationships, including sexual relationships, were increasingly mediated through objects. Embodying universal promises of freedom and mobility, motor vehicles, especially motorcycles, were quintessential forms of modern, masculine-dominated, sexually potent capital.

Notes

1. W. Doernhöffer, "Mit Gori im Beiwagen," *Das Motorrad*, 1929: 1540–41.
2. In the first chapter of her study on *Sex after Fascism*, Dagmar Herzog addresses aspects of the liberalization of sexual mores during the Weimar Republic and the continuities and ruptures to the Third Reich. See Dagmar Herzog, *Sex after Fascism: Memory and Morality in Twentieth-Century Germany* (Princeton, NJ: Princeton University Press, 2005), 10–63.
3. Gijs Mom also provides a reading of *Garage 13*; see Mom, *Atlantic Automobilism*, 454–55.
4. Julius Donny, *Garage 13* (Berlin: Georg König Verlag, 1930), 1–20. Donny was also the author in 1919 of a short pamphlet, "The Program of Dictatorship," that stated: "It will depend a lot on the man ... Manliness alone leads to barbarism, when it is not bound in the iron grips of a lasting and moral culture." Julius Donny, "Programm der Diktatur" (Berlin: Verlag Georg König, 1919). For bibliographic information on Donny, see Oberschlep, *Gesamtverzeichnis*, vol. 28, 358.
5. The deception, however, does later make Cläre uneasy: "In her soul, the doubts grew stronger about the man who sat next to her with his carefree demeanor. That, as a lady from a good family, she had kept her name secret, was easy enough to understand, but that he hadn't found it necessary to name his seemed a lot less harmless to her. Weren't there enough adventurers in a cosmopolitan city, who with intellect and wit and perfect manners were able to hide their pranks?" Donny, *Garage 13*, 24.
6. Ibid., 17–18.
7. However, part of the appeal "Wolf" has for Cläre is that he presents himself as a "bandit" and a "dangerous man," and so she also feels herself to be dangerous and calls herself "the bandit's bride." Ibid., 15.
8. "Die 'Panne,'" *Motorrad-Sport, -Verkehr und -Technik*, no. 35, 1925, 9.
9. "Cajus Jul. Cäsar," *Motorrad-Sport, -Verkehr und -Technik*, no. 7, 1926, 18.
10. The reference to the "tastiness" of the car and its occupants is a reference to the nickname of the Hanomag, *Kommissbrot* (pan loaf of bread) after its "loaf of bread"–like form.
11. Olex was a brand of petrol product available during the Weimar Republic. The company's name was Olex Deutsche Petroleum-Verkaufs G.m.b.H., and was later acquired by British Petroleum.
12. A Russian mixed snack of pickles, sausage, salads, etc., eaten with vodka.
13. "Liebe im Viertakt" *Motor und Sport*, no. 25, 1927, 37–39.
14. "Der Soziussitz als Liebesfalle; 'Drum prüfe wer sich ewig bindet,'" *Auto-Magazine*, no. 1, 1928, 797–99.

15. For an exploration of the cinematic genre of melodrama in film, see Petro, *Joyless Streets*. Lothar Sachs, "Sie fährt Motorrad," *Der Herrenfahrer*, no. 1, 1926, 60–62.
16. See Lynne Frame, "Gretchen, Girl, Garçonne? Weimar Science and Popular Culture in Search of the Ideal New Woman," in von Ankum, *Women in the Metropolis*, 12–13.
17. Carl G.P. Henze, "Susi gewinnt ein Motorrad," *Motorrad-Sport, -Verkehr und -Technik*, no. 6, 1930, 20–21.
18. On the concept of "mansplaining," see Rebecca Solnit's essay, "Men Who Explain Things," in *Los Angeles Times*, 13 April 2008; republished in Rebecca Solnit, *Men Explain Things to Me* (Chicago: Haymarket Books, 2014), 6–17.
19. "Die Motorbraut," *Auto-Magazin*, no. 8, 1928, 579. The woman, Ellen Douglas, and the two men, Harry Frank and Hanskarl Georg, bear the markings of modernity, and all three acted in films.
20. Herzog, *Sex after Fascism*, 16.
21. On cocooning, see Mom, "Encapsulating Culture." Georg O. Bayer, "Die Eheliebste treibt Autosport," *Der deutsche Motorfahrer*, no. 7, 1928, 18–19.
22. Lundberg and Rockenfeller married each other at some point before 1937 and were pioneers of the "Recreational Vehicle" movement, traveling in 1938 to the Algerian desert. Nicola Wohllaib, "Die Wanderniere" *Die Zeit*, 24 October 1997. Known as "Thero the Travel Uncle," Theo Rockenfeller published widely on both motoring and photography. See, for example, *Als Autozigeuner durch die Bergen* (1934); *Autokarte von Deutschland Kurzführer* (1954); *Fotobaby in der Dunkelkammer* (1951). For Lundberg's publications, see also Chapter 6 here.
23. In another article, Lundberg described the honeymoon "back then and now." She described a progression from travel by stagecoach to travel by train, and then by automobile, the motorcycle, and, finally, the airplane. Ilse Lundberg, "Die Hochzeitsreise, Einst und Jetzt," *ADAC-Motorwelt*, no. 4, 1926, 29–30.
24. This is similar to the way that Nina Sylvester positions the ubiquitous Weimar figure of "Das Girl" in terms of automobility: "The car is the space that assists the girl in her move away from the confined, supervised spaces of the domestic." Sylvester, *Das Girl*, 33.
25. See, for example, Lundberg, "Sozia," 24; Lundberg "Hochzeitsreise," 30; Ilse Lundberg, "Hausfrau, Kindererziehung und Motorsport," *ADAC-Motorwelt*, no. 2/3, 1930, 29.
26. Ilse Lundberg, "Er–Sie–Es," *BMW-Blätter*, no. 3, 1930, n.p.
27. Theo Rockenfeller, "Er, Sie und das Motorrad," *ADAC-Motorwelt*, no. 10, 1925, 17–19.
28. Irmgard Keun, *Gilgi – Eine von Uns* (Hildesheim: Classen, 1993), 88. First published in 1931.
29. Lundberg, "Er–Sie–Es."
30. See Karl Marx, "The Fetishism of Commodities and the Secret thereof," in *Capital: A Critique of Political Economy*, vol. 1, part 1, section 4. See also Jacques Derrida's reading of this passage in *Specters of Marx*: "It is quite different when it becomes a commodity, when the curtain goes up on the market and the table plays actor and character at the same time, when the commodity-table, says Marx, comes on stage (*auftritt*), begins to walk around and to put itself forward as a market value. Coup de theatre: the ordinary, sensuous thing is transfigured (*verwandelt sich*), it becomes someone, it assumes a figure. This woody and headstrong denseness is metamorphosed into a supernatural thing, a sensuous non-sensuous thing,

sensuous but non-sensuous, sensuously supersensible (*verwandelt er sich in ein sinnlich übersinnliches Ding*)." Jacques Derrida, *Specters of Marx: The State of the Debt, the Work of Mourning, and the New International* (New York: Routledge, 1994), 150.

31. "Hat das Motorrad eine Seele?," *Motorrad-Sport, -Verkehr und -Technik*, no. 9, 1925, 21.

32. Artur Vieregg, "Motorradfahrers Frühling," *Motorrad-Sport, -Verkehr und -Technik*, no. 9, 1924, 15.

33. The phrase "feelings of joy" is likely an oblique reference to the effects of stimulating vibrations on females, while the reference to the "cannon-like motorcycle" may hint at a penile form.

34. Engelbert Zaschka, "Die Dame und das Motorrad," *Motorrad-Sport, -Verkehr und -Technik*, no. 4, 1924, 18–19.

35. Gustav Gibim, "Jugendglück und Soziussitz," *Sportpolitisches Rundschau*, no. 3, 1930, 2.

Epilogue
The Will to Motor

The lived experience of modernity during the Weimar Republic was shaped by social and economic transformations readily graspable for everyday men and women in the form of technology and commodities. As a mass-produced industrial object, the motorcycle, as I hope to have shown in the previous chapters, stood for these changes and served as a carrier of multiple social meanings. Like the automobile, the motorcycle represented a kind of special commodity. As Herbert Marcuse remarked in reference to the automobile in "Some Social Implications of Modern Technology," "The machine that is adored is no longer dead matter but becomes something like a human being."[1] Motorcyclists likewise remarked on this peculiar bond, for example, when arguing that the "true" practice of motorcycling was tied to a spiritual union between man and his machine. In euphoric, quasi-religious terms, one everyday motorcyclist describes the experience of motorcycling, a state of being he imagined intrinsic to motorcycling:

> Has [the motorcycle skeptic] ever taken a motorcycle ride on a bright summer morning through God's nature? What does he know of the feeling to be human and still master over something that gives way to the slightest application of pressure? Does he know the song of a well-tuned sports machine, which sings "we are both one and I want what you want," elevated above time and space, the eye intoxicated and yearningly takes in the changing scenes. The heart rejoices – oh how glorious the world is!

His feeling that he is in complete control over the machine allows the motorcyclist to believe he has achieved mastery over time and space. Through envisioning a metaphysical bond between the man and the motorcycle, the motorcyclist imagines the motorcycle's materiality transcended through the creation of a mystical bond between the rider and the ridden. Framed in terms of a spiritual relation, the motorcyclist as a consumer is obscured.[2]

The peculiarity of the motorcycle as a thing provoked Martin Heidegger to ruminate on its phenomenological characteristics. Indeed his work from the 1920s to the 1960s is punctuated with references to motorcycles.[3] Not only in the "authentic experience" of hearkening, addressed in both *Being and Time* and in various tracts on metaphysics, but also in terms of his understanding of "truth" and the relationship between Nietzsche's concept of will and his own concept of "resoluteness" (*Entschlossenheit*), Heidegger chose the motorcycle to illustrate his concepts. For example, in his lectures at Freiburg in 1936 on Nietzsche's *The Will to Power*, he commented:

> But we can also "want" [i.e. will-to-have, "*wollen*" in original] something, e.g. a book or a motorbike. A boy "wills" to have a thing, that is, he would like to have it. This "would like to have" is no mere representation, but a kind of striving after something . . . Is willing then a wishing to which we add our own initiative? No, willing is not wishing at all. It is the submission of ourselves to our own command, and the resoluteness of such self-command, which already implies our carrying out the command.[4]

Not only did Heidegger's understanding of resoluteness echo the mental characteristics attributed to the "true motorcycle sportsman," but his interpretation of the willing and the willed is captured in the vision of the animated motorcycle, as in the quote above —"we are both one and I want what you want." The act of consumption is yet again veiled, this time behind a resolute will.

The attempt to combine *Technik* and *Kultur*, an aim that distinguished the reactionary modernists of the Weimar Republic, filtered down into everyday motorcycling rhetoric.[5] Gustav Stratil-Sauer, a geologist and motorcyclist adventurer, described his "struggle in the desert" between Tabriz and Teheran, imparting the bond with his motorcycle world-historical significance:

> My machine was not alone materialized spirit; it was also for me a manifestation in which the spirit continued to take effect . . . The motor is the second Promethean gift given to us. The spiritual awakening still floats above humanity, and already in the motor the pure animation of the spirit comes into being. Forward then! . . . We are not slaves of the machine; we have become supermen [*Übermenschen*] since having animated the torpid material, the dead metal, with our spirit. I lift the machine over the edge and jump into the saddle—forward![6]

Based on a reconciliation of *Technik* and *Kultur*, Stratil-Sauer followed a logic of German anti-rationalist nationalism that, hostile to materialism, situated technology within the realm of the spiritual. Imagining himself as one of Nietzsche's Promethean *Übermenschen*, as Stratil-Sauer motored through the "Orient," he asserted a renewed claim for German economic and political power.[7]

Such expansionist visions were more than abstract desire. Even before the official end of republican democracy in 1933, authoritarian solutions to the unraveling economic and social order gained support while, at the same time, apathy and antipathy towards the republic grew. By the end of the 1920s, the Reichswehr was confidently reasserting itself as a necessary social institution and was an increasingly significant site for constructing motorcycling masculinity. Motorized divisions of the Reichswehr took part in motorcycle races and staged public events at which its members would perform stunts on motorcycles. A magazine titled *Der Kraftzeug in Wirtschaft und Heer* ["The Motor Vehicle in Industry and the Military"] featured illustrated reports on the performance of the Reichwehr at competitions: "The quality and skills of the riders varied greatly. The factory workers [from factory-sponsored teams] were the tried and tested practitioners, familiar with all technical details. The Reichswehr riders were bodies in peak condition. Nothing was too difficult for them. Here service was sport. Strictest belief in service, discipline, and sport idealism had an exemplary effect on their ability to endure the challenges."[8] The Weimar era Reichswehr interpreted new technologies of the body, optimized through "machine sports," as a way of securing the health of the nation. In a 1929 article, "Thoughts on Technology and the Military" in *Der Kraftzeug in Wirtschaft und Heer*, the author professed technology would "prevent or at least delay the party-political poisoning of the youth," as "the same duties affect the sons of the employer and the employee, the proletariat and the capitalist during their teenage years." On the question of what was more important for building an effective modern army, materiel (meaning technology) or morale (meaning human character), the author remarked: "Morality is an expression of the people's spirit [*Volksseele*] and the result of a methodical education of the people [*Volkserziehung*]. That is the first priority of a people, to fight for their existence and non-existence [*das um Sein oder Nichtsein*]—war is not made for other reasons these days."[9] Voices within the Reichswehr increasingly called for a military solution to thwarted expansionist aims, and by 1929, motorcycle firms such as Wanderer and BMW cooperated in the Reichswehr's "Airplane Engine and Motorization Program."[10]

When the economic bubble burst, Germans faced their second economic cataclysm within ten years. Newspapers reported about armed robberies carried out with help of motor vehicles, while at the same time thousands if not tens and hundreds of thousands of Germans

Image 8.1. Motorized Christmas. Cover *ADAC-Motorwelt*, December 1928.

decided not to purchase a motorcycle, and dreams of a motorized Christmas melted into thin air.

As unemployment and bread lines grew longer, radical and violent resolutions to economic and social disorder became increasingly popular. There were frequent clashes between motorized divisions of paramilitary organizations affiliated with the NSDAP, the KPD, and the SPD-affiliated Reichsbanner during the final years of the Weimar Republic.[11] While violent confrontations probably did nothing to improve the reputation of motorcyclists among the wider public, the open conflict on the streets between bands of mostly young men doubtlessly appeared to the non-involved as manifestations of the dissolution of political authority.

Motorized paramilitary organizations were not only "flying squads" engaged in violence against political opponents. They also disseminated propaganda and performed ideologies, providing physical instantiations of alternatives to a system in crisis.[12] These groups also served to create a sense of political purpose and internal belonging for their members. In 1932 the Motor-SA and the NSKK organized an excursion to Upper Silesia: "A two-kilometer-long column ventured forth into the glorious autumn morning. Nieborwitz, the first town driven past—20 meters away from the Polish border—'Versailles' reads the memorial stone and calls into our memory that we find ourselves in the furthest corner of the Reich. To our left, forests and meadows, stolen German land that we must retake—'Versailles!'"[13] Communist motorcycle organizations also organized "military sport events" (*Wehrsportveranstaltungen*) and "rejected solidarity with the exploiters and parasites of human society," calling for "proletarian motorists, who still stand aloof, to join the ranks of the proletarian class front!"[14] Yet all groups, including the KPD-affiliated Roter Frontkämpferbund [Alliance of the Red Front Fighters], relied on the concept of comradeship to foster a sense of belonging. The concept of comradeship during the Weimar Republic was, however, polyvalent, open to multiple and at times contradictory interpretations. As historian Thomas Kühne argues, when invoked by the left, it served "as a model of *international* conciliation," whereas the right sought to "extend front comradeship into *national* unity."[15]

The image of a soldierly bond between motorcyclists was central to Walter Julius Bloem's 1927 novel *Motorherz*.[16] In this Ernst Jüngeresque melodrama, Bloem repeatedly refers to motorcyclists as "soldiers of speed," claiming motorcyclists were "a strange youth, a whole new race."[17] When the protagonist, Thomas Themal, reflects on the meaning of motor sport, he explicitly ties the bond of comradeship to military and *völkisch* ideologies: "What happens here is equivalent to real war:

steadfastness, courage, and ability decide the battle. There are heavy losses; there are wounds and blood. But it is like a war in Walhalla: the dead rise again and shake the winner's hand." Through the thoughts of Themal, Bloem insists that motorcycling represents a different kind of war: "In *this* war the best blood is not murdered for all times and for the eternal *curse* of the race—we practice a selection [*Auslese*] of the most thoroughbred blood and we breed iron health, determined derring-do, and hot, unbridled power for the *benefit* of the whole race."[18] The hearts of the sportsmen, and also women, that Bloem describes are filled with the "pure flame of comradeship."[19]

Despite the rhetoric of comradeship and unity, conflicts between the motorized and non-motorized divisions of the Nazi party during the last years of the Republic—NSKK, the Motor-SA, and the "Foot-SA"—provide a fitting example of the types of conflicts that arose from the social instability of Weimar society, and how they were expressed, in part, through the language of motorization. As Dorothee Hochstetter has argued, "Older and more settled motorists" sought membership in the NSKK, because they viewed it as *"gemütlich"* (comfortable), and because, "as well-situated citizens, they sought contact with other well-situated citizens." In contrast, members of the Motor-SA "felt a certain antipathy towards the 'clubbiness' of the NSKK and the petty-bourgeois circles that dominated the NSKK."[20] The Silesian Motor-SA's song "What Rattles and Roars" captured their desire to be members of a "brown, wild, swash-buckling army":

> What ratters and roars and thunders so,
> as if the devil came riding
> Criss-cross through Salesia's land?
> A brown, wild, swashbuckling army!
> And you ask what are these troops?
> Then it rings out in jubilance,
> tari, tara, It is, it is Hitler's Silesian
> Motor-SA . . .[21]

Sharing aspects of the language of the *Freikorps*, the Motor-SA nurtured an image of "lansquenet-like bravado and readiness for violence."[22] The Motor-SA habitus "helped to valorize long-standing links between masculinity and brutality."[23]

Deploying transgressive behavior, noise, and the threat of violence were obviously central to the Motor-SA's political tactics of intimidation during the *Kampfzeit*. Even within the *Volksgemeinschaft* of the SA, however, the Motor-SA was not above differentiating itself from the "Foot-SA":

Whomever God wants to show grace to,
He sends to the Motor-SA,
He doesn't make him travel by foot
At full throttle we are there quicker!
The Foot-SA has to sweat terribly
They greatly resent our ride,
And when we whiz by
They curse after us.[24]

Legitimizing hierarchies drawn between the motorized and the non-motorized, the song deemed the foot soldiers of the movement inferior to the motorized SA. The performance of masculinity by SA motorcyclists asserted itself on the one hand through violence and noisemaking, and was on the other hand based on their access to motorcycles and the opportunities for accelerated mobility that they offered.

While motorcycling during the Weimar Republic was marked by diversity, some of the voices in this cacophony, namely the *völkisch*-nationalist voices, saw this diversity as damaging the German *Volk*. Carl Eduard, Duke of Sachsen-Coburg and Gotha, believed that German motorists had to "stand shoulder to shoulder to fight for internal and external liberation," whereas another author claimed that, "in long years of Marxist slavery," he had learned to "become more serious, tougher, stronger, and more impersonal":

We threaten the politics of the economy that has savaged Germany like a catastrophe. You have forgotten honor. We have not. You nurture your skin and face into peachy velvet—but you do not nourish the soul, the German soul. That is who you are: greedy, spiritless, bloodless, and concealed completely behind business. And between you we stand, sneeringly laughed at, the lone one's true love of the people in ever-bursting strength of blood.[25]

Vocal activists of an anti-Republican and anti-Semitic platform could be found among motorcyclists, above all in motorized organizations associated with the military, such as the Stahlhelm and the Wehrwolf organizations, the Nationalen Deutschen Automobilklub, and the NSKK and the SA- and SS-Motorsturm, who banded together to fight the republic in order to create a motorized *Volksgemeinschaft*.[26]

Motorcycling under National Socialism and Beyond

Examining motorcycling in the Weimar Republic tells us much about how everyday men and women experienced the advent of mass-motorized modernity. Consumer choices proliferated. Lifestyles were expressed to a growing extent through purchasing consumer products. I have argued that because motorcycling facilitated individual spatial, social, and sexual mobility, it offers a particularly salient field for exploring the dreams and fears generated by new freedoms. For many Germans, motorcycles mediated how they experienced modernity. And although National Socialism only represented one possible future during the Weimar Republic, the process of motorization clearly did not end with the demise of the Weimar Republic. To end my history with the demise of the republic, however, would preclude the opportunity to make some initial and brief observations on changes and continuities between motorcycling and masculinity in Germany during the Third Reich and beyond.

Soon after assuming state power on 30 January 1933, the Nazis not only shut down motorcycle clubs that belonged to political opposition groups and religiously affiliated sport clubs, but also imposed the Nazi principle of "unity" on motorcycle associational life. The ADAC assumed the mantle, maintaining their headquarters in Munich and holding the leadership in the newly configured Der Deutsche Automobil Club [The German Automobile Club, DDAC]. The club's leadership not only agreed to shut out Jewish members, also required "promises of loyalty" and "evidence of national tradition" from all members.[27] Within a year, the umbrella organization of Weimar motorcyclists, the DMV, dissolved itself under pressure from the regime, and urged its members to "join the DDAC or the NSKK."[28] The new regime disallowed many forms of motor- cycling sociability that were not a part of the Nazi apparatus, including banning clubs that were organized around motorcycling brands, as well as forcing long-standing anti-democratic conservative motorcycling clubs such as the Motorclub von Deutschland to change its statutes and reconfigure itself as a "fellowship" (*Kameradschaft*) instead of a club.[29] Thus, the Nazi restructuring of the organization of the associational system on the principle of *Gleichschaltung* represented a radical break with prior periods, although sometimes continuities in personnel and organizational mechanisms were maintained.[30] Both the national DDAC organization and local DDAC groups organized motorcycling socia- bility under the principle of exclusionary and expansionist-imperialist comradeship.[31]

The Nazi's policy of racial exclusion silenced the voices of Paul Friedmann and Josef Ganz, two prominent journalists in the world of motorcycling. Despite writing a lead editorial in favor of "community goals over individual interests" and dedicating much space during 1931 and 1932 to both praising Mussolini's approach to motorization and an authoritarian solution to promoting motorization in Germany, Paul Friedmann, longtime editor of *Das Motorrad*, was ousted from his position in May 1933 and replaced by his "Aryan" colleague Gustav Müller.[32] Nevertheless, Friedmann's awareness of the surge in xenophobia and anti-Semitism as official policy can be gleaned from his lead article, "What is German." Responding to a military decree issued in August 1931 by the Reich minister of defense that forbade members of the Reichswehr from using foreign cars for official purposes or from parking or repairing foreign vehicles on military-owned premises, including army barracks, the editor of *Das Motorrad* questioned what made a motorcycle "German" or not, expressing shock and dismay that the Reich minister of defense could decide that "all these old-established motorcycle companies" were "suddenly no longer German."[33] His New Year 1933 editorial, one of his last, conveys an apprehension about the future: "It doesn't appear peaceful in this world. Everywhere there is crisis. Hardly is it my intention to climb up to the heights or descend into the depths of politics. But we feel in our bodies that a crisis is approaching."[34] Josef Ganz, a Jewish automotive engineer and the editor of *Klein-Motor-Sport* and *Motorkritik*, critical journals that mainly addressed engineering and industrial issues, was arrested by the Gestapo in May 1933, and was forced to flee to Switzerland.[35]

Jewish owners of motorcycle firms were likewise divested of their businesses over the course of the 1930s. One example is Hanni Köhler's motorcycle dealership and repair shop in Berlin. When Köhler decided to leave Berlin to live on her husband's estate in Sudetenland in 1935, she transferred ownership of her motorcycle store to her longtime Jewish friend, Kurt Birnholz. In 1939, he was forced to emigrate and to sell off his store.[36] Birnholz was only one Jewish motorcycle businessman who suffered under the Nazi rule. In Nuremberg, the "Coventry" of Germany, the Nazi policy of Aryanization compelled the Jewish owners of Mars, Hercules, Victoria, and Ardie to sell their shares.[37] Motorcycles of political opponents were also confiscated and handed over to members of the Nazi organizations such as the Deutsche Arbeitsfront [German Labor Front, DAF], the Hitler Jugend [Hitler Youth, HJ], the NSKK, the SA, and the SS.[38] During the first years of the Third Reich, not only were communist and socialist motorcyclists affected by the physical terror meted out by SA-troops operating in "wild" concentration camps, but Jewish-German motorcyclists were also subject to an insidious and incremental social death that intensified over the course of the 1930s, which included exile for some and culminated in the Holocaust for others.[39]

Thus, the Nazi variant of consumerism was, despite continued possibilities for enacting consumer choice, constricted by the project of creating a narrowly defined *Volksgemeinschaft*. The Christmas 1933 issue of the then titled *DDAC-Motorwelt* depicts an image of a family out Christmas shopping. A man and a woman gaze through a shop window at the latest limousines. In the background, a sign lettered in Gothic print proclaims "German Labor" (*Deutsche Arbeit*).[40] At the automobile and motorcycle exposition held in Berlin in February 1933 and again in March 1934, Hitler declared motorization key to the new regime's strategy of modernization and of economic renewal.[41] Only in Hitler's imagination, Germans would be riding in cars on newly built autobahns, not on motorcycles.[42] A dramatic recounting of the "origin story" of the Volkswagen is captured in Horst Mönnich's 1951 documentary-novel about Wolfsburg and the VW factory, *Die Autostadt*. The anecdote is set in a schoolroom in Wolfsburg, with a teacher recalling to her young pupils when and why the Führer decided to have the VW factory built:

> And down the twisting road rolls a big black car, a Mercedes, and through the drenched windshield that the electric wipers have trouble keeping clear, the eyes of the Führer stare into the grayness, into the rain, into the storm. And just as these eyes seek to penetrate this gray, they are met with a terrible sight. A motorcycle, on which three people sit: a man, a woman, and a child.... They aren't equipped for the weather, they must be soaked to the bone and cower together ... exposed to the elements, a picture of misery.

The teacher continues her vivid story: "This picture, dear children cut through the Führer's heart. The chauffeur passed the poor motorcyclist, and the Führer raised his hand and waved at the three, filled with pity for them." At this point Hitler turns to his fellow passenger, Jakob Werlin, on the board at Mercedes Benz and a longtime Nazi brother-in-arms, and says, "We must find a way to make it possible for these people to have a car." An enclosed vehicle, the car "protects from the wind and rain." He dreamed of Germans driving "after a workday, to be uplifted by the beauties of our country, to gather new energy, a car that makes it possible for them to live happier. I want a happy people, Werlin. And damn the devil if we can't make it happen."[43] Despite Hitler's grandiose plans, unlike the mass-produced *Volksempfänger* radios or the *Volksgasmaske*, gas masks that sold for 5 RM, or even the limited-availability *Volkskühlschrank* refrigerators and *Volkswohnung* apartments, the Nazi plans for the mass production of the Kraft durch Freude [Strength through Joy, KdF] Volkswagen car never came to fruition. Instead, expansionist war aims were prioritized and the giant factory at Wolfsburg, erected between 1938 and 1939, while impressive in its monumentality, was not fully fitted with the necessary equipment for assembly-line production of automobiles, and no more than 630 civilian automobiles were manufactured before the Third Reich fell.[44]

Motorcycle manufacturers, however, continued to apply the sobriquet "*Volks*" to their wares to indicate their affordability.[45] While Hitler's tax alleviations for motor vehicles did increase the numbers of automobiles, motorcycles remained the most affordable and widely dispersed form of individual motorized transportation under the National Socialist regime.[46] Adding to the number of two-wheelers on the road, the motorcycle industry had already begun manufacturing large numbers of motorized bicycles in the last years of the Weimar era, and this segment expanded significantly during the Third Reich. Thus, as the costs of maintaining an automobile remained prohibitively high and in light of wage stagnation with full employment, motorcycles and motorized bicycles continued to offer the easiest access to individual motorized mobility.[47] Motorcycling endured as an important site for consumption, with motorcycles most often being used for leisure and recreational purposes. The DDAC and the KdF tourist organization incorporated motorized leisure into their programs, while the NSKK hosted motorcycling events that drew hundreds of thousands.[48] State-directed and private opportunities for leisure "sustained" the regime's "deliberate pursuit of everyday normality."[49] They also offered the Nazi state a means of organizing consent and managing consumption. Although the reality of a production program aimed towards rearmament often conflicted with the regime's stated goals of raising the standard of living for members of the *Volksgemeinschaft*, and despite their ideological aversion to the mass-consumption of the Weimar era, the Nazis propagated their own version of a society of consumers.[50]

Although the importance of consumption and leisure grew as a compensatory strategy under Nazism, normative masculinity was simultaneously defined more rigidly. "National Socialism presented to the world a seamless front of dominant masculinity—hard, decisive, armed, modern, organized. The soldier image of the SA-man, later polished up as the image of the hyper-Aryan SS-man, was perhaps as important in Nazi iconography as the image of the leader, and has been carried forward into contemporary right-extremism."[51] In the National Socialist cult of masculinity, "iron-hard" masculinity trumped all other types of motorcycling masculinity. Labeled feminine, homosexual, and Jewish, non-conformist masculinities that had been permissible during the Weimar Republic were now excluded from the social body and stood to suffer persecution under the Nazi regime.[52] Speaking to an international committee that organized motorcycle racing during the 1930s, the Nazi minister of transportation, Baron Peter Paul von Eltz-Rübenach, proclaimed that he "could not imagine a more impressive symbolization of technically intensified life than a motorcycle race. It is the culmination of the collaboration between man and machine." In the motorcycle racer, he saw "a figure contorted into a black rune, which crouches over a fire-spewing racing machine, striving in the center of the howling motor with cold and clear reason. Hot and passionately pulses the will."[53] Motorcycle races offered the National Socialists a stage to promote their ideological platform and an opportunity to invoke racist and militaristic rhetoric.[54] The establishment of the Motor-Hitlerjugend [Motor Hitler Youth, Motor-HJ], an extremely popular division of the HJ, allowed the regime to capitalize and intensify the technical enthusiasm of boys and young men.[55] The Motor-HJ provided young men not only opportunities to obtain a driver's license but also a "hint of freedom and adventure in the 1930s."[56] The twin-pillars of National Socialist constructions of masculinity were self-discipline and comradeship, concepts central to forming an exclusionary *Volksgemeinschaft*.[57]

The Nazi state thus operated according to coercion, self-coercion, and consent. Alongside exclusion and direct persecution of those outside the *Volksgemeinschaft*, certain lifestyle choices available during the Weimar Republic were restricted, and mechanisms of both internal and external discipline served to police appropriate boundaries; however, those who conformed gained greater social, sexual, and spatial mobility during the Third Reich. Despite the rants of some Nazi ideologues against "American promiscuity" and the accelerated sexual mobility offered by motorization, in reality, trips sponsored by the DAF, the KdF, and the DDAC offered both men and women opportunities for sexual adventures, and the regime's attitude towards non-marital heterosexual sex was far more liberal than is often portrayed.[58] Although "cosmopolitan" aspects of modern femininity were eradicated from representations of modern German womanhood under the National Socialists, women who conformed to the Nazi interpretation of Germanness were not forced wholesale to abandon the modern ways of living they had grown accustomed to.[59] As Irene Guenther argues, "Whether stylishly elegant or youthfully sporty, many German women fashioned themselves according to the newest styles, popular trends, their individual tastes, and their financial means."[60] Indeed, females continued to be active in motorcycle racing during 1930s. Ilse Thouret, for example, was already an active motorcyclist during the Weimar Republic, winning her first race as a 30 year old in 1927. Married to a naval officer and mother of two daughters, she continued racing until the outbreak of World War II as a member of the Auto Union-DKW racing team. The author of a 1936 article in the *DDAC-Motorwelt* portrayed Thouret and the Swiss sidecar motorcycle racer Cilly Stärkle as "women who can take on men." Nonetheless, despite competing with and against men, the author repeatedly stressed their status as heterosexual wives and, above all, their femininity. "Ilse Thouret in leather dress and Ilse Thouret the lady after the race are hardly recognizable as the same person ... Little Ilse [*Ilschen*] is only afraid of one thing: that she could be taken for a virago [*Mannweib*]; because she wants to be a woman, only woman. What her male comrades achieve through strength, she achieves through skill and tough endurance." The accompanying photograph of Ilse Thouret shows her with shortly cropped hair, wearing a masculine tailored collar under her coveralls, getting ready to mount her motorcycle. While women could be comrades, the Nazi ideal of femininity sought to contain the masculine woman through asserting her femininity and her role as a mother and wife.[61] Coercion, self-coercion, and consent thus also determined the range of femininities available to women during the Third Reich.

The ability of the motorcycle to "conquer time and space" was connected not only to mastery over nature, but increasingly to Nazi German aspirations for world domination. In his 1938 memoirs of his travels to North Africa by motorized bicycle, Franz Münnich wrote, "Above the ride was the guiding star of the will ... We Germans will forever go out into the vast distance, we will always bring other peoples news [*Kunde*] of the German being, the German character, of the greatness of our people."[62] Soon enough, motorized German battalions were swarming over many parts of the globe on BMW, Zündapp, and DKW motorcycles, bringing "the German character" to bear brutally on millions. The Wehrmacht alone had over a quarter million motorcycles at its disposal.[63] This was the first war in which motorized warfare played a significant role, and Nazi hubris was in part based on the special relationship it envisioned between the German man and the machine, and between technology and culture. The NSKK had trained hundreds of thousands of men in the military uses of motorcycles over the 1930s, and continued military instruction into the war. Motorized divisions of the German military contributed to the total war and were complicit in crimes against humanity. For example, the NSKK played a role both in dispossessing Polish civilians in 1939 and 1940, as well as in the genocide against the Jewish population in the Soviet Union in 1941.[64]

In the first years following the defeat of the Nazi regime, all of the Allied occupying forces were concerned with turning German soldiers into citizen-civilians. Initially all clubs and associations were banned, and publication of motoring magazines that had all been halted during the war did not immediately resume. In the three "West Zones," associations and clubs reestablished themselves as soon as possible: the ADAC already in 1946 and the DMV in 1949 as an umbrella motor sport organization.[65] Sports organizations affiliated with religious and political organizations were revived in post–WWII West Germany, never, however, to achieve the same membership numbers as before the war.[66] On 1 August 1948, the *ADAC-Motorwelt* issued its first number after the war; and in 1949, the first postwar issue of *Das Motorrad* hit the stands. Although motorcycles continued to outnumber automobiles in the Federal Republic of Germany into the late 1950s, the foundations for the shift to mass motorization via the automobile had already been laid during the Nazi regime.[67] In postwar West Germany, the *Volkswagen*, cleansed of its National Socialist origins through willful forgetting, was coded as a domestic space of respectable femininity and masculinity, and as an anchor of the family. Imagined as non-ideological, it was viewed as the appropriate vehicle for the citizen of the new Federal Republic of Germany and served as a demonstration of the postwar "economic miracle" and personal freedom.[68] Thus, the practice of motorcycling was gradually marginalized and became more individualistic than it had been during either the Nazi period or the Weimar Republic. The rise of the figure of the male rebel youth on a motorcycle—the *Halbstarke* with his leather jacket—was in part imported from the United States, and in part a product of social anxiety about young male motorcyclists that had existed since the Weimar Republic.[69] In the two postwar Germanys, the mainstream appeal and the social and cultural significance of motorcycling gradually faded. The motorcycle no longer made the man.[70]

Notes

1. Herbert Marcuse, "Some Sociological Implications of Modern Technology," in *The Essential Franfurt School Reader*, ed. Andrew Arato and Eike Gebhardt (London and New York: Continuum, 1982), 144. Originally published in *Studies in Philosophy and Social Science* 9, no. 3 (1941).
2. "Die Öffentliche Meinung 219," *Das Motorrad*, 1929: 163.
3. See, for example, Martin Heidegger, "Leitgedanken zur Entstehung der Metaphysik, der neuzeitlichen Wissenschaft und der modernen Technik," in *Gesamtausgabe*, vol. 76 (Frankfurt am Main: Vittorio Klostermann, 2009), 295; Martin Heidegger, *Parmenides* (Frankfurt am Main: Vittorio Klostermann, 1982), 21.
4. Martin Heidegger, "The Will as the Will to Power," in *Nietzsche I* (San Francisco: Harper and Collins, 1991), 40.
5. See Herf, *Reactionary Modernism*.
6. Gustav Stratil-Sauer, *Fahrt und Fessel: Mit dem Motorrad von Leipzig nach Afghanistan* (Berlin: August Scherl, 1927), 100.

7. See Sasha Disko, "The World Is My Domain: Technology, Gender, and Orientalism in German Interwar Motorized Adventure Literature," *Transfers* 1, no. 3 (2011): 44–63.

8. "Der Kraftradsport," *Der Kraftzug in Wirtschaft und Heer*, no. 12, 1930, 268–70.

9. "Gedanken über Technik und Heer," *Der Kraftzug in Wirtschaft und Heer*, no. 8, 1929, 178–80.

10. Ernst Willi Hansen, *Reichswehr und Industrie: Rüstungswirtschaftliche Zusammenarbeit und wirtschaftliche Mobilmachungsvorbereitungen 1923–1932* (Boppard am Rhein: Harald Boldt Verlag, 1978), 139.

11. "Die Schlacht an der Sternschanze, 7.9.1930," from *Erlebnisbericht des SA-Sturmführers Conn aus Hamburg* (DHM-Bestand) http://www.dhm.de/lemo/forum/kollektives_gedaechtnis/092/, accessed 13 July 2012; *Die Rote Fahne*, no. 111, 25.5.1932; Landesarchiv Berlin A Rep 358 01 1546; A Rep 358 01 1639; Landesarchiv Berlin A Rep 358 01 1881; Landesarchiv Berlin A Rep 358 01 2584 (1); Landesarchiv Berlin A Rep 358 01 2584 (2); Staatsarchiv München, Pol.-Dir-München Sachakten, 6833: SA-Motorsturm; Hochstetter, *Motorisierung und "Volksgemeinschaft"*, 42–44.

12. Hochstetter, *Motorisierung und "Volksgemeinschaft*," 53–66; *AIZ*, no. 40, 1930, 795; *AIZ*, no. 16, 1930, 318.

13. *Motorschau: National Deutsche Motorfahrt Zeitung*, no. 12, 1932, n.p.

14. Bundesarchiv, BA-SAPMO, SgY2/V/DF/III/38ü, *Neuköllner Kraftfahrer*, nos. 1 and 2, 1931. In the second issue they report on having held a "herring and potato ride" and taking part in the filming of *Kuhle Wampe* on the Storkower Chaussee in Berlin.

15. Kühne, *Belonging and Genocide*, 25. Ettelson, "The Nazi 'New Man,'" 270.

16. Gijs Mom also discusses this novel; see Mom, *Atlantic Automobilism*, 452–54.

17. Walter Julius Bloem, *Motorherz* (Berlin: Julius Scherl-Verlag, 1927), 40, 80, 204.

18. Ibid., 100.

19. Ibid., 75. Here he also asserts "sport is thoroughly non-erotic."

20. Hochstetter, *Motorisierung und "Volksgemeinschaft*," 27.

21. "Was ratter und knattert," first verse, reprinted in Hochstetter, *Motorisierung und "Volksgemeinschaft*," 36.

22. "*landknechthaftes Draufgängertum und Gewaltbereitschaft.*" See Matthias Sprenger, *Landknechte auf dem Weg ins Dritte Reich? Zu Genese und Wandel des Freikorpsmythos* (Paderborn: Schöningh, 2008), 59.

23. Ettelson, "The Nazi 'New Man,'" 53.

24. As quoted in Hochstetter, *Motorisierung und "Volksgemeinschaft*," 36–37.

25. Carl Eduard, "Das Jahr 1931," *Motorschau*, no. 1, 1932, n.p.; and "13 Jahre Rebell," *Motorschau*, no. 4., 1932, n.p.

26. See also Hochstetter, *Motorisierung und "Volksgemeinschaft*," 62–66.

27. See Steinbeck, *Das Motorrad*, 276–82, here 277.

28. Landesarchiv Berlin B Rep 042 26616 "Deutscher Motorradfahrer Verband DMV Berlin."

29. See, for example, Landesarchiv Berlin, B Rep 042 Nr 26905 "AJS Motorrad Club-Berlin (DMV)"; Landesarchiv Berlin, A Pr.Br. Rep 030-04 1437, "Motorclub von Deutschland" also Staatsarchiv München Pol-Dir. Sachakten 6318, 5898, 5995; also Hochstetter, *Motorisierung und "Volksgemeinschaft*," 209–29.

30. Hochstetter, *Motorisierung und "Volksgemeinschaft,"* 209.
31. Local subsidiaries of the DDAC, for example, organized "Border Tours" to Pomerania, and the DDAC also organized a "Comradeship Cruise" to West Africa in 1938. "Aus dem Leben des DDAC," no. 134, 1938, 100; "DDAC-West Afrika-Äquator Fahrt," *DDAC-Motorwelt*, no. 21, 1938, 754.
32. Paul Friedmann, "Die Aufgabe der Verbände," *Das Motorrad*, no. 31, 1932, 1237; "Italienischer Motorsport und italienische Industrie; Konzentration und Zusammenarbeit ein Ziel aufs innigste zu wünschen – für Deutschland," *Das Motorrad*, 1932: 1250; Paul Friedmann, "Dacho-Kraft," *Das Motorrad*, 1931: 1223. See also Steinbeck, *Das Motorrad*, 276.
33. Paul Friedmann, "Was ist eigentlich deutsch?," *Das Motorrad*, 1931: 1607.
34. Paul Friedmann, " . . . Und Frieden auf Erde," *Das Motorrad*, 1932: 1941. Friedmann emigrated from Germany to Palestine in 1935. He died in Israel in 1982. See Flik, *Von Ford lernen?*, 21, fn 3.
35. Phil Patton, "In Beetle's Creation Story, A Plot Twist," *The New York Times*, 22 January 2012.
36. See the online database of Jewish-owned businesses in Berlin 1930–1945, compiled by the Institute for Contemporary History at the Humboldt University. http://www2.hu-berlin.de/djgb/www/find, accessed 19 June 2015.
37. Julius Streicher personally seized stocks that banker Anton Kohn held in the Mars factory. Carl and Heinrich Marschütz, members of the Hercules factory board of directors, were forced to dump their stocks in 1938 when the company was "Aryanized," and their cousins, Ernst und Fritz Marschütz, who had managed the company since the late 1920s, were replaced by the "Aryan" Konrad Schmidt. Victoria, owned by Max Frankenburger and Max Ottenstein, and Ardie, owned by Leo Bendit, were two other Jewish-German-owned factories that were forcibly "Aryanized" after the Nazi seizure of power. Diefenbacher and Endres, *Stadtlexicon Nürnberg*, 60, 84, 438–39, 673–74.
38. Steinbeck, *Das Motorrad*, 274–75.
39. Hochstetter, *Motorisierung und "Volksgemeinschaft,"* 403–20.
40. Cover image, *DDAC-Motorwelt*, nos. 48–49, 1933, 1.
41. Hochstetter, *Motorisierung und "Volksgemeinschaft,"*153–76; Bernhard Rieger, *The People's Car: A Global History of the Volkswagen Beetle* (Cambridge, MA: Harvard University Press, 2013), 47, 57–60.
42. Steinbeck, *Das Motorrad*, 233.
43. Hans Mönnich, *Die Autostadt* (Munich: Paul List Verlag, [1951] 1958), 19.
44. The only truly successful Nazi *"Volks"* product was the radio. See Wolfgang König, *Volkswagen, Volksempfänger, Volksgemeinschaft: "Volksprodukte" im Dritten Reich; vom Scheitern einer nationalsozialistischen Konsumgesellschaft* (Paderborn: Schöningh, 2004); Rieger, *The People's Car*, 81.
45. The regime fought against this practice in the courts, as they had legally protected the designation "*Volks-*" to indicate that it was a product that was initiated by the state and the DAF. König, *Volkswagen, Volksempfänger, Volksgesmeinschaft*, 234–42. See Steinbeck, *Das Motorrad*, 235.
46. In 1936, 35 percent of the total number of motorcycles in the world were owned by Germans, but by 1939 this percentage had increased to over 45 percent. See König, *Volkswagen, Volksempfänger, Volksgesmeinschaft*, 188–90. Annexed Austria and Sudetenland also had a high ratio of motorcycles to automobiles.
47. Steinbeck, *Das Motorrad*, 239–44.

48. "Aus der Kraft des deutschen Volkes, Zur Freude des deutschen Volkes!," *DDAC-Motorwelt*, no. 12, 1938, 445. Steinbeck, *Das Motorrad*, 262–68. Hochstetter, *Motorisierung und "Volksgemeinschaft,"* 314–18.

49. On "seemingly normal tourism" in the Third Reich, see Kristin Semmens, *Seeing Hitler's Germany* (New York: Palgrave Macmillan, 2005), 72–97, here 128.

50. Shelley Baranowski, *Strength through Joy: Consumerism and Mass Tourism in the Third Reich* (Cambridge: Cambridge University Press, 2004), 25–39. The advertising industry was likewise reworked to fit the Nazi image. See Swett, Wiesen, and Zatlin, *Selling Modernity*.

51. Raewyn Connell, "Masculinity and Nazism," in *Männlichkeitskonstruktionen im National-Sozialismus*, ed. Anette Dietrich and Ljiljana Heise (Frankfurt am Main: Peter Lang, 2013), 38.

52. See also Ettelson, "The Nazi 'New Man,'" 219.

53. "Männer im Wettkampf; Der Reichsverkehrsminister über Motorradrennen," *DDAC-Motorwelt*, no. 24, 1935, 6; see also Hochstetter, *Motorisierung und "Volksgemeinschaft,"* 297–99.

54. See Hochstetter, *Motorisierung und "Volksgemeinschaft,"* 314–25; and Steinbeck, 283–88.

55. A cover image of the *DDAC-Motorwelt* from 1935 shows a group of young boys enthusiastically viewing a motorcycle. *DDAC-Motorwelt*, no. 10, 1935, 1.

56. Hochstetter, *Motorisierung und "Volksgemeinschaft,"* 231–35.

57. See Ettelson, "The Nazi 'New Man'"; and Kühne, *Belonging and Genocide*.

58. Herzog, *Sex after Fascism*, 10–63, here 25.

59. Poiger, "Fantasies of Universality?," 334–42; Lynn, "Contested Femininities," 227–38; Sutton, *The Masculine Woman*, 61.

60. Irene Guenther, *Nazi Chic? Fashioning Women in the Third Reich* (Oxford: Berg, 2004), 267.

61. K.G. von Stackelberg, "Zwei Interviews: Ilse Thouret, Cilly Stärkle," *DDAC-Motorwelt*, no. 10, 1936, 17–18. See also Sutton, *The Masculine Woman*, 82–86.

62. Franz Münnich, *Ein Motorfahrrad fährt nach Afrika* (Böhm-Leipa: Küstner, 1938), 109.

63. See Steinbeck, *Das Motorrad*, 288–91.

64. See Hochstetter, *Motorisierung und "Volksgemeinschaft,"* 421–72.

65. "Der DMV wird 90!," *DMV-Inside*, no. 4, 2012, 12.

66. See Eisenberg, "Massensport," 137–77.

67. In 1960, automobiles first surpassed the number of motorized two-wheelers on the roads of West Germany. See Steinbeck, *Das Motorrad*, 301–6.

68. Rieger, *The People's Car*; Sachs, *For the Love of the Automobile*, 63–88.

69. Poiger, *Jazz, Rock, and Rebels*, 80.

70. In order not to exceed the limits of what is possible in this short epilogue, I see myself unfortunately forced to leave the East German case aside. Motorized two-wheelers certainly continued to play a central role in individual motorized travel throughout the German Democratic Republic's 40-year history, as the East German state was unable to fulfill the consumer desires of its citizens by filling the countless orders for its Trabant automobile. This is clearly an aspect of the German history of motorization and consumer culture that deserves greater attention. See Steinbeck, *Das Motorrad*, 308–9.

Appendix: Tables

Table 1 Comparative Numbers of Registered Motorcycles, Automobiles, and Trucks in Germany 1907/1914

	1907	1914
Motorcycles	15,000	20,620
Automobiles	9,200	55,000
Trucks	950	9,100

Source: "Die Verbreitung des Motorrades seit dem Jahre 1907," in *Motorrad-Sport, -Verkehr und -Technik* 3 (1924): 12–13.

Table 2 Comparative Numbers of Registered Motorcycles, Automobiles, and Trucks in Germany 1921–1923*

	1921	1922	1923	With baseline of 100 in 1921		
Motorcycles	26,666	38,048	59,409	100	143	223
Automobiles	60,611	82,692	100,329	100	136	166
Trucks	30,267	43,711	51,737	100	144	171

* Statistics for small-powered motorcycles are only available after 1926.
Source: "Die Verbreitung des Motorrades seit dem Jahre 1907," in *Motorrad-Sport, -Verkehr und -Technik* 3 (1924): 12–13.

Table 3 Comparative Numbers of Registered Motorcycles, Automobiles, and Trucks in Germany 1924–1928

	1924	1925	1926	1927	1928
Total Motor Vehicles (including special vehicles and tractors)	293,032	425,790	571,893	723,935	933,312
Total Motorcycles	97,965	161,508	263,345	339,226	438,288
Small Powered Motorcycles	———	———	26,934	44,040	103,974
Large Powered Motorcycles	97,965	161,508	236,411	295,186	334,314
Automobiles	132,179	174,665	206,487	267,774	351,380
Trucks	60,629	80,383	90,029	100,969	121,765

Source: Flik, "Anhang 1: Kraftfahrzeugbestand," *Von Ford lernen?*, 280–82.

Table 4 Yearly Sales of DKW Motorcycles 1928–1930

	1928	1929	1930
Tax Free, under 200 ccm	22,587	51,413	11,575
Motorcycles over 200 ccm	20,468	10,227	6,619
Total	43,055	61,640	18,194

Source: "Stückmäßige Jahres Motorrad Umsätze," Akte 104, Firmengeschichte, 31070, Bestand Zschopauer Motorenwerke J.S. Rasmussen AG (DKW), Zschopau 1913–1932, Sächsische Staatsarchiv Chemnitz.

Table 5 Comparative Numbers of Registrations of Motorcycles, Automobiles, and Trucks 1929–1932

	1929	1930	1931	1932
Total Motorcycles	608,342	731,237	792,075	819,178
Small-Powered Motorcycles	222,479	309,052	374,506	433,559
Large-Powered Motorcycles	385,863	422,185	417,569	385,619
Automobiles	433,205	501,254	522,943	497,275
Trucks	143,952	157,432	161,072	152,420

Source: Flik, "Anhang 1: Kraftfahrzeugbestand," *Von Ford lernen?*, 280–82.

Table 6 Motorcyclists by Profession 1924

Commercial Sector	205
Mechanics/Metalworkers	86
Factory Owners/Directors	61
Engineers/Technicians	30
Master Craftsmen	20
Foremen	17
Military/Police	17
Service Industry	16
Liberal Professions	16
Students/Interns	12
Bankers	11
Women	8
Total	499

Source: *Der Motorradsport; motorsportliche Mitteilungen bayrischer Motorradklubs*, VNFM, Verlag Druck A. Mayer [1924].

Table 7 Motorcycle Registrations 1929 by Occupation

Workers (skilled, semi-skilled, unskilled)	217
Agricultural	20
Artisans (including master)	66
State Employment	21
Liberal Professions	17
New White Collar	14
Service Industries	40
Commercial Sector	76
Total	471

Source: *Straße und Verkehr*, Nr. 1–3, January 1929.

Table 8 Occupations of Skilled, Semi-Skilled, and Unskilled Workers, 1929

Miners	48
Metalworkers	75
Masons	22
Workers	14
House painters	18
Electricians	12
Construction workers	12
Plumbers	5
Others	11
Total	217

Source: *Straße und Verkehr*, Nr. 1–3, January 1929.

Bibliography

Archives

Sächsisches Staatsarchiv Chemnitz
Bayerisches Hauptstaatsarchiv
Stadtarchiv München
Bundesarchiv
Staatsarchiv München
Stiftung Deutsches Technikmuseum Berlin, Historisches Archiv
Deutsches Historisches Museum
Landesarchiv Berlin

Internet

historischesarchiv.bmw.de
ijms.nova.edu/IJMS_Archives.html
motorcyclestudies.org
motorradonline.de
www2.hu-berlin.de/djgb/www/find
tukutuku.de

Periodicals

ADAC-Motorwelt
AIZ
Auto-Magazin
Berlinische Monatsschrift
BMW-Blätter
Concordia
Das Auto
Das Motorrad (Berlin)
Das Motorrad (Vienna)
DDAC-Motorwelt
Der deutsche Motorfahrer
Der Kraftzug in Wirtschaft und Heer
Der Motorradsport; motorsportliche Mitteilungen bayrischer Motorrad Klubs
Der Motorsportler
Der Motorwagen

Der Pioneer: Zeitschrift zur Förderung der Nüchternheit und Sicherheit im Verkehr
Der Schlossermeister
Die Arbeit
Die Epoche: Das Magazine des Werbefilms
Die Weltbühne
Dixi Magazin
DMV-Inside
Echo Continental
Emelka-Woche
FKZ
Geschäftsbericht der Handelskammer Nürnberg
Jahrbuch der Reichsverband der Automobilindustrie
Klein-Motor-Sport
Motor
Motor und Sport
Motor-Kritik
Motor-Tourist
Motorcycling
Motorrad-Markt
Motorrad-Sport, -Verkehr und -Technik
Motorschau
Münchner Post
New York Times
NSU-Mitteilungen
Rad-Welt
Rheinische Heimatsblätter
Sportpolitisches Rundschau
Statistisches Taschenbuch der Stadt Berlin
Straße und Verkehr
Tatsachen und Zahlen der Reichsverband der Automobilindustrie
Technik Voran!
Tempo

Books, Book Chapters, Journal Articles, and Films

Acutus [Kurt Lubowsky, pseud]. *Knigge für industrielle Beamte: Zeitstudien von Acutus, eine lustige Darstellung bitterer Erfahrungen gewidmet allen Berufsfreunden zum Verständnis ohne Brille.* Berlin: Verlag Walter Fiebig & Co., 1931.
Alford, Steven E., and Suzanne Ferriss. *Motorcycle.* London: Reaktion Books, 2007.
Alt, John. "Popular Culture and Mass Consumption: The Motorcycle as Cultural Commodity." *Journal of Popular Culture* 15, no. 4 (Spring 1982): 129–41.
Appadurai, Arjun, ed. *The Social Life of Things: Commodities in Cultural Perspective.* Cambridge: Cambridge University Press, 1986.
Audi AG, ed. *Das Rad der Zeit, Die Geschichte der Audi AG.* Bielefeld: Delius Klasing, 2000.
AvD, ed. *100 Jahre AvD: 100 Jahre Mobilität.* Königswitter: Heel 1999.
Baranowski, Shelley. *Strength through Joy: Consumerism and Mass Tourism in the Third Reich.* Cambridge: Cambridge University Press, 2004.

Baudrillard, Jean. *America*. London: Verso, [1968] 1988.

Beck, Ulrich, and Wolfgang Bonß. *Die Modernisierung der Moderne*. Frankfurt am Main: Surkamp, 2001.

Bertschik, Julia. *Mode und Moderne: Kleidung als Spiegel des Zeitgeistes in der deutschsprachigen Literatur (1770–1945)*. Cologne: Böhlau, 2005.

Beynon, John. *Masculinities and Culture*. Buckingham, Open University Press, 2002.

Biernacki, Richard. *The Fabrication of Labor: Britain and Germany, 1640–1914*. Berkeley: University of California Press, 1995.

Bijker, Wiebe E., Thomas Parke Hughes, and T.J. Pinch, eds. *The Social Construction of Technological Systems: New Directions in the Sociology and History of Technology*. Cambridge, MA: MIT Press, 1987.

Birkefeld, Richard. "Spektakel im Stadtwald: Die Motorradrennen in der Eilenriede." In *Wochenend und Sonnenschein: Freizeit und modernen Leben in den Zwanziger Jahren: das Beispiel Hannover*, edited by Adalheid von Saldern and Sid Auffarth, 15–23. Berlin: Elefanten Press, 1991.

Birkefeld, Richard, and Martina Jung, eds. *Die Stadt, der Lärm und das Licht: Die Veränderung des öffentlichen Raumes durch Motorisierung und Elektrifizierung*. Seelze: Kallmeyer, 1994.

Biro, Matthew. "The New Man as Cyborg: Figures of Technology in Weimar Visual Culture." *New German Critique* 62 (Spring/Summer, 1994): 71–110.

Bloch, Ernst. *Erbschaft dieser Zeit*. Frankfurt am Main: Suhrkamp, 1985.

Bloem, Walter Julius. *Motorherz*. Berlin: Julius Scherl-Verlag, 1927.

Bönig, Jürgen. *Die Einführung von Fließbandarbeit in Deutschland bis 1933: Zur Geschichte einer Sozialinnovation*. 2 vols. Münster: LIT-Verlag, 1993.

Bonß, Wolfgang, Joachim Hohl, and Alexander Jakob. "Die Konstruktion von Sicherheit in der reflexiven Moderne," in *Die Modernisierung der Moderne*, edited by Ulrich Beck and Wolfgang Bonß, 147–59. Frankfurt am Main: Surkamp, 2001.

Bourdieu, Pierre. *Distinction: A Social Critique of the Judgment of Taste*. London: Routledge, 1984.

Boveri, Margret. *Verzweigungen, Eine Autobiographie*. Munich: R. Piper & Co., 1977.

Bowlby, Rachel. *Carried Away: The Invention of Modern Shopping*. New York: Columbia University Press, 2001.

Braun, Hans-Joachim. "Lärmbelästigung und Lärmbekämpfung in der Zwischenkriegszeit." In *Sozialgeschichte der Technik, Festschrift für Ulrich Troitzsch*, edited by Günter Bayerl and Wolfhard Weber, 251–58. Münster: Waxman, 1998.

Braun, Helmut, and Christian Panzer. "The Expansion of the Motor-Cycle Industry in Germany and Great Britain 1918–1919." *Journal of European Economic History* 32, no. 1 (Spring 2003): 25–59.

Braunbeck, Gustav. *Braunbecks Addressbuch der Motorfahrzeug- und verwandten Industrie für Deutschland*. Berlin: Gustav Braunbeck, 1925, 1929.

Breward, Christopher. *The Hidden Consumer: Masculinities, Fashion and City Life 1860–1914*. Manchester: Manchester University Press, 1999.

Brunotte, Ulrike, and Rainer Herrn, eds. *Männlichkeiten und Moderne: Geschlecht in den Wissenskulturen um 1900*. Bielefeld: transcript Verlag, 2008.

———. "Statt einer Einleitung. Männlichkeiten und Moderne–Pathosformeln, Wissenskulturen, Diskurse," in *Männlichkeiten und Moderne: Geschlecht in den Wissenskulturen um 1900*, edited by Ulrike Brunotte and Rainer Herrn, 9–24. Bielefeld: transcript Verlag, 2008.

Buck-Morss, Susan. *Dreamworld and Catastrophe: The Passing of Mass Utopia in East and West.* Cambridge, MA: MIT Press, 2002.

Butler, Judith. *Undoing Gender.* London: Routledge, 2004.

Büttner, Alexander. *Mein Motorrad und Ich: Ein Buch von Sport und Wandern.* Stuttgart: Dieck & Co., 1924.

———. *Das Knipsbuch des Sportmanns.* Stuttgart: Dieck & Co., 1927.

Campigotto, Antonio, and Enrico Ruffini. "Le veterane degli anni '20: Agli albori dell'industria motociclistica Bolognese." *Scuola Officina: Museo del Patrimonio Industriale di Bologna* 1 (2004): 9–17.

Canning, Kathleen. *Gender History in Practice: Historical Perspectives on Bodies, Class, and Citizenship.* Ithaca, NY: Cornell University Press, 2006.

Christenn, Willi. "Die deutsche Motorrad-Industrie und ihre Steuerliche Belastung." Inaugural dissertation. Munich: Ludwig-Maximillians-Universität, 1929.

Clarsen, Georgine. *Eat My Dust: Early Women Motorists.* Baltimore, MD: John Hopkins University Press, 2008.

Connell, R.W. *Masculinities.* Cambridge: Polity, 1995.

———. "Hegemonic Masculinities: Rethinking the Concept." *Gender & Society* 19, no. 6 (2005): 829–59.

———. "Masculinity and Nazism." In *Männlichkeitskonstruktionen im National-Sozialismus*, edited by Anette Dietrich and Ljiljana Heise, 37–42. Frankfurt am Main: Peter Lang, 2013.

Das deutsche Heer im Manöver. Dresden: Cigaretten Bilddienst, 1936.

Davis, Belinda. "Police and Patterns of Street Conflict in Berlin in the Nineteenth and Twentieth Centuries." In *Polizei, Staat, Gewalt im 20. Jahrhundert*, edited by Alf Lüdtke, Heinrich Reinke and Michael Sturm, 81–103. Wiesbaden: VS-Verlag für Sozialwissenschaften, 2011.

Day, Uwe. "Mythos ex machina: Medienkonstrukt 'Silberpfeil' als massenkulturelle Ikone der NS-Modernisierung." PhD dissertation, Kulturwissenschaften, Universität Bremen, 2004.

de Certeau, Michel. *The Practice of Everyday Life.* Berkeley: University of California Press, 1984.

de Grazia, Victoria, and Ellen Furlough, eds. *The Sex of Things: Gender and Consumption in Historical Perspective.* Berkeley: University of California Press, 1996.

Derrida, Jacques. *Specters of Marx: The State of the Debt, the Work of Mourning, and the New International.* New York: Routledge, 1994.

Diefenbacher, Michael, and Rudolf Endres, eds. *Stadtlexicon Nürnberg.* Nürnberg: W. Tümmels, 2000.

Disko, Sasha. "The Image of the 'Tourist Trophy' and British Motorcycling in the Weimar Republic." *The International Journal of Motorcycling Studies* 3, no. 3, Special 100-year-TT-Issue, November 2007, Accessed 14 March 2016, http://ijms.nova.edu/November2007TT/IJMS_Artcl.Disko.html

———. "The World Is My Domain: Technology, Gender, and Orientalism in German Interwar Motorized Adventure Literature." *Transfers* 1, no. 3 (2011): 44–63.

Donny, Julius. *Garage 13.* Berlin: Georg König, 1930.

Doyle, J.A. *The Male Experience.* Dubuque, IL: William C. Brown, 1989.

Dudow, Slatan, dir. *Kuhle Wampe oder: Wem Gehört die Welt?* (1932). British Film Institute, 1999.

Edelmann, Heidrun. *Vom Luxusgut zum Gebrauchsgegendstand: Die Geschichte der Verbreitung von Personenkraftwagen in Deutschland.* Frankfurt am Main: Verband der Automobil Industrie, 1989.

Egert, Hugo. *Der Kraftwagen im deutschen Verkehrswesen.* Halle an der Saale: Martin Boerner, Verlagsbuchhandlung, 1929.

Eisenberg, Christiane. "Massensport in der Weimarer Republik," *Archiv für Sozialgeschichte* 33 (1993): 137–77.

———. *"English Sports" and deutsche Bürger: Eine Gesellschaftsgeschichte 1800–1939.* Paderborn: Schöningh, 1999.

Elias, Norbert. *The Civilizing Process. Vol. 2. State Formation and Civilization.* Oxford: Blackwell, 1982.

Ermanski, J. *Theorie und Praxis der Rationalisierung.* Berlin: Verlag für Literatur und Politik, 1928.

Ettelson, Todd. "The Nazi 'New Man': Embodying Masculinity and Regulating Sexuality in the SA and SS, 1930–1939." PhD dissertation, University of Michigan, 2002.

Featherstone, Mike, Nigel Thrift, and John Urry, eds. "Special Issue on Automobilities." *Theory, Culture & Society* 21 (October 2004).

Feldman, Gerald. *The Great Disorder: Politics, Economics, and Society in the German Inflation, 1914–1924.* New York and Oxford: Oxford University Press, 1993.

Findeisen, Franz. *Die Markenartikel im Rahmen der Absatzökonomik der Betriebe.* Berlin: Industrieverlag Spaeth & Linde, 1924.

Fleißer, Marieluise. *Die List, Frühe Erzählungen.* Frankfurt am Main: Suhrkamp, 1995.

Flik, Reiner. *Von Ford lernen? Automobilbau und Motorisierung in Deutschland bis 1933.* Cologne: Böhlau, 2001.

Ford, Henry (with Samuel Crowther). *My Life and Work.* Garden City, NY: Doubleday, 1923.

Frame, Lynne. "Gretchen, Girl, Garçonne? Weimar Science and Popular Culture in Search of the Ideal New Woman." *Women in the Metropolis: Gender and Modernity in Weimar Culture,* edited by Katharina von Ankum, 12–40. Berkeley: University of California Press, 1997.

Franz, Kathleen. *Tinkering: Consumers Reinvent the Early Automobile.* Philadelphia: University of Pennsylvania Press, 2005.

Fraunholz, Uwe. *Motorphobia: Anti-automobiler Protest in Kaiserreich und Weimarer Republik.* Göttingen: Vandenhoeck & Ruprecht, 2002.

Frehill, Lisa M. "The Gendered Construction of the Engineering Profession in the United States, 1893–1920." *Men and Masculinities* 6, no. 4 (2004): 383–403.

Frevert, Ute. *Mann und Weib und Weib und Mann: Geschlechterdifferenz in der Moderne.* Munich: C.H. Beck, 1995.

———. "Soldaten, Staatsbürger: Überlegungen zur historischen Konstruktion von Männlichkeit." In *Männergeschichte, Geschlechtergeschichte: Männlichkeit im Wandel der Moderne,* edited by Thomas Kühne, 69–87. Frankfurt am Main: Campus Press, 1996.

Fritzsche, Peter. *A Nation of Fliers: German Aviation and the Popular Imagination.* Cambridge, MA: Harvard University Press, 1992.

Gartman, David. "Three Ages of the Automobile: The Cultural Logics of the Car," *Theory, Culture & Society* 21, no. 4/5 (2004): 169–95.

Geiger, Theodore. *Die soziale Schichtung des deutschen Volkes. Soziographischer Versuch auf statistischer Grundlage.* Stuttgart: Ferdinand Enke Verlag, 1932.

Geisthovel, Alexa. "Das Auto." In *Orte der Moderne: Erfahrungswelten des 19. und 20. Jahrhundert*, edited by Alexa Geisthovel and Habbo Knoch, 37–46. Frankfurt am Main and New York: Campus, 2005.

Gimmel, Jürgen. *Die politische Organisation kulturellen Ressentiments: der "Kampfbund für Deutsche Kultur" und das bildungsbürgerliche Unbehagen an der Moderne*. Münster: LIT Verlag, 2001.

Goltermann, Svenja. *Körper der Nation: Habitusformation und die Politik des Turnens 1860–1890*. Göttingen: Vandenhoeck & Ruprecht, 1998.

Gömmel, Rainer, and Helmut Braun. "Aufstieg und Niedergang der deutschen Motorradindustrie." In *Struktur und Dimension. Festschrift für Heinrich Kaufhold zum 65. Geburtstag*, vol. 2, edited by Hans-Jürgen Gerhard, 167–94. Stuttgart: Steiner, 1997.

Gräf, J.W. *Die Hupe*. Radolfzell am Bodensee: Hein Verlag, 1933.

Grossmann, Atina. *Reforming Sex: The German Movement for Birth Control and Abortion Reform, 1920–1950*. New York: Oxford University Press, 1995.

Guenther, Irene. *Nazi Chic? Fashioning Women in the Third Reich*. Oxford: Berg, 2004.

Gumbrecht, Hans Ulrich. *In 1926: Living at the Edge of Time*. Cambridge, MA: Harvard University Press, 1997.

Hagemann, Karen, and Stefanie Schüler-Springorum, eds. *HOME/FRONT, The Military, War and Gender in 20th Century Germany*. Oxford: Berg, 2002.

Hake, Sabine. "Urban Spectacle in Walther Ruttmann's Symphony of the Big City." In *Dancing on the Volcano: Essays on the Culture of the Weimar Republic*, edited by Thomas W. Kniesche and Stephen Brockmann, 127–42. New York: Camden House 1994.

Hanfland, Curt. *Das Motorrad und seine Konstruktion unter Berücksichtigung des Fahrrad- und Seitenwagenbaues sowie der Sonderkonstruktion*. Berlin: M. Krayn Verlag, 1925.

Hansen, Ernst Willi. *Reichswehr und Industrie: Rüstungswirtschaftliche Zusammenarbeit und wirtschaftliche Mobilmachungsvorbereitungen 1923–1932*. Boppard am Rhein: Harald Boldt Verlag, 1978.

Harootunian, Harry. *Histories Disquiet: Modernity, Cultural Practice, and the Question of Everyday Life*. New York: Columbia University Press, 2001.

Harvey, David. *The Condition of Postmodernity: An Inquiry into the Origins of Social Change*. London: Blackwell Publishers, 1989.

Haubner, Barbara. *Von Nervenkitzel zur Freizeitvergnügen, Automobilismus in Deutschland, 1860–1914*. Göttingen: Vandenhoeck & Ruprecht, 1998.

Hebdige, Dick. "Object as Image: The Italian Motor Scooter Cycle." In *Hiding in the Light: On Images and Things*, 77–115. London: Comedia, 1988.

Heidegger, Martin. "Von Wesen und Wirklichkeit der Kraft." In *Die Grundbegriffe der Metaphysik, Aristoteles: Metaphysik IX 1–3*. Frankfurt am Main: Vittorio Klostermann, 1981.

——. *Parmenides*. Frankfurt am Main: Vittorio Klostermann, 1982.

——. "The Will as the Will to Power." In *Nietzsche I*. San Francisco: Harper and Collins, 1991.

——. *Introduction to Metaphysics*. Translation by Gregory Fried and Richard Polt. New Haven, CT: Yale University Press, 2000.

——. "Leitgedanken zur Entstehung der Metaphysik, der neuzeitlichen Wissenschaft und der modernen Technik." In *Gesamtausgabe*, vol. 76. Edited by C. Strube. Frankfurt am Main: Vittorio Klostermann, 2009.

Herf, Jeffrey. *Reactionary Modernism: Technology, Culture and Politics in Weimar and the Third Reich*. Cambridge: Cambridge University Press, 1984.

Herzog, Dagmar. *Sex after Fascism: Memory and Morality in Twentieth-Century Germany*. Princeton, NJ: Princeton University Press. 2005.

Hochstetter, Dorothee. *Motorisierung und "Volksgemeinschaft": Das NSKK 1931–1945*. Munich: C.H. Beck, 2005.

Horowitz, Roger, ed. *Boys and Their Toys? Masculinity, Technology and Class in America*. New York: Routledge, 2001.

Horowitz, Roger, and Arwen Mohun, eds. *His and Hers: Gender, Consumption and Technology*. Charlottesville: University of Virginia Press, 1998.

Hounshell, David. *From the American System to Mass Production, 1800–1932: The Development of Manufacturing Technology in the United States*. Baltimore, MD: Johns Hopkins University Press, 1984.

Jacob, Wilson Chacko. *Working out Egypt: Effendi Masculinity and Subject Formation in Colonial Modernity, 1870–1940*. Durham, NC: Duke University Press, 2011.

Jarausch, Konrad. *The Unfree Professions: German Lawyers, Teachers and Engineers, 1900–1950*. Oxford: Oxford University Press, 1990.

Jensen, Erik Norman. *Body by Weimar: Athletes, Gender and German Modernity*. Oxford: Oxford University Press, 2010.

Keun, Irmgard. *Gilgi – Eine von Uns*. Hildesheim: Classen, 1993.

Kirchberg, Peter. "Die Motorisierung des Straßenverkehrs in Deutschland von den Anfängen bis zum Zweiten Weltkrieg." In *Die Entwicklung der Motorisierung im Deutschen Reich und den Nachfolgestaaten*, edited by Harry Niemann and Armin Hermann, 9–22. Stuttgart: Steiner Verlag, 1995.

Kocka, Jürgen. "Zur Problematik der deutschen Angestellten 1914–1933." In *Industrielles System und Politische Entwicklung in der Weimarer Republic*, edited by Hans Mommsen, 792–810. Düsseldorf: Droste, 1974.

Koerner, Steve. "Four Wheels Good, Two Wheel Bad: The Motor Cycle versus the Light Motor Car 1919–1939," in *The Motor Car and Popular Culture in the 20th Century*, edited by David Thoms, Len Holden, and Tim Claydon, 151–76. Aldershot: Ashgate, 1998.

———. "Whatever Happened to the Girl on the Motorbike? British Women and Motorcycling, 1919 to 1939." *International Journal of Motorcycling Studies* (March 2007), n.p. Accessed 14 March 2016, http://ijms.nova.edu/March2007/IJMS_Artcl.Koerner.html.

König, Wolfgang. *Volkswagen, Volksempfänger, Volksgemeinschaft: "Volksprodukte" im Dritten Reich: vom Scheitern einer nationalsozialistischen Konsumgesellschaft*. Paderborn: Schöningh, 2004.

Koshar, Rudy. *German Travel Cultures*. Oxford and New York: Berg, 2000.

———. "On the History of the Automobile in Everyday Life." *Contemporary European History* 10, no. 1 (2001): 143–54.

———. "Cars and Nations: Anglo-German Perspectives on Automobility between the World Wars." *Theory, Culture & Society* 21 (2004): 121–44.

Kracauer, Siegfried. *From Caligari to Hitler: A Psychological History of German Film*. Princeton, NJ: Princeton University Press, (1947) 1974.

———. "Film 1928." In *The Mass Ornament*. Cambridge, MA: Harvard University Press, 1995.

———. *The Salaried Masses: Duty and Distraction in Weimar Germany*. London: Verso, 1998.

Kraft, Reinhold, Thomas Müller, and Georg Solms, eds. *Ernst Neumann-Neander, 1871–1954*. Düren: Hahne & Schloemer Verlag, 2004.

Kroeker, Konrad. *Fabrik- oder Handwerksbetrieb: Ein Versuch zur Aufstellung leicht anwendbarer Unterscheidungsmerkmale der beiden Betriebsformen*. Berlin: Carl Heymanns Verlag, 1927.

Kubisch, Ulrich, Andreas Curtius, and Joachim Dufner. *Das Automobil als Lesestoff: zur Geschichte der deutschen Motorpresse, 1898–1998*. Vol. 29. Berlin: Staatsbibliothek zu Berlin, 1998.

Küchler, Susanne, and Daniel Miller, eds. *Clothing as Material Culture*. Oxford: Berg, 2005.

Kugler, Anita. "Von der Werkstatt zum Fließband, Etappen der frühen Automobil-produktion." *Geschichte und Gesellschaft* 13, no. 3 (1987): 324–28.

Kühne, Thomas. "Männergeschichte als Geschlechtergeschichte." In *Männergeschichte – Geschlechtergeschichte; Männlichkeit im Wandel der Moderne*, edited by Thomas Kühne, 7–30. Frankfurt am Main: Campus Press, 1996.

——. *Kameradschaft: Die Soldaten des nationalsozialistischen Krieges und das 20. Jahrhunderts*. Göttingen: Vandenhoeck & Ruprecht, 2006.

——. *Belonging and Genocide: Hitler's Community, 1918–1945*. New Haven, CT: Yale University Press, 2010.

——, ed. *Männergeschichte – Geschlechtergeschichte: Männlichkeit im Wandel der Moderne*. Frankfurt am Main: Campus, 1996.

Ladd, Brian, *Autophobia: Love and Hate in the Automotive Age*. Chicago: University of Chicago Press, 2008.

Lamberty, Christiane. *Reklame in Deutschland 1890–1914, Wahrnehmung, Profession-alisierung und Kritik der Wirtschaftswerbung*. Berlin: Duncker und Humblot, 2000.

Laux, James M. *The European Automobile Industry*. New York: Twayne Publishers, 1992.

Lefebvre, Henri. *Everyday Life in the Modern World*. New Brunswick, NJ: Transaction Publishers, [1968] 1994.

Lerner, Paul. *Hysterical Men: War, Psychiatry, and the Politics of Trauma in Germany, 1890–1930*. Ithaca, NY: Cornell University Press, 2003.

Leßmann, Peter. *Die preussische Schutzpolizei in der Weimarer Republik: Streifendienst und Strassenkampf*. Düsseldorf: Droste, 1989.

Lethen, Helmut. *Cool Conduct: The Culture of Distance in Weimar Germany*. Berkeley: University of California Press, 2002.

Lüdke, Alf. "The 'Honor of Labor': Industrial Workers and the Power of Symbols under National Socialism." In *Nazism and German Society, 1933–1945*, edited by David Crew, 67–109. London: Routledge, 1994.

Lützen, Wolf-Dieter, "Radfahren, Motorsport, Autobesitz. Motorisierung zwischen Statuserwerb." In *Die Arbeiter: Lebensformen, Alltag und Kultur*, edited by Wolfgang Ruppert, 369–77. Munich: C.H. Beck, 1986.

Lynn, Jennifer M. "Contested Femininities: Representations of Modern Women in the German Illustrated Press, 1920–1945." PhD dissertation. Chapel Hill: University of North Carolina, 2012.

Maier, Charles S. "Between Taylorism and Technocracy: European Ideologies and the Vision of Industrial Productivity in the 1920s." *Journal of Contemporary History* 5, no. 2 (1970): 27–61.

Marcuse, Herbert. "Some Sociological Implications of Modern Technology." In *The Essential Frankfurt School Reader*, edited by Andrew Arato and Eike Gebhardt, 138–62. London: Continuum, 1982.

Marx, Karl. "The Fetishism of Commodities and the Secret thereof." In *Capital: A Critique of Political Economy*, vol. 1, 71–83. New York: International Publishers, 1967.

McShane, Clay. *Down the Asphalt Path: The Automobile and the American City*. New York: Columbia University Press, 1994.

Merki, Christoph Maria. *Der holprige Siegeszug des Automobils, 1895–1930: Zur Motorisierung des Straßenverkehers in Frankreich, Deutschland und der Schweiz*. Vienna: Böhlau, 2002.

Merriman, Peter. *Mobility, Space and Culture*. London: Routledge, 2012.

Merz, Fritz, ed. *Deutscher Sport*, Vol. 1. Berlin: Deutscher Sport-Verlag, 1926.

Miller, Daniel. *Material Culture and Mass Consumption*. Oxford: Blackwell Publishers, 1987.

——. *Car Cultures*. Oxford: Berg, 2001.

Mom, Gijs. "Encapsulating Culture: European Car Travel, 1900–1940." *Journal of Tourism History* 3, no. 3 (2011): 289–307.

——. *The Electric Vehicle: Technology and Expectations in the Automobile Age*. Baltimore, MD: John Hopkins University Press, 2012.

——. *Atlantic Automobilism: Emergence and Persistence of the Car 1985-1940* (New York: Berghahn Books, 2015

Mönnich, Hans. *Die Autostadt*. Munich: Paul List Verlag, 1958.

Möser, Kurt. "World War I and the Creation of Desire for Automobiles in Germany." In *Getting and Spending: European and American Consumer Societies in the 20th Century*, edited by Susan Strasser, Charles McGovern, and Matthias Judt, 195–222. Cambridge: Cambridge University Press, 1998.

——. *Geschichte des Autos*. Frankfurt am Main: Campus, 2002.

——. "The Dark Side of 'Automobilism', 1900–30: Violence, War, and the Motor Car." *Journal of Transport History* 24, no. 2 (2003): 238–58.

——. *Fahren und Fliegen in Frieden und Krieg: Kulturen individueller Mobilitätsmaschinen 1880–1930*. Heidelberg: Verlag Regionalkultur, 2009.

Mosse, George L. *Fallen Soldiers: Reshaping the Memory of the World Wars*. New York: Oxford University Press, 1990.

——. *The Image of Man: The Creation of Modern Masculinity*. Oxford University Press, Oxford: 1996.

Münnich, Franz. *Ein Motorfahrrad fährt nach Afrika*. Böhm-Leipa: Küstner, 1938.

Murko, Matthias. *Motorrad Legenden*. Nuremberg: W. Tummels, 1994.

Nabinger, Manfred. *Deutsche Fahrradmotoren, 1898 bis 1988*. Brilon: Pozdun Motorbücher, 1988.

Neuendorff, Edmund. *Geschichte der neueren deutschen Leibesübung vom Beginn des 18. Jahrhunderts bis zum Gegenwart*, 4 vols. Volume 4, *Die Zeit vom 1860 bis 1932*. Dresden: Limpert, 1932.

Neumann-Neander, Ernst. "Mit dem Motorrad durch Eis und Schnee." In *Auf dem Motorrad durch Eis und Schnee: die Geschichte der Deutschlandfahrt, 1924*, edited by Cölner Club für Motorsport. Düsseldorf: Mittag-Verlag, 1924.

Niptsch, R. *Marktbeobachtung und Wirtschaftsführung in der Kraftfahrzeugindustrie Amerikanische Methoden und deutsche Gemeinschaftsarbeit*, edited by Institut für Konjunkturforschung. Berlin: Reichsverband der Automobilindustrie, 1930.

Nolan, Mary. *Visions of Modernity: American Business and the Modernization of Germany.* Oxford: Oxford University Press, 1994.

Norton, Peter D. "Street rivals: Jaywalking and the invention of the motor age street." *Technology and Culture* 48, no. 2 (2007): 331–359.

———. *Fighting Traffic: The Dawn of the Motor Age in the American City.* Cambridge, MA: MIT Press, 2008.

Oberschlep, Reinhard, ed. *Gesamtverzeichnis des deutschsprachigen Schriftums.* Munich: Saur, 1976–81.

O'Connell, Sean. *The Car and British Society: Class, Gender and Motoring, 1896–1939.* Manchester: Manchester University Press, 1998.

Oldenziel, Ruth. *Making Technology Masculine: Men, Women and Modern Machines in America, 1870–1945.* Amsterdam: Amsterdam University Press, 1999.

Packer, Jeremy. *Mobility without Mayhem: Safety, Cars, and Citizenship.* Durham, NC: Duke University, 2008.

Paulitz, Tanja. *Mann und Maschine: eine genealogische Wissenssoziologie des Ingenieurs und der modernen Technikwissenschaften 1850–1930.* Bielefeld: transcript Verlag, 2012.

Petermann, Fred. *Der PS-Narr: Sportroman.* Berlin: Georg König Verlag, 1930.

Petro, Patrice. *Joyless Streets: Women and Melodramatic Representation in Weimar Germany.* Princeton, NJ: Princeton University Press, 1989.

Petzina, Dietmar, Werner Abelshauser, and Anselm Faust. *Sozialgeschichtliches Arbeitsbuch: Materialien zur Statistik des Deutschen Reiches 1914–1945.* vol. 3. In *Statistische Arbeitsbücher zur neueren deutschen Geschichte*, edited by Jürgen Kocka and Gerhard A. Ritter. Munich: C.H. Beck, 1978.

Peukert, Detlev J.K. *The Weimar Republic: The Crisis of Classical Modernity.* New York: Hill and Wang, 1989.

Pirsig, Robert M. *Zen and the Art of Motorcycle Maintenance: An Inquiry into Values.* New York: Morrow, 1974.

Poiger, Ute G. *Jazz, Rock, and Rebels: Cold War Politics and American Culture in a Divided Germany.* Berkeley: University of California Press, 2000.

———. "Fantasies of Universality? *Neue Frauen*, Race and Nation in Weimar and Nazi Germany." In *The Modern Girl around the World: Consumption, Modernity and Globalization*, ed. Alys Eve Weinbaum, Lynn M. Thomas, Priti Ramamurthy, Uta G. Poiger, Madeleine Yue Dong, 315–44. Durham, NC: Duke University Press, 2008.

Potter, Christopher Thomas. "An Exploration of Social and Cultural Aspects of Motorcycling during the Interwar Period." Doctoral thesis. Newcastle: Northumbria University, 2007.

Preussisches Ministerium für Volkswirtschaft, ed. *Sport-Statistik: Amtliches Quellenwerk, Quellenwerk zur 1. amtlichen Statistik des Freistaates Preussen über Turnen, Sport, Wander Übungsstättenbau-Vereinswesen, nach dem Stande vom 1. Januar 1928.* Kassel: Rudolph'sche Verlagsanstalt, 1928.

Rabinbach, Anson. *The Human Motor: Energy, Fatigue, and the Origins of Modernity.* Berkeley: University of California Press, 1992.

Radkau, Joachim. *Das Zeitalter der Nervösität: Deutschland zwischen Bismarck und Hitler.* Darmstadt: Wissenschaftliche Buchgesellschaft, 2002.

Rapini, Andrea. "La Vespa: histoire sociale d'une innovation industrielle." *Actes de la recherche en sciences sociales* 4 (2007): 72–93.

Reuveni, Gideon. *Reading Germany: Literature and Consumer Culture in Germany before 1933*. New York: Berghahn Books, 2006.

Rieger, Bernhard. *Technology and the Culture of Modernity in Britain and Germany, 1890–1945*. Cambridge: Cambridge University Press, 2005.

——. *The People's Car: A Global History of the Volkswagen Beetle*. Cambridge, MA: Harvard University Press, 2013.

Röder, Werner, and Herbert A. Strauss, eds. *Biographisches Handbuch der deutschsprachigen Emigration nach 1933 / International Biographical Dictionary of Central European Emigrés 1933–1945*. Vol. 2. Munich: Saur, 1983.

Rohrkrämer, Thomas. *Eine andere Moderne? Zivilisationskritik, Natur und Technik in Deutschland 1880–1933*. Paderborn: Schöningh, 1999.

Ross, Kristin. *Fast Cars, Clean Bodies: Decolonization and the Reordering of French Culture*. Cambridge, MA: MIT Press, 1995.

Rothe, E. *Schönheitspflege des Mannes*. Berlin: Max Hesses Verlag, 1927.

Sachs, Albert. *Motorradunfälle*. Berlin: R.C. Schmidt & Co., 1929.

Sachs, Wolfgang. *For the Love of the Automobile: Looking Back into the History of our Desires*. Berkeley: University of California Press, 1992.

Salweski, Michael. "Das Weimarer Revisionssyndrom." *Aus Politik und Zeitgeschichte* 2, no. 80 (1980): 14–25.

Schalcher, Traugott. *Die Reklame der Straße*. Vienna: C. Barth Verlag, 1927.

Scharff, Virginia. *Taking the Wheel: Women and the Coming of the Motor Age*. New York: Free Press, 1991.

Schivelbusch, Wolfgang. *The Railway Journey: The Industrialization of Time and Space in the 19th Century*. Berkeley: University of California Press, 1986.

Schmeling, Max. *Max Schmeling: An Autobiography*. Translated by Georg B. von der Lippe. Chicago: Bonus Books, 1994.

Schmidt, Jens. *Sich hart machen, wenn es gilt: Männlichkeitskonzeptionen in Illustrierten der Weimarer Republik*. Münster: LIT-Verlag, 2000.

Schmitt, Julius. *Musterbetriebe deutscher Wirtschaft*. Vol. 27, *Die Motorradfabrikation, NSU Vereinigte Fahrzeugwerke AG, Neckarsulm/Württbg*. Leipzig: J.J. Arnd, Verlag der Übersee-Post, 1932.

Schneider, Peter. *Die NSU-Story: Die Chronik einer Weltmarke*. Stuttgart: Motorbuch Verlag, 1999.

Scholz, Wilhelm. *Festschrift der Reichverband der Automobilindustrie zum fünfundzwanzigjährigen Bestehen 1901–1926*. Berlin: Reichsverband der deutschen Automobilindustrie, 1926.

Schüler-Springorum, Stefanie. "Flying and Killing: Military Masculinity in German Literature, 1914–1939." In *HOME/FRONT: The Military, War and Gender in 20th Century Germany*, edited by Karen Hagemann and Stefanie Schüler-Springorum, 205–32. Oxford: Berg, 2002.

Schulte, Robert. *Körper-Kultur: Versuch einer Philosophie der Leibesübungen*. Munich: Ernst Reinhardt Verlag, 1928.

Schulz, Horst-Peter, and Hermann Rösch, eds. *Der Arbeiter Rad und Kraftfahrbund "Solidarität": ein Verzeichnis seiner Bestände im Archiv der Sozialen Demokratie und in der Bibliothek der Friedrich-Ebert-Stiftung*. Bonn: Historisches Forschungszentrum, 1996.

Schwarte, Max, ed. *Technik im Weltkriege*. Berlin: E.S. Miller, 1920.

Schwiglewski, Katja. *Erzählte Technik: Die literarische Selbstdarstellung des Ingenieurs seit dem 19. Jahrhundert*. Cologne: Böhlau Verlag, 1995.

Schwitters, Kurt. *Das literarische Werk, Vol. 2, Prosa 1918–1930*. Edited by Friedhelm Lach. Cologne: Verlag M. Dumont, 1974.

Seely, Bruce E. "Engineers and Government–Business Cooperation: Highway Standards and the Bureau of Public Roads, 1900–1940." *Business History Review* 58, no.1 (1984): 51–77.

———. "The Scientific Mystique in Engineering: Highway Research at the Bureau of Public Roads, 1918–1940." *Technology and Culture* 25, no. 4 (1984): 798–831.

———. *Building the American Highway System: Engineers as Policy Makers*. Philadelphia: Temple University Press, 1987.

Seiler, Cotton. *Republic of Drivers: A Cultural History of Automobility in America*. Chicago: University of Chicago Press, 2008.

Semmens, Kristin. *Seeing Hitler's Germany*. New York: Palgrave Macmillan, 2005.

Sheller, Mimi. "Bodies, Cybercars and the Mundane Incorporation of Automated Mobilities." *Social & Cultural Geography* 8 no. 2 (2007): 175–97.

Siegelbaum, Lewis S. *Cars for Comrades: The Life of the Soviet Automobile*. Ithaca, NY: Cornell University Press, 2008.

Sievers, Immo. *Jørgen Skafte Rasmussen: Leben und Werk des DKW-Gründers*. Bielefeld: Delius Klasing, 2006.

Simmons, Sherwin. "Ernst Neumanns 'Neuwerte der bildenden Kunst': Kunsttheorie und –praxis um 1900." In *Ernst Neumann-Neander, 1871–1954*, edited by Reinhold Kraft, Thomas Müller, and Georg Solms, 34–59. Düren: Hahne & Schloemer Verlag, 2004.

Simsa, Paul. "Ein Leben wie sonst keines." In *Ernst Neumann-Neander, 1871–1954*, edited by Reinhold Kraft, Thomas Müller, and Georg Solms. Düren: Hahne & Schloemer Verlag, 2004.

Siodmak, Robert, dir., *Menschen am Sonntag*. Filmstudio 1929 (1929/2006).

Solnit, Rebecca. *Men Explain Things to Me*. Chicago: Haymarket Books, 2014.

Sombart, Nicholas. "Männerbund und Politische Kultur in Deutschland." In *Männergeschichte, Geschlechtergeschichte: Männlichkeit im Wandel der Moderne*, edited by Thomas Kühne, 136–55. Frankfurt am Main: Campus Press, 1996.

Sprenger, Matthias. *Landknechte auf dem Weg ins Dritte Reich? Zu Genese und Wandel des Freikorpsmythos*. Paderborn: Schöningh, 2008.

Steinbeck, Frank. *Das Motorrad: Ein deutscher Sonderweg in die automobile Gesellschaft*. Stuttgart: Franz Steiner Verlag, 2012.

Strasser, Susan, Charles McGovern, and Matthias Judt, eds. *Getting and Spending: European and American Consumer Societies in the 20th Century*. Cambridge: Cambridge University Press 1998.

Stratil-Sauer, Gustav. *Fahrt und Fessel: Mit dem Motorrad von Leipzig nach Afghanistan*. Berlin: August Scherl, 1927.

Sun, Raymond C. "'Hammer Blows': Work, the Workplace, and the Culture of Masculinity among Catholic Workers in the Weimar Republic." *Central European History* 37, no. 2 (2004): 245–71.

Sutton, Katie. *The Masculine Woman in Weimar Germany*. New York: Berghahn Books, 2011.

Swett, Pamela E. *Neighbors and Enemies: The Culture of Radicalism in Berlin, 1929–1932*. Cambridge: Cambridge University Press, 2004.

Swett, Pamela E., S. Jonathan Wiesen, and Jonathan R. Zatlin, eds. *Selling Modernity: Advertising in Twentieth-Century Germany*. Durham, NC and London: Duke University Press, 2007.

Sylvester, Nina. "'Das Girl': Crossing Spaces and Spheres: The Function of the Girl in the Weimar Republic." PhD dissertation. University of California, Los Angeles, 2006.

Tergit, Gabriele. *Atem einer anderen Welt: Berliner Reportagen*. Edited by Jens Brüning. Frankfurt am Main: Suhrkamp, 1994.

Terry, Alan, et al. "Spectators' Negotiations of Risk, Masculinity and Performative Mobilities at the TT Races." *Mobilities* (2014): 1–21.

Theweleit, Klaus. *Male Fantasies*. Minneapolis: University of Minnesota Press, 1987.

Thompson, Lana. *The Wandering Womb: A Cultural History of Outrageous Beliefs about Women*. Amherst, NY: Prometheus, 1999.

Tooze, Adam. *The Wages of Destruction: The Making and Breaking of the Nazi Economy*. New York: Penguin, 2006.

Trapp, Thomas. "Ernst Neumann-Neander und die Fahrzeugtechnik." In *Ernst Neumann-Neander, 1871–1954*, edited by Reinhold Kraft, Thomas Müller, and Georg Solms. Düren: Hahne & Schloemer Verlag, 2004.

Ugolini, Laura. *Men and Menswear: Sartorial Consumption in Britain, 1880–1939*. Aldershot: Ashgate, 2007.

Vaukins, Simon. "The Isle of Man TT Races: Politics, Economics and National Identity." *International Journal of Motorcycle Studies* 3, no. 3 (2007). Accessed 14. March 2016, http://ijms.nova.edu/November2007TT/IJMS_Artcl.Vaukins.html.

VDI, eds. *Technik, Ingenieure und Gesellschaft: Geschichte des Vereins Deutscher Ingenieure 1856–1981*. Düsseldorf: VDI-Verlag, 1981.

Vetter, Karl, and K.A. Tramm. *Das Wochenende: Anregungen zur praktischen Durchführungen*. Berlin: Rudolf Mosse Buchverlag, 1928.

Vieregg, Artur. *Der Sport und seine Ziele: Unter besonderer Berücksichtigung der Gegenwartsfragen*. Berlin: Fischer Sport-Verlag, 1924.

Virilo, Paulo. *Speed and Politics: An Essay on Dromology*. New York: Semiotext(e), 1977.

von Ankum, Katharina, ed. *Women in the Metropolis: Gender and Modernity in Weimar Culture*. Berkeley: University of California Press, 1997.

von Saldern, Adelheid. "Cultural Conflicts, Popular Mass Culture, and the Question of Nazi Success: The Eilenriede Motorcycle Races, 1924–39." *German Studies Review* 15, no. 2 (1992): 317–38.

Wagner, Helmut. *Sport und Arbeitersport*. Berlin: Büchergilde Gutenberg, 1931.

Wajcman, Judy. *Feminism Confronts Technology*. University Park, PA: Pennsylvania State University Press, 1991.

Ward, Janet. *Weimar Surfaces: Urban Visual Culture in 1920s Germany*. Berkeley: University of California Press, 2001.

Wehler, Hans-Ulrich. *Deutsche Gesellschaftsgeschichte 1914–1949*. Munich: C.H. Beck, 2003.

Weinbaum, Alys Eve, Lynn M. Thomas, Priti Ramamurthy, Uta G. Poiger, Madeleine Yue Dong. *The Modern Girl around the World: Consumption, Modernity and Globalization*. Durham, NC: Duke University Press, 2008.

Weisbrod, Berndt. "Military Violence and Male Fundamentalism: Ernst Jünger's Contribution to the Conservative Revolution." *History Workshop Journal* 49 (Spring 2000): 68–94.

Weitz, Eric D. *Weimar Germany: Promise and Tragedy*. Princeton, NJ: Princeton University Press, 2007.

Wheeler, Robert F. "Organized Sport and Organized Labor: The Workers' Sports Movement." *Journal of Contemporary History* 13, no. 2 (1978): 191–210.

Widdig, Bernd. *Männerbund und Massen: Zur Krise Männlicher Identität in der Literatur der Moderne*. Opladen: Westdeutscher Verlag, 1992.

Williams, Raymond. *Marxism and Literature*. Oxford: Oxford University Press, 1977.

Zatsch, Angela. *Staatsmacht und Motorisiserung am Morgen des Automobilzeitalters*. Konstanz: Hartung-Gorre, 1993.

Index